9/11

Enemies
Foreign and Domestic

Secret Evidence Censored from the Official Record
Proves Traitors Aided Israel in Attacking the USA

"For we are opposed around the world by a monolithic and ruthless conspiracy that relies primarily on covert means for expanding its sphere of influence, on infiltration instead of invasion, on subversion instead of elections, on intimidation instead of free choice, on guerrillas by night instead of armies by day. It is a system which has conscripted vast human and material resources into the building of a tightly knit, highly efficient machine that combines military, diplomatic, intelligence, economic, scientific and political operations. Its preparations are concealed, not published. Its mistakes are buried, not headlined. Its dissenters are silenced, not praised. No expenditure is questioned, no rumor is printed, no secret is revealed. It conducts the Cold War, in short, with a war-time discipline no democracy would ever hope or wish to match."
John F. Kennedy, President of the United States.

**P.O. Box 503
Garrisonville, Virginia 22463**

Second Edition
Copyright © 2010, 2011 by Edward Hendrie
All rights reserved.
All Scripture references are to the Authorized (King James) Version of the Holy Bible, unless otherwise indicated.

Printed in the U.S.A.

ISBN-13: 978-0-9832627-3-2
ISBN-10: 098326273X

www.911enemies.com

edwardhendrie@gmail.com

Other books by Edward Hendrie:

● Antichrist Conspiracy
● The Anti-Gospel
● Solving the Mystery of BABYLON THE GREAT
● Bloody Zion
● What Shall I Do to Inherit Eternal Life?

Available at: www.antichristconspiracy.com, www.mysterybabylonthegreat.net, www.911enemies.com, www.antigospel.com, www.amazon.com, www.barnesandnoble.com, and www.lulu.com

Table of Contents

Introduction iii

1   Seven Alleged Hijackers are Still Alive 1

2   American Airlines Flights 11 and 77 Did Not Exist 7

3   No AA Flight 77 Wreckage at the Pentagon 14

4   Decoy Plane 22

5   2.3 Trillion Reasons for the Pentagon Attack 28

6   A Patriotic Witness Steps From the Rubble 29

7   What Happened to UA Flight 93? 34

8   Impossible Speeds 49

9   Rock, Scissors, Planes 51

10   Media Participation in 9/11 Attacks 57

11   Eyewitness Accounts 77

12   The Man Who Knew Too Much 91

13   Evidence of Directed Energy on 9/11 103

14   The Destruction After the Destruction 124

15   What Did Bush Know and When Did He Know It? 129

16   Mossad Involvement in the 9/11 Attacks 135

17   Able Danger 153

18   A Nest of Spies 161

19   Israel is Our Enemy 165

20	Silverstein and Friends	179
21	Osama Bin Patsy	186
22	The Real Reason for the Invasion of Iraq	199
23	Is Iran Next?	203
24	The Media Lap Dogs	209
25	The Core of the Conspiracy	218
Endnotes		251

Introduction

The official government conspiracy theory is that on the morning of September 11, 2001, 19 Arabs nearly simultaneously hijacked four planes using box cutters and purposely crashed one plane into the Pentagon, crashed two others into each of the World Trade Center Twin Towers, and the fourth plane crashed in Shankesville, Pennsylvania as a result of the passengers rising up and trying to get control of the plane from the hijackers. This book will prove beyond any reasonable doubt that the government's conspiracy theory is a preposterous cover story. The truth is that the attacks on 9/11 were perpetrated by Israel, aided and abetted by high officials in the U.S. Government.

Article VI of the Constitution requires the following:

> The Senators and Representatives before mentioned, and the Members of the several State Legislatures, and all executive and judicial Officers, both of the United States and of the several States, shall be bound by Oath or Affirmation, to support this Constitution; but no religious Test shall ever be required as a Qualification to any Office or public Trust under the United States.

U.S. CONST. art. VI

There are millions of Americans who have taken that constitutionally required oath or affirmation to defend the Constitution against all enemies foreign and domestic:

> I do solemnly swear (or affirm) that I will support and defend the Constitution of the United States against all enemies, foreign and domestic; that I will bear true faith and allegiance to the same; that I take this obligation freely, without any mental reservation or purpose of evasion; and that I will well and faithfully discharge the duties of the office on which I am about to enter: So help me God.

We need to uphold the letter and spirit of that oath. This book provides evidence that identifies the true foreign and domestic enemies who attacked America on September 11, 2001. The Constitution states: "Treason against the United States, shall consist only in levying war against them, or in adhering to their enemies, giving them aid and comfort." U.S. CONST. art. III, sec. 3. The 9/11 attacks were surprise acts of war by foreign enemies who were aided by domestic traitors. Their purpose was to accelerate the transformation of the United States from a constitutional republic to a despotic oligarchy under Zionist control. I call on those who take their solemn oath seriously to defend the Constitution of this great republic against those foreign and domestic enemies.

1   Seven Alleged Hijackers are Still Alive

According to the government conspiracy theory, 19 middle eastern men worked in concert to hijack four planes in the morning of 9-11-01. They allegedly did so at the instigation of the mastermind, Osama Bin Laden. Two of the planes were purposely crashed into each of the two World Trade Center Towers, one plane was crashed into the Pentagon, and the fourth hijacking was thwarted by passengers and crashed in Stoney Creek Township near Shanksville, Pennsylvania.

Suspicions about the government conspiracy theory were voiced as soon as it was publicized. The most notable problem with the theory was how quickly the hijackers were identified by the FBI. The FBI was able to identify the hijackers and even send photos to the news media within days of the attacks. The personal details of the accused hijackers were given, including their names, places and dates of birth, and occupations. One former FBI official with extensive experience in counter-terrorism stated in an interview with New American: "Obviously this information was available in the files and somebody was sitting on it."[1]

Another problem with the government conspiracy theory is that seven of the 19 identified hijackers were confirmed to be alive after they were supposed to have died in the four plane crashes on 9-11.[2] Four of the falsely accused Saudi Arabian citizens were interviewed by *The Telegraph*.[3] One of the alleged hijackers, Ahmed Al-Nami from Riyadh, is an administrative supervisor with Saudi Arabian Airlines. He was in Riyadh when the terrorists struck.

The Telegraph premised their article upon the theory that the still-alive subjects had their identities stolen by the real hijackers in order for the real hijackers to cover their tracks. The FBI, which could not refute the fact that seven of their identified hijackers were alive, have also floated the stolen identity theory.

The stolen identity theory does not hold up to scrutiny in the case of Ahmed Al-Nami. Al-Nami stated that he had never had his passport stolen and therefore cannot account for how he was identified as a hijacker. Another alleged hijacker, Salem Al-Hamzin, who works at a petrochemical complex in the industrial eastern city of Yanbou, stated that he had not been outside of Saudi Arabia in the two years prior to the 9/11 attacks and had never ever been to the United States.

While it is likely that some of the persons portraying the alleged hijackers assumed false identities, there is a problem with the FBI's and *The Telegraph's* version of the false identity theory. The problem with their false identities theory is that it makes no sense, because they assume (or rather would like people to believe) that the alleged hijackers were Arabs. If the hijackers used false identifications in order to steer the authorities away from the alleged mastermind (Osama Bin Laden), why would they use Saudi Arabian identities in 10 of the 19 cases, when such identities would point in the direction of Bin Laden, who is a Saudi Arabian?

If the hijackers were truly Saudi Arabian citizens as alleged by the government, why wouldn't they use Russian false identities or even Israeli false identities? There is no doubt that false identities were used, as would be expected with any covert operation. In order for the false identities to be effective in this case, the actors playing the role of Arab hijackers would be doing so in order to point the blame on Arabs. It would make no sense for an Arab hijacker to assume the false identity of another Arab. One acting as an *agent provocateur* would desire the victim of the attack to retaliate against his enemies, not his friends.

These alleged hijackers were supposedly on a *Jihad,* and they were headed to a certain suicidal death. Why would they not want to take credit for their alleged martyrdom? It makes no sense for the alleged hijackers to use false identities if they were Muslims on a suicidal mission. It makes perfect sense, however, for the terrorists to use false identities if there were not on a suicide mission; if instead, the mission was a false flag operation designed to make it look like a Muslim suicide mission.

The identities were certainly false, that much is clear, and the false identities accomplished the task of pointing the finger at Osama bin Laden and Muslim extremists. That means that the true identities of the terrorists were other than Muslim extremists. The FBI was stating the obvious when it revealed that the false identities were for the purpose of throwing the investigation off the trail of the actual perpetrators.

The issue is then who were the real perpetrators? This book will answer that question. The real perpetrators would certainly want the authorities and the public to continue to believe that the falsely accused Arab hijackers are the true hijackers. The real perpetrators then would not have been Arab Muslims and certainly not from Saudi Arabia.

Once it became public knowledge that the FBI list was wrong, the FBI made no effort to identify the real alleged hijackers. The suspicious lack of curiosity by the FBI speaks volumes. It suggests that they know that their list is completely fabricated. It points to them as the fabricators. The FBI has not withdrawn or revised the list, which suggests that the list was floated to serve the purpose of convincing the general public to believe the official fictional conspiracy theory. The fact that the FBI is not looking for the actual hijackers suggests that they know that such an investigation would be futile. Why would it be futile? The only plausible explanation is that there were no hijackers at all.

As of October 2010, the FBI still has posted on its official FBI website a formal press release with the names and pictures of the 19 hijackers.[4] That is more than nine years after it was publicly revealed that seven of the listed hijackers were alive after their supposed suicidal plane crashes.

The FBI press release containing the hijacker list[5] was dated September 27, 2001, which is four days after *The Telegraph* article was posted on the internet (September 23, 2001), wherein four of the purportedly deceased hijackers were interviewed. An official spokesman for the FBI was contacted and interviewed for the article, and so the FBI knew that the hijacker list was in error when it was published in the FBI news release four days later.

The FBI states in the press release that "attempts to confirm the true identities of these individuals are still under way."[6] The FBI implies that the "true identities" of the listed individuals have not been confirmed. It is true that the identities of the hijackers have not been confirmed, but the FBI is being disingenuous, because before the press release was issued, seven of the listed individuals were confirmed to be still alive and therefore not among the hijackers. Why did the FBI continue to list seven of the hijackers on the list that they know were not among the hijackers?

The press release further states: "The FBI requests the public's assistance in obtaining more information about these individuals."[7] Notice that the request for assistance is only for assistance "about *these* individuals." That is an odd request, when only days before the press release was issued the FBI was informed that seven of the listed hijackers were still alive. Yet all seven of the living suspects were still listed as dead hijackers in the press release. The FBI asks the public for assistance in the press release in obtaining information about the listed dead hijackers, knowing full well that seven of the persons on the list could not possibly be among the hijackers, because they were confirmed as still being alive.

The FBI has not asked for any assistance about any other individuals. That request for assistance by the FBI in the September 27, 2001 press release makes no sense if one views the FBI as conducting a legitimate investigation into 9-11. It makes perfect sense, however, if the FBI is engaging in a cover-up designed to deceive the public. The FBI is pushing the 19 hijackers conspiracy theory, because if that theory is proven false, the public might realize that there were no hijackers at all.

The request for assistance about the individuals listed as hijackers is clearly insincere, because they know with certainty that Waleed Al Sheri, whose actual picture and biographical information are posted on the FBI website, is definitely not one of the alleged hijackers. The

BBC reported: "Saudi Arabian pilot Waleed Al Shehri was one of five men that the FBI said had deliberately crashed American Airlines flight 11 into the World Trade Centre on 11 September. His photograph was released, and has since appeared in newspapers and on television around the world."[8] Shehri is still alive and well. On September 23, 2001, the BBC reported that Shehri protested his innocence. Shehri acknowledged that he was indeed the same Waleed Al Shehri listed by the FBI as one of the hijackers, but he had nothing to do with the 9/11 attacks.

Who can doubt his claim? Because if he was a hijacker, as alleged by the FBI, he'd be dead. When Sheri, who is one of the hijackers on the list, turns up alive and says publicly "that is me," the FBI leaves him on the dead hijacker list and ignores the fact that he is still alive. The FBI then asks for the "public's assistance in obtaining more information about these individuals," which includes Sheri. The fact that the FBI has never tried to contact or interview any of the listed hijackers who have been identified as still being alive indicates that the FBI is not sincerely trying find the truth.

You would think that the FBI would have all of this sorted out and have an updated and corrected hijacker list to submit to the 9/11 Commission. Instead, the FBI submitted the same list of allegedly dead hijackers, knowing that seven of the persons on the list are still alive and therefore could not have been among the alleged hijackers. Oddly, the 9/11 Commission followed the party line and kept with the original list of the 19 hijackers.[9] In 2006, approximately two years after the 9/11 Commission report was issued, the BBC updated their original report about some of the hijackers being still alive. They asked the FBI for comment about the still living hijackers.

> We recently asked the FBI for a statement, and this is, as things stand, the closest thing we have to a definitive view: **The FBI is confident that it has positively identified the nineteen hijackers responsible for the 9/11 terrorist attacks. Also, the 9/11 investigation was thoroughly reviewed by the National Commission on Terrorist Attacks Upon the United States and the House and Senate Joint Inquiry. Neither of these reviews ever raised the issue of doubt about the identity of the nineteen hijackers.**[10] (bold emphasis in original).

That statement must be kept in historical perspective. When doubts were raised about the identities of the hijackers, the FBI admitted that its list was in doubt. On or September 20, 2001, only nine days after the 9-11 attacks "FBI Director Robert Mueller acknowledged on Thursday that the identity of several of the suicide hijackers is in doubt."[11] Why did the FBI five years later, after the doubts became even more pronounced and solidified, retreat from its statement of doubt and instead claim that there was no doubt about the accuracy of their list of 19 hijackers?[12] The reason for the FBI's initial vacillation and subsequent entrenchment over the hijacker list is that if it is discovered that any one of the alleged hijackers on the list is wrong, it calls into question all other names on the list. If any single thread of the hijacker identity is pulled, the whole "19 hijackers" story comes unraveled.

If that list is in doubt, then the existence of the hijackers is in doubt. The FBI cannot allow the list to be undermined, because if people doubt the hijack list, they will doubt the existence of hijackers. If they doubt the existence of hijackers, they will doubt the existence of planes. If people were to find out there were no planes, they will discover that 9/11 was a massive conspiracy involving the highest levels of the government and media. That is why the government dropped FBI Director Robert Mueller's initial vacillation over the accuracy of the hijacker list. Initially, Director Mueller would have looked foolish if he maintained the accuracy of the list in the face of clear evidence of hijackers being still alive. However, it was later determined that to doubt the list would create deep problems with the official story. The hijacker list is the cornerstone of the government's official conspiracy theory. It is the orthodoxy of the 9/11 conspiracy theory and any attempt to attack the list is viewed as heresy.

The BBC in a desperate effort to quash any discussion of a U.S. Government conspiracy, took the unusual step of altering the posted archive of the original October 23, 2001, article. "Under the FBI picture of Waleed al Shehri we have added the words A man called Waleed Al Shehri ... to make it as clear as possible that there was confusion over the identity."[13]

The BBC revised their original story in order to spin it to give some plausible explanation for the fact that the FBI hijacker list is inaccurate. The problem with the BBC approach is that in making the alteration they assumed facts that are not in evidence. The BBC claims that it altered its original story because of confusion over the identity of the hijackers. The FBI, however, to this day refuses to say that there is any confusion about the identity of the hijackers. The FBI claims that the original list is accurate and that two official reviews have not raised any doubt as to the accuracy of the listed hijackers.

The fact is that the FBI identified Waleed Al Shehri as one of the hijackers, and they posted his picture on their official website. Waleed Al Shehri later acknowledged that he was in fact the person identified by the FBI as one of the hijackers. Quite simply, the FBI identified the wrong person. Waleed Al Shehri was not one of the hijackers. Yet, the FBI, the 9/11 Commission, and the BBC want to continue with the charade that the original list was accurate. That is not confusion, that is deception

The BBC admits that it altered its article in order to point away from U.S. Government involvement in a conspiracy, because "[t]he story has been cited ever since by some as evidence that the 9/11 attacks were part of a US government conspiracy."[14] The BBC cares not what the facts are, they are not reporting news, they view their job as pointing people away from certain conclusions and supporting the official view of 9/11 as presented by the government. There is only one conspiracy theory allowed and that is the one propounded by the government and broadcast by its shills in the media. The media's mission is to protect the government from any blowback.

One live terrorist patsy was already in custody prior the September 11 attack. Zacarias Mousaui was arrested on August 16, 2001 by the FBI after he attempted to receive flight training for a Boeing 747 jumbo jet. Mousaui was not the brightest bulb in this terror chandelier. He claimed he was from France, but when the flight instructor spoke French to him he did not understand what the instructor was saying. He discussed with the flight instructors the amount of fuel carried by a 747 and how much damage that would do if it hit something. Mousaui was not concerned with learning how to take off or landing, he only wanted to learn how to steer the plane. It was so obvious to the flight school employees that Mousaui was a potential hijacker that they called the FBI, who in turn arrested him. Mousaui was obviously being "sheep dipped," which is the process used by the intelligence community to color an unwitting patsy in advance and make him look like a conspirator in the chosen crime.

When Pan Am International Flight Academy raised questions with the FAA about another patsy's inability to speak English, the international language of aviation, an FAA representative sat in class and observed Hani Hanjour and discussed with the school getting someone to tutor him in English. Hanjour allegedly plowed American Airlines flight 77 into the Pentagon. The allegation that Hanjour piloted flight 77 is a rather clumsy cover for what really happened. Hanjour was a patsy. Testimony from those who tried to teach Honjour to fly indicates that Hanjour was incompetent to pilot even a small plane. It is incredible to believe that he could fly a Boeing 767 in a death spiral and hit a target that even the most skilled pilot would find almost impossible to reenact.

Photographs and videos of the second plane crashing into the World Trade Center South Tower indicate the plane was not a Boeing 767. A conventional Boeing 767 passenger jet has built in failsafe computers programed to prevent the pilot from making sharp high "G" turns that might injure elderly or frail passengers. The sharp turn allegedly made by the 767 before it struck the south tower could not have been by a pilot at the controls of a conventional Boeing 767.

2   American Airlines Flights 11 and 77 Did Not Exist

On the next page is a screen shot of the first few flights listed by the Bureau of Transportation Statistics on its official website listing all the flights in ascending order of flight number flying out of Boston Logan Airport on 9-11-2001. The screen shot is of a chart from an archive created on or about November 2003. Notice that the alleged American Airlines (AA) flight 11 that was supposed to have taken off from Boston Logan Airport on 9-11-2001 before being hijacked is missing from the list. American Airlines Flight 11 is the plane that is supposed to have hit the World Trade Center's North Tower. If the fight had existed, it would have been listed in numeric order as the first flight on the list, but it is not there.

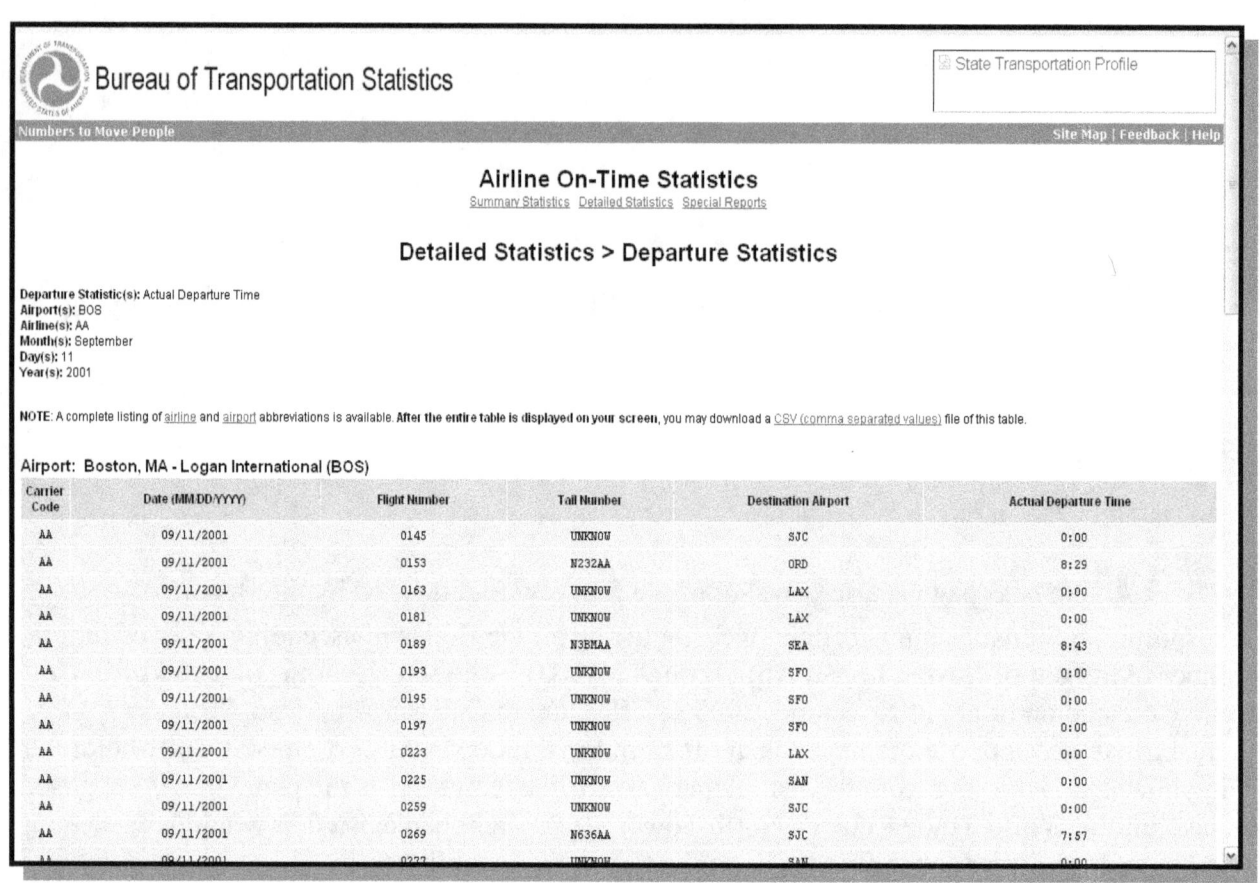

ORIGINAL Bureau of Transportation Statistics Chart Showing <u>No</u> American Airlines (AA) Flight 11 Scheduled to Depart Boston Logan Airport on 9-11-2001

Similarly, American Airlines Flight 77 is not found on the Bureau of Transportation Statistics page listing for American Airlines flights that were scheduled to take off out of Washington Dulles Airport on 9-11-2001. The screen shot below is of the chart from an internet archive created on or about November 2003. The alleged American Airlines Flight 77 that was supposed to have taken off from Washington Dulles Airport on 9-11-2001 before being hijacked and crashed into the Pentagon should be listed as the second flight on the list, but it is missing.

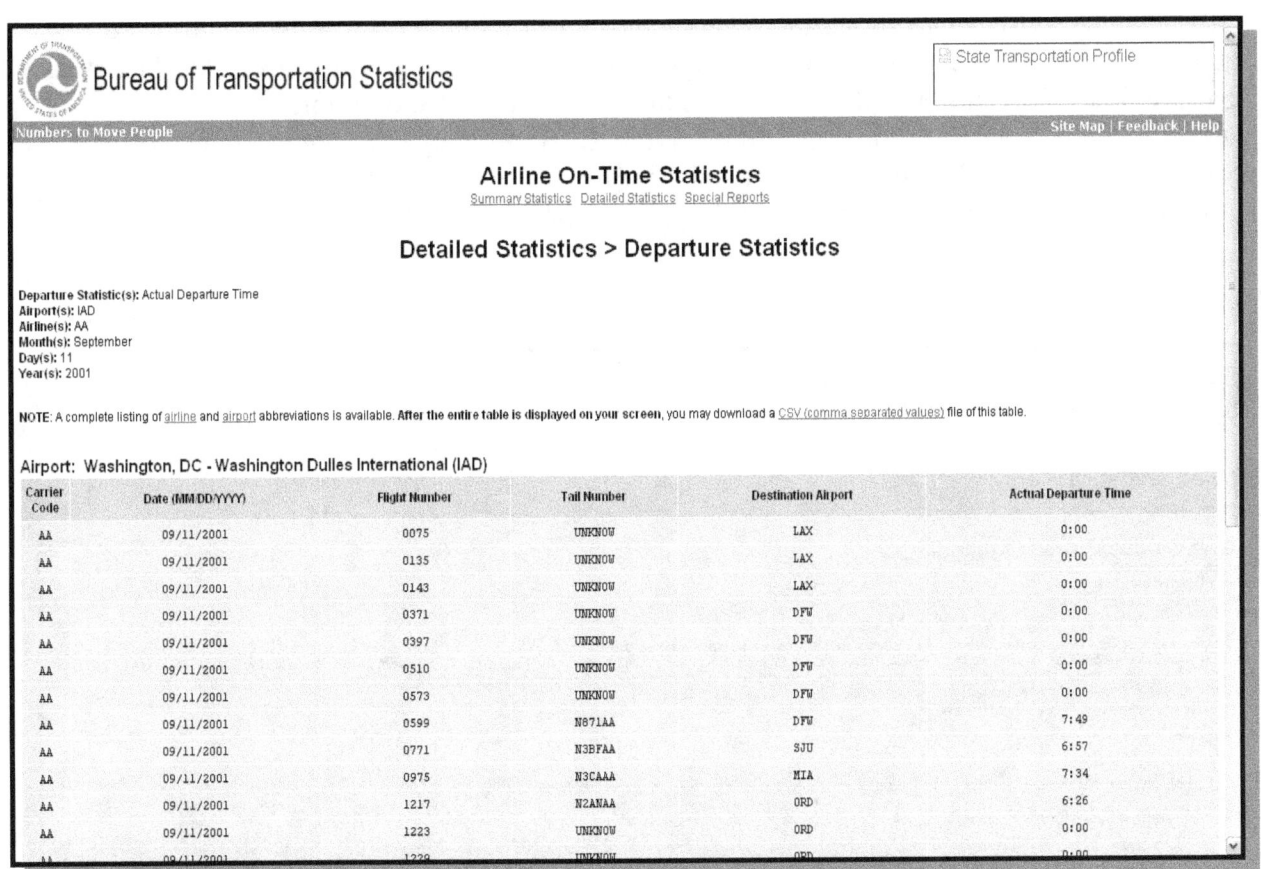

ORIGINAL Bureau of Transportation Statistics Chart Showing No American Airlines (AA) Flight 77 Scheduled to Depart Washington Dulles Airport on 9-11-2001

Notice that there are a number of flights listed in the charts above where there are no departure times, nor are there any tail numbers. A review of the BTS charts makes clear that the only time the departure time and the tail numbers are missing is if the flight does not take off. One can see in the charts above a large number of flights with no take off times or tail numbers. That is because after the attacks in the morning of 9-11-2001 all flights were cancelled and all planes en route were grounded.

Approximately 10 months after it was broadcast on the internet that AA flights 11 and 77 were missing from the Bureau of Transportation Statistics charts, the Bureau of Transportation Statistics revised it charts and added both American Airlines Flights 11 and 77 to its lists of flights on 9-11-2001.[15] In addition, the above internet archive charts (obtained on or about October 2010) showing no flights 11 and 77, were made inaccessible by the internet archive website some time after this book was initially published in 2010. The above charts can no longer be accessed from the internet archives.

On the next page is a screen shot taken in October 2010 of the first few flights listed on the revised BTS chart showing the flights departing from Boston Logan Airport on 9-11-2001.

Notice that the revised chart shows the scheduled departure time for AA Flight 11 from Boston Logan Airport on 9-11-2001 (it is the first flight listed), but there is no time given for the actual departure time. Further notice that there is no tail number reported or a time given for the "wheels-off time," nor is the "taxi-out time" given. BTS routinely does not report any of that information for flights that do not actually take off from an airport. The ineluctable conclusion is that flight 11 did not take off from Boston Logan Airport on 9-11-2001.

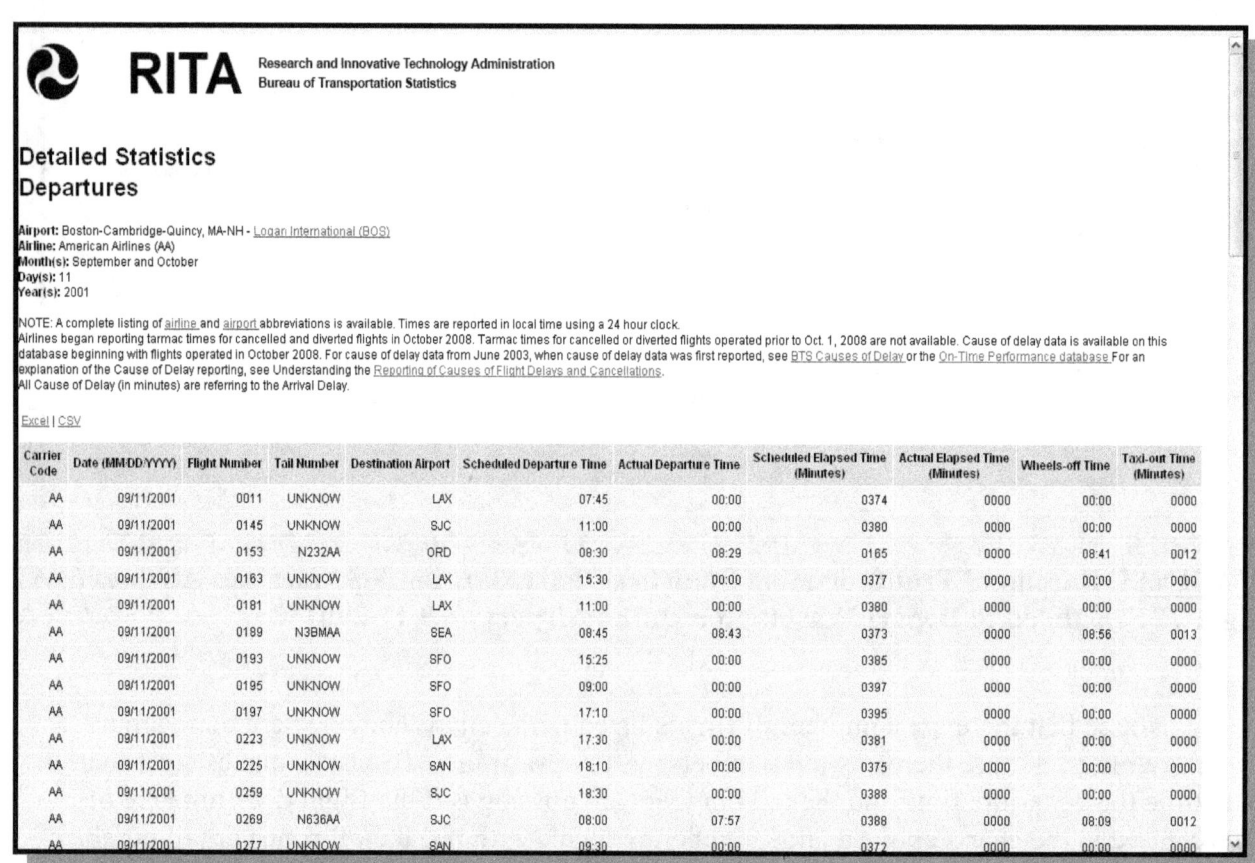

REVISED Bureau of Transportation Statistics Chart Showing American Airlines (AA) Flight 11 Existing But Without Tail Number or a Departure From Boston Logan Airport on 9-11-2001

On the next page is a screen shot taken on October 2010 of the first few listed flights on the revised BTS chart showing the flights departing from Washington Dulles Airport on 9-11-2001. Notice that the scheduled departure time is given for AA Flight 77 in the second line down from the top, but there is no time given for the actual departure time. Notice also that there is no tail number reported, nor is there a time given for the "wheels-off time" or the "taxi-out time" for AA Flight 77. BTS routinely does not report any of that information for flights that do not actually take off from an airport. We can only conclude that the information is not listed, because flight 77 did not take off from Washington Dulles Airport on 9-11-2001.

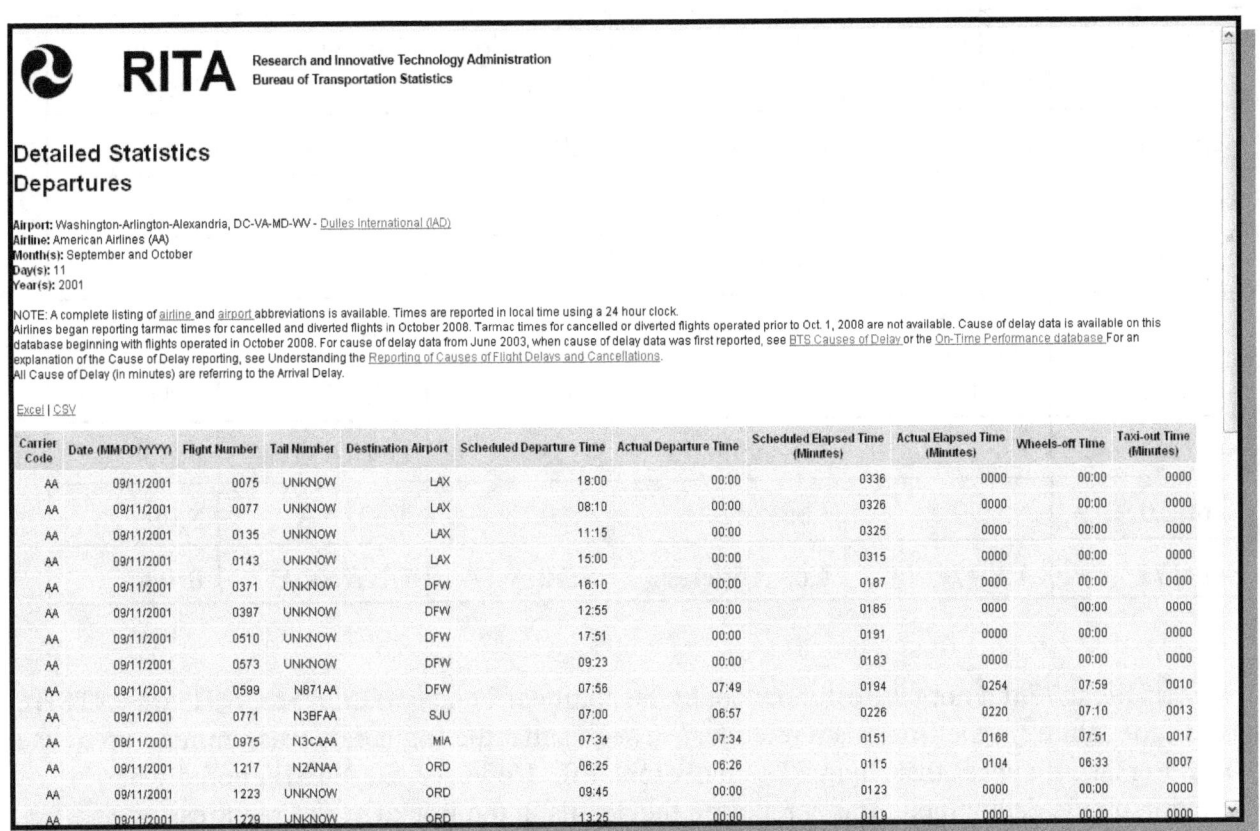

REVISED Bureau of Transportation Statistics Chart Showing American Airlines (AA) Flight 77 But Without Tail Number or a Departure From Washington Dulles Airport on 9-11-2001

On the next page is a chart of the information presented on the Bureau of Transportation Statistics for both 9-10-2001 and 9-11-2001. The chart shows that on 9-10-2001, the actual departure time and the tail numbers on the planes were both listed for both flights on 9-10-2001. Yet, when the Bureau of Transportation Statistics jimmied-up the new list and added flights 11 and 77 on 9-11-2001, they did not have a tail number or an actual departure time for 9-11-2001.[16] The present charts follow the Bureau of Transportation Statistics consistent pattern of not reporting tail numbers (listing them as "unknow") or departure times (listing them as 0:00) for flights that do not take off. A reasonable conclusion is that there are no tail numbers or actual departure times listed for flights 11 and 77, because those flights did not take off on 9-11-2001.[17]

Flight Date	Flight Number	Destination	Scheduled Departure	Tail Number	Actual Departure
Sept. 10	UA 93	San Francisco	8:00	N570UA	7:57
Sept. 11	UA 93	San Francisco	8:00	N591UA	8:01
Sept. 10	UA 175	Los Angeles	8:00	N618UA	7:59
Sept. 11	UA 175	Los Angeles	8:00	N612UA	7:58
Sept. 10	AA 11	Los Angeles	7:45	N321AA	7:41
Sept. 11	**AA 11**	**Los Angeles**	**7:45**	**UNKNOW**	**0:00**
Sept. 10	AA 77	Los Angeles	8:10	N632AA	8:09
Sept. 11	**AA 77**	**Los Angeles**	**8:10**	**UNKNOW**	**0:00**

If flight 77 did not take off, how could the National Transportation Safety Board (NTSB), have flight data from the flight data recorder? It seems that the flight data was jimmied up by the NTSB to make it appear that flight 77 actually took off. However, the NTSB goofed when jimmying up the data. Sheila Casey reported the details in the Rock Creek Free Press:

> Pilots for 9/11 Truth has reported that the data stream from the flight data recorder (FDR) for American Airlines flight 77, which allegedly struck the Pentagon on 9/11, shows that the cockpit door never opened during the entire 90 minute flight. The data was provided by the National Transportation Safety Board (NTSB), which has refused to comment.
>
> The FDR is one of two "black boxes" in every commercial airliner, which are used after accidents to help determine the cause of a crash. One black box records flight data, the other records voice data (everything said in the cockpit during the flight). With those two sets of data, NTSB investigators can usually piece together the events that led to a crash. The status of the door to the cockpit is checked every four seconds throughout a flight and relayed as a simple 0 or 1, where 0=closed and 1=open, with approximately 1,300 door status checks performed during AA77's 90 minute flight. Every one of those door status checks shows as a 0, indicating that the door to the cockpit never opened during the entire flight.
>
> Accident investigators monitor the cockpit door with the FDR

because it may yield clues to pilot error in a crash. The FDR begins recording once the pilots are in their seats and readying for takeoff, and the plane cannot take off unless the FDR is working.[18]

It seems that flight 77 did not take off, and to hide that fact the NTSB jimmied up phony flight data, but the NTSB forgot to include phony data that the cockpit door was opened. Instead, the NTSB has come up with data that indicates that there was no hijacking at all. In order for the hijackers to commandeer the plane as claimed in the official government conspiracy theory, they would have had to open the flight deck door. The data provided by the NTSB, however, shows that the flight deck door was never opened. Hence, no hijacking - Oops!

Sheila Casey further reveals that the flight voice recorder (which is separate and distinct from the flight *data* recorder) for flight 77 could not be found. She states in her report: "The government claims that the voice data recorder was damaged during the crash and that no usable data was retrieved from it. If true, this would be the first time in aviation history that a solid-state data recorder was destroyed during a crash."[19] Apparently, it is easier to fabricate fake flight data than it is to fabricate the voices of the pilots and ground control.

3   No AA Flight 77 Wreckage at the Pentagon

If AA Flight 77 did not take off from Washington Dulles Airport, what, if anything, struck the Pentagon? We know that if a large Boeing 757 crashed into the Pentagon, there would be huge amounts of aircraft debris everywhere.

At right is the massive tail section of the Boeing 737-T43 that carried U.S. Commerce Secretary Ron Brown and 34 others when it crashed into a mountainside in Croatia on April 3, 1996.[20] That plane is similar in size to a Boeing 757. The plane crashed directly into the mountain at a similar impact trajectory as did the alleged 757 which supposedly crashed into the Pentagon. If one reviews airplane crash pictures, one aspect of those crashes becomes clear. First there is a large debris field with obvious airplane remnants strewn about, and second, the massive tail section almost always remains intact as it is the last point of impact.

Tail Section of Boeing 737-T43 Crashed in Croatia

Let us see if we can detect evidence that a large Boeing 757 struck the Pentagon. Let's try to find the large tail section, which should be adjacent to the alleged point of impact. Below are several photographs of the front of the Pentagon shortly after the explosion that ripped a hole in the building.[21] As one looks at the photographs, the most surprising feature of each of the photographs is not what is seen but rather what is missing. There is no visible plane debris in any of the photos. The large tail section is nowhere in sight. The only way to account for that is that whatever caused the damage to the Pentagon was not a Boeing 757.

A closeup of that same area a little later in the day does not seem to help.[22] There is no plane debris in sight. The alleged impact site included the ground level floors, which would have required the plane's large engines that hung from each wing to have skidded on the lawn before impact. Yet, there is no visible damage to the lawn.

Let's try a different angle.[23] Perhaps the plane is hidden behind the fire truck. No, it is not there.

Be aware that the large gaping hole was not immediately caused by the alleged plane. The collapse of the building took place approximately 45 minutes after the alleged plane impact. At right is a picture of the Pentagon before the collapse.[24] There is no way to account for there not being any large plane debris outside the building as there is no place for the plane to fit in the limited opening caused by the alleged plane impact.

Compare the pristine Pentagon lawn in the pictures above with what the debris one might expect to find at a crash site. At left is a picture of the crash site in Russia of a Tupolev TU-154M, which crashed on July 3, 2001, killing all 143 aboard.[25] With a maximum seating capacity of 180, the Tupolev TU-154M has a similar seating capacity to that of the Boeing 757 that was alleged to have been AA Flight 77, which had a seating capacity of 176.[26] Notice the large tail section is still intact. The frequent survival of the tail section is why the black box recorder is always placed in the tail section of commercial aircraft.

Tupolev TU-154M Crash in Russia

The picture at right is a closeup of the bottom of the tail section of the crashed Tupolev TU-154M.[27] Notice the large size of the debris and compare that with the very few pieces of small debris found at the Pentagon.

Tupolev TU-154M Crash in Russia

At left is an ariel view of the Pentagon impact zone.[28] The building is still smoking, so we know that the picture was taken later in the day on 9-11-2001. Notice, there is no plane wreckage at the point of impact, which is where one would expect to find plane wreckage. There are only two conclusions, 1) either the plane magically disintegrated or 2) there was no plane impact at the site. The government and the media say that there was a huge Boeing 757 that struck the building. The government and the media are like the husband and paramour who are caught in *flagrante delicto* in bed together by the husband's wife; they deny having an affair and argue "are you going to believe us or your lying eyes?"

Much has been made of the statements from CNN reporter Jamie McIntyre, where he explained that there was no evidence of a plane crashing anywhere near the Pentagon. However, closer examination of his statement in context makes clear that he was indicating that in his view the plane crashed into the Pentagon, not short of the Pentagon.

> Judy WOODRUFF: Jamie, Aaron was talking earlier -- or one of
> our correspondents was talking earlier -- I think -- actually, it was
> Bob Franken – with an eyewitness who said it appeared that that
> Boeing 757, the American jet, American Airline jet, landed short

of the Pentagon. Can you give us any better idea of how much of the plane actually impacted the building?

Jamie MCINTYRE: You know, it might have appeared that way, but from my close-up inspection, there's no evidence of a plane having crashed anywhere near the Pentagon. The only site is the actual site of the building that's crashed in, and as I said, the only pieces left that you can see are small enough that you can pick up in your hand. There are no large tail sections, wing sections, fuselage, nothing like that anywhere around, which would indicate that the entire plane crashed into the side of the Pentagon and then caused the side to collapse.[29]

Before the above colloquy, McIntyre stated that the largest piece of wreckage that he saw was only 3 feet long. He described that piece as being silver and painted green and red, but he did not see any identifying markings on the object. The picture on the right seems to match the description of the largest piece seen by McIntyre.[30] Indeed, it is the largest piece of the aircraft photographed on the exterior of the Pentagon on 9-11-2001.

The significance of what McIntyre said was that his eyewitness account matches what is seen in the above photograph of the exterior of the Pentagon. It is clear that there were no large plane sections in or around the crash site. McIntyre indicated that except for the three-foot section all other plane pieces that he saw were big enough to pick up in your hand. If in fact a huge Boeing 757 crashed into the Pentagon, one would expect to find large pieces of the aircraft around the crash scene. Yet, there were none. There were only small scraps. That defies logic and experience. How could a 250,000 pound aircraft vanish and leave only scattered small pieces behind? It makes no sense and suggests that there was no Boeing 757 that struck the Pentagon. If no Boeing 757 struck the Pentagon, we are left to conclude that the small bits of plane debris must have been planted at the scene.

Bodies From Henan Airlines Crash

Another thing that McIntyre does not mention is the presence of any bodies. The picture at left is of a crash of Henan Airlines aircraft that crashed at Yichun City's airport in the northeastern Chinese province of Heilongjiang on August 24, 2010, killing 42 of the 91 people aboard.[31] Notice the bodies wrapped and lined up at the crash site. According to the official conspiracy theory there were 64 passengers on AA Flight 77. While 64 is well below the capacity of 176, 64 passengers would be a sufficient number to leave a gruesome scene of dead bodies and body parts everywhere. The 64 people were not just seated on the plane, they were traveling across country to Los Angeles. They would have packed lots of luggage. There was not a single picture or sighting of any luggage. In addition, one would think that with 176 seats that there would be at least one extant picture of an airline seat from the Pentagon crash, yet there are no pictures of a single seat or even the remnant of a single metal seat frame. There was no visual evidence of any bodies at the Pentagon on 9-11-2001. In addition, we see that the large tail section of the Chinese plane survived the horrific crash. That is common with airplane crashes, and it is notable that the common occurrence of a surviving tail section was not present at the Pentagon.

Freelance videographer, Bob Pugh who was on the scene within five minutes of the attack on the Pentagon, stated that he was looking for airplane wreckage but did not see anything discernable from an airplane.[32] Pugh stated that he did not see any airplane seats, tail, wheels, engines, luggage, or airline logo. He filmed the Air Florida plane crash and expected to see similar airplane wreckage at the Pentagon, but there was none, and he was looking for it so that he could film it. He was surprised that there was no damage to the grass or heliport in front of the alleged impact area. One notable unexplained fact is that the heliport tower on the left of the picture above has no damage to it whatsoever.

Pugh opined that the hole in the Pentagon was approximately 16 feet, but no more than 20 feet, in diameter. The hole was so small that close examination of the picture above does not reveal anything close to being large enough to absorb a large plane into the building.[33] Compare that picture to later pictures of the Pentagon and it becomes clear that the secondary explosions that were heard by the witnesses caused more damage to the Pentagon than the initial explosion. In fact, later in the day a whole section of the building approximately 50 feet to the right of the alleged impact point collapsed as a result of the later secondary explosions.

One thing is clear, there is no plane wreckage visible. Major General Albert Stubblebine, U.S. Army Ret., is of the opinion that no plane hit the Pentagon.[34] He states that the hole is not big enough to account for the impact of a Boeing 757. He is an expert who knows what he is talking about. One of his many assignments was to be in charge of scientific analysis of images depicted in photographs, in particular Russian military equipment.

General Stubblebine retired as the Commanding General of the United States Army Intelligence and Security Command (INSCOM). In that capacity he was responsible for all of the U.S. Army's strategic intelligence forces around the world. "He had responsibilities for the signals intelligence, photo intelligence, counter-intelligence and human intelligence. Prior to this assignment he commanded the US Army Electronics Research and Development Command (ERADCOM). During his active duty career he commanded soldiers at every level. One of his experiences in the Army was being in charge of the Army''s imagery interpretation for scientific and technical intelligence during the Cold War."[35]

You don't need a photographic expert like General Stubblebine to point out the obvious fact that it is impossible for a Boeing 757 to have hit the Pentagon. You can see in the picture below where the hole is framed by the square that there is no way a Boeing 757 could completely fit in that hole and leave no wreckage outside.[36]

The Pentagon is one of the most secure facilities in the world with virtually every square inch of the exterior under constant video surveillance. Yet, one of the few Pentagon videos of the 9/11 attack contained only five frames released in March 2002. Those frames are of rather poor quality, with an obstructed view. The video has allegedly altered frames showing a white smoke trail, which is an impossible exhaust for a turbofan jet engine at sea level. The time stamp on the video was "Sep. 12, 2001, 17:37:21," which indicates that it was an after-the-fact fabrication.[37]

The surrounding businesses that had surveillance cameras had their videos quickly seized by the FBI. "The FBI visited a hotel near the Pentagon to confiscate film from a security camera which some hotel employees had been watching in horror shortly after the attack. The FBI denied that the footage captured the attack."[38] In addition, the "FBI visited the Citgo gas station southwest of the Pentagon within minutes of the attack to confiscate film that may have captured the attack."[39]

Lawsuits had to be filed by various parties in order to obtain the videos. The Department of Justice was forced to admit on September 9, 2005, that "85 videotapes in the FBI's possession are 'potentially responsive'" to the request for videos. On September 15, 2006, the Department of Justice released parts of the Citgo gas station video, which for the most part showed the interior and limited portions of the exterior, but not any view of the Pentagon.

The Department of Justice finally released a video from the Double Tree Hotel to Judicial Watch on December 2, 2006, which showed the explosion at the Pentagon, but did not show the plane.[40] If there had been a plane, it would have been revealed on the video flying into the Pentagon.[41] Once more, the evidence points to the fact that AA Flight 77 did not strike the Pentagon.

4 Decoy Plane

One might ask about all of the witnesses who saw a plane strike the Pentagon. Craig Ranke and Aldo Marquis traveled to Arlington, Virginia, where the Pentagon is located and interviewed many of those witnesses. Their interviews of the witnesses were videotaped and have been posted on the internet.[42] They have uncovered irrefutable evidence of a decoy plane that witnesses saw fly at a low level toward and over the Pentagon at precisely the time that the west wing of the Pentagon exploded into a fireball. The plane then continued on its path and flew away. The decoy plane served its purpose of convincing many witnesses that it in fact struck the Pentagon. However, when questioned on that point most of the witnesses admitted that they did not actually see the plane strike the Pentagon, they just assumed it did when they saw the explosion after the plane passed overhead very close to the ground.

Below is a chart showing the path of the decoy airliner as described by 13 different witnesses who saw the jet from five different vantage points.[43] The trajectory of the plane is depicted by the witnesses flying north of the Citgo gas station. The government conspiracy theory is that the plane followed the path depicted on the chart knocking over the light posts depicted as white dots. The government is locked into the path south of the Citgo station, since there are light posts that were knocked down as an apparent staging of the event to convince the public that the damage to the Pentagon was due to a low flying airliner. The only light poles knocked down were the five light poles depicted as large white dots on the picture. The key landmark in the picture is the Citgo gas station. All of the witnesses, including several at the Citgo station itself, were positive that it passed north of the station. The government conspiracy theory is that the plane passed south of the station.

One notable witness was Sgt. William Lagasse, who is an officer with the Defense Protective Service Police at the Pentagon. Sgt. Lagasse, who was at the Citgo gas station on 9-11-2001, stated that he was 100% sure and that he would bet his life on his observation that the plane flew between Arlington Cemetery and the Navy Annex, north of the Citgo gas station. He was at the gas pump on the north side of the station when the plane flew by him. It would have been impossible for him to have seen the plane if it passed to the south of the station, because his view to the south was blocked by the station building and the large expansive canopy over the pumps. Sgt. Lagasse can be seen at the north gas pump at the Citgo in a surveillance video that was released years later by the government as a result of a Freedom of Information Act request by Judicial Watch. The surveillance video verifies that Sgt. Lagasse could only have seen the plane if it had passed to the north of the station. Sgt. Lagasse's observations were corroborated by Sgt. Chadwick Brooks of the Defense Protective Service, who also saw the plane pass to the north of the Citgo station.

Another thing mentioned by Sgt. Lagasse is that after leaving the Citgo gas station to render assistance at the Pentagon, he heard what he called secondary explosions. He concluded that those secondary explosions were from compressed natural gas and welding equipment. However, they were so significant that he said that the explosions and smoke forced him to leave the area. In fact, one of the explosions was caught on a news broadcast at approximately 10:10 a.m. It was described as "another loud explosion" by the FOX5 newscaster, Audrey Barnes, who was on the scene.[44] Barnes stated that "you could hear it very clearly, it was a loud boom!" The secondary explosions explain the collapse of the section of the Pentagon at about that time.

The key witness that establishes that the plane seen by the other witnesses was a decoy plane is Roosevelt Roberts. Upon hearing the explosion he took seven steps from his booth to look out of the loading dock where he worked and saw a large commercial jet flying very low banking over the south Pentagon parking lot. He stated that it was flying just above the light poles. He stated that it took him approximately 10 seconds after he heard the explosion at the Pentagon to walk to the loading dock platform where he saw the plane banking hard and flying away from the Pentagon in a southwesterly direction.[45] That means that the plane that was seen by the other witnesses did not in fact hit the Pentagon but flew over the Pentagon at the moment that the side of the building exploded and then immediately turned and flew away.

Another important witness is Erik Dihle, who was an Arlington National Cemetery employee. He was interviewed by the Center for Military History on December 13, 2001. Dihle stated that within seconds of the huge explosion that nearly knocked him out of his chair, "some people were yelling that a bomb had hit the Pentagon and a jet kept on going."[46]

The striking thing about Dihle's testimony is that he is explaining what people said they saw within seconds of the event in a state of excitement without any time to reflect. Hearsay is usually not admissible in evidence. Hearsay is an out-of-court statement being introduced to prove the truth of the matter asserted. However, there is an exception to the hearsay rule, which allows a hearsay statement into evidence if it has objective indicia of reliability. In virtually all state and federal courts excited utterances like the ones heard by Dihle are considered reliable and therefore admissible. An excited utterance is "a statement relating to a startling event or condition made while the declarant was under the stress of excitement caused by the event or condition."[47] The reason courts allow excited utterances into evidence is that the person does not have an opportunity to reflect and fabricate a false declaration while they are explaining an exciting event while under the stress of that exciting event. Dihle would be able to testify in court regarding the excited utterances by the people who explained that a jet flew away after the explosion. The inherently reliable statements of the witnesses to the Pentagon indicate that the witnesses honestly perceived that a jet kept on flying away after the explosion at the Pentagon.

American Airlines Flight 77 allegedly struck the portion of the Pentagon that had undergone a billion-dollar renovation. That section had been reconstructed with a web of steel columns and bars to withstand bomb blasts. The outer walls were 24 inches thick (10 inches of concrete + 8 inches of brick + 6 inches of Indiana limestone).[48] The building contained steel reinforcement, bolted together to form a continuous structure through all of the Pentagon's five floors. The area allegedly struck by the plane also had blast-resistant windows that were 2 inches thick and weighed 2,500 pounds each.[49] September 11, 2010, was the day that the contract for the renovation of that section of the Pentagon was officially complete.[50]

What are the chances that a terrorist attack takes place on the very day on the section of a building on which a huge renovation project has just been completed? One would think that if any building could withstand a strike from an aircraft it would be the newly reinforced section of the Pentagon. Yet the building was severely damaged all the way through to the C ring. If this were a true terrorist attack, the terrorists could not have picked the worst location to hit with a plane. If, however, the 9/11 attacks were planned ahead of time by elements within the government, then the renovation of the Pentagon would have been the perfect cover to plant explosives in the building.

Supposed Path of Alleged Plane to C Ring Hole

At left is a picture showing the official version of the trajectory of the alleged plane showing where the hole in the C ring of the Pentagon is located.[51] Below right is a closeup picture of the hole in the C ring.[52] Explosives experts who have looked at the hole in the C ring of the Pentagon have concluded that it was made with an explosive shaped charge.[53] A symmetrical hole is a telltale characteristic of a rapid wall breaching shaped charge used by the military.[54]

The official story is that an aircraft made of thin aluminum was able to pierce through a 24-inch thick bomb resistant brick, concrete, and limestone wall and continue through nine more feet of reinforced concrete in five more walls in three other buildings before punching out a nearly Symmetrical hole with the thin aluminum nose of the plane, leaving no evidence of the plane near the impact area or the exit hole.[55] That is simply impossible!

Closeup of C Ring Hole

If an aircraft did not strike the Pentagon, that points directly to high treason by government officials. There would have had to have been access to the Pentagon to set up explosives. Access to a secure facility like the Pentagon, would mean that elements of the government had to be involved. The suspicious behavior of high officials in the U.S. Government points to their guilt in the 9/11 attacks. On September 11, 2001, U.S. Representative Christopher Cox gave the following account of his observations of what U.S. Defense Secretary Donald Rumsfeld said on that day.

> At 9 a.m. EDT Tuesday, as a hijacked Boeing 767 slammed into the World Trade Center, I was in the Pentagon in the private dining room of the Secretary of Defense. Don Rumsfeld, the Secretary, and Paul Wolfowitz, the Deputy Secretary, and I were discussing how to win votes for the Bush defense plan that is now pending in the House and Senate.

> When minutes later, the Pentagon itself was hit by a Boeing 757 loaded with civilian passengers, virtually the entire building was immediately evacuated. I escaped just minutes before the building was hit. Most of those who remained were huddled in the National Military Command Center in a basement bunker of the building. From there, America's military response is being directed even now.
>
> Ironically, just moments before the Department of Defense was hit by a suicide hijacker, Secretary Rumsfeld was describing to me why America needs to abandon its decade-old two-major-war strategy, and focus on the real threat facing us in the 21st century: terrorism, and the unexpected.[56]

* * *

> "And let me tell you, I've been around the block a few times. There will be another event." He [Rumsfeld] repeated it for emphasis: "There will be another event." Within minutes of that utterance, Rumsfeld's words proved tragically prophetic.[57]

That blockbuster revealed by Representative Cox points to Rumsfeld as having foreknowledge of the 9/11 attacks. Foreknowledge by Secretary of Defense Rumsfeld implicates him in the attacks. Rumsfeld's behavior was even more suspicious than his statements. Rumsfeld knew that America was under attack, yet after the Pentagon was struck he abandoned his post as the chief civilian officer in charge of military defense of the country. One unnamed White House official said: "What was Rumsfeld doing on 9/11? He deserted his post. He disappeared. The country was under attack. Where was the guy who controls America's defense? Out of touch!"[58]

After the two alleged planes were reported to have struck the World Trade Center, Rumsfeld continued with his usual scheduled appointments and did not immediately go to the Executive Support Center (ESC), located near his office, which would have been the ordinary protocol in the event of a terrorist attack.[59] Rumsfeld did finally show up at the ESC, but not until around 10:15 a.m., which was a full hour and 15 minutes after being notified of the alleged second plane hitting the World Trade Center and approximately 45 minutes after the attack on the Pentagon.[60]

Paul Wolfowitz, who was Rumsfeld's immediate subordinate as Deputy Secretary of Defense, came up with this account of why he took no immediate action after he found out that two alleged planes struck the World Trade Center:

> We were having a meeting in my office. Someone said a plane had hit the World Trade Center. Then we turned on the television and

> we started seeing the shots of the second plane hitting, and this is
> the way I remember it. It's a little fuzzy.... There didn't seem to be
> much to do about it immediately and we went on with whatever the
> meeting was.[61]

Wolfowitz said "there didn't seem to be much to do about it!" That is not the response from a loyal Deputy Secretary of Defense! That is the statement of a treasonous accomplice who is trying to explain his unexplainable failure to act in the face of obvious terrorist attacks!

Instead of manning his post and coordinating the nation's defenses to what to all appeared to be a massive attack, Rumsfeld ran outside the Pentagon and made himself unavailable to coordinate anything. Mathew Everett concluded that "a closer analysis shows, Rumsfeld's behavior that morning was sinister and highly suspicious. The fact that an individual in such a position of responsibility should have acted as Rumsfeld did at such a critical moment should be of concern to us all."[62] Why would he seemingly remove himself from any ability to coordinate a defense? Because he knew that the attacks would happen and his job was to delay making any important defense decisions until the coordinated attacks were played out and those that performed the dirty deeds were given an opportunity to get away without being discovered.

Both Defense Secretary Rumsfeld and Deputy Defense Secretary Wolfowitz are listed as signatories on the June 3, 1997, Statement of Principles for the Project for a New American Century.[63] Vice President Dick Cheney is also listed as a signatory on that Statement of Principles. The Project for a New American Century (PNAC) issued a paper (Rebuilding America's Defenses) on September 2000, one year before the 9-11-2001 attacks. That document advocated transforming the United States politically and militarily.

In that report, PNAC stated that the United States must increase its defense budget, transform the military to use advanced technologies, redefine the military to perform constabulary missions throughout the world, and maintain sufficient forces to fight and win multiple large scale wars. The September 2000 paper stated: "Further, the process of transformation, even if it brings revolutionary change, is likely to be a long one, absent some catastrophic and catalyzing event - like a new Pearl Harbor."[64] The 9/11 attacks would certainly qualify as a new Pearl Harbor.

The strange inaction of Wolfowitz and Rumsfeld on 9-11-2001 is revealing when it is viewed in the light of the need for a "new Pearl Harbor" expressed by their September 2000 PNAC report. The 9/11 attacks certainly brought about a political and military "revolutionary change" as envisioned in their report. The proof is in the pudding. The United States has in fact been transformed politically and militarily as a result of the 9/11 attacks.

5   2.3 Trillion Reasons for the Pentagon Attack

The day before 9/11, on September 10, 2001, Secretary of Defense Rumsfeld held a press conference at which he acknowledged that "according to some estimates we cannot track 2.3 trillion dollars in transactions."[65] That is not some accounting rounding error. That's trillion with a "T." That is $8,000 for every man, woman, and child in the United States. It is incomprehensible that the Pentagon would lose track of $2.3 trillion. Rumsfeld's newspeak about failing to "track" $2.3 trillion dollars in transactions really means that someone stole $2.3 trillion.

    Such a huge theft would have to be investigated. Auditors investigating the theft were in the financial management/audit area, which is contiguous to the Army personnel offices, which were heavily damaged in the Pentagon attack. It seems that the attack targeted the computers and personnel that were tracking the massive theft.[66]

    The Pentagon's top financial officer at the time was Dov Zakheim, who was a Jewish rabbi and reportedly a dual citizen of Israel. He is a staunch supporter of Israel who was instrumental in Israel receiving squads of F-15s and F-16s at a fraction of their true cost by having them classified as surplus military equipment.[67] Zakheim began his stint as Pentagon comptroller in May 2001. By the time Zakheim left his position in March 2004, there was an additional $1 trillion dollars missing, for which there was no accounting. He was unable to explain the missing money.[68]

    Zakheim, along with Rumsfeld, Wolfowitz, and Cheney, was a member of PNAC. As a member of PNAC, he was listed as a contributor to the September 2000 paper, Rebuilding America's Defenses. As mentioned above, that document stated that it would take a long time for the political and military transformation of the U.S. advocated by PNAC "absent a catastrophic and catalyzing event - like a new Pearl Harbor."[69] It was no coincidence that a year after that article, when the PNAC members were in places of power in the government, the United States was subjected to the well orchestrated insider 9/11 attacks.

6   A Patriotic Witness Steps From the Rubble

April Gallop was a Pentagon employee who was present in the Pentagon when it was attacked on 911. She was an administrative specialist with the U.S. Army, with a top secret special compartmented information clearance. Her first-hand eyewitness experience corroborates the evidence listed in the previous chapters. Gallop and her infant child were injured in the explosion that enveloped her office. After the attacks she was in the hospital and was visited by civilian and military personnel who were not concerned with her well-being or that of her child. Neither were they interested in hearing what she had to say about what happened. Instead, they were there to inform her of what happened at the Pentagon that day. They told her that a plane had struck the Pentagon.[70] It is apparent that their job was to give her the company line, so to speak, and that she should adhere to that story.

When she later raised questions about the lack of any plane parts at the alleged crash site, the Department of Defense retaliated against her. She was wrongfully denied medical care and other benefits she should have received since the attack. She was refused service at the VA medical center, on grounds that she supposedly owed the Defense Department more than $14,000; for which no documentation has ever been provided.[71] Officials from the Department of Defense have acted to discourage others from helping her. When she was discharged from the army, the Department of Defense closed out her account with a zero balance.

Gallop's desk on 9-11-2001 was roughly 40 feet from the hole in the outer wall of the Pentagon. She was returning from maternity leave and was instructed by her supervisor to immediately go to her office as soon as she arrived at work to perform an urgent document clearing job. She was told that she should not drop her baby off at child care until she was finished with the job. Following those instructions, she was able to get her child cleared through security. She sat down at her desk, and as soon as she turned on her computer she heard and felt two explosions in succession.[72] Flames shot out of her computer, the walls collapsed and the ceiling fell in. She was dazed, but ultimately found her baby and made her way toward the daylight showing through a blasted opening in the outside wall.

When making her way to safety through the building and out the hole she saw no airplane wreckage, no seats, no luggage, no burning airplane fuel anywhere. There was no evidence of a plane inside the building. She saw only rubble and dust. When she made it outside the building, she saw no evidence of any plane parts anywhere outside the Pentagon.

If a plane had struck the building Gallop was in a position to see its wreckage as she traversed the area immediately inside and outside the alleged impact zone. She explained in an interview that she was concentrating on what was on the ground because she lost her shoes and was therefore walking barefooted with her baby son on her shoulder. She was being watchful and careful not to cut her feet on the debris.[73] Consequently she was focused on the debris and what type of debris it was. Gallop never at any time saw any plane debris or any sign whatsoever that an airliner had struck the Pentagon. A significant point is that in talking with her coworkers who also survived the blast, it was unanimous among them that there was no visible plane debris immediately inside or outside the impact zone.[74]

In 2008, Gallop filed a federal lawsuit against Vice President Dick Cheney, Secretary of Defense Donald Rumsfeld, General Richard Myers, U.S.A.F. (Ret.), and others unknown for their complicity in the 9/11 attacks. Her lawsuit was dismissed, and she has appealed that dismissal. One of the three judges hearing her appeal in the U.S. Court of Appeals for the Second Circuit is none other than Judge John Walker, who is President George Walker Bush's cousin.[75] As of this writing, her appeal is pending.

Gallop's original complaint sets forth compelling facts in support of her claim. Her most significant charge is that the official story that a hijacked plane crashed into the Pentagon and exploded is false. Her claim is supported by clear and convincing evidence. She bases that claim in pertinent part on the following first-hand observations:

> At the building, inside or outside of the wall the plane supposedly hit, there was no wreckage, no airplane fragments, no engines, no seats, no luggage, no fuselage sections with rows of windows, and especially, no blazing quantities of burning jet fuel. The interior walls and ceilings and contents in that area were destroyed, but there was no sign of a crashed airplane. A number of those present inside the building and out have attested to this fact in published reports.[76]

Gallop's complaint points out the obvious impossibility of the government's official plane-impact conspiracy theory:

> The nose of such a plane contains radar equipment, and the outer shell is made of a porous, composite material that allows the radar to function. Therefore, the nose was not capable of surviving an impact with the outer wall without being crushed, let alone penetrating all the way inside to the C-Ring wall, 300 feet away.[77]

If a plane did not strike the Pentagon, what caused the damage? Gallop points out:

> Several trained and experienced military personnel at the scene noted the distinctive odor of cordite, a high explosive used in gunpowder, in the aftermath of the attack at the Pentagon. This suggests explosives as the cause for the destruction rather than the impact and fire resulting from burning jet fuel.[78]

Her complaint raises an issue that few have touched. If, as has been reported, it was known that there was an unidentified jet plane approaching the Pentagon, after all domestic flights had been grounded, and the twin towers had allegedly been struck by two planes, why were there no efforts made to sound the alarm and evacuate the Pentagon?

> If an unauthorized non-military plane was headed towards the building, on a day when two apparently hijacked planes had hit the Twin Towers, why wasn't she evacuated, with her baby, instead of hurried inside? Why weren't alarms going off, and all the people in the building rushing to safety? Due to the conspiracy, and defendants' actions and flagrant failures to act, in furtherance of it, one hundred and twenty-five people, members of the Military and civilian employees, died in the bombing; and many more including plaintiff and her child were seriously hurt.[79]

Her complaint points out the black box data from the alleged plane released by the National Transportation Safety Board (NTSB) indicates that "the plane passed over the building at very low altitude, just as an explosion and fireball were engineered by other means, a planted bomb or bombs and/or a missile."[80] Regarding the flight data, Gallop further points out:

> The "black box" flight data recorder identified by the Government as coming from Flight 77, and reportedly recovered from the wreckage at the scene, bears data, according to pilots who have examined printouts provided by the National Transportation Safety Board (NTSB), which contradict various aspects of the official account, — and indeed the very notion that a plane struck the Pentagon — in crucial ways, viz:
>
> It is a fundamental premise of airliner manufacture and operation that the black box only stops recording data when a flight is terminated — by the pilot turning off the engines at the gate, or by a crash. According to the pilots who studied the printouts, however, the record showing the path of Flight 77, etched with codes which connect it to that plane that day, cuts off, unaccountably, some 4-500 yards short of the building

Gallop points out contradictions between the 9/11 Commission Report and the NTSB conclusions:

> The Safety Board has released a computer simulation of the flight path of Flight 77, allegedly based on the data from the flight recorder, which contradicts a simulation adopted by the 9/11 Commission. The Commission simulation shows the flight path of the official story, at an angle reflected by the damage inside the building, consistent with the downed light poles, and to the south of two nearby buildings housing the Navy Annex and a Citgo gas station. The NTSB simulation shows the plane headed towards the building on a path north of the two buildings and the line of lampposts.[81]

Notice the key point made in the complaint that the NTSB simulation, based upon the flight data in the black box, shows the plane headed toward the building on a path north of the Citgo gas station. That is directly contrary to the path as portrayed in the official story by the 9/11 Commission, which has the plane traveling south of the Citgo station. The northern path is consistent with the 13 eyewitnesses who saw the decoy plane approach the Pentagon north of the Citgo gas station prior to the explosion. Obviously, the NTSB simulation was based upon the black box data in the decoy plane. The decoy plane never actually struck the building, which is why the data on the black box terminated 400 to 500 yards short of the Pentagon.

Gallop raises questions about the very existence of highjackers:

> There have also been repeated reports since 9/11 that several of the other men named and pictured by the FBI as the hijackers were still alive after 9/11, and living in various locations in the world — including one, Waleed Al-Shehri, who was said to be a working pilot for Moroccan Air Lines, correctly shown in the FBI photo, whose identity and location have been verified by at least one major press outlet, the BBC. This information has not been pursued by U.S. investigators, or media.[82]

Most significant is the missing $2.3 trillion that Defense Secretary Rumsfeld announced at a press conference on September 10, 2011, which has all been forgotten about after the 9/11 attacks.

> Further, it should be noted that on September 10, 2001, the day before the attack, Defendant Rumsfeld conducted a press conference at the Pentagon in which he publicly announced that auditors had determined that some 2.3 trillion dollars in Defense Department funds —$2.300,000,000,000 — could not be accounted for. To plaintiff's knowledge and belief, part of the area

of the ground floor of the Pentagon that was destroyed in the bombing is a location where records were kept that would be used to trace those funds, and where people worked who knew about them. On information and belief, there has been to this day no public report concerning the fate of those records, or that money.[83]

7 What Happened to UA Flight 93?

Below is a picture of the alleged crash site for United Airlines Flight 93 near Shankesville, Pennsylvania.[84] Notice that, as with the Pentagon, there is no sign of a plane anywhere. This is supposed to be the scene of a Boeing 757 crash, yet there are no engines, no wings, no seats, no fuselage, no tail section or any of the parts one would expect to find from a 115-ton aircraft.

Alleged UA Flight Point of Impact - No Plane Debris

Eyewitnesses on the scene saw no sign of an aircraft anywhere. Chris Konicki, a photographer, was interviewed by a local FOX News affiliate reporter and asked "Any large pieces of debris at all?... Smoke? Fire?" Konicki stated: "No, there was nothing, nothing that you could distinguish that a plane had crashed there. ... No smoke. No fire."[85]

The Mayor of Shanksville, Ernie Stull, in an interview with a German reporter in March 2003 stated: "My sister and a good friend of mine were the first ones there," Stull said. "They were standing on a street corner in Shanksville talking. Their car was nearby, so they were the first here - and the fire department came. Everyone was puzzled, because the call had been that a plane had crashed. But there was no plane. They had been sent here because of a crash, but there was no plane."[86]

Dennis Roddy who is managing editor of the Pittsburgh Post Gazette sent a team of reporters to the crash site, which was one and 1/2 hours by automobile. Upon arrival Roddy stated that there was no airplane debris that he could identify.[87]

Somerset county coroner, Wallace Miller, was one of the first persons on the crash scene. The Washington Post reported:

> Miller was among the very first to arrive after 10:06 on the magnificently sunny morning of September 11. He was stunned at how small the smoking crater looked, he says, "like someone took a scrap truck, dug a 10-foot ditch and dumped all this trash into it." Once he was able to absorb the scene, Miller says, "I stopped being coroner after about 20 minutes, because there were no bodies there."[88]

Coroner Miller was interviewed a year later, on September 11, 2002, by the Pittsburgh Tribune Review: "He takes off his glasses, cleans them with his T-shirt. 'This is the most eerie thing,' he says. 'I have not, to this day, seen a single drop of blood. Not a drop.'"[89] Miller said something during the interview that seemed incongruent with an airline crash scene. He said "he saw shreds of that white cloth they put over the headrests."[90] Reflect on that for a minute; large steel wheel struts, titanium engine parts, huge aluminum wings, hundreds of aluminum seats, and 40 bodies, all totaling 115 tons disappeared, and yet the thin disposable cloth headrest covers survived. The only conclusion to draw from such a circumstance is that no Boeing 757 crashed, and the scene was staged (apparently not very convincingly) by planting bits of aircraft scraps to make it appear that a plane crashed there.

There is more direct evidence of a staged scene and planted evidence. The investigators who run the website www.killtown.com have discovered clear evidence that the cockpit voice recorder alleged to be from UA Flight 93 was in fact planted on the site. Below is a picture of a cockpit voice recorder (CVR) that was introduced as an exhibit during the *United States v. Moussaoui* trial.[91] That CVR depicted in the exhibit photograph is supposed to have been found at the scene of the alleged crash in Shanksville. The perpetrators of the 9/11 crimes, however, made a mistake. They planted the wrong CVR at the Shanksville alleged crash site.[92] Look closely at the H in the picture. It is the remnant of a manufacturer's label, indicating it was made by Honeywell.

M-CSP-00009733

Plane N591UA, which is the plane that was allegedly United Airlines Flight 93, went into service in 1996.[93] The flight data recorder is supposed to be labeled "Allied Signal," not "Honeywell." That is because it was not until 1999, when Allied-Signal acquired Honeywell and took its more recognizable name, that it made CVRs under the brand name Honeywell. In fact, the Flight Data Recorder (FDR), which is a separate instrument, allegedly recovered for the plane that was flight 93 was listed by the NTSB as manufactured by Allied Signal. Apparently, the perpetrators planted a CVR without realizing that it was manufactured after the plane that allegedly crashed at Shanksville was built.

Honeywell

If UA Flight 93 did not crash at Shanksville, what happened to it? Cincinnati News station WCPO "9News" reported on 11:43:57 AM on 9-11-2001 that United Airlines Flight 93 landed at Cleveland Airport on 9-11-2001. The report stated in pertinent part: "A Boeing 767 out of Boston made an emergency landing Tuesday at Cleveland Hopkins International Airport due to concerns that it may have a bomb aboard, said Mayor Michael R. White. White said the plane had been moved to a secure area of the airport, and was evacuated. United identified the plane as Flight 93."[94]

The 9News report was later deleted from the internet with an explanation that it was an erroneous report from the AP. The problem with that explanation is that it was posted as a report from the "9News Staff." Nowhere in the article was there an attribution to the AP. Furthermore, there are two sources for the information named in the article 1) Mayor Michael R. White, and 2) United Airlines (who identified the plane as flight 93). Nothing can be determined with certainty from the above information alone. However, when presented with evidence that there were no bodies or any obvious plane debris at the alleged crash site for flight 93 in Shanksville, Pennsylvania, it seems like a plausible explanation for what actually happened to flight 93.

Christopher Bollyn called White at his 45-acre alpaca ranch, Seven Pines Alpacas in Newcomerstown, Ohio, to inquire about the events at the Cleveland airport on 9-11-2001. "White, however, was unwilling to discuss anything and cut the conversation short saying, 'I'm out of the interview business.'"[95]

Some have claimed that Mayor White was confused, that the flight was actually Delta Flight 1989. In fact, Delta Flight 1989 did land at Cleveland-Hopkins Airport on 9-11. Delta Flight 1989 was one of several flights that were diverted to Cleveland-Hopkins Airport. The media reported that Delta Flight1989 landed at Cleveland-Hopkins Airport at 10:10 a.m. and was evacuated at approximately 12:30 p.m. into the FAA headquarters building.[96]

Another plane landed at 10:45 a.m., and at 11:15 a.m. approximately 200 passengers were reportedly evacuated into the NASA Glenn Research Center located on the far west end of the airport.[97] It is possible that the other flight that was evacuated into the NASA Glenn Research Center was UA Flight 93. News accounts indicated that the NASA Glenn Research Center itself had been evacuated prior to the arrival of Flight 93.

One plane contained approximately 200 passengers, which was reportedly evacuated to the NASA research center. Another plane contained 78 passengers (69 passengers + 9 crew =

78), which the Cleveland Plain Dealer identified as Delta flight 1989, and reported that its passengers were taken to the FAA headquarters.[98] However, the Akron Beacon Journal, apparently referring to Delta Flight 1989, reported that 78 passengers "were taken to NASA Glenn Research Center to be interviewed by FBI agents."[99] Either that is the same plane being inconsistently reported or there were two planes with the same number of passengers reported to have been evacuated to two different locations. Mary Ethridge, one of the journalists who worked on the story for the Akron Beacon Journal, when questioned on the accuracy of the report, stood by the paper's report that the passengers had been interviewed by the FBI in the vacated NASA facility.[100]

That confirmation by Ethridge raises two possibilities: 1) two planes were unloaded into the NASA facility, one plane with approximately 200 passengers and another with 78 passengers, or 2) only one plane was evacuated into the NASA facility and the reporters simply got the number of passengers on each plane wrong. It is unclear how to resolve the seeming contradictory report that a 78-passenger flight was evacuated into the FAA Headquarters and also into the NASA facility. One thing is clear, at least one plane was evacuated into the NASA facility, and that plane was a different plane from the Delta Flight 1989 that was evacuated into the FAA facility.

Those that argue that witnesses have confused UA Flight 93 with Delta Fight 1989, do not address the reports that two different planes landed at two different times (10:10 a.m. and 10:45 a.m.) and they were evacuated to two different locations (NASA building and FAA building), over an hour apart from one another (the NASA facility at 11:15 a.m. and the FAA building at 12:30 p.m.). There is no confusing the NASA building with the FAA building, because they are a mile apart, at opposite ends of the airport.

Flight 93 and Flight 1989 drew special attention because they were surrounded by law enforcement and quarantined away from the terminal. All other flights were evacuated to the airport terminal. The time and distance between Delta Flight 1989 and UA Flight 93 is too great for anyone to have confused flight 1989 for flight 93. In order to argue there was confusion between flights, the government must identify some flight other than Delta Flight 1989, and then explain why that plane was evacuated into the NASA Research Center rather than the terminal building. There was no other flight that matches those facts, which is why that argument has not been made.

Devvy Kidd filed an FOIA request for FAA records of arrivals and departures of planes on 9-11-2001 from Cleveland-Hopkins Airport. The FAA initially lied to her by telling her that they did not have any such documents. Later, they reversed their position and stated that they had the documents after all and agreed to send them to her.[101] The FAA record reflects that Delta Flight 1989 landed at 10:11 a.m.[102] Continental Airlines Flight 3742 flying out of Cleveland is recorded as landing at Cleveland-Hopkins Airport at 10:10 a.m.[103] There was no record of the landing of UA Flight 93. That is not surprising. If UA Flight 93 had in fact landed at the Cleveland-Hopkins Airport, the government would certainly not produce a record confirming that fact; it is easy to delete entries from a government record and then produce the redacted record portraying it as genuine.

The news reported that Cleveland-Hopkins Airport was ordered closed, while other airports throughout the country were busting at the seams with planes when the order came to ground all commercial aircraft. However, the record received by Kidd was that there were other flights that landed at Cleveland-Hopkins Airport after the 9/11 attacks. In fact, 13 other flights landed at Cleveland-Hopkins Airport after Delta Flight 1989 landed at 10:11 a.m., with the Continental flight landing one minute prior, at 10:10 a.m.[104] One of those 13 flights was a military F-16 fighter jet, which landed at 12:31 p.m.

There was no report that any of the 13 other flights were quarantined at the FAA building or the NASA facility. It seems that the government is pretending that the flight that was seen being evacuated to the NASA building did not exist and that people are confusing flight 1989 with flight 93. In order to abide by the government version of events, one must conclude that no plane was evacuated to the NASA facility. That simply does not hold water as there were specific times of the landing and evacuation given by witnesses. The evacuation of the plane to the NASA facility was one hour and fifteen minutes before flight 1989 was evacuated into the FAA building a mile away. There is just too much time and space separating the events for witnesses to have confused the two flights.

The news estimate that there were approximately 200 passengers aboard UA Flight 93 being evacuated to the NASA facility would put the plane above its maximum capacity, since the UA Flight 93 Boeing 757 only had the capacity to carry 182 passengers (not including the seating available for the seven crew members).[105] The media story is that UA Flight 93 was alleged to have had only 44 passengers (that number includes seven crew members and four highjackers). How then did the passenger list balloon to an estimated 200 passengers? Some have speculated that the plane was loaded with passengers from other alleged highjacked planes at another site.

Would such a theory even make mathematical sense? If the Boeing 757 that was UA Flight 93 landed at Cleveland-Hopkins Airport, it would only have had capacity to carry 182 passengers. If we assume, as the evidence suggests, that the highjackers did not in fact truly exist, we are left with 256 passengers on the four planes (275 total reported passengers - 19 fictional highjackers = 256).[106] A Boeing 757 configured like UA Flight 93 is not large enough to carry 256 passengers. While the UA Flight 93 Boeing 757 was configured to only carry 182 passengers, it should be noted that the Boeing 757 has many different seat layouts available and can be configured to carry as many as 279 passengers.

The above calculation is premised on assumption that American Airlines flights 11 and 77 actually existed. As discussed in a previous chapter, the evidence suggests that AA flights 11 and 77 never existed on 9-11-2001. If flights 11 and 77 did not exist, that would eliminate 146 passengers from the equation. Only one plane (containing 110 passengers) would need to be evacuated into the NASA facility. The UA Flight 93 Boeing 757, which was configured to carry 182 passengers, would have had the capacity to carry 110 passengers.

Why would the government want to evacuate passengers from a flight into a NASA facility? Cathy O'Brien in her book, Trance-Formation of America, explained that she was often brought to NASA facilities to undergo tortuous mind-control programing. She stated that part of the process of mind-control involved the use of CIA designer drugs which rendered her helpless and compliant.[107] Brice Taylor corroborates O'Brien's experience. Taylor stated that she would travel to NASA bases where she was subjected to high-level mind-control programming.[108] If the NASA facilities have been used for criminal kidnaping and mind-control programing, it would not be a stretch to have the same facilities used for other criminal purposes. Who knows what capabilities they have at the NASA Glenn Research Facility at Cleveland-Hopkins Airport.

There is one witness to Delta flight 1989 having landed at Cleveland-Hopkins Airport, who has written about her experience aboard that plane on 9-11.[109] The witness does not explain into which facility she was evacuated, but the time of events and the other details in her account suggest that her flight was evacuated into the FAA facility. It is interesting that the posting of the information was not made by the passenger herself, but rather by someone who says he is her friend. He states that the passenger gave him permission to post her open letter of the events on 9-11. However, he clearly has an agenda to debunk any view of the evidence that contradicts the official government story.[110] He calls those who question the official government conspiracy theory of the 9/11 attacks "9/11 skeptics/tinfoil-hat-types."[111]

It seems that the major media outlets in the area were all over the Cleveland-Hopkins Airport events of 9-11-2001; however, after the official story came out they lost interest. There was a rather suspicious lack of curiosity by the media about what took place inside the NASA facility. We don't need to theorize about what happened inside the NASA facility; all we need to know is that none of passengers who entered the NASA facility have ever been heard from again. As of this writing, it has been almost 10 years since 9-11-2001, and there are no survivor stories from any member of the crew or among the passengers from the other flights off-loaded into the NASA facility.

A fact cannot be proven from a lack of evidence, except the nonoccurrence of an event, when evidence of the event would be expected. The lack of evidence can be the basis for disproving a theory. There is a lack of evidence that a large plane crashed in the crater near Shanksville; the items that have turned up were so obviously planted, only the most gullible would believe they were evidence of a plane crash. We can reasonably infer, therefore, that the UA Flight 93 Boeing 757 did not crash at Shanksville. It is on that basis that the government's conspiracy theory can easily be disproved. We do not know for sure what happened to the plane or the passengers that were supposed to be aboard the flight. The disputed report that UA Flight 93 landed at Cleveland-Hopkins Airport and was evacuated to the NASA Research Center is a significant clue, but more evidence is needed.

The initial conspiracy theory by the government and broadcast through major media outlets was that the passengers made cell phone calls to others from the hijacked airplanes. Legitimate research indicates that the cell phone calls supposedly made from the airliners would have been impossible. One plausible explanation is that the calls were the result of voice-morphing technology that allows one person to sound exactly like another person once a voice exemplar is taken. The exemplars must have been taken prior to UA Flight 93 alleged crash time of 10:06 a.m.

A. K. Dewdney, Professor Emeritus at the University of Western Ontario, has concluded from his research that the cell phone calls allegedly made from hijacked airplanes on September 11, 2001 were nearly impossible.[112] Professor Dewdney conducted trials that confirmed the near physical impossibility of the cell phone calls.[113] A number of factors contribute to the impossibility of the calls. The metal skin on the aircraft has a Faraday effect of degrading the signal; while calls can be made from a plane parked on the ground, the weakened signal has difficulty reaching a cell tower once the plane reaches an altitude higher than 8,000 feet. Furthermore, the speed of the aircraft at more than 500 mph at cruising altitude will cause towers to drop calls. Typically, a Boeing 757 has a cruising altitude of between 30,000 and 39,000 feet. According to Professor Dewdney, the likelihood of successfully making a call at 32,000 feet is .006. That is, a cell connection could only be made in 6 out of 1,000 attempts.

According to the official 9/11 Commission Report the hijackers attacked the cockpit of UA Flight 93 at 9:28 a.m. when the plane was traveling at 35,000 feet. The plane dropped 700 feet during the struggle. At 9:32 one of the hijackers made an announcement to the Flight 93 passengers. "Shortly thereafter, the passengers and flight crew began a series of calls from GTE airphones and cellular phones."[114] In the 9-11-2001 FBI report of an interview with Deena Lynne Burnett, she told the FBI that she received a series of three to five cellular phone call from her husband, Thomas Edward Burnett, Jr., beginning at approximately 9:30 a.m. EST (6:30 PST), with the last call being at approximately 9:45 a.m. EST (6:45 a.m. PST).[115] She told the FBI Agent that she knew that her husband was using his own cellular phone because her husband's cellular phone number appeared on the caller identification. She said that only one call did not show up on caller identification because she was on the line with another call.

Here the government has a problem. According to the official 9/11 Commission Report, the plane was flying at approximately 34,300 feet (35,000 - 700 foot drop = 34,300 feet). We know that it is almost impossible for Edward Burnett to make a call from that altitude. Yet, he not only made one call, he allegedly made a series of three to five calls. According to Professor Dewdney, the chances of successfully making three successive phone calls from an altitude higher than 32,000 feet is 1 in 5 million. ($.006 \times .006 \times .006 = .0000002$).

The government had to do something about this problem. They decided to simply continue their practice of adding one lie on top of another. In 2006 during the trial in *United States v. Moussaoui*, the U.S. Department of Justice simply ignored Mrs. Burnett's account and implied that her husband called from an onboard air-phone.[116]

CeeCee Lyles, a UA flight attendant, also called from her cell phone starting at 9:47 a.m. She initially left a message. Her husband finally woke up to take her call at approximately 9:51 a.m. She told him that she was calling from the plane and that the plane had been hijacked. He looked at the caller identification and noticed that the call was from her cell phone. Her husband thought that was unusual, since he knew that cell phones do not work from planes in flight.[117]

What is very odd about the phone message left on the recorder is that she repeats three times that she is on the plane, as though she is trying to convince her husband of that fact. She states: "I am on a plane that's been hijacked, I'm on the plane, I'm calling from the plane."[118] Another thing that is odd, you can hear a voice from a person standing close by faintly whispering in the background what sounds like: "you did great."[119]

Below is a picture of the personal effects from Cee Cee Lyles. The plane, aluminum wings, titanium engines parts, fuselage, steel landing gear, tail section, 282 seats, and all the passengers completely vanished. Her body allegedly disintegrated in the crash. The coroner stated that he could not find a single drop of blood from any of the passengers. Yet, Cee Cee Lyles' thin plastic driver's license and her fragile paper receipts survived unscathed and were not even singed. That is more than incredible; it is impossible! It simply does not pass the smell test.

The Impossible Survival of CeeCee Lyles' Thin Plastic Driver's License and Paper Receipts

Certainly, Mrs. Burnett and Mr. Lyles could recognize their spouses' voices. Their spouses actually made the purported calls, right? Not necessarily. A little known technology exists that allows a person to mimic the exact sound of a person after taking a sample of only ten minutes of his voice.[120] In February 1999 the Washington Post reported that Gen. Carl W. Steiner, former Commander-in-chief, U.S. Special Operations Command was broadcast as saying: "Gentlemen! We have called you together to inform you that we are going to overthrow the United States government." The statement, however, was not made by General Steiner. It was a demonstration recording by a computer program that morphed General Steiner's voice to sound exactly like him saying something that he would never be expected to actually say. General Steiner was so impressed by the demonstration that he asked for a copy of the tape. The article presciently stated: "For Hollywood, it is special effects. For covert operators in the U.S. military and intelligence agencies, it is a weapon of the future."[121]

The future came just two years later on 9-11-2001, when the voices of passengers of the allegedly hijacked planes were morphed to sound like them making calls from planes that were supposed to have been hijacked. The author of the article explains:

> Digital morphing — voice, video, and photo — has come of age, available for use in psychological operations. PSYOPS, as the military calls it, seek to exploit human vulnerabilities in enemy governments, militaries and populations to pursue national and battlefield objectives.

* * *

> Voice-morphing? Fake video? Holographic projection? They sound more like Mission Impossible and Star Trek gimmicks than weapons. Yet for each, there are corresponding and growing research efforts as the technologies improve and offensive information warfare expands.

> Whereas early voice morphing required cutting and pasting speech to put letters or words together to make a composite, Papcun's software developed at Los Alamos can far more accurately replicate the way one actually speaks. Eliminated are the robotic intonations.[122]

The perpetrators of 9/11 could not risk having the real persons make the calls, they would have no control of what might be blurted out. The voice morphing technology explains perfectly how calls were made by persons portraying the callers who described hijackings that never took place. Below is a colloquy between a man claiming to be Mark Bingham, who called Bingham's sister-in-law, Cathy Hoglan; Bingham's mother was visiting her. Bingham's mother is Alice Bingham. Cathy Hoglan initially took the call and then handed the phone to Alice, telling her "Alice, talk to Mark. He's been hijacked." Bingham's mother made a point of stating that her son made the call from an air-phone in the plane. Below is the conversation that Alice Bingham had with the person portraying himself as her son:

Caller: "Mom? This is Mark Bingham."

Caller: "I want you to know that I love you. I'm on a flight from Newark to San Francisco and there are three guys who have taken over the plane and they say they have a bomb."

Alice: "Who are these guys?"

Caller: (after a pause) "You believe me, don't you?"

Caller: "Yes, Mark. I believe you. But who are these guys?"

(After another pause the line went dead.)[123]

Who calls his mother and gives his last name? Nobody! Someone who is portraying the son, however, would make that mistake. "Mom? This is Mark <u>Bingham</u>." The actor was a little befuddled, he was so uncertain of his success in deceiving Mark Bingham's mother that he actually asked: "You believe me, don't you?"

There is more to the mystery of Mark Bingham than the strange phone conversation he had with his mother. A groundbreaking discovery was made by Phil Jayhan. He came across information imbedded in the IPTC code of Bingham's picture posted on the CNN September 11 Memorial website which indicated that the picture and the obituarial information in the sidebar to the photograph were prepared for posting by CNN 12 days prior to 9-11-01.[124] The IPTC metadata for the posted 1993 college graduation photograph of Bingham indicated that the photograph had an IPTC title of "ATTACKS AIRLINE VICTIMS BINGHAM."[125]

The International Press Telecommunications Council (IPTC) is an organization that, among other things, sets standards for the use of metadata imbedded into a digital image.[126] Metadata is data that is usually not visible but can be read with special software by computers or humans that describes "what you can see on the photo, either using free text or codes from a controlled vocabulary."[127]

According to the IPTC, the information in the metadata includes "administrative information about the photo like who has taken it, when and where it was taken, etc."[128] The IPTC standard is designed for the international exchange of news photographs among newspapers and news agencies. Information such as the name of the photographer, copyright information, date, and the caption or other description can be embedded either manually or automatically into the digital photograph by most popular digital editing software.

The IPTC is very careful about the accuracy of the information contained in the metadata, because that is critical in establishing the legal intellectual property rights of the creator, which is why the IPTC has regular meetings with industry groups when establishing standards for the IPTC.

The IPTC metadata in the Bingham photo posted on the CNN 9/11 Memorial website (Figure 29 below) indicates that the photograph was prepared on August 30, 2001, which was 12 days prior to the September 11, 2001 attacks. The obituary, which is embedded into the digital coding of the picture stated:

> FILE--Mark Bingham, 31, shown in this 1993 graduation photograph from the University of California, Berkeley, was killed aboard United Flight 93 from Newark, N.J. to San Francisco Tuesday, Sept. 11, 2001, after it crashed outside of Pittsburgh (AP Photo/Contra Costa Times, handout)[129]

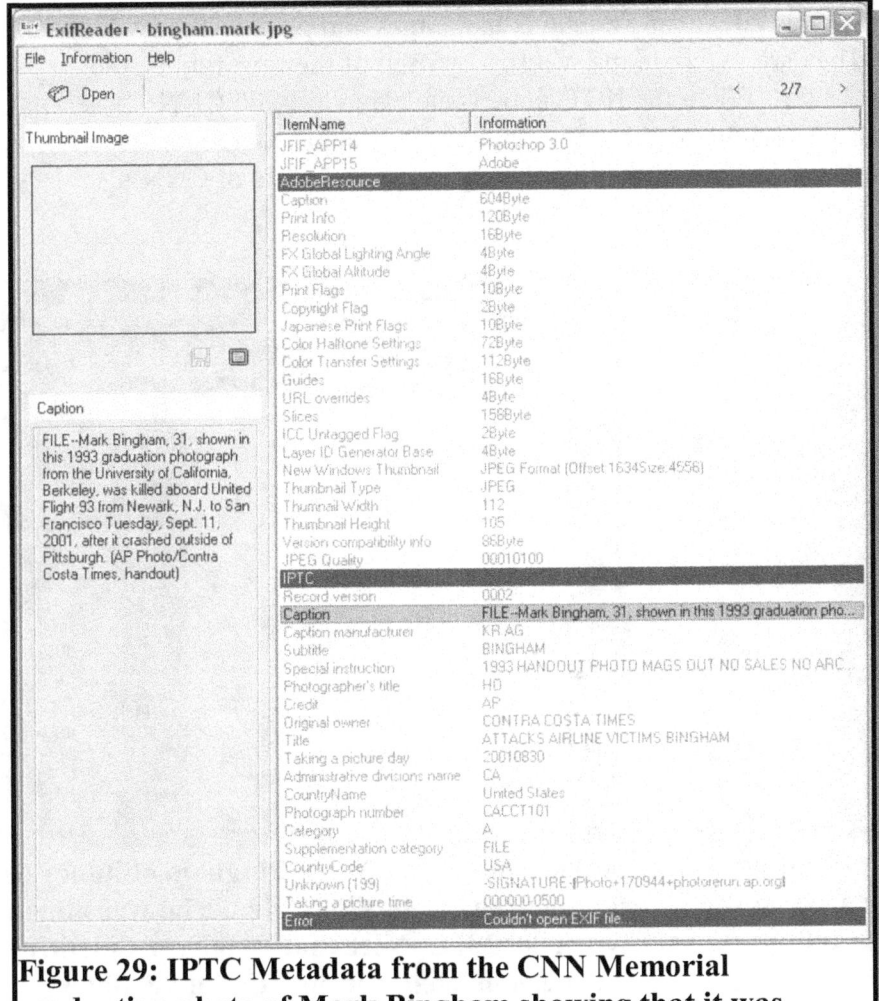

Figure 29: IPTC Metadata from the CNN Memorial graduation photo of Mark Bingham showing that it was created on August 30, 2001.

Editing a photo by using a photo editing program such as Adobe Photoshop affects the IPTC data when the person enters or updates the IPTC data manually or clicks the "Today" button to display the current date, which is standard procedure. When that is followed by clicking on the "Write" button the date is changed to the present date. That means at the very least, some or all of the IPTC metadata was entered or altered by the AP in Bingham's graduation photograph on August 30, 2001.[130]

Bingham's graduation photo was purportedly originally taken in 1993. Why would the AP show an interest in Mark Bingham on August 30, 2001? Even if the AP had an interest in Bingham, why choose an eight year old graduation photograph? Certainly they were not going to run a story about his 1993 graduation on or after 8-30-2001. The very idea is preposterous. The only logical explanation is that whoever entered the IPTC caption data, and the "ATTACKS AIRLINE VICTIMS

BINGHAM" data made a huge blunder by having the IPTC data reflect the date he made the edits, which was on August 30, 2001. The August 30, 2001 IPTC metadata clearly points to foreknowledge of the 9/11 attacks by the AP.[131]

Researchers have discovered many more persons whose photographs posted by CNN have imbedded IPTC metadata that indicate that CNN, AP, or other affiliated news entities knew in advance about the 9/11 attacks and had identified those who would be the victims of the attacks. The conclusion that the AP and CNN had prior knowledge and were in fact accomplices in the 9/11 attacks is supported by the suspicious conduct of CNN after it found out about the IPTC anomalies in the Bingham photograph.

The CNN September 11 Memorial website contains the names and obituaries for all of the victims of the 9/11 attacks. They are listed on the website by each of the four flights, the Pentagon, and the World Trade Center. When the IPTC code issue came to light, CNN responded by not only deleting Mark Bingham's photograph, but CNN also scoured its 9/11 Memorial website and deleted many other incriminating photographs. The scale of CNN's photographic redactions is surprising.

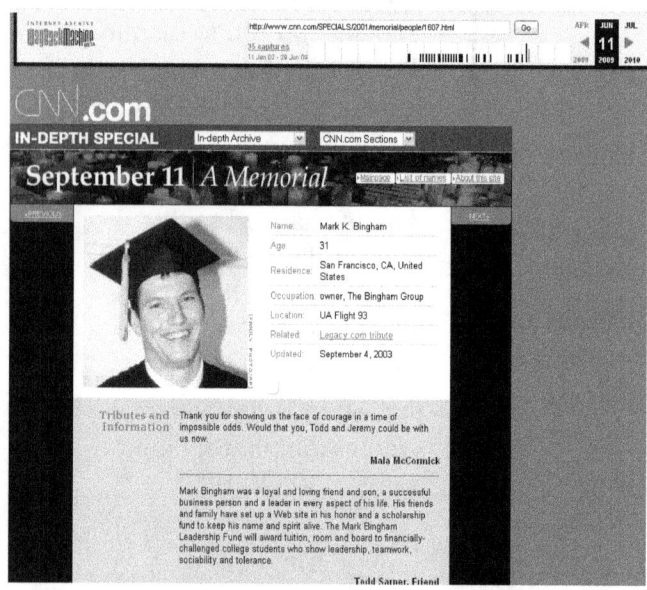

Screen shot of the Mark Bingham Obituary from the internet archive as it appeared on the CNN Memorial website on June 11, 2009.

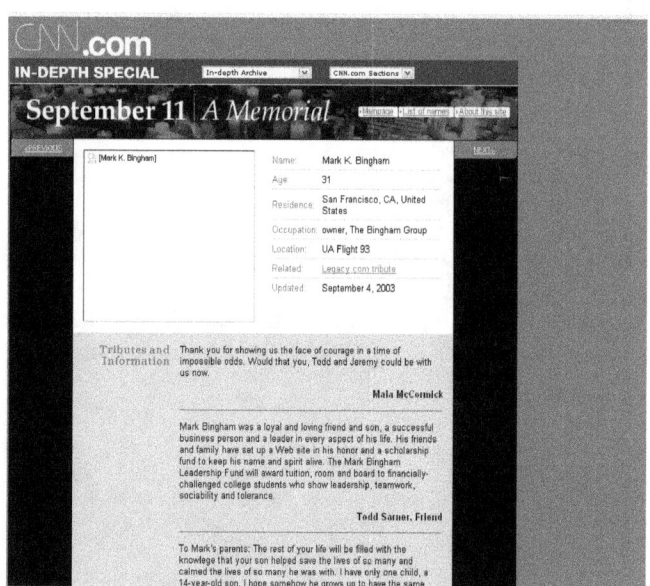

Screen shot of the Mark Bingham obituary as it appeared on the CNN Memorial website on April 30, 2011. Note that Bingham's picture has been deleted, yet the "Updated" date remains unchanged, even though the obituary has clearly been changed by deleting the picture.

The CNN September 11 Memorial website has listed the names of the 40 victims that were allegedly aboard UA Flight 93. Using the Wayback Internet Archive, one can find that on June 11, 2009, the CNN website had photographs posted for 32 out of the 40 victims allegedly aboard flight 93.[132] However, after the IPTC code issue came to light, CNN deleted Bingham's photo and the photos of 26 other victims, leaving only 5 victims with photos displayed. As of this writing (April 25, 2011), the CNN Memorial website contains only the photos of UA Flight victims Christian Adams, Colleen Fraser, Leroy Homer, Waleska Rivera, and Christine Snyder.[133]

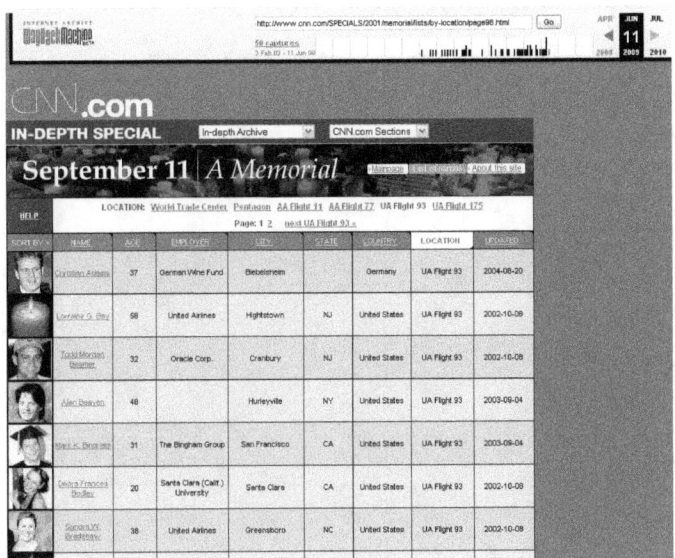

Screen shot of Internet Archive of UA Flight 93 first page on the CNN Memorial website as it appeared on June 11, 2009.

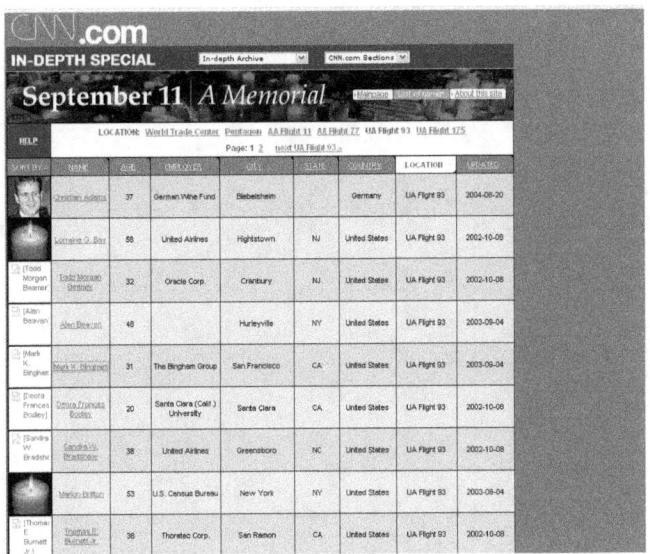

Screen shot of UA Flight 93 first page on the CNN Memorial website as it appeared on April 30, 2011. Note that most of the pictures have been deleted, yet the "Updated" date for each person remains unchanged.

As of June 11, 2009, CNN had photographs for 72 out of the 87 alleged victims for American Airlines Flight 11 on its memorial website.[134] After the IPTC metadata anomalies came to light, CNN stripped 56 of the pictures of the AA Flight 11 alleged victims. The website now depicts only 16 pictures for the 87 alleged victims of AA Flight 11.[135]

As of June 11, 2009, CNN had photographs of 40 out fo the 59 alleged victims of American Airlines flight 77 on its memorial website.[136] After the IPTC metadata information came to light, CNN deleted 33 out of the 40 pictures, leaving only 7 pictures of the alleged victims of AA Flight 77 posted on its memorial website.[137]

As of June 11, 2009, CNN had photographs of 41 out fo the 60 alleged victims of United Airlines flight 175 on its memorial website.[138] After the IPTC metadata anomalies came to light, CNN stripped 31 of the pictures of the UA Flight 175 alleged victims, leaving only 10 pictures of the 60 alleged victims of UA Flight 175 posted on its memorial website.[139]

It is quite suspicious and incriminating for CNN to delete all of those photographs. That is conduct indicating a cover-up. It is evidence that CNN and AP had prior knowledge of the

9/11 attacks, which when viewed in light of other evidence suggests that the news media was complicit in the crime of 911.

8 Impossible Speeds

The 9/11 Commission Report states that "[a]t 9:37:46, American Airlines Flight 77 crashed into the Pentagon traveling at approximately 530 miles per hour."[140] The 9/11 Commission obtained its information about the speed of alleged Flight 77 from the official reports by the National Transportation Safety Board (NTSB) and the Federal Aviation Administration (FAA). The 9/11 commission further concluded that United Airlines Flight 93 "plowed into an empty field in Shanksville, Pennsylvania, at 580 miles per hour."[141]

The NTSB concluded that alleged United Airlines Flight 175 Boeing 767, which allegedly struck the South Tower, was traveling at 510 knots (586 miles per hour) and that the alleged American Airlines Flight 11 Boeing 767, that allegedly struck the North Tower, was traveling at 430 knots (494 miles per hour).[142]

There are two "V" (velocity) speeds to which pilots must adhere. One is the "Va" speed, which is the maximum design maneuvering speed. If the pilot exceeds that speed, he risks crashing if he tries to maneuver the plane because beyond that speed he cannot maneuver the plane without losing control or causing structural failure. The other "V" speed is the "Vmo" (Velocity Maximum Operating) speed. That is the maximum operating speed limit of the aircraft, beyond which there is a danger of exceeding the design structural integrity or design stability and control of the plane (i.e., there is a danger the plane will fall apart and crash).

The Va of a Boeing 767 at sea level is 360 mph.[143] The alleged plane that struck the South Tower at a supposed speed of 586 mph, exceeded the Va of that plane by 206 mph! The Vmo of a Boeing 767 is 414 mph.[144] The alleged South Tower plane exceeded the Vmo by 172 mph! The speeds reported by the government for the airplanes on 9-11-2001 are impossible!

Keep in mind that aircraft have safety alarms required by the FAA that go off when the aircraft exceeds the Vmo. The alarm is a loud "clacker" that would be sounding in the cockpit. The idea that inexperienced pilots could fly a plane with any accuracy with a loud distracting clacker is simply incredible.

One might say that the Va and Vmo speeds seem too low, and that they have read that the Boeing 767, and similar planes, can cruise at speeds in excess of 500 mph. It is true that airliners like the 767 can cruise at such speeds, but when doing so they are traveling at altitudes greater than 30,000 feet. At such high altitude, the air is much less dense than it is at sea level. Planes therefore can travel at much greater speeds at higher altitude because there is less air resistance. The added resistance at lower altitude is similar concept to the added resistant that a runner would feel if he were to try to run the 100-yard dash while chest deep in a swimming pool. The resistance caused by the much denser water slows down the runner in much the same way as the denser air at sea level slows down a plane.

Joseph Keith, who is an aerospace engineer and the lead designer for the shaker system for Boeing Aircraft, stated that the maximum speed for the Boeing 767 at 700 feet is 330 mph. He stated that it would be impossible for a Boeing 767 to fly at 500 mph at sea level, since at that altitude the air is so thick that the turbine blades on the engine turbine would actually act as brakes and prevent the plane from going faster than 330 mph. The engines are incapable of pushing enough thick air at low altitude through the jet turbines to allow the planes to go any faster.[145] He stated that the plane at an altitude of 700 feet would begin the process of shaking itself apart at about 220 mph.[146] Even if the planes were to travel 500 mph at 700 feet, which is impossible, those planes would have shaken themselves apart before they hit the buildings.

On September 17, 2007, Jeffrey Hill contacted Leslie Hazard, a spokesman for Boeing, and asked her if a Boeing 767 could travel 500 mph at an altitude of 700 feet. Her immediate response to the question was to laugh and say "not a chance!"[147] She stated that the cruising speed of a Boeing 767 is 530 mph, but that is attained at an altitude of 35,000 feet.

9 Rock, Scissors, Planes

"Rock breaks scissors, scissors cut paper, paper covers rock – and aluminum TRANSCENDS steel?"[148] The official conspiracy theory is that the planes pierced into the building and then exploded after penetrating the outer skin of the buildings. The 9/11 Commission Report misrepresents the twin towers as hollow steel shafts. The report states:

> [T]he outside of each tower was covered by a frame of 14-inch-wide steel columns; the centers of the steel columns were 40 inches apart. These exterior walls bore most of the weight of the building. The interior core of the buildings was a hollow steel shaft, in which elevators and stairwells were grouped.[149]

The WTC Towers were not hollow steel shafts as alleged in the 9/11 Commission Report. That statement conceals the existence of 47 massive box columns, which were the real strength of the building, as seen in the picture below of the initial floors of one of the twin towers under construction. Notice in the picture below the less robust steel structure appurtenant to the tower on the left used for the portion of the sub-basements that were not directly underneath the tower.[150]

The National Institute of Standards and Technology (NIST) acknowledged the core columns and theorized that the first Boeing 767-200 strike shredded 6 of the 47 core columns in the Tower 1 (North Tower) and damaged three additional columns. The NIST report states that the outer columns acted as knife edges that shredded the planes, yet the shreds of the planes were able to cut through 6 of the inner core columns. The NIST report further states that the second Boeing 767-200 severed 10 of the 47 core columns in Tower 2 (South Tower), and damaged one additional column in that tower.[151]

The NIST report is simply ludicrous. NIST would have us believe that an aircraft made of a light skeletal structure covered with a thin aluminum skin was able to pierce through thick steel columns. For example, the aluminum skin on a Cessna Citation corporate jet ranges from 0.06 inches for high speed transport wings to approximately 0.05 inches for the fuselage.[152] That aluminum skin is placed over aluminum and alloy ribs and spars that can be as thin as 0.025 inches with spar webs 0.06 inches at the wing tips.[153] The plane must be made light so that it can fly. The same light construction on a different scale is found in commercial jets.

Large passenger jets are essentially flying hollow tubes filled with passengers, having hollow wings filled with fuel. Below is an Airbus A340-600, which is the largest passenger aircraft in the world. It crashed into a blast barrier due to alleged negligence by the pilots. Notice how the plane did not fare very well against the blast barrier; it was only able to break the relatively thin lightweight panel attacked to the top of the barrier. While the plane is designed to be very strong for its weight, it is no match for the blast barrier or the reinforced concrete at the Pentagon, or the large structural steel at the World Trade Center.

When I was 13 years old I was told by a football coach before tackling practice that the harder I hit someone the less it will hurt. I found out quickly that he lied. I learned a hard lesson that day in Newton's third law of motion: for every action there is an equal and opposite reaction. A light aluminum plane hitting a thick steel beam will have the same effect a steel beam being swung at the same speed and hitting the plane. It makes no difference which one is moving as to the effect on the plane and the beam. In both cases the thick steel beam will do damage to the plane and the beam will emerge relatively undamaged. The faster the speed at the point of impact, the more damage that will be done to the plane. Try punching a steel girder. No matter how fast your hand is traveling, you will not be able to break through it; you will eventually break your hand. It matters not if the girder is swung at your hand or you swing your hand at the girder; assuming the impact is at the same speed, the injury to your hand would be the same.

One of the 47 Massive WTC Core Columns

The massive core columns of the World Trade Center were anchored to bedrock. Thirty one of the columns were 36-by-16-inch box shaped columns made of two-inch thick solid steel at the foundation.[154] Sixteen of the columns measured 52 inches by 22 inches triple thick steel boxes that were 5 inches thick at two ends matched perpendicularly with one 6 ½-inch and two 6-inch thick slabs of steel.[155]

The box columns reduced in size and thickness at the upper floors, but were still substantial steel columns for which an aircraft of any size would not pose any serious threat. The minimum thickness was 2.25 inches for the columns between the impact zone for the alleged plane that supposedly hit Tower 2 (South Tower) between the 77th and 85th floors. The diagram

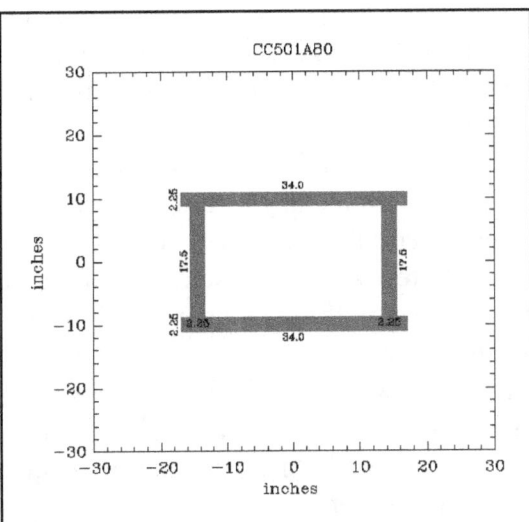

Dimensions of one of the 47 steel core columns between the 77th and 80th floors as reported by NIST

depicts the dimensions as reported by NIST of one of the 16 larger box columns for the 77th through the 80th floors.[156]

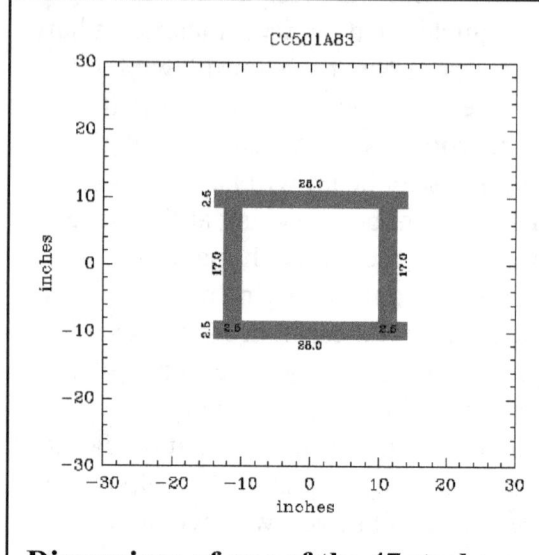

Dimensions of one of the 47 steel core columns between the 80th and 83rd floors as reported by NIST

As the core columns progressed to the upper floors, they became smaller in size as seen in the diagram of the columns for WTC floors 80 to 83.[157]

The core columns transitioned to massive I beams that spanned from the 83rd to the 86th floor, as depicted in the diagram of the dimensions of those I beams.[158] There is no way in this physical world that a light aluminum aircraft is capable of breaking such thick columns of steel.

In fact, the WTC Towers were designed to withstand the impact of a Boeing 707 (the largest passenger aircraft then flying at the time the WTC Towers were designed).[159] The Boeing 767s that struck the twin towers were only slightly larger than a Boeing 707. The Boeing 707 length is 153 feet with a wingspan of 146 feet, whereas the Boeing 767 length is 159 feet, with a wingspan of 156 feet. The engineers were not making guesses about its strength. In the mid-1960's, the structural engineers who designed the Twin Towers carried out studies to determine how the buildings would fare if hit by large jetliners. "In all cases the studies concluded that the Towers would survive the impacts and fires caused by the jetliners."[160]

Before the alleged planes even got to the inner core columns they would have had to get past the outer columns. That would be an impossible feat in and of itself. The inner core was interlaced with steel and connected to 240 (59 on each side and one on each corner) outer box columns that were 14 ½ inches by 13 ½ inches on the lower floors with 2 ½-inch thick steel on two sides and .875-inch thick steel on the other two sides.[161] The outer box columns tapered to 13 ½-by-14-inch box columns that were 1/4-inch thick at the upper floors.[162]

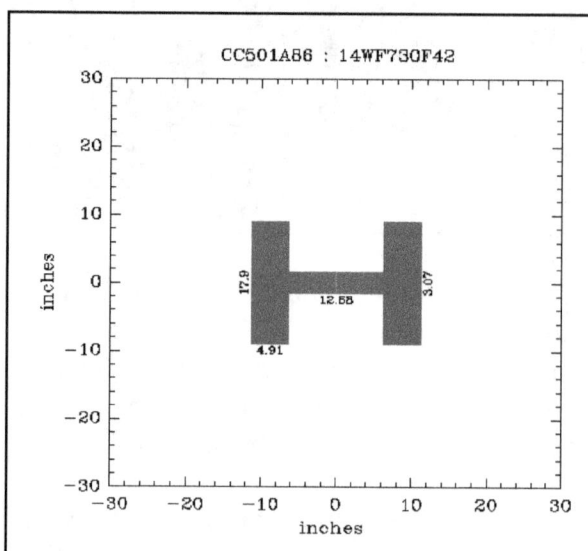

Dimensions of one of the 47 steel core columns between the 83rd and 86th floors as reported by NIST

Even though the outer columns did not have the strength of the inner columns they would have been an insurmountable barrier for any plane. They have traditionally used 1/4 inch steel chest plates as impenetrable protection against rifle bullets in bullet proof vests.[163] National Institute of Justice (NIJ) rated Level III body armor1/4 (.25) inch steel plate protects against all handgun bullets, including .44 magnum rounds, and against rifle bullets 9.6g (148 gr) 7.62x51mm NATO M80 ball bullets at a velocity of 847 m/s ± 9.1 m/s (2780 ft/s ± 30 ft/s).[164]

Note in the diagram below how the columns each had two 13.5-inch plates that were 1/4 inch thick steel facing edgewise toward the alleged plane. Those two 13.5-inch steel plates were framed by two other steel plates that were 13 inches wide in the exterior and 14 inches wide in the interior. They were also 1/4 thick. Those columns would have resisted penetration by the plane into the towers and any pieces that made it through the openings between the columns would have been for the most part shredded pieces of the aircraft.

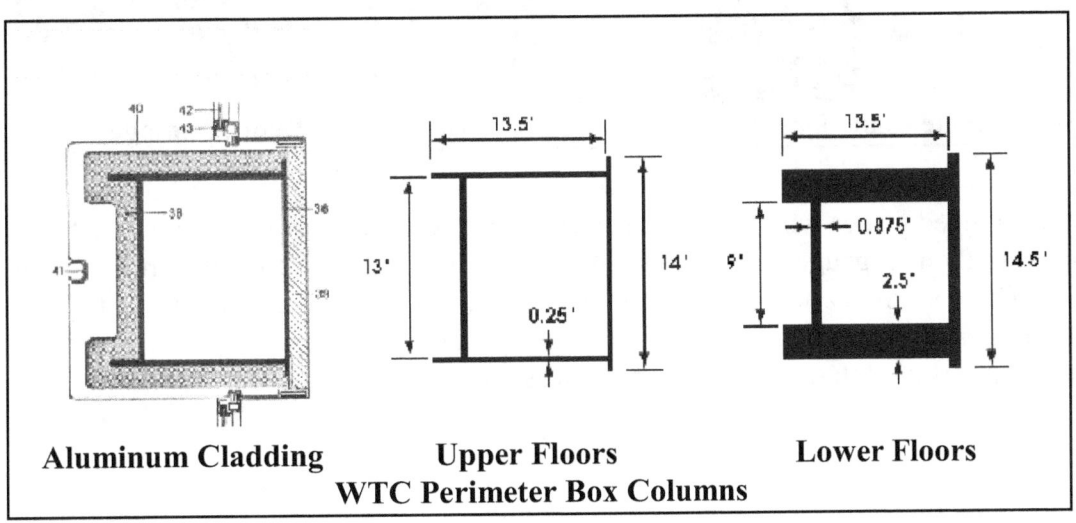

Aluminum Cladding   **Upper Floors**   **Lower Floors**
WTC Perimeter Box Columns

The media and the government would have the public believe that an aluminum plane can pierce into a building ringed with steel columns, and after cutting through those columns, continuing to cut through even thicker columns in the core of the building. Below are examples of what happens to a plane when it collides with a bird. Birds are light, which is how they are able to fly.[165] Yet, look at the damage the birds do to an aircraft. If a bird can do that degree of damage to a plane what chance would a plane have against robust steel columns at the World Trade Center?

Bird Strike Plane Damage

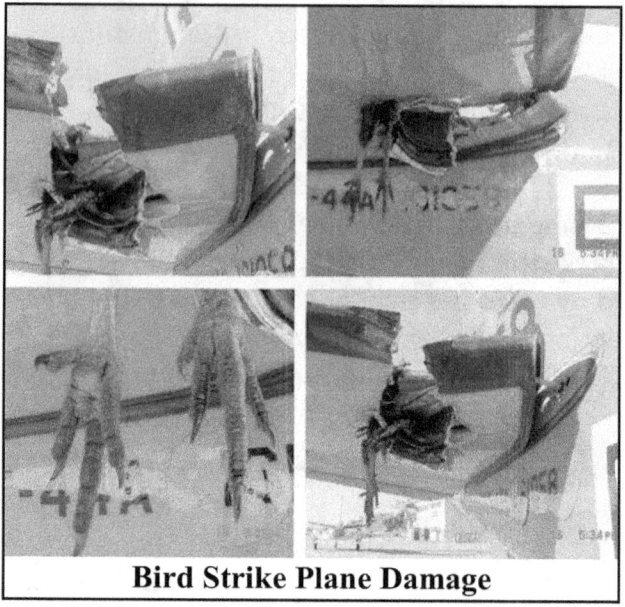
Bird Strike Plane Damage

    The alleged planes would have struck floors that contained at minimum 4 inches thick of concrete poured on 22-gauge fluted steel plates interwoven underneath with supporting steel trusses.[166] There is simply no possible way that any part of an aluminum plane, especially not the wings, striking such a building could pierce edgewise through the barrier posed by the concrete floors and supporting fluted steel flooring and trusses.

10 Media Participation in 9/11 Attacks

The evidence clearly points to the fact that no plane struck the Pentagon and there was no plane that crashed near Shanksville, Pennsylvania. It is impossible that aluminum planes could pierce large buildings made of thick construction steel. What about the planes that we saw on television striking the twin towers? Certainly those planes existed, didn't they? The media had video of the planes piercing through the twin towers like a knife through butter. Let's look at the evidence and see if in fact the evidence points to actual planes or computer generated images (CGI).

As amazing as it sounds the objective evidence clearly and irrefutably points to the fact that the planes that were seen on television crashing into the Twin Towers were in fact computer generated images (CGI). Below is a frame from an ABC News broadcast of the second plane hitting the south tower. Notice that the plane clearly has a wing missing. There is a point in the video where the wing simply disappears from view. That is evidence that the major media outlets were in on the conspiracy, and that they used CGI to cover the fact that no airliners struck the WTC towers on 911. ABC claimed that they received the video from a person free of charge.[167]

Below the larger image there are three sequential frames from the video broadcast by ABC. The frames clearly show that the wing is intact in frame 1, it disappears in frame 2, and it then reappears in frame 3. The wing blinks off and then back on again, within approximately one second. It is almost too fast for the eye to see when it is in motion, unless a person was focused upon seeing it.

Image of Alleged Plane Attack on 9/11 From ABC News Video

1: Wing Present   **2: Wing Missing**   **3: Wing Back Again**

    In the frames from the film sequence below, which is supposed to show the second plane crashing into WTC 2, you can see how the CGI of the plane becomes corrupted before it even reaches the building. The sequence begins at frame # 1, with both wings of the aircraft clearly visible. However, as the dark gray left wing and the light gray right wing intersect with the dark gray background on the left and light gray background on the right, the computer is unable to distinguish the wings from the background. Consequently, the computer leaves the right wing behind in the light background of the clouds, and it leaves the left wing behind in the dark gray background at the top of the tower. By the time the plane passes the mixed shade backgrounds and emerges into the uniform mid-gray background of the middle section of the tower at frame # 4, the left wing from the engine onward has completely disappeared and the right wing has only a small remnant remaining. This is clear indication that the media broadcast CGIs of planes on 9-11. There were no real planes used.

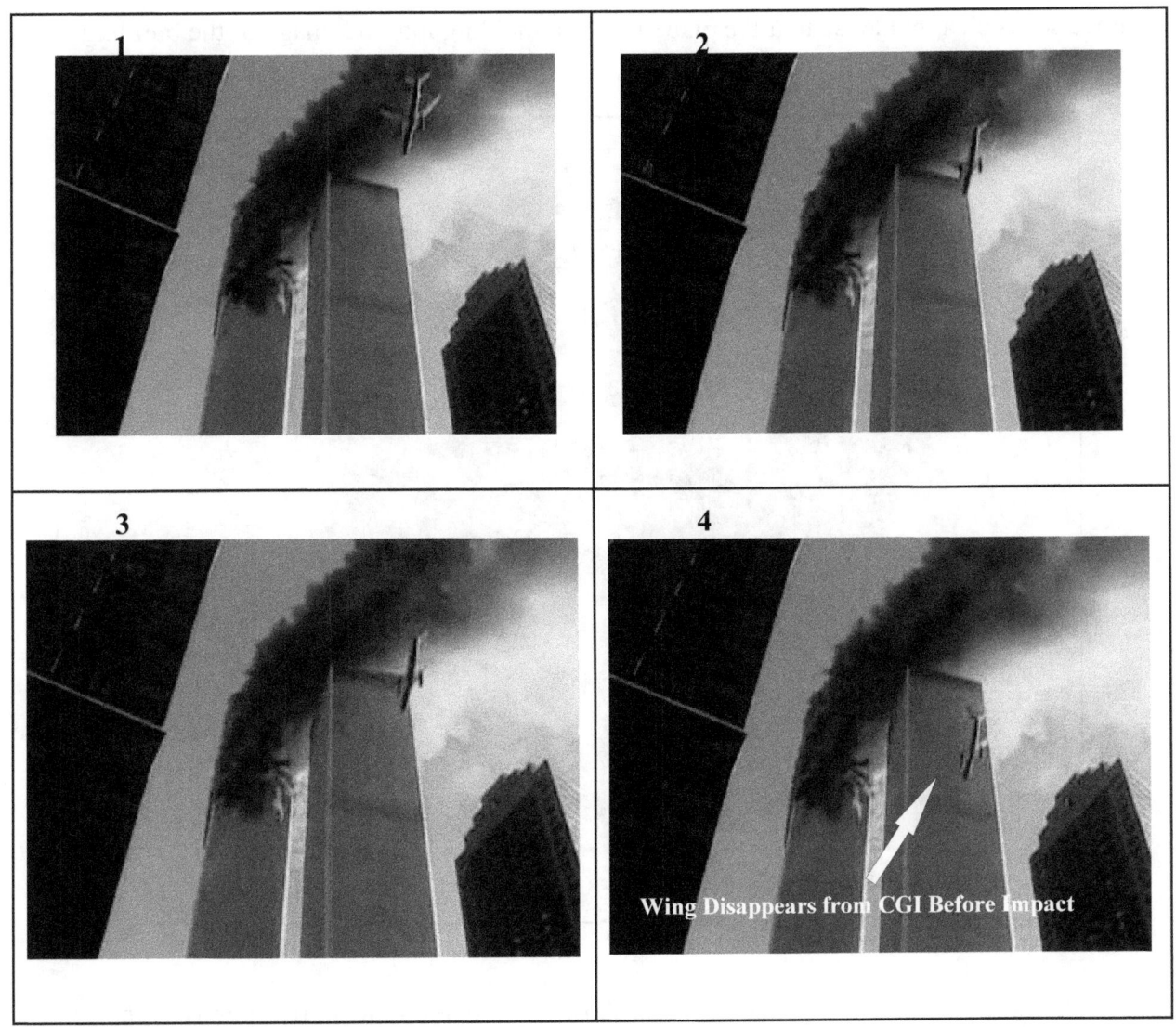

Further evidence of media involvement in the 9/11 attacks is found in the frame below, which is from yet another video broadcast over the major media networks after the 9/11 attacks. Notice that the building between the port (left) engine and the fuselage (passenger compartment) of the plane is not damaged at all. That is impossible in the physical world. The wing between the engine and the fuselage has supposedly just pierced the building, yet the building is undamaged. Either the WTC Tower 2 is self-healing or the plane is a computer generated image (CGI). Proof that the plane is a CGI is the fact that an aluminum plane simply cannot pierce inside a building ringed by thick steel columns braced by steel girders and concrete floors. An aircraft is built to be as light as possible so it can fly. It is basically a flying aluminum can; there is no way in the physical world that a plane can slice into a massive building as though it were a knife going though butter. Notice that there is no distortion of the building or the plane; there is no explosion; there is no visible damage; there is no fragmentation. If a real plane had struck the building, there should have been an immediate explosion of the aircraft upon impact with the side of the building, with very little penetration of the plane inside the building itself. Instead, what we see is clear evidence that the plane is a CGI melding into the image of the building.

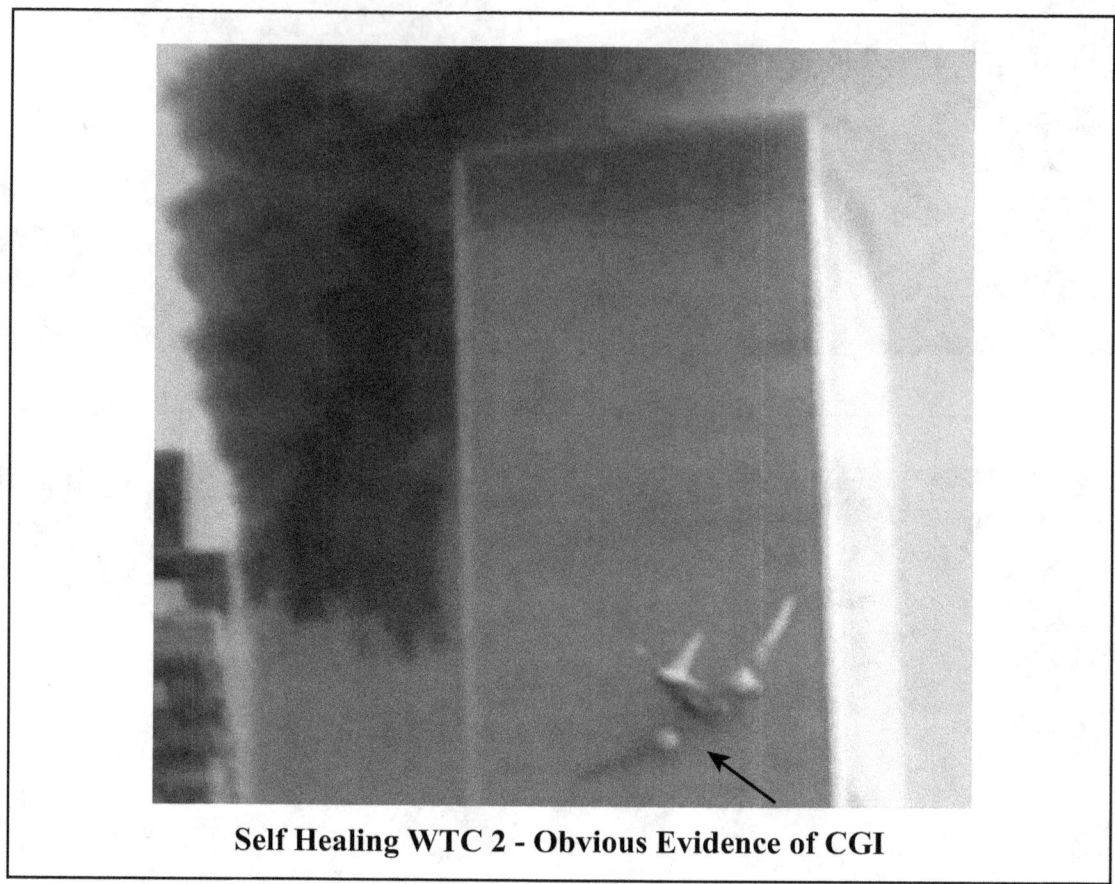

Self Healing WTC 2 - Obvious Evidence of CGI

Below is more evidence that the plane shown by the news media flying into tower 2 in their many videos were not live videos of a plane, but rather computer generated imagery (CGI) used to deceive the public. "Several videos clearly show a fully-intact 'plane' exiting the north face of WTC2. For these images to be real, steel beams would have to be shorn, just as they seemingly were on the entry face. However, there are clearly no sections of steel beams missing from the picture on the right."[168] It is astounding that anyone would believe that the nose of a thinly clad aluminum plane would slice through huge steal columns made of inches thick steel that ring both buildings and fill their infrastructure. The videos broadcast by the major media outlets on 9-11-01 and thereafter were clearly not real videos of planes, but rather computer generated images designed to deceive the public.

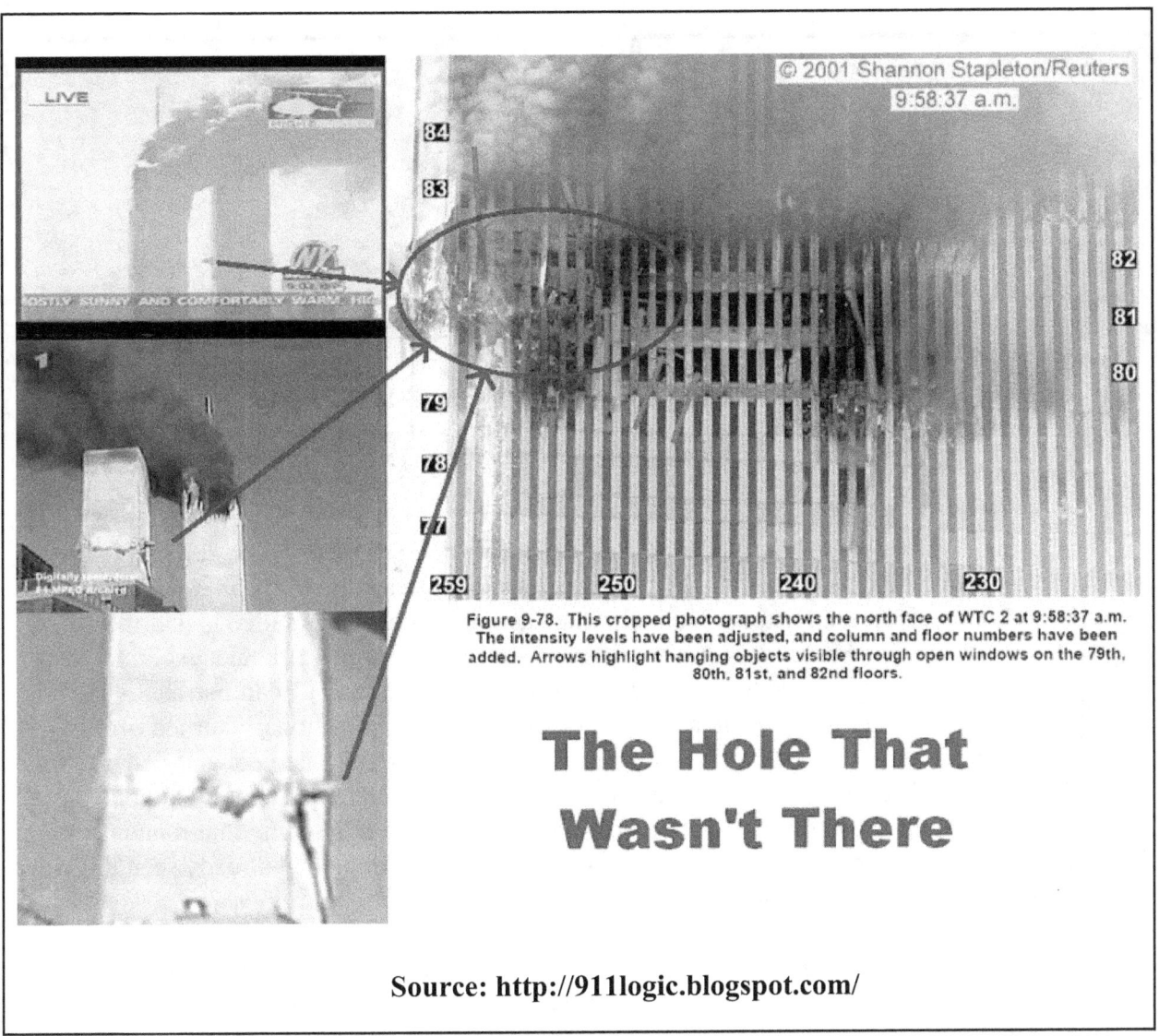

Figure 9-78. This cropped photograph shows the north face of WTC 2 at 9:58:37 a.m. The intensity levels have been adjusted, and column and floor numbers have been added. Arrows highlight hanging objects visible through open windows on the 79th, 80th, 81st, and 82nd floors.

The Hole That Wasn't There

Source: http://911logic.blogspot.com/

The infamous Evan Fairbanks video is so obviously a fabrication, it is a wonder that the conspirators ever allowed it to be aired. Fairbanks himself described it as "like a bad special effect." The video supposedly shows the second plane impacting the South Tower. The problem is that the computer artists used to implant the computer graphics into the video got so hung up on their artistry that they forgot some basic laws of nature.

The video displays something that any child would understand is impossible. The perpetrators showed a windshield reflecting an event that is taking place behind it. As everyone knows a mirror or a window can only reflect the light from something that is in front of it. In the Fairbanks video of the towers, the plane and the explosion all take place behind the car windshield. Yet those things are seen being reflected in the windshield. That is impossible.

Impossible Reflection in Windshield of Tower and Smoke Behind It

Impossible Reflection in Windshield of Plane Flying Into View Behind It

During a subsequent History Channel airing of the video, the editors took pains to crop out the bottom of the video so the impossible reflection in the windshield would not show.[169] Another odd thing about the History Channel broadcast of the Fairbanks video is that the video also had audio. The first broadcasts of his video had no sound. Evan Fairbanks explained that there was no sound recorded due to operator error on his part. Although Evan Fairbanks is a professional videographer and photographer, he claims that he unintentionally turned off the sound. He claimed that it was the first time he had used that particular camera and he was unfamiliar with it.[170] It turns out, however, there was sound, which means that he did not inadvertently turn the sound off, as he claimed.[171] He knew when explaining that it had no sound that was not true, because he told Peter Jennings on 9-11-2001 that he had already seen the video 6 to 7 times. Clearly, he heard the sound when reviewing it those 6 or 7 times.

Why did Fairbanks claim that he inadvertently turned off the audio when there was in fact audio on the tape? The events on the video give us a clue. In the full Fairbanks video that has no sound Fairbanks is seen crossing paths with many people discussing the first tower explosion and even talking directly to him.[172] However, there is no audio and so the viewer does not know what is being said. The History Channel cut out those sections from their audio/video broadcast. For some reason the media does not want it broadcast what those people are saying.[173] That is probably because the witnesses are discussing the fact that the initial damage to the first tower appeared to be from bombs, because there was no plane.

ABC News Anchor Peter Jennings interviewed Evan Fairbanks on 9-11-2001. During the interview Fairbanks stated that the video looked like a bad special effect, that what is depicted is "uncomprehensible."

> Peter Jennings: Watch how the aircraft penetrates the building, completely in one side and out the other.
> Evan Fairbanks: **It disappears like a bad special effect.** It disappeared right into the building. I've seen it 6,7 times now. **It**

is still uncomprehensible what is actually happening there.[174]

During an interview with Connie Chung, Fairbanks characterized what is seen on the video as appearing "artificial" as though it was a Hollywood movie. He stated:

> The image of that plane coming out of nowhere, coming into the frame and disappearing into the side, south side of the tower as though a floor had been hollowed out and it is a hanger that it is landing in. We have seen these images in movies and we know that it's artificial, and Hollywood makes it, and it's hard to put together that it's real this time.[175]

The pictures below are frames from a BBC live broadcast on 9-11-01 that announces the collapse of WTC building 7 (also known as the Solomon Brothers Building).[176] The announcer, Phil Hayton, had earlier told the audience that the Solomon Brothers Building (WTC 7) had collapsed (20 minutes before the actual collapse). Hayton repeats the announcement again at 5:07 p.m. EST. At approximately 5:07 p.m. EST, the newscaster states: "Now more on the latest building collapse in New York, you might have heard a few moments ago us talking about the Solomon Brothers Building collapsing, and indeed it has. . . . Jane what more can you tell us about the Solomon Brothers Building and its collapse?" The curious thing about the broadcast video is that the building did not collapse until 13 minutes later, at approximately 5:20 p.m. EST.

After the announcer tells the audience that Solomon Brothers Building (WTC 7) had collapsed, he goes to a live feed to Jane Standley on the scene in New York. Initially her head blocks WTC 7, but she later moves and shows the audience the smoke rising from towers 1 and 2. When she does that you can see WTC 7 clearly standing in the background. When she resumes her appearance on the screen you can see WTC 7 in the background over her left shoulder and to the left of her left ear.

Someone at the BBC jumped the gun and had the script read too early. This is evidence that 9/11 was scripted in advance, and that the major media outlets were part of the conspiracy.

BBC Broadcasting the Collapse of the 47 story WTC 7 (Solomon Brothers Building) 13 Minutes Before its Collapse

Later in the BBC broadcast there is a studio shot live from England, with Phil Hayton sitting at his studio desk, showing the live feed from New York of Jane Standley with WTC 7 Still standing behind her to the left of her left ear. However, the screen script announces that the Solomon Brothers Building (WTC 7) "has also collapsed."

The BBC has received much attention and a lot of inquiries over their 9-11-2001 broadcast predicting the collapse of WTC Tower 7. It took the BBC until February 27, 2007, to respond to the inquiries, by publishing a short response from Richard Porter.[177] Think about that. This is a news organization that is supposed to be in the business of gathering news and rapidly disseminating an accurate account of events to the public. It took them years to respond to inquiries about their prediction of the collapse of Tower 7. That is the behavior that is consistent with someone who is not quite sure what to say and wants to take their time to ensure that they do not say anything that might later turn out to be incriminating.

The problem in which the BBC finds itself is that the circumstances of the pre-reporting on 9-11-2001 are so compellingly incriminating that no explanation will mitigate its guilt. They have, so to speak, been caught red-handed. The only thing that they can do is either admit guilt, which they are not going to do, or try to cover their tracks with lies, which is what they have done. The BBC response is quite revealing and incriminating. The most notable thing in its response is that the BBC simply makes assertions without any supporting evidence, as though a denial is sufficient. The BBC stated:

> We're not part of a conspiracy. Nobody told us what to say or do on September 11th. We didn't get told in advance that buildings were going to fall down. We didn't receive press releases or scripts in advance of events happening.[178]

The BBC states that they are not part of a conspiracy and that nobody told them in advance that the buildings would fall down on September 11th. However, if they broadcast an event that nobody could possibly foresee, and then the event takes place exactly as they pre-reported, that clearly indicates that they had prior knowledge of the event.

Their pre-reporting was more than a prediction of the event, it was a reporting of the event before it happened. If the BBC had said that Tower 7 "would soon collapse" they would have some explaining to do. People would want to know how they knew it was going to collapse. However, the BBC did not say Tower 7 would "soon collapse;" the BBC announced that Tower 7 had already collapsed. That is doubly suspicious, because it proves that they had a script about the collapse of Tower 7 and were reading from the script. The BBC made a mistake by reading the script too early.

The BBC premature reporting of Tower 7's collapse is more than a mere prediction of an event; it is a reporting of an unforeseeable event that actually occurred just as it was reported, but the report was aired before the unforeseeable event occurred. The only way that could happen is if the BBC had a script of the planned events of 9-11-2001 ahead of time. The only source for such a script had to be from the perpetrators. That puts the BBC in the middle of the 9/11 conspiracy and cover-up. The BBC denial does not address that point at all.

When Phil Hayton, the BBC announcer who is seen on screen speaking with Jane Stadley, was apprised of the suspicious collapse of WTC and the BBC broadcast suggesting foreknowledge by the BBC, he did not even try to argue the point. Hayton had to agree that it seems there is a conspiracy. He said: "I sense that you think there's a conspiracy here-but you might be right."[179]

The official BBC response through Richard Porter gets worse:

> We no longer have the original tapes of our 9/11 coverage (for reasons of cock-up, not conspiracy).[180]

A cock up? That is quite simply incredible. The BBC, which is known for its meticulous record keeping and storage of news archives going back over 50 years, inexplicably loses live news footage documenting the crime of the century! That explanation does not pass the smell test. How could the news agency of record for Britain, who is by law required to keep records of broadcasts, lose those records? The answer is that they did not lose them; the records are clear evidence that support a finding that the BBC was part of the 9/11 conspiracy.

Paul Joseph Watson reported on February 28, 2007, which was a day after Richard Porter revealed that the BBC had lost its tapes, that Prison Planet received the following email from a CNN archivist. The archivist's email eviscerates the BBC claim that they lost the tapes of their 9-11-2001 broadcast:

> I'm an archivist with the CNN News Library in Atlanta, and I can tell you with absolute certainty, the mere idea that news agencies such as ours would "misplace" any airchecks from 9/11 is preposterous. CNN has these tapes locked away from all the others. People like myself, who normally would have access to any tapes in our library, must ask special permission in order to view airchecks from that day. Multiple tapes would have been recording their broadcast that day, and there are also private agencies that record all broadcasts from all channels - constantly - in the event that a news agency missed something or needs something. They don't just have one copy. . . . they have several. It's standard procedure, and as soon as the second plane hit, they would start recording several copies on other tapes machines all day long.[181]

The BBC, like CNN, has a very strict policy on retaining recordings of all television and radio broadcast outputs. That rigid policy explicitly states:

> The following components to be retained:-
> -Two broadcast standard copies of all transmitted/published TV, Radio and BBC output – one to be stored on a separate site as a master
> -One browse-quality version for research purposes, to protect the broadcast material
> -All supporting metadata to enable research and re-use
> -A selection of original (i.e., unedited) material for re-use/re-versioning purposes
> -Hardware/software/equipment to enable replay/transfer of the media[182]

* * *

> A retention schedule for each set of records kept /archived must be created as defined in the Core Records Policy. Retention periods are set according to the status and value of the record.[183]

As reported by Steve Watson: "Even more remarkable is the fact that if the BBC maintains that its footage is indeed lost, this means that at least THREE copies have been lost from DIFFERENT LOCATIONS."[184] Watson is absolutely correct. As the above BBC regulations attest, in order for the BBC to no longer have the broadcast, they would have had to lose the tapes from three different locations! That is simply unimaginable. It gets worse, after making the incredible statement that the BBC no longer has the tapes of their 9-11-2001 broadcasts, Porter, as official spokesman for the BBC, makes the following ridiculous statement:

> So if someone has got a recording of our output, I'd love to get hold of it. We do have the tapes for our sister channel News 24, but they don't help clear up the issue one way or another.[185]

How can Porter make such a ridiculous statement? By the time he made that statement, the tapes of the BBC broadcast had been plastered all over the internet. He then states that he has the tapes from his sister channel News 24, but they do not clear up the issue. In fact, the News 24 tapes absolutely prove foreknowledge by the BBC. Below is a frame from that broadcast with a time stamp indicating 21:55 (9:55 p.m. BST, which is London time), which would be 4:55 p.m. EST, (New York time), clearly depicting the announcement in a caption on the screen that accompanied the news reported by the BBC that "Another building near the World Trade Center in New York has collapsed."[186] That is 25 minutes before the actual collapse of the building.

Frame from BBC News 24 broadcast. The time stamp indicates 21:55 (9:55 p.m. BST, which is London time), which would be 4:55 p.m. EST, (New York time). This confirms that the broadcast of the collapse of Tower 7 was at least 25 minutes before it occurred.

Richard Porter concludes the February 27, 2007, official BBC response with this gem:

> If we reported the building had collapsed before it had done so, it would have been an error - no more than that. As one of the comments on You Tube says today "so the guy in the studio didn't quite know what was going on? Woah, that totally proves

conspiracy. . . ."[187]

This is the representative of the BBC giving an official response to a legitimate inquiry and he quotes a juvenile statement by an anonymous poster to conclude his explanation. That is what is called a smokescreen. Notice, he said: "If we reported the building had collapsed before it had done so." He suggests by using the word "if" that perhaps the internet archives are wrong and in fact the BBC didn't do what is claimed. He puts it that way because he knows that nobody is going to get their hands on the original time stamped video of he broadcast, because they have publicly stated that they are lost. In any event, the time stamped original is not needed, because the taped broadcast clearly shows WTC 7 in the background as the BBC is broadcasting live news of it supposedly having collapsed.

The strangest thing is the explanation he gives as his conclusion. Porter states that the broadcast of the tower collapse in advance was an error and no more than that. Think about that. The BBC broadcasts something that is totally unforeseeable in advance of it happening, and the BBC calls it an error! It is not an error! It would be an error if the BBC was wrong, but they got it right. The report was early, not wrong. The building did collapse just as they reported it. The BBC demonstrated that they had foreknowledge of the collapse by reporting the event before it took place.

The BBC early report of the WTC collapse would be tantamount to reporting the assassination of a President before it happened. Such a thing would be clear evidence of foreknowledge. Foreknowledge of a crime is evidence that the person is an accomplice in the crime. Tower 7 was only the third steel structured skyscraper to have ever collapsed from fire; the other two were WTC Towers 1 and 2 on 9-11-2001. Yet, the BBC was able to broadcast in advance an event that could only have been foretold if the event was planned and the BBC knew about the plans.

There was such a furor over the inadequacy of Porter's response that he was compelled to post a second comment on March 2, 2007.[188] In that response he tried to explain the reporting of the collapse of Tower 7 before it happened by citing to two previous reports by the BBC stating that Tower 7 had collapsed. He is just throwing up a smokescreen. It does not explain how BBC knew in advance that the towers were going to collapse by admitting that the BBC knew about it earlier. An earlier broadcast of the collapse by the BBC makes the case stronger that the BBC had prior knowledge.

Porter ends his story by saying: "But there was no conspiracy in the BBC's reporting of the events. Nobody told us what to say. There's no conspiracy involving missing tapes. There's no story here."[189] He is fearfully whistling in the dark, hoping we just go away so the BBC can continue doing its job of spreading propaganda for the ruling class.

Porter makes another odd statement: "Because three BBC channels were saying this in quick succession, I am inclined to believe that one or more of the news agencies was reporting this, or at least reporting someone saying this."[190] He has the resources of the BBC at his disposal, and he states a conclusion based upon no evidence but only what he is "inclined to believe." With all of the news resources and connections at the disposal of the BBC, why did he not check out if there were other news agencies that reported the collapse before it happened? Because, his statement is yet another smokescreen. Because, if other news agencies reported the collapse before the BBC then that would expand the suspicions about the complicity in 9/11 beyond the BBC to other media outlets. Porter's job is to limit damage, not to expose other accomplices. As we will see, he is forced in a later response to drag other news agencies into the fray in order to cover for the BBC.

Porter and the BBC have reason to keep a lid on things, because it turns out that other news outlets reported the collapse of WTC Tower 7 before it happened. The newscaster for Fox5 News in Washington, D.C., Shawn Yancy, in her second day on the job[191], narrated the collapse of WTC 7 as she watched a live feed of its collapse being broadcast. She had minutes earlier announced that the building had already collapsed as that same live feed was broadcast on screen showing Tower 7 still standing.[192] She didn't miss a beat and played off her earlier announcement by not mentioning the inconvenient fact that she had already announced the collapse. She seemed clearly flustered and stunned as she tried to act calm in front of the camera.

The furor over the BBC broadcast would not go away, and so on or about July 2, 2008, the BBC felt compelled to present a short video denial of being involved in a conspiracy.[193] Interesting, that in this version, the BBC suddenly announced that it had not lost its tapes of 9/11 after all. They claimed that the tapes were simply mislaid on the wrong shelf in the archives.

It is reasonable to infer that what has happened is that the BBC realized that the unwashed public did not need the original tapes to prove that the BBC broadcast Tower 7's collapse before it happened. It became clear that the BBC knew that the story that the tapes were lost was simply not being believed, so to put an end to the controversy they pretended to find the tapes, which they truly never lost and in fact had all along.

The BBC then blames its pre-reporting of the WTC 7 collapse on a Reuters newswire that they claim was withdrawn when it was realized that WTC 7 was still standing. But that raises more questions than it answers. On the BBC video, one can see clearly the date of the email from Reuters. The BBC received the email from Reuters on 10 May 2007.[194] Why did it take the BBC over a year to report the discovery about the Reuters newswire?

The Reuters email stated that the story was picked up from a local news station. Who knew with such certainty that WTC 7 was going to collapse that it sent out a story explaining the collapse before it happened? Didn't the BBC think to ask for the identity of the local news source? The BBC, would like to be known as an objective news agency that digs for the truth, however, it has displayed a suspicious lack of curiosity about the ultimate source of the WTC collapse story. That is not the conduct of a news agency, it is the conduct of the propaganda arm of a huge criminal conspiracy trying to parcel out little dribs and drabs of information in order to convince the public to let go of a news story.

The BBC claim as to how the tapes went missing and how they found them again simply does not add up. The BBC claimed: "They'd just been put back on the wrong shelf - 2002 rather than 2001."[195] The statement that they were "put back" on the wrong shelf suggests that at some point they were taken off the 2001 shelf. That would mean the tapes were taken off the 2001 shelf after 2002 and then placed on the wrong 2002 shelf when being re-shelved. That is because the 2002 shelf may not have existed in 2001 when the tapes were initially shelved. Even if a 2002 shelf did exist in 2001, it would be obvious that it was the wrong shelf in 2001, since there would be no other tapes on the 2002 shelf to confuse the worker if he were shelving the tapes in 2001. That means that the tapes would have to have been re-shelved after the year 2002 in order for the worker to be confused by similar appearance of the shelves. That raises another question: why were the tapes taken off the shelf and not returned until after 2002?

Furthermore, the purported BBC scenario would only be plausible if one assumes that there was only one tape. We know that there were three separate sets of tapes at three different locations, which makes the entire story about misfiling impossible. The BBC staff would have had to put the tapes on the wrong shelves on three separate locations, since the BBC policies require them to maintain and store at least three full sets of tapes at three different locations.

The BBC has been caught in another lie. Why would they lie about such a thing? The ineluctable conclusion is that they are part of the 9/11 conspiracy, and are trying to use deception to hide that fact from the public.

The deafening silence in the mainstream media outlets about this major story of the impossible disappearance (and then the strange reappearance) of the BBC tapes was noted by Steve Watson:

> It has come to light this week that the most pre-eminent broadcasting company in the world has lost the original recordings of its output for the entire day on September 11th 2001, just over five years on, yet no major news agency has even bothered to report the fact.
>
> Despite being currently the biggest story on the internet and in the alternative media, the only place in the mainstream the story has appeared is on a small German news website.
>
> This highlights the fact that the mainstream media is not free to report events. The information it disseminates is strictly controlled and regulated.[196]

Steve Watson's conclusion that the media is not free to report events is accurate, and there is a reason for that lack of freedom. He who pays the piper calls the tune. Evidence presented before United States Congress in 1917 proved that J.P. Morgan, who was the American agent for the international Jewish (Rothschild) banking interests, purchased control over the major media in the United States.[197] That control continues today. According to some researchers, Jews own or control 96 % of the world's major media outlets to include newspapers, television, movies, and other media.[198] The mass media was instrumental in the deception of the American people. The major media outlets played a key role in the deception of attacks of 9-11, by laying the blame on innocent patsies, concealing the treasonous conduct of government officials and the acts of war against the United States by agents of a foreign nation (Israel), and actively relaying false and deceptive portrayals of what really took place on 9-11.

On February 17, 1917, Congressman Oscar Callaway presented the following facts before the United States Congress which explained the successful efforts of J.P. Morgan and his cabal to control public opinion in order to involve the United States in World War I.

> Mr. CALLAWAY. Mr. Chairman, under unanimous consent, I insert in the record at this point a statement showing the newspaper combination, which explains their activity in this war matter, just discussed by the gentleman from Pennsylvania,
>
> [Mr. Moore]: In March, 1915, the J.P. Morgan interests, the steel, shipbuilding, and powder interests, and their subsidiary organizations, got together 12 men high up in the newspaper world and employed them to select the most influential newspapers in the United States and sufficient number of them to control generally the policy of the daily press of the United States.
>
> These 12 men worked the problem out by selecting 170 newspapers, and then began, by an elimination process, to retain only those necessary for the purpose of controlling the general policy of the daily press throughout the country. They found it was only necessary to purchase the control of 25 of the greatest newspapers.
>
> The 25 papers were agreed upon; emissaries were sent to purchase the policy, national and international, of these papers; an agreement was reached; the policy of the papers was bought, to be paid for by the month; an editor was furnished for each paper to properly supervise and edit information regarding the questions of preparedness, militarism, financial policies, and other things of national and international nature considered vital to the interest of the purchasers.
>
> This contract is in existence at the present time, and it accounts for the news columns of the daily press of the country being filled with all sorts of preparedness argument and misrepresentations as to the present condition of the United States Army and Navy and the

> possibility and probability of the United States being attacked by foreign foes.
>
> This policy also included the suppression of everything in opposition to the wishes of the interests served. The effectiveness of this scheme has been conclusively demonstrated by the character of stuff carried in the daily press throughout the country since March, 1915. They have resorted to anything necessary to commercialize public sentiment and sandbag the national congress into making extravagant and wasteful appropriations for the Army and Navy under the false pretense that it was necessary. Their stock argument is that it is "patriotism." They are playing on every prejudice and passion of the American people.[199]

How successful have the Jews and their fellow conspirators been in controlling public knowledge and opinion? Read and weep over the sad truth as John Swinton, the former Chief of Staff for the New York Times, explains the state of the supposed free press in the United States in a speech before the New York Press Club in 1953.

> There is no such thing, at this date of the world's history, in America, as independent press. You know it and I know it. There is not one of you who dares to write your honest opinions, and if you did, you know beforehand that it would never appear in print. I am paid weekly for keeping my honest opinion out of the paper I am connected with. Others of you are paid similar salaries for similar things, and any of you who would be so foolish as to write honest opinions would be out on the streets looking for another job. If I allowed my honest opinions to appear in one issue of my paper, before twenty-four hours my occupation would be gone. The business of the journalists is to destroy the truth; to lie outright; to pervert; to vilify; to fawn at the feet of mammon, and to sell his country and his race for his daily bread. You know it and I know it and what folly is this toasting an independent press? We are the tools and vassals of rich men behind the scenes. We are the jumping jacks, they pull the strings and we dance. Our talents, our possibilities and our lives are all the property of other men. We are intellectual prostitutes.[200]

If an event cannot be spun to conceal the true nature of the threat to our liberties, it is simply ignored. The experience of Sibel Edmonds reveals how the major media outlets conceal information from the general public. Mrs. Edmonds was a contract translator for the FBI who exposed the involvement of high government officials in the 9/11 attacks. Mrs. Edmonds had appealed the district court dismissal of a whistleblower lawsuit brought by her. The U.S. government had obtained the dismissal of her suit, by alleging that the information revealed in the lawsuit constituted "state secrets."

The information she has constitutes state secrets only in the sense that it exposes the involvement of high government officials in the 9/11 attacks, and the government wants to keep that secret from the citizens. Her court hearing on the appeal of the dismissal was supposed to be an adversarial hearing, with each side presenting their arguments. Yet, the hearing turned into a secret *ex parte* conference between government lawyers and the judges. Amazingly, she and her lawyers were dismissed by the judges from the courtroom so the government lawyers could be alone to present their case to the judges.

The major media was notably absent; not a single newspaper reporter covered the hearing, even though it was scheduled in advance on the court docket for all to see. Consequently, there was no reporting by major media outlets of the government shenanigans and the complicity of the federal court in what is a coverup of high treason by government officials. Tom Flocco interviewed Mrs. Edmonds who explained the events as follows:

> Washington -- Former FBI contract translator and whistleblower Sibel Edmonds and her attorneys were ordered removed from the E. Barrett Prettyman U.S. Courthouse so that a three-judge U.S. Court of Appeals panel could discuss her case in private with Bush administration lawyers.
>
> In an exclusive interview on Saturday, we asked Edmonds if she would deny that laundered drug money linked to the 911 attacks found its way into recent House, Senate and Presidential campaign war-chests, according to what she heard in intelligence intercepts she was asked to translate.
>
> "I will not deny that statement; but I cannot comment further on it," she told TomFlocco.com, in a non-denial denial.
>
> Edmonds is appealing the Bush administration's arcane use of "state secrets privilege," invoked last year to throw out her U.S. District Court lawsuit alleging retaliation for telling FBI superiors about shoddy wiretap translations and allegations that wiretap information was passed to the target of an FBI investigation. Given our multiple reports and numerous other interviews, Edmonds heard much more--but enough to warrant public suppression of criminal evidence by a wholly Republican appeals court panel?
>
> **"Tom, I'm telling you that not a single newspaper covered what happened to me on Thursday when I went into court,"** said the exasperated translator, adding, "[Judge David] Ginsberg kicked everyone out, cut off my lawyer's arguments and told us 'we

have questions to ask the government's attorneys that you cannot hear.' "

Criminal evidence in Edmonds' explosive case is apparently getting too close to Washington officials, since the former contract linguist also told us she would not deny that "once this issue gets to be . . . investigated, you will be seeing certain [American] people that we know from this country standing trial; and they will be prosecuted criminally," revealing the content of the FBI intercepts she heard indicates that recognizable, very high-profile American citizens are linked to the 911 attacks.

Edmonds implied that legislators and even lobbyists were benefitting from laundered narcotics proceeds in an earlier interview with the Baltimore Sun, "...this money travels. And you start trying to go to the root of it and it's getting into somebody's political campaign, and somebody's lobbying. And people don't want to be traced back to this money."

So the Bush administration's Department of Justice enlisted its taxpayer-funded lawyers to petition a Republican U.S. Appeals Court to suppress Sibel Edmonds' criminal evidence allegations--linked to a 3,000 death mass murder--in the name of "state secrets."

When we asked how many Americans were named in the intercepts, Edmonds said "There is direct evidence involving no more than ten American names that I recognized," further revealing that "some are heads of government agencies or politicians--but I don't want to go any further than that," as we listened in stunned silence.

* * *

"I cannot be present at my own hearing; and not a single paper was there Thursday to cover the story--even though all of my allegations were supported by the FBI Inspector General's report and my case involves 911 and national security," said Edmonds.

When asked in 2002 by CBS 60 Minutes co-host Ed Bradley, "did she seem credible to you? Did her story seem credible?" Senator Charles Grassley (R-IA) said "Absolutely, she's credible. And the reason I feel she's very credible is because people within the FBI have corroborated a lot of her story."[201]

The presence of the opposing party serves as a check on any misrepresentation that might be made by a party to the action. If the adversary is removed from the proceedings, then the remaining party is in a position to misrepresent the case and even exercise undue influence over the court. No entity in the world is more able to present an undue influence than the government of the United States. When (or rather if) the judgment of the court is reported by the media, there will likely not be any mention of the kangaroo nature of the court proceedings. The uninformed citizens will be left with the impression that the court made a well reasoned judgment based upon an adversarial proceeding where both parties were able to present their arguments in the presence of the other.

The media is part of the conspiracy. They are selling the story of 19 Arab hijackers. That story was prepared as the official story of what happened on 9-11-2001 by the conspirators behind the attacks. The 9/11 attacks were a well scripted psychological operation. The conspirators have more such operations in store for us.

> "Within weeks of the Sept. 11 attacks, reports surfaced that military-intelligence experts had convened a secret meeting of Hollywood screenwriters to brainstorm possible terrorist scenarios," says the *Seattle Times*. "Almost two years later, security officials across the country are taking a more mathematical approach to guarding the homeland. It's called 'risk-based methodology,' and it's a way of thinking about the unthinkable to best deploy limited funds and manpower."[202]
>
> According to Variety, the FBI, in reaction to the events of September 11, approached some of Hollywood's top writers to help them come up with possible terrorist attack scenarios, in order to aid in preparation of homeland security.[203]

It is ridiculous to think that Hollywood script writers would be able to assist in securing the homeland by somehow being able to predict the next terrorist attack. They write fiction! They do not investigate facts and review hard intelligence! A script writer would be no better at predicting the next terrorist attack than a painter would be at painting next years World Series winner. The only rational explanation for consulting with Hollywood script writers would be for the writers to help script the next "terrorist" attack in order to gain maximum psychological impact. Script writers know next to nothing about national security, but they know plenty about mass emotion and hysteria. They know how to put together a scenario that would create the required emotional response from the general population.

11 Eyewitness Accounts

If the planes were only CGIs, how does one explain the eyewitnesses who saw a plane? Let's examine some of the key early first hand witnesses one at a time. Rick Leventhal was a reporter for FOX news who was on the streets of New York shortly after the second explosion. A bystander overheard Leventhal tell the television audience that there was a second plane that struck the towers. The witness to the second explosion interrupted Leventhal and stated:

> Witness: **"No second plane, it was a bomb. Bomb that went off in the building, not second plane. It was a bomb. Who said a second plane?"**
>
> Leventhal: That's what we were told, a second plane, we saw it on television.
>
> Witness: No! I saw everything!
>
> Leventhal: All right. Thanks a lot.[204]

There are a couple of important facts that come out during this colloquy. First, when hearing Leventhal say there was a second plane, the eye-witness corrects him. The witness is adamant that there was no second plane. Second, he asks Leventhal who said there was a second plane. Apparently, the witness was incredulous that anyone would claim that there was a second plane. How could the witness be so sure? He explained to Leventhal that he **"saw everything."**

What is even more revealing is the response by Leventhal. He responded by saying "that's what <u>we</u> were told" and that "<u>we</u> saw it on television."[205] Apparently, Leventhal, the news man on the street, only knew that there was a plane because he was part of a group ("we") who were told that there was a second plane. It seems at this point no actual eyewitness on the street has told Leventhal that there was a second plane.

What is most astounding, however, is that Leventhal has no interest in continuing the conversation with this man who is contradicting the plane myth. Leventhal is supposed to be a news reporter, and he has someone standing in front of him who has stated emphatically that he "saw everything," yet Leventhal is quick to end the interview and walk away, with a dismissive statement: "All right. Thanks a lot." That is the strangest lack of curiosity ever displayed by someone who is supposed to be a reporter on the scene assigned to find first hand eyewitness accounts of the one of the worst tragedies in American history.

If Leventhal was actually interested in gathering the facts, he would want to get the witness's name, and go over the details of what he saw. Instead, after the witness tells him that he saw everything, Leventhal dismissively walks away. Clearly, what we have is an actual eyewitness on live television throwing a monkeywrench into the carefully crafted plane impact story.

There was another witness who did not see a plane. He was interviewed by a local Channel 7 reporter.[206] The witness's name was Kenny Johannemann. The reporter begins questioning by mentioning the second airplane, however Johannemann at no time confirmed that there was an airplane. He simply stated what he saw: that about 10 minutes later the building "blew up" and that there was a "big explosion." 10 minutes later than what? Obviously, Johannemann was referring to the first building explosion and thought the reporter was referring to the first alleged plane strike, because he was now explaining what happened 10 minutes after the first attack.

>Reporter: Were you there for the second hit by the plane?
>Johannemann: Yeah about ten minutes later the second building went off
>Reporter: Did you see it?
>Johannemann: **Yes I saw it. It just blew up. A big explosion.** People started running, there was chaos everywhere. People jumping out. People just kept jumping and jumping and jumping and you could still see they were alive because they were flailing around.
>Reporter: The FBI has already stepped in to investigate, it could be possibly a terrorist strike.
>Johannemann: It could be. It could be, because **the first one went off and then ten minutes later this just blew up out of nowhere**.
>Reporter: Hard to think that would be just accidental.
>Johannemann: No, I don't think it could be accidental.
>Reporter: Spell your name
>Johannemann: J o h a n n e m a n n
>Reporter: And you were working there?
>Johannemann: Yes, I was right there. I was in the B, I was down in the basement, came down, all of a sudden **the elevator blew up**, smoke, I dragged a guy out. His skin was hanging off, and I

dragged him out and I helped him out to the ambulance.[207]

Johannemann was there and saw the building blow up. He described it as a big explosion. He did not say it was hit by a plane; he stated that "it blew up out of nowhere." At no time did he mention a plane hitting the building. He also mentions that the elevator blew up in the basement area (apparently referring to the first explosion in the North Tower), because he was outside when he saw the second explosion. William Rodriguez also heard and experienced huge explosions in the basement floors seconds *before* the first explosion higher up in the North Tower.[208] Incidently, Rodriguez was with Johannemann as they both helped the badly burned victim to the ambulance. Kenny Johannemann died on August 31, 2008. He is alleged to have committed suicide by shooting himself.[209]

The live television coverage was proving to be a problem for the media conspirators. Don Dahler was being interviewed over the telephone as he is describing the scene from his vantage point on the street to the studio announcer, Charles Gibson. Suddenly, the second tower exploded; the video feed shows what appears to be a plane impacting the tower as Dahler is being interviewed. The following exchange takes place.

> Dahler: "Oh my God!"
> Gibson: "That looks like a second plane."
> Dahler: **"I did not see a plane go in, that just exploded."**
> Gibson: "I just saw another plane coming in from the side."
> Dahler: **"You did? Because that was out of my view."**
> Gibson: "You could see the plane come in from the right hand side of the screen.
> * * *
> Gibson: Don, could you hear that plane as it came in?"
> Dahler: **"I did not hear that plane."**[210]

It is revealing that Dahler, who is on the street and watching the tower, does not see the plane impact the tower or hear the plane approach. However, a large airliner is clearly seen in the video feed by the studio announcer.

Jennifer Oberstein was interviewed by phone on NBC4 by Katie Couric. She was being interviewed about the alleged first plane impact. She began by saying that she walked out of the subway at Bowling Green and was walking to work at the Ritz Carleton in Battery Park, heard a boom, looked up and saw a big ball of fire. She was on the opposite side of the tower from the alleged plane impact.[211]

> Couric: Do you have any idea what kind of plane it was?
>
> Oberstein: I'm sorry?
>
> Couric: Do you have any idea what hit the World Trade Center?

> Oberstein: What it was?
>
> Announcer: Yeah, what kind of plane? We're getting reports that an airplane hit the building.
>
> Oberstein: **Oh, I didn't even know that**. Honestly, I was walking up, and it, looked up and saw a big boom, and fire. You know, I gotta tell you, we were all saying around here, that it was very interesting that it would be a bomb and it would be so high up. So perhaps it was a plane. **We have no, no talk of a plane**. However, I have to tell you, there are still things flying in the air. I mean, it's mind boggling, and it's horrifying.[212]

Oberstein was surprised to hear that it was a plane. One could argue that she was on the south side opposite where the alleged plane hit the tower and so could not have seen a plane if that is what impacted the tower. However, she states clearly that "we have no talk of a plane." It was later during the interview that Oberstein revealed that a police officer had just told her that he "heard" it was a plane. Apparently, the media story of a plane was starting to filter to the street.

Steve Evans was introduced by a BBC announcer. Immediately prior to him coming on the air the second tower exploded. Evans gives his excited account of the events. He makes no mention of a plane, only explosions. He states clearly that the initial assumption was that it was a bomb. He is standing at the base of the tower when it exploded. He was in a position to see a plane if it was there, but he makes no mention of a plane. He only mentions explosions. He was looking at the building as he was about to come on the air.

> There are more explosions further down the building. It was calm until we came on the air now. But I am now looking up at this building. There is smoke billowing from the very top, but then here is a fire and an explosion about 20 stories further down. **I was at the base of the building when it happened. There was a huge bang and the building physically shook, then there were two or three bangs and the building again shook. . . . Initially the assumption was that it was a bomb**.[213]

Jeane Yurman, a CNN reporter, was interviewed by CNN at 8:56 a.m. EST. Yurman was a witness to the first explosion in the North Tower. The announcer introduces Yurman as an eyewitness who is on the phone.

> Yurman: I can tell you that I was watching TV, and there was this sonic boom, and the TV went out. And I thought maybe the Concorde was back in service, because I've heard about that sonic

boom. And I went to the window -- I live in Battery Park City, right next to the twin towers -- and **I looked up, and the side of the World Trade Center exploded right when I looked up.** At that point, debris started falling. I couldn't believe what I was watching.

* * *

Announcer: Jeanne, we are continuing to look at pictures of this devastating scene, according to Sean Murtagh, vice president of finance, who witnessed what he described as a twin-engine plane, possibly a 737. He was almost absolutely sure it was a large passenger jet that went into that plane. Jeanne, you are saying you didn't see anything initially. You didn't see a plane approach the building?

Yurman: **I had no idea it was a plane. I just saw the entire top part of the World Trade Center explode. So I turned on the TV when I heard they said it was a plane. It was really strange.**[214]

Yurman looked out her window and saw the North Tower explode. She saw no plane and "had no idea it was a plane." Her response to hearing that it was a plane was to say "it was really strange."

Johannemann, Dahler, Oberstein, Evans, Yurman, and the other witnesses on the street presented a problem for the conspirators. Later that day they decided to firmly implant the plane story in the minds of the American people by using a shill. The alleged eyewitness was so clearly a shill who was playing a role that virtually nobody believes that he saw what he claimed. The infamous "Harley Guy" showed up on scene to reveal not only what he saw, but to also explain the cause of the collapse. The "Harley Guy" had it all figured out the day of the attacks. His demeanor was an odd mixture of a dispassionate observer and an excited participant. His voice inflection seemed out of place for someone who had just witnessed a historically tragic event "from beginning to end," as he put it. While he delivered his lines flawlessly, he came across as an insincere shill.

The interview starts with Rick Leventhal introducing Mark Walsh (the Harley Guy), who is described by Leventhal as a "freelancer for FOX."[215] It is obvious that the interview of Walsh was arranged ahead of time because at no time on camera do we see Leventhal speak with Walsh before his introduction of him, and Walsh is seen standing nearby waiting to be interviewed. Walsh was apparently an alias used by Harley Guy for his role as an eyewitness to the 9/11 attacks. If in fact there was a freelancer for FOX named Walsh one would expect to find some work for FOX by Mark Walsh somewhere on the internet, however, there is no such work found anywhere on the internet.

Rick Leventhal: We want to bring in Mark Walsh, who's a Freelancer for FOX. You live just a few blocks away and witnessed.

Mark Walsh: Dude, I was - I - I live on the 43rd floor of a building which is five blocks from the Trade Center itself. I witnessed the entire thing from beginning to end.

Rick Leventhal: People talk about how it looked like a movie. I know when I came walking down here early this morning and saw both towers on fire and people on every street corner it was -- it was -- it was like a movie but you watched the planes hit the towers

Mark Walsh: I was watching with my roommate. It was approximately several minutes after the first plane had hit. **I saw this plane come out of nowhere and just ream right into the side of the Twin Tower exploding through to the other side, and then I witnessed both towers collapse, one first, and then the second, mostly due to structural failure because the fire was just too intense.**[216]

How could he know the reason for the collapse of the towers within minutes when everyone else in the world was mystified by their collapse? Because, that was the story scripted by the conspirators before the 9/11 attacks, and he was just following the script. Notice, he explains that the second plane exploded through the other side. That was a glitch in the video CGI and so he apparently was informed to go with the glitch before he was interviewed.

Mark Walsh a/k/a "Harley Guy" (left) being interviewed by Rick Leventhal (right)

A strange event happened toward the end of the video. A man wearing a black suit and tie with a surgical mask came up to Leventhal, touched his arm to get his attention, and guided him by pointing back behind Leventhal. Leventhal followed his direction but apparently did not understand what the man was trying to get him to do so he turned to the man and asked him a question:

Leventhal: "Could we talk to you? What's your role out here right now?"

The masked man nervously stated in response:

Masked Man: "Just standing by right now. Can't say what role I'm playing right now."[217]

Masked Man in Black directing Rick Leventhal

It was obvious that the man was doing something official as he had just touched Leventhal's arm and was just directing and pointing for Leventhal to do something, but when Leventhal unexpectedly turned to him and asked him what his role was he stated he was "just standing by." That statement was not true. He was obviously there to do something, and in fact just moments earlier tried to guide Leventhal. That is why Leventhal asked him what his role was. Why didn't he explain himself? He further stated: "can't say what role I'm playing right now." Why couldn't he say? His actions and his responses to the questions were very suspicious.

The Harley Guy was not the only person to claim to have seen a plane. In fact the first witness to the alleged plane crash broadcast by CNN was Sean Murtagh. Murtagh claimed that he saw the first alleged plane impact the North Tower.[218] He was interviewed live at 8:50 a.m. on CNN, which was within 4 minutes of the first explosion in the North Tower. Murtah is believed to be the first eyewitness to see the alleged first plane.

Masked Man in Black to Rick Leventhal: "Can't say what role I'm playing right now."

Murtah said he had just seen a two engine jet that he described as "maybe a 737" slam into one of the World Trade Center Towers.[219] Murtagh was introduced by the newscaster as a CNN producer on the line, but Murtagh himself stated that he was Vice President for Finance at CNN.[220] The very first news of a commercial jet hitting the North Tower came from the Financial Vice President for CNN.

After Murtagh, the next witness that was interviewed by CNN was Jeanne Yurman at 8:56 a.m. eastern time. Yurman's account of hearing a sonic boom and seconds later looking at the twin towers and seeing one of them explode is recounted above. She did not see a plane.

FOX had Owen Moogan on the line within minutes of the first explosion. Before they even brought Moogan on the air and asked him a single question, there is a banner on the screen announcing: "FOX NEWS ALERT, PLANE CRASHES INTO WORLD TRADE CENTER." Moogan came on the air and stated that "I was lying in bed, and all of a sudden I heard what sounded like a plane or something coming extremely low and then we just heard this shattering explosion."[221] Moogan was introduced as one of the producers of the "FOX Report."[222]

At 9:02 a.m. Mark Obenhaus was on the line with Peter Jennings. Oberhaus stated that he saw the plane impact the first tower. He describes hearing a loud roar and seeing a large commercial jet flying low overhead. He then states:

> My eyes followed it because this is approximately fifteen blocks from the World Trade Center and it, it just slammed right into it and it was completely engulfed by the building. It was extraordinary. No wings flew off. Nothing like that. It just went directly in creating this cavern like hole. It reminds you of the worst kinds of effects in movies, but you are reassured that you are watching a movie, that it's an effect, but this is not.[223]

Mark Obenhaus echoes the sentiment of Evan Fairbanks about the appearance of special effects. Both Obenhaus and Fairbanks know a little something about special effects in movies. Fairbanks is a professional photographer and videographer, and Peter Jennings introduced Obenhaus as a Senior ABC Producer.[224]

At approximately 9:05 a.m., CNN broadcasts a call from Dr. Jay Adlersberg who claimed to have seen a second plane that hit the World Trade Center. Dr. Adlersberg stated that he saw what looked like a small propeller plane come in from the west and while he did not see it impact the World Trade Center, he believed that is what happened. "It was very visible that a plane had come in at a low altitude and appeared to crash into the World Trade Center."[225] Dr. Adlersberg is the Medical reporter for ABC's Eyewitness News.

Within one minute of the second explosion a FOX News announcer identifies Osama Bin Laden as a key suspect, and has on the line Eric Shawn, who is portrayed as a terror expert and war correspondent for FOX News, who had covered the 1993 WTC bombings, the Waco siege, TWA Flight 800, the Anthrax threat, and lastly, but most importantly, the "Hunt for Bin Laden."[226] Oddly, Shawn is not on the phone to opine about the involvement of Bin Laden, but rather to give his eyewitness account of the alleged second plane strike.

Shawn gave a rambling account of what he saw:

> I was walking down Fifth Avenue, er, which is close to our studios and I heard a jet, perhaps a 737 or a small airbus, er, flying low, unusually low over Fifth Avenue, making a right. I am not going to er say, I don't know, I don't have any reports on what kind of plane hit the world trade center. But people looked up and it made a right toward the, toward the building. John, what we just saw though, was obviously if that would be a second aircraft that hit the southern Tower of the World Trade Center. That obviously raises the specter of an intentional terrorist attack, here, if that is indeed

what we are looking at. I don't know what the reports say, what type of plane hit the Tower, but I did see a jet airliner that was fairly low.[227]

Most of the first hand witnesses who jump started the plane scenario were corporate media executives, producers, or reporters.[228] Below is a partial list of some of the notable first-hand witnesses affiliated with the corporate mass media who reported seeing or hearing an airplane strike the Pentagon, or one or both World Trade Center Towers:

Sean Murtagh - CNN Vice President of Finance

Mark Obenhaus - ABC Senior Producer

Owen Moogan - FOX Senior Producer

Sid Bedingfield - CNN Executive Vice President

Richard Davis - CNN Executive Vice President New Standards and Practices

Rose Arce - CNN Producer

Winston Mitchell - ABC/CNN Producer

Eric Shawn - FOX TV Senior Correspondent

Jane Derenowski - MSNBC Producer

Dr. Jay Adlersberg - ABC medical reporter

Elliot Walker - NBC NEWS reporter

Theresa Renaud - Wife of CBS Producer Jack Renaud (The Early Show)

Mark D. Birnbach - FOX TV employee

Mike Walter - USA Today Reporter

Joel Sucherman - USA Today.com Editor

Steve Anderson - USA Today, Director of Communications

Fred Gaskins - USA Today National Editor

Juxtapose the media executives against NY Daily News Photographer, David Handschuh.

He was interviewed in 2001 by Charlie Rose. The interview took place before there were any substantial questions raised about the existence of planes. Handschuh was looking at the building and snapped a picture of the explosion just as it happened. This is what he said in a 2001 interview.

> I got down there at 8:53 a.m. . . . I was less than 100 yards from the building, I was standing on West Street. . . . **The South Tower just exploded. It just blew up**, and somebody said that was a plane. I was underneath it, I was looking at the tower, I had my camera in my hand, I heard the noise, **I never saw the airplane**. And didn't realize I had that picture until a neighbor brought the Daily News over the next day and it had my byline underneath it.[229]

Hanschuh did not see the plane. If there had been a plane, he would have seen it. As you can see from the photograph he snapped his picture within seconds of the explosion. He was in the perfect position to see a plane had there been one. Note that Handschuh was not questioning the existence of the plane, he was simply and honestly recounting the notable fact that he never saw a plane.

Handschuh mentions in his statement that he heard the noise. One would think in the context that he was referring to the noise of an aircraft. However, he explained on another occasion what that noise was:

David Handschuh took this picture of the south side of the south tower within a moment of the explosion and was clearly in position to see a plane if there was one, but he "never saw the airplane."

> **Then this noise filled the air that sounded like a high-pressure gas line had been ruptured.** It seemed to come from all over, not one direction. Everyone was looking around thinking, "What was that?" **And the second tower explodes.**[230]

Clearly the sound he heard was not the sound of a jet since everyone was looking around and thinking "what was that?" At the time he heard that noise the propaganda about a plane hitting the first tower had been broadcast far and wide and the first thought would be that it is a jet if it at all sounded like one. It sounded like a high-pressure gas line, which sounds nothing like the roaring engines of a low flying airliner. Notice that Handschuh explains that "the second tower explodes." He does not say the plane hit the tower. In fact if one looks closely at

86

Handschuh's photograph, it clearly looks like an explosion expectorating building material outward. None of the material even remotely resemble plane parts.

On another occasion Handschuh stated: **"I did not see the plane despite the fact that I was looking at the tower at the time."**[231] Handshuh was not the only photographer to be looking directly at the towers and not see a plane. David Thom, who was also in a position to see the plane, stated: **"I did not see a plane and assumed a bomb or something had gone off."**[232] Victor Cruzate, who was with several others who were all in a position to see a plane, stated: **"I did not see the plane neither did any of the other guys on the roof."**[233] The photographs of Handschuh, Thom, and Cruzate, that day indicate that from their vantage point if there was in fact a plane, they would have seen it.[234]

Victor Cruzate has posted a reply to those who have quoted his statement as evidence that there were no planes on 911. While he does not retract his statement of not seeing a plane, he posted comments indicating that he was upset by having his name associated with those who question the existence of the second plane on 911. Cruzate states in pertinent part: "I find it very upsetting to find my name associated with videos trying to prove that there wasn't a second plane on the 9/11 attacks. I totally reject that view."[235] Regardless of the fact that Cruzate is upset, his original statement stands, with the most significant part being that not only did he not see a plane but "neither did any of the other guys on the roof."[236]

Gary Welz on the other hand has retracted his earlier statement of having seen a plane crash into the second tower. In an interview by a news station CW11 Welz originally stated: "this is where I and many of my neighbors gathered around 9 o'clock on the morning of September 11th . . . the second plane actually flew over our heads, it flew directly down there and impacted the second tower, the south tower."[237]

Later in an interview with Jeffrey Hill, Welz denied that he saw the crash. He stated: "I wasn't on the roof at the time of the crash."[238] Hill asked him about the inconsistency with his previous statement that he was in fact on the roof and saw the plane impact the second tower. Welz explained that in the CW11 interview he meant that it flew over the heads of people on the roof. He told Hill that he was not on the roof until later. He stated that the plane flew over his head in the literal sense in that he was inside the building at the time the plane flew over the building.

The problem with Welz's retraction is that in his original statement he stated he was on the roof with his neighbors at around 9 o'clock. The second plane hit the South Tower at 9:03 a.m. That suggests that in his CW11 interview he intended to convey that he saw the plane fly over their heads at around 9 o'clock. His later retraction seems to be based upon the fact that he knows there were no planes on 9/11 and has come to understand that more and more people are becoming aware that the evidence does not support the presence of planes on 911. He does not want to be exposed as a false eyewitness.

Clifton Cloud's statements present compelling evidence that a CGI of a plane was inserted into his video. On 9/11 Cloud was in position to take video of the second tower explosion. As can be seen from the frame from his video, the plane is clearly in view flying toward the tower before the explosion. If the plane was in fact in the original video, it would have been seen by Cloud for approximately four seconds before its impact with the tower.[239] The video has been in the possession of the government until the government was forced to release the video in 2010, pursuant to a Freedom of Information Act request.[240] Why did the government drag its feet for nine years before releasing the video and then only doing so because it was required to by the FOIA laws? Because the spontaneous statements heard in the audio contradict the video and consequently impeach the video's authenticity.

The audio suggests that the video has been altered by having a CGI of a plane inserted. The audio not only demonstrates that Cloud did not see a plane, but also his adamant certainty that there was no plane. Cloud is heard on the tape talking on the phone, and he clearly states that there was no plane. When the person on the phone tells Cloud that a plane struck the towers, Cloud contradicts the person and states that **"no plane hit, nothing, the building exploded."**[241]

Clifton Cloud did not see the plane appearing in the video he shot, even though it was visible for four seconds during its approach. Cloud was adamant that "no plane hit" the building, which suggests that the plane was a CGI inserted later.

Cloud calls his office and asks to speak with Joe Maltha and he talks with Lloyd. **"The Second tower just exploded**. . . . Just caught the second explosion on videotape."[242] The person on the phone asks about a plane, apparently passing on the initial media reports of a plane, and Cloud responds by saying: **"No, a bomb, I saw it, no plane hit, nothing, the building exploded, the other tower, floors down."**[243]

After Cloud gets off the phone, people can be heard in the audio portion of the tape talking to Cloud in the background. Apparently, the people in the background are passing on information that they are receiving from the mass-media outlets. On the tape persons standing nearby tell Cloud they think it was a plane. Cloud cannot be convinced there was a plane. He knows what he saw and is certain that the building just exploded. He responds to those claiming it was a plane:

> **I saw it. Nothing hit it, I didn't see anything hit it, I got it on video, I didn't see another plane, It looked like it exploded. . . . I'm telling you I didn't see a plane the second time. . . . The**

> second one was a white flash, if it was a plane it was packed
> with explosives. . . . but the second was a bomb, I didn't see a
> plane. I saw the second one explode, I was in shock. [244]

On the tape you can hear the others nearby saying that "they said it was possibly another plane."[245] Clifton cannot be convinced, he saw the building explode and there was no plane. He states:

> I didn't see one dude, I was here. . . . It looked like a bomb
> went off inside. . . . dude that was no plane on that second one.
> . . . Dude I saw the second explosion, there was no plane that
> hit that second building, it exploded from the inside out. . . . I
> didn't see a plane, I was here watching it.[246]

A person can be heard in the background saying it was a twin engine plane that hit it. Cloud cannot be swayed from what he saw. He responds: **"I don't believe it, man I can't imagine, look at the size of that hole."**[247]

Another video released by the government in 2008 pursuant to an FOIA request also has the same characteristics of the Clifton Cloud video. The audio impeaches the video. The witness explains that she just saw an explosion and makes no mention of the huge plane seen in the video crashing into the tower. She does not mention the plane because it was not there; it was a CGI added to the video tape later. The unidentified witness is on the phone with her mother when she sees the second explosion:

> **Oh my God! I just got an explosion on it! Oh my God it is
> exploding!** I just got it on video! Jesus Christ! Oh my God! It is
> the worst thing I have ever seen in my life mom! It's like the end of
> the world![248]

Furthermore, the perpetrators of 9/11 slipped up with one of their video feeds. In one telecast from "Chopper 4" someone dropped the ball and did not insert the CGI into the telecast. Consequently the telecast did not show a plane hitting the tower. The studio announcers confirm that there was no plane seen. Neither of the news announcers who were commentating mentioned anything about a plane. Below is what they said as they watched the explosion of the South Tower on their video monitor.

> Announcer 1: Oh! Uh, if you are taking a look now, you see that
> **we have just had another explosion**, and that is considerably
> lower. And is that in the other building? Is that I am witnessing?

> Announcer 2: That apparently looks like it is in the other
> building![249]

In the series of frames below we see in the top frames what the announcers were looking at during their live broadcast.[250] Notice there is no sign of a plane approaching the towers. Shortly after midnight, NBC broadcast a video from virtually the exact same perspective showing a plane crashing into the South Tower.[251] When NBC broadcast the videotape with the CGI plane they did so at ½ speed. That may have been to compensate for the impossible speeds of the plane CGIs in their previous broadcasts.

Each frame from that later videotape has been synchronized and paired with live broadcast; the synchronization compensates for the ½ speed replay and so the synchronization is accurate. When comparing the frames from the live video with the later broadcast video, it becomes clear that the plane in the later broadcast is a CGI. The background has been completely taken out of the late video tape. There is no water or skyline.

The objective evidence points to the planes being CGIs; that conclusion becomes more compelling when the supposed eyewitness accounts of planes hitting the towers are scrutinized more closely. The major media involvement in the 9/11 deception is the holy grail of the 9/11 cover-up. The conspirators cannot allow the general population to find out that the media outlets are propaganda tools used by them to deceive the world. They will do anything to keep a lid on that fact.

12 The Man Who Knew Too Much

If the BBC had advance notice of Tower 7 collapsing, that suggests that it was planned well in advance of 9-11-2001. Barry Jennings reveals some strange conduct of New York city officials, which implicates them in the 9/11 attacks. Barry Jennings was Deputy Director of Emergency Services Department for the New York Housing Authority, which was one of the component agencies of the New York City Office of Emergency Management. Upon being informed about the first explosion at the World Trade Center on September 11, 2001, he responded to the unfolding emergency as he was trained to do.[252]

Jennings immediately reported to the Emergency Operations Center (EOC) for the Office of Emergency Management located on the 23rd floor of Tower 7 at the World Trade Center. When he arrived at the WTC 7, he was met there by Michael Hess, New York City Corporate Counsel. When they arrived at the EOC, they noticed that the EOC was empty. It was evident to them that people had been at the EOC and had left it shortly before he and Hess arrived, because Jennings could see on desks half-eaten sandwiches and hot coffee with steam still wafting from the cups. He stated that he was inside on the 23rd floor when the alleged second plane hit the South Tower.

Jennings called several people, one of whom told him to "leave and leave right away." He and Michael Hess began walking down the stairwell and when he reached the 6th floor there was a huge explosion that caused the stairwell beneath him to collapse. Jennings was clear that the explosion came from beneath him. He and Hess then went up to the 8th floor. It was from the 8th floor that he heard additional explosions inside Tower 7. It was after he reached the 8th floor and was waiting to be rescued that WTC Towers 1 and 2 collapsed. Jennings and Hess were finally rescued from Tower 7. Jennings noted that as he was being escorted from Tower 7 he was stepping over dead bodies. He stated that the lobby of the building was in such "total ruins" that he did not even recognize it as the lobby of Tower 7. Just hours earlier he passed through that same lobby, which at that time was magnificent and beautiful.

Jennings statements pose a problem for the government 9/11 conspiracy theory. That is because he clearly remembers that the explosion that caused the stairwell to collapse under him came from underneath him and it was before Towers 1 and 2 collapsed. The explosions in Tower 7 mean that the destruction of Tower 7 began before Towers 1 and 2 collapsed and were unrelated to the collapse of either building. That is because at the time of the collapse of the stairwell, the attacks on WTC Towers 1 and 2 were purportedly to the upper floors of those buildings and thus separated by a road (Vesey Street), a building (WTC 6), and at least 77 floors from WTC 7. The explosion that caused the stairwell of Tower 7 to collapse under Jennings' feet came from lower in WTC 7. The dead bodies that Jennings stepped over while being rescued means that the government story that nobody was killed in Tower 7 is a lie.

Another revelation that is a fly in the ointment of the official story of 9/11 is that he revealed that New York Mayer Rudolph Giuliani was present at the EOC on 9-11-2001. He said that it was unusual for the EOC to be unoccupied, and he was told that the reason that nobody was there when he arrived was because they had to take the mayor and evacuate. Jennings stated that he personally did not see Giuliani at the EOC, but that other staff members told Jennings that Giuliani was there that morning. Jennings explained that Giuliani's presence was the reason that Hess was at the EOC that day. He explained that Hess was Giuliani's lawyer, and he had gone to the EOC in order to meet with Giuliani, but apparently Giuliani had left before Hess arrived. If Giuliani was at the EOC, it means that Giuliani lied about his whereabouts on 9-11, because he stated that he never went to the EOC on the day. Why would Giuliani want to deny he was in the EOC on 9-11-2001, if he was in fact there that day?

Barry Jennings mysteriously died on August 19, 2008. He was 53 years old at the time, with no history of life-threatening illness. Mr. Jennings died within days of the NIST report being issued on the cause of the Tower 7 collapse. Mr. Jennings was married and had four children, but there is no obituary or public record of his death. Dylan Avery went to Mr. Jenning's home, and found the residence vacant with a "For Sale" sign out front. A friend of Dylan Avery hired a private detective who is reputed to be the best P.I. in New York to find out how Mr. Jennings died. Within 24 hours the P.I. contacted the client to refund his money and told him not to ever contact her again, that it was a police matter. To this day there has been no reported cause of death for Barry Jennings.[253]

Jennings died on August 19, 2008; two days later, on August 21, 2008, NIST called a press conference to release a draft of its report on the collapse of Tower 7.[254] The final NIST report was released in November 2008.[255] NIST did no materials testing, but instead relied upon a computer model that supported its theory.[256] NIST refuses to release the model to the public for review. Engineers that have read the NIST report noted that the computer model misrepresents the fires that actually occurred in Tower 7.[257] Barry Jennings spent hours in the buildings and heard numerous explosions. Jennings was a fly in the ointment of the NIST computer modeling assumptions. With Barry Jennings now dead, there are no first-hand witnesses around to refute the false data used in the NIST computer model.

Barry Jennings posed a threat to two main points made in the NIST report. The NIST report states:

> Simulations of hypothetical blast events show that no blast event played a role in the collapse of WTC 7. NIST concluded that blast events did not occur, and found no evidence whose explanation required invocation of a blast event.[258]

Jennings was in the building and heard repeated explosions. An explosion took out the stairwell beneath his feet at the sixth floor of the building. He was trapped in the building because of the explosions. The stairwell explosion happened before either tower collapsed.

The second main point of the NIST report that Jennings could refute was the claim that nobody died in WTC 7. The NIST report states:

> There were no serious injuries or fatalities, because the estimated 4,000 occupants of WTC 7 reacted to the airplane impacts on the two WTC towers and began evacuating before there was significant damage to WTC 7.[259]

The NIST report states that building 7 was completely evacuated within an hour of the first alleged plane impact on WTC 1. However, we know that Jennings and Hess were still in the building long after that and were there when both Towers 1 and 2 collapsed. Jennings was told by a fireman do not look down because they were stepping over dead bodies as he was being rescued from the building by the firemen.

Jennings was put under tremendous pressure at his job and told Dylan Avery that he was threatened to be fired over his statements about the events of 9-11-2001. Jennings was afraid of being fired and asked Avery not to use his interview in an upcoming update to his *Loose Change* video. Avery agreed, and the interview was not placed in the video. Under continuing pressure, Jennings later equivocated in a BBC interview. Jennings stated: "I didn't like how I was portrayed. I was portrayed as seeing dead bodies. I never saw dead bodies. I said it felt like I was stepping over them, but I never saw them."[260]

It is reasonable to conclude that Jennings was under pressure to equivocate his earlier account. Jennings' original interview has now been posted on the internet by Dylan Avery. In the video, Jennings clearly states that he was stepping over bodies as he was being rescued from building 7.[261] He stated: "we were stepping over people, and you know you can feel when you are stepping over people."[262]

While Jennings may in fact not have "seen" bodies he "knew" he was stepping over dead bodies because he could "feel" them. He did not "see" the dead bodies, because he was told by the fireman who rescued him not to look down, so that he would not see the dead bodies. Jennings later equivocation is not a retraction of his earlier statement. He did not retract that he was told not to look down by the fireman, and he did not retract that he felt the bodies as he was stepping over them. His testimony remains as evidence of those facts.

The NIST theory is that the entire destruction of Tower 7 was caused by fire. The NIST report states that the fires were caused by the impact of debris from the collapse of Tower 1.[263] NIST claims that the collapse resulted from fire that caused the buckling of an interior column in the northeast region of the building.[264] A problem with the NIST report is that it claims that among the principal fires that caused the collapse were fires on floors seven through nine.[265] Barry Jennings was trapped for several hours on the 8th floor. He was on the 8th floor when Towers 1 and 2 collapsed and remained there until his eventual rescue.

If there was such a raging inferno in floors 7 through 9, Jennings, who was on floor 8, would have died. In fact, the rescuers would have had to go past the supposed raging inferno on the 7th floor to get to him. Yet, they did not need any fire hoses because there was no fire there. Finally NIST claimed that the raging fires caused the collapse, which started in the northeast side of the building. Jennings was on the north side of the building when he was rescued.

That NIST theory is not only contrary to the eyewitness account of Barry Jennings but is also contrary to the clear evidence of a total simultaneous structural failure of the entire building causing it to free-fall collapse into its own footprint. Scientists and engineers have severely criticized the NIST report for being unscientific and based upon unfounded theory and false assumptions and data.[266] It took the federal government 7 years to come up with some explanation for the collapse of Tower 7. Scientists and engineers that have reviewed the report have found it scientifically unsupportable.

Prior to 9-11-01 there had never been a case where a steel structured high-rise tower has collapsed as a result of fire. On 9-11-2001, three steel structured towers all fell. The government would have us believe that they all collapsed as a result of fire. The collapse of World Trade Center Tower Seven on September 11, 2001, at 5:20 p.m. was particularly unusual. Tower Seven had 47 stories, which made it 600 feet tall. Aside from the WTC Twin Towers, it was one of the tallest buildings in lower Manhattan. It was separated from Twin Towers by a city block. Tower 7 was fully 355 feet away from the north face of the North Tower, and Tower 6 stood between it and the North Tower. The South Tower was even further away. Tower 7 was no closer to the Twin Towers than any of the other surrounding buildings which suffered only superficial damage. Tower 7 was not struck by either of the alleged planes (which we now know didn't exist) or significant debris from Towers One or Two, yet mysteriously two limited fires broke out in the building and it suddenly collapsed later in the evening of September 11.

Interestingly, the 23rd floor of Tower Seven received 15 million dollars worth of renovations, including independent and secure air and water supplies and bullet and bomb resistant windows designed to withstand 200 MPH winds. The renovation was intended to be used by the Mayor of New York, Rudolph Giuliani, as an emergency command center. Part of the reason for the command center was the 1993 bombing of the World Trade Center. The 23rd floor was ideal for a command center because it had an unobstructed view of the north sides of the Twin Towers, which since the 1993 bombing were considered prime terrorist targets. Tower 7 was a well-built 100% steel-framed skyscraper. It had a series of 58 columns ringing its perimeter, and a bundle of 25 columns in its core.[267] Suspiciously, on the day of the 9/11 attacks,

Mayor Giuliani and his entourage alleged that they set up shop in a different location and did not use the special bunker designed precisely for such an event. Giuliani stated that Tower 7 was evacuated immediately upon the first plane impact.

> The command center was at 7 World Trade Center, which is the building that was north of the World Trade Center that went down in the afternoon. It went down maybe 4 or 5 o'clock in the afternoon. **But from the very moment that the first plane hit, 7 World Trade Center was evacuated.**[268]

The bodies that Barry Jennings stepped on as he was rescued from the building puts the lie to the statement that Tower 7 was immediately evacuated. Giuliani claims that Tower 7 was evacuated immediately upon the impact of the first plane, but no order had been given to evacuate the South Tower, which had not yet been struck by the second plane, even though it was right next to the North Tower. At that time only the North Tower was burning; many thought it was just a tragic accident and not a concerted attack that would eventually involve the South Tower. In fact, many people in the South Tower were told by security personnel to stay put and go back to their offices after the first plane struck the North Tower. WTC Security felt the damage was limited to the upper floors of the North Tower and there was no threat to the South Tower. Tower 7 was much further from the burning North Tower than was the South Tower. In fact, Tower 7 was not even in the same complex of buildings as the rest of the WTC towers. Tower 7 was across Vesey Street from Tower 6 which stood between Tower 7 and the North Tower. Tower 7 was not even located in the WTC Plaza.

While the six buildings in the WTC Plaza were constructed in the 1970's, construction on Tower 7 did not even begin until 1985. It had a completely different architectural style. At the time Tower 7 was allegedly ordered evacuated on 9-11, there were no fires present in that building and no damage to the building. The fires in Tower 7 did not appear until after its alleged evacuation and after the second plane hit the South Tower. When Tower 7 ultimately collapsed, there were no firemen in the building fighting the fires. There was only superficial damage to the building, and the fires were limited to two isolated pockets. Except for the rescue of Jennings, Hess and others earlier in the day, it seemed that the firemen had advance notice that the building would collapse later in the day and stayed clear of it. How did they know? Who told them?

Furthermore, Jennings' revelation that he was told that Guiliani was at the Tower 7 command center during the morning of 9-11-2001 contradicts Guiliani's claim that he never went to the command center that day. Giuliani ultimately went to an alternative command center a block away at 75 Barclay Street. He let the cat out of the bag when he explained to Peter Jennings of ABC News the morning of 9-11: "I went down to the scene and we set up headquarters at 75 Barclay Street which was right there with the police commissioner and the fire commissioner, the head of emergency management. We were operating out of there [75 Barclay Street] when **we were told that the World Trade Center was gonna collapse**, and it did collapse before we could get out of the building."[269]

Notice that Giuliani did not say he was warned that it might collapse, he was "told the World Trade Center was gonna collapse." In the history of the world no steel framed building has ever collapsed from fire. In fact, the WTC Twin Towers were specially designed to withstand the damage caused by the midair impact of a Boeing 707, a plane substantially the same size as the Boeing 767's that crashed into the North and South towers on 9-11.[270] Who then could know in advance that the World Trade Center was going to collapse? The answer is obvious: the ones who planned on destroying the towers. Giuliani was in the emergency headquarters along with both the police and fire commissioners. They were in direct radio contact with the firemen who were bravely still climbing the stairs to fight the fires in the Twin Towers. Giuliani and others were "told the World Trade Center was gonna collapse" yet nobody warned those courageous firemen of the imminent collapse of the South Tower.

Prior to the collapse of each tower, there was a large explosion. It is notable that the mass media calls the site of the destruction of the WTC Twin Towers "ground zero," which is a designation traditionally used to describe the point where a nuclear device is detonated. That large base explosion was followed by a series of smaller explosions as the buildings turned to dust and dissolved into their own footprints. Investigative reporter Alexander James summarizes the eyewitness account of the large explosion taking out the foundation of one of the towers.

> USA Today Interviews Final Survivor of WTC Disaster "As he left the building, (Ronald DiFrancesco) saw a fireball rolling toward him. He put his arms in front of his face. He woke up three days later at St. Vincent's hospital. His arms were burned. Some bones were broken. His lungs were singed. But he was alive - the last person out of the south tower."
>
> The Account of Two Photographers of 911 Don Halasy: "As I turned to run, a wall of warm air came barrelling toward me. I tried to outrace it, but it swept me up and literally blew me into the wall of a building. By the time I regained my footing, a hailstorm of debris was falling from the sky." (Notice how the "hailstorm of debris" fell from the sky moments AFTER Halasy was thrown to the ground. This is a crucial detail!)
>
> David Handschuh: "Instinctively I lifted the camera up, and something took over that probably saved my life. And that was to run rather than take pictures. I got down to the end of the block and turned the corner when a wave - a hot, solid, black wave of heat threw me down the block. It literally picked me up off my feet, and I wound up about a block away."
>
> What each of these witnesses are describing is known as the "shockwave effect." When an explosion goes off, extremely high temperatures are generated in a small amount of time and space.

This abrupt shift in temperature causes the air to push outwards with violent force, seeking to stabilize itself. The result is a blast of hot air radiating in all directions.[271]

Following the large base explosion a fireman described smaller sequential explosions taking out each floor seriatim as the building collapsed in on itself. Two firemen were recorded discussing their eyewitness account of the collapse of one of the Twin Towers:

Fireman1: Floor by floor it started popping out . . .
Fireman2: It was almost like they had detonators. . .
Fireman1: Yeah, detonators . . .
Fireman2: . . .planted to take down the building. boom-boom-boom-boom-boom . . .
Fireman1: All the way down. I was watching it and running.[272]

Why haven't more New York Firemen come out and explained what they saw and heard? Because they are under a gag order on threat of being fired if they reveal what they know. Reporter Randy Lavello explains:

I met Auxiliary Lieutenant Fireman and former Auxiliary Police Officer, Paul Isaac Jr. at the World Trade Center Memorial. Paul, along with many other firemen, is very upset about the obvious cover-up and he is on a crusade for answers and justice. He was stationed at Engine 10, across the street from the World Trade Center in 1998 and 99; Engine 10 was entirely wiped out in the destruction of the towers. He explained to me that, "many other firemen know there were bombs in the buildings, but they're afraid for their jobs to admit it because the 'higher-ups' forbid discussion of this fact." Paul further elaborated that former CIA director Robert Woolsey, as the Fire Department's Anti-terrorism Consultant, is sending a gag order down the ranks. "There were definitely bombs in those buildings," he told me. He explained to me that, if the building had 'pancaked' as it's been called, the falling floors would have met great resistance from the steel support columns, which would have sent debris flying outward into the surrounding blocks. I asked him about the trusses and quoted the history channel's "don't trust a truss" explanation for the collapses. He responded in disbelief, and told me, "You could never build a truss building that high. A slight wind would knock it over! Those buildings were supported by reinforced steel. Building don't just implode like that; this was a demolition."

Just after the disaster, Firefighter Louie Cacchioli said, "We think there were bombs set in the building." Notice he said "we." At 9:04, just after flight 175 collided with the South Tower, a huge explosion shot 550 feet into the air from the U.S. Customs House known as WTC 6. A huge crater scars the ground where this building once stood. Something blew up WTC 6 - it wasn't a plane; it must have been a bomb of some sort.[273]

Furthermore, it is certain that Tower Seven was also deliberately demolished. What is the evidence of that? For one thing, the leaseholder of the World Trade Center, Larry Silverstein, slipped up and admitted to it during an interview. In the documentary "America Rebuilds", aired September 2002, Silverstein stated:

I remember getting a call from the, er, fire department commander, telling me that they were not sure they were gonna be able to contain the fire, and I said, 'We've had such terrible loss of life, maybe the smartest thing to do is pull it.' And they made that decision to pull and we watched the building collapse.[274]

Another smoking gun in the demolition of Tower 7 is the fact that the two buildings that framed Tower 7 on both sides remained standing. Closely next door immediately to the west of WTC Tower 7 was the 32 story Verizon Building. Virtually all of the significant damage suffered by the Verizon Building was a result of the collapse of Tower 7, not from the collapse of the North or South Towers. In fact the Verizon Building is slightly closer to the North Tower and therefore would have suffered at least as much damage from the collapse of that tower as was suffered by Tower 7. However, the Verizon building remained standing and no fires broke out in the building. The U.S. Post Office Building, which was immediately next door on the east side of Tower 7, remained standing. Both the Verizon and U.S. Post Office buildings were repaired and reopened.

The World Financial Center (WFC) was directly across the street to the west from the World Trade Center. Building 2 of the World Financial Center was approximately as close to the North WTC Tower 1 as was WTC Tower 7, yet WFC building 2 did not suffer any significant damage from the collapse of the WTC Twin Towers. The only notable damage to any of the World Financial Center buildings was some damage to the southeast corner of building 3, apparently from falling debris.[275] That damage could accurately be described as superficial and was certainly not even close to the damage required to cause the total collapse of the building; it was repaired in due course. The WFC buildings were approximately the same vintage as WTC Tower 7, with all of them being built in the mid 1980's. They were all subject to the same construction codes and standards. The WFC buildings are standing today as strong as the day they were built. WTC Tower 7 would be standing right along with them if it had not been purposely demolished.

The clearest evidence that the 9-11-2001 attacks were deliberately orchestrated by elements in the government is that the official 9/11 Commission Report issued by the government does not even mention Tower 7. Stop and reflect upon that; the commission set up by the government to find out what happened, how it happened, and who did it, did not mention the collapse of a 47 story skyscraper! That silence in the report speaks louder than words ever could.

The 585 page 9/11 Commission Report contains no date of publication. The report was issued by a commission that was reluctantly called together by the Bush Administration, which only called the commission together after a public clamor for an investigation. The commission did not convene until November 26, 2002, which was 441 days after the attacks. That delay is clear evidence of foot-dragging and suggests that the government was in no hurry to find out what truly happened on 9-11-2001. The 9/11 Commission Report was issued on July 22, 2004. The commission spent more than 1 ½ years studying the events of 9-11-2001, with all of the resources of the federal government at its disposal, yet it decided not to even discuss Tower 7. Tower 7 is the elephant in the room; the failure to even mention Tower 7 in the 9/11 Commission Report is clear evidence of a cover-up.

Barry Jennings revealed in an interview with Dylan Avery that he was interviewed by the 9/11 Commission and told them about the stairwell collapsing up to the 6th floor, that he was trapped on the 8th floor, that he heard repeated explosions over several hours, stepping over dead bodies, and the devastation he witnessed in the lobby. The 9/11 Commission knew about what happened to Tower 7. The evidence pointed to WTC 7 being purposely brought down by those with access to the inside security of the building. They could not reveal that, so they did not even discuss WTC 7.

The 9/11 Commission's failure to address the collapse of Tower 7 speaks volumes. The commission could not reveal what happened to WTC 7, because it pointed directly to the involvement of high officials in the federal government. WTC 7 was one of the most secure buildings in New York. It was the home of the CIA, IRS Regional Council, U.S. Secret Service, ATF, the SEC, and the Mayor's Office of Emergency Management. Security in that building was very tight. Not anyone could just walk into that building. It would require security clearances and coordination from high officials in the federal government. If there were explosions going off in the building as reported by Barry Jennings, high officials in the federal government made it happen. The purposeful refusal by the commission to address WTC 7 is clear proof of a cover-up.

It was left to NIST to conjure up a theory for the collapse of Tower 7. NIST did not issue its report until November 2008, which was four years after the 9/11 Commission Report was issued and seven years after the 9/11 attacks. Suspiciously, NIST did no materials testing.[276] The NIST report was based entirely upon a computer model that included assumptions that supported its theory of collapse due to fire.[277]

Whom do we find in charge of security at the World Trade Center, including Tower 7? A company called Securacom (since renamed Stratesec), which had on its board of directors on 9-

11-2001 none other than Marvin Bush, the brother of President George W. Bush.[278] In addition, the chairman of the board of Stratesec is Wirt D. Walker III, a cousin of Marvin and George W. Bush.[279] After the 9/11 attacks the then existing video recordings made by the security cameras during the attacks and destruction all disappeared.

Those behind the conspiracy were so concerned about keeping a lid on things that President Bush and Vice President Cheney lobbied Congress not to look too hard at the cause of the 9-11 attacks. The lame excuse Bush gave for the lobbying effort was that a full investigation would "take resources and personnel away from the effort in the war on terrorism."[280] Their lobbying effort was in reality a rather transparent attempt to get Congress to go along with a cover-up.

Congress seemed willing to honor Bush's request. Senate Majority Leader Tom Daschle promised that he would "limit the scope and overall review of what happened."[281] What Daschle meant by that was that he will ensure that they would never get to the bottom of what really happened.

Congressman Porter Goss and Senator Bob Graham, who each headed the intelligence committees in their respective houses of Congress, both assured the president that the joint congressional investigation that began in February 2002 would be a forward-looking inquiry only. The congressional joint committee agreed to only look deep enough to bring about needed government intelligence reforms.

The question is how could Congress determine what reforms need to be made without first thoroughly understanding what went wrong? The obvious answer is they did not care to find out what went wrong, because either they are afraid what it may turn up or they know what it will turn up because they are in on it. In essence, President Bush, Vice President Cheney, and the Congressional leadership agreed to a cover-up. The joint congressional report was issued on December 20, 2002, and was limited to intelligence community activities.[282] The 9/11 Commission investigation was a separate investigative body from the joint congressional investigation. The 9/11 commission was not established until November 27, 2002.

What is the evidence that Congress and the President are trying to hide from the American public? For starters, six weeks prior to the WTC destruction, David Schippers, chief investigative counsel for the Clinton impeachment, had learned from FBI agents in Minnesota and Chicago that a massive attack had been planned for lower Manhattan. Schippers attempted to warn Attorney General John Ashcroft. Department of Justice officials, however, spurned Schippers' attempt to forward the information to Ashcroft.[283] The reason that Schippers tried to warn Ashcroft directly was that the FBI agents, whom he was representing, were frustrated by the lack of action being taken by the FBI and the Department of Justice when they went through their chain of command to try to put a stop to the obvious threat.

Significant evidence was uncovered that pointed to Israel as the prime perpetrator of the 9/11 attacks. At first, Henry Kissinger was appointed as the Executive Director of the 9/11

Commission. However, due to the enormous protest over his appointment, he surrendered the post. Henry Kissinger is a Jew and ardent supporter of Israel. Kissinger was replaced as Executive Director with yet another Zionist Jew, Philip Zelikow.[284] As Executive Director, Zelikow was the most powerful person on the committee.

The appointment Zelikow was a perfect choice if the objective of the commission was to cover-up the involvement of Israel. Not only is Zelikow a Zionist Jew, he is also a dual citizen of Israel. From his position as Executive Director of the 9/11 Commission, Zelikow ensured that none of the evidence implicating Israel was mentioned in the commission's report. It is possible, the 9/11 Commission could become even more infamous than the Warren Commission that covered-up the conspiracy in the Kennedy assassination.[285]

It is not hyperbole to call the 9/11 Commission Report a cover-up. A former member of that commission agrees that it was a cover-up. Former U.S. Senator Max Cleland served on the 9/11 Commission for over a year. He resigned because he determined that the White House knew more about 9/11 than it was revealing and was delaying access to information in order to run out the clock so the commission would be required to submit its report to congress by the mandated deadline without vital information.

The 9/11 Commission was used in much the same fashion as the Warren Commission investigation of the Kennedy assassination. Senator Cleland saw clearly that the commission was designed not to reveal evidence, but to conceal evidence, and not to inform the public, but to misinform the public.[286] Senator Cleland stated: "One of these days we will have to get the full story because the 9-11 issue is so important to America. But this White House wants to cover it up."[287] Senator Cleland wanted no part of the cover-up and so resigned his position on the commission.

The 9/11 Commission is one of many instances of Israeli control over the U.S. Government. Israel has complete control over the U.S. Government. The CIA, the State Department, and the FBI have been infiltrated by Zionist agents and their fellow travelers. The policies of the U.S. government, consequently, have been subverted to the benefit of the Zionists and to the detriment of the U.S. citizens.

On March 9, 1978, Michael Saba witnessed firsthand the power and influence of the Jews in the United States government. He happened to be seated out of view but adjacent to a table where Stephen Bryen, an official of the U.S. Senate Foreign Relations Committee met with official representatives of Israel at the Madison Hotel in Washington, D.C.[288] What struck Mr. Saba was that the conversation between Bryen and the Israeli officials was not a general discussion but rather a strategy meeting on how the Israeli delegation could affect United States foreign policy to the benefit of Israel.

What surprised Mr. Saba was that Bryen used the pronoun "we" when he expressed the position of the Israeli government and the pronoun "they" when he described the position of the United States government. Mr. Saba had the distinct impression that Mr. Bryen's loyalties were to Israel rather than to the United States. In other words, Mr. Bryen was a spy. During the discussion Mr. Bryen offered top-secret Pentagon documents regarding Arab military bases in the Middle East.

Once Mr. Saba revealed the events to the U.S. Justice Department, he found out the power that the Jews have in the United States government. At every turn, the investigation of his allegations was thwarted. In addition, despite the ongoing investigation of Mr. Bryen by the U.S. Justice Department, Bryen was allowed to become the Deputy Assistant Secretary of Defense in the Reagan Administration.

The handling of the Bryen espionage revealed that the highest levels of the U.S. government were infiltrated by a network of Jews that were beholden to Israel. Not only were elements in the U.S. government working to protect Bryen, but the major media did everything possible to kill the story. While initially reporters were very interested in the story, suddenly they became uninterested once they returned to their offices. Mr. Saba labeled this interlocking Jewish web the Armageddon Network.

The following October 2001 colloquy between Israeli Foreign Minister Shimon Peres and Israeli Prime Minister Ariel Sharon reveals from the horse's mouth the Jewish power in the United States.

> According to the Israeli Hebrew radio Kol Yisrael Wednesday, Peres warned Sharon that refusing to heed incessant American requests for a cease-fire with the Palestinians would endanger Israeli interests and turn the US against us. At this point, a furious Sharon reportedly turned toward Peres, saying "every time we do something you tell me America will do this and will do that . . . I want to tell you something very clear: Don't worry about American pressure on Israel. We, the Jewish people, control America, and the Americans know it." The radio said Peres and other cabinet ministers warned Sharon against saying what he said in public, because "it would cause us a public relations disaster."[289]

The control of the 9/11 Commission through its executive director is just one example of the influence that Zionist Jews have over the government of the United States. Explosions in WTC 7 would point directly to Larry Silverstein and George Bush, which would in turn ultimately lead to Israel, so the 9/11 Commission did not even address the collapse of Tower 7. The implication of explosions occurring in WTC 7 is why the NIST report expressly ruled out explosions as the cause of WTC 7 collapse. It was not until November 2008 that NIST issued its final report on the collapse of Tower 7.[290] It took the federal government more than seven years to issue a report on the collapse of a 47 story skyscraper. Yet the report is not based upon a true investigation, because NIST did not test any materials from the collapse. Instead, the report is based upon a computer model. That computer model has been criticized severely by engineers for being based upon false data.[291]

13 Evidence of Directed Energy on 9/11

Eyewitness accounts of explosions inside the World Trade Center before the collapse of the Twin Towers of the WTC have been completely ignored by the major media outlets. Christopher Bollyn, a reporter for the American Free Press, published a report on October 22, 2001, regarding ear and eyewitness accounts of explosions before and at the time of the collapse of the WTC Towers.

> Despite reports from numerous eyewitnesses and experts, including news reporters on the scene, who heard or saw explosions immediately before the collapse of the World Trade Center, there has been virtual silence in the mainstream media.

* * *

> Van Romero, an explosives expert and former director of the Energetic Materials Research and Testing Center at New Mexico Tech, said on Sept. 11, "My opinion is, based on the videotapes, that after the airplanes hit the World Trade Center there were some explosive devices inside the buildings that caused the towers to collapse."

* * *

> Romero is vice president of research at New Mexico Institute of Mining and Technology, which studies explosive materials and the effects of explosions on buildings, aircraft and other structures, and often assists in forensic investigations into terrorist attacks, often by setting off similar explosions and studying the effects.
>
> After being hit by the aircraft, the twin towers appeared to be

stable. Then without warning, at 9:58 a.m. the south tower imploded vertically downwards, 53 minutes after being hit. At 10:28, 88 minutes after being struck, the north tower collapsed.

"It would be difficult for something from the plane to trigger an event like that," Romero said. If explosions did cause the towers to collapse, "It could have been a relatively small amount of explosives placed in strategic points," he said.

"One of the things terrorist events are noted for is a diversionary attack and secondary device," Romero said. Attackers detonate an initial, diversionary explosion, in this case the collision of the planes into the towers, which brings emergency personnel to the scene, then detonate a second explosion.

Ten days after the attack, following criticism of his initial remarks, Romero did an about-face in his analysis of the collapse, "Certainly the fire is what caused the building to fail," he told the Journal on Sept. 21.

* * *

However, there is other information that lends credence to Romero's controversial [first] scenario. One eyewitness whose office is near the World Trade Center told AFP that he was standing among a crowd of people on Church Street, about two-and-a-half blocks from the South tower, when he saw "a number of brief light sources being emitted from inside the building between floors 10 and 15." He saw about six of these brief flashes, accompanied by "a crackling sound" before the tower collapsed. . . . One of the first firefighters in the stricken second tower, Louie Cacchioli, 51, told People Weekly on Sept. 24: "I was taking firefighters up in the elevator to the 24th floor to get in position to evacuate workers. On the last trip up a bomb went off. We think there were bombs set in the building."

Kim White, 32, an employee on the 80th floor, also reported hearing an explosion. "All of a sudden the building shook, then it started to sway. We didn't know what was going on," she told People. "We got all our people on the floor into the stairwell . . . at that time we all thought it was a fire . . . We got down as far as the 74th floor . . . then there was another explosion."

The accepted theory is that as the fires raged in the towers, the steel cores in each building were heated to 2,000 degrees Fahrenheit, causing the support beams to buckle.

A lead engineer who designed the World Trade Center Towers expressed shock that the towers collapsed after being hit by passenger jets. "I designed it for a 707 to hit it," Lee Robertson, the project's structural engineer said. The Boeing 707 has a fuel capacity of more than 23,000 gallons, comparable to the 767's 23,980-gallon fuel capacity.

Another architect of the WTC, Aaron Swirski, lives in Israel and spoke to Jerusalem Post Radio after the attack: "It was designed around that eventuality to survive this kind of attack," he said.

Hyman Brown, a University of Colorado civil engineering professor and the World Trade Center's construction manager, watched in confusion as the towers came down. "It was over-designed to withstand almost anything including hurricanes, high winds, bombings and an airplane hitting it," he said.

Brown told AFP that although the buildings were designed to withstand "a 150-year storm" and the impact of a Boeing 707, he said the jet fuel burning at 2,000 degrees Fahrenheit weakened the steel. Brown explained that the south tower collapsed first as it was struck lower with more weight above the impact area. Brown told AFP that he "did not buy" the theory that the implosion was caused by the fires sucking the air out of the lower floors, which has been speculated.

The contractor who is reported to have been the first on the WTC collapse scene to cart away the rubble that remains is a company that specializes in the scientific demolition of large buildings, Controlled Demolition, Inc. (CDI) of Baltimore, headed by Mark Loizeaux.

CDI is the same contractor that demolished and hauled away the shell of the bombed Oklahoma City Murrah building, actions that prevented independent investigators from pursuing evidence on leads suggesting that there were bombs set off inside the building.

In February 2000, a federal grand jury indicted Mark Loizeaux, Douglas Loizeaux and Controlled Demolition, Inc. on charges of falsely reporting campaign contributions by asking family members and CDI employees to donate to the campaign of Rep. Elijah E.

Cummings (D-Md.).

The Baltimore Sun reported that the illegal contributions allegedly occurred between 1996 and 1998. The Loizeaux brothers and CDI were acquitted in September 2000.

Cleaning up the estimated 1.2 million tons of rubble will reportedly cost $7 billion and take up to a year.[292]

Below are three different photographs of a woman standing in the gash left by the explosion that was alleged to be the impact of the second plane that hit the north tower of the World Trade Center on 9-11-01. The woman has been tentatively identified by some as Edna Cintron (but that identity has not been confirmed and is in dispute). Cintron was allegedly an administrative assistant for Marsh & McLennan.[293] In order to get to the opening, the woman would have had to walk through the floor upon which she is standing. According to the official story, however, that area of the tower was a raging inferno, hot enough to melt solid steel girders (approximately 2,700°F; 1,500°C is required to melt steel), which ultimately caused the buildings to collapse one floor at a time in a pancaking sequence.

The official scenario is impossible, since commercial jet fuel (Jet-A), which is pure kerosene, burns in the air at a maximum temperature of approximately 1,500°F; 800°C. Experts have calculated that the temperature of a burning floor at the WTC was not even close to the temperature needed to weaken, let alone melt, steel girders.[294] That conclusion would seem to be supported by the appearance of the woman. As you can see, the woman appears to be in good health; neither her hair nor her clothing is even singed. So we know that the fire was localized and not a raging inferno sufficient to melt steel girders.

Victim Standing in Gash of WTC 2 - Clearly the Heat Was not Sufficient to Melt Steel

It is impossible for a burning hydrocarbon of any kind, without supplementation from pure oxygen, to melt steel. If it were possible for a hydrocarbon fire to cause steel to melt, then we would find people who cook on natural gas stoves melting their steel pots and pans. That would happen with regularity since natural gas stoves are very efficient and burn much hotter than jet fuel, which is essentially kerosene. In fact, if the official WTC fiction were true, stove burners themselves, which are made of rather thin steel would be melting with regularity. We know that is not the case; so also we know that the fires at the WTC did not cause the steel in the towers to melt or even weaken.

What most people do not realize is that 0n February 13, 1975, the North Tower of the World Trade Center survived a three alarm fire that spread between the 9th and 14th floors.[295] The fire was a raging inferno, because at that time there was no sprinkler system in the North Tower. The fire was put out in a few hours and the towers did not suffer any structural damage.

It has been alleged that pools of red hot molten steel were found at the base of each of the collapsed twin towers six weeks after the collapse. However, there has been no physical evidence presented to support those claims. It sounds incredible that there would be molten pools of steel at the base of the world trade center six full weeks after their collapse. In order for the steel to remain molten for that length of time would require a continuous source of high heat or an energy process that would keep the steel in a molten state.

A momentary explosion six weeks earlier would not be sufficient to keep the steel in a red hot molten condition for six weeks. Some have theorized that a thermite bomb, a micro-nuclear device, or a barometric bomb was used to knock the towers off their foundations, causing them to collapse.[296] As we will see, those theories are not supported by the physical evidence, which points to something even more exotic used to disintegrate the towers. The exotic method of destruction may explain the alleged molten steel phenomenon.

The sounds of explosions heard by witnesses seems to point to internal explosives as the cause for the collapse of the towers. However, more information has since come to light that indicates that something much more advanced than conventional internal explosives were used on WTC towers 1 and 2. It is possible that conventional explosives were used for the initial explosions filmed in the towers when the supposed planes (which were obviously CGIs) were suggested in the videos to have impacted the towers. However the photo-sequence below indicates that there was another technology that was the primary cause for the collapse of the towers.

Notice in the picture sequence below how the South Tower is turning to dust.[297] It is disintegrating; it is not a pancake collapse as portrayed by the government and news media.

The same "dustification" phenomenon is seen below in the photo sequence of the second tower disintegration (North Tower).[298] This is not a pancake collapse of a building. There is a 96 foot tall spire at the top of the North Tower. That spire was not exposed to any of the flames and it is clearly visible in the below left photo as the tower begins disintegrating. That spire should have been that last thing to hit the ground and should have been laying at the top of the rubble from the destruction of both towers. However, the spire was not found anywhere in the rubble. That spire simply disappeared. The reason it was not found is because it turned to dust before it reached the ground.

Seismographs at Columbia University's Lamont-Doherty Earth Observatory in Palisades, N.Y., 21 miles north of the WTC, recorded two spikes in the seismic record from Sept. 11, which indicate two bursts of energy shook the ground beneath the World Trade Center's twin towers. An event measuring 2.1 on the Richter scale was recorded during the collapse of the first (south) tower. A second event which registered 2.3 on the Richter scale was detected during the collapse of the second (north) tower. According to Dr. Judy Wood, if the towers had actually collapsed in a pancake fashion with the rubble hitting the ground, rather than disintegrate and turn to dust, the Richter reading should have been 3.8 for each tower, and not 2.1 or 2.3.[299]

Dr. Wood further states that if the towers had collapsed in a pancake fashion as theorized by the government, the relatively fragile cement bathtub at the base of the towers would have been severely damaged by the 500,000 tons of rubble from each tower striking the bathtub. The so-called bathtub was found to have been relatively undamaged after the debris from the disintegrated towers was removed.[300] Why? Because the towers were turned to dust which did not have near the force of rubble from a collapsing building.

The photo-sequence below is the smoking gun (or rather smoking steel) of the 9/11 attack. Notice in the photo-sequence how the approximately 60-story tall steel remnant of the superstructure of the North Tower (WTC 1) suddenly turns to dust. You can see that the steel column is taller than the 47 story WTC Tower 7, which is the foreground in the right-hand side of the photographs. It is hard to conceive that the steel would turn to dust when you consider that the columns were 36-inch by 16-inch rectangular columns of steel that had 4-inch-thick steel walls.

These are massive columns of steel turning to dust within seconds. How can that happen? Dr. Judy Wood[301] (Ph.D. in Materials Engineering Science) opines that the towers could only turn to dust if there is molecular disassociation. The only technology that can cause such a drastic molecular disintegration from solid to dust is a directed energy weapon.[302] Directed energy weapons are not science fiction, they are science reality. Read through the material from the U.S. Air Force Research Laboratory, Directed Energy Directorate.[303] The use of directed energy on 9-11 would explain why there was so little rubble from the collapse of the two 1/4 mile high towers. Most of the concrete, steel columns, and steel beams were turned to dust.[304] The more mass an object has the more energy is absorbed. That explains why there were sheets of paper floating to the ground on 9-11, because they have little mass to absorb directed energy.

50-story tall steel spire remnant of the North Tower (WTC 1) suddenly turns to dust

Below is a photo of the collapse area of World Trade Center Towers 1 & 2, taken on September 13, 2001, two days after the destruction of the WTC towers. The remnant of the west wall from WTC 2 (South Tower) can be seen in the foreground at the bottom of the picture. The WTC 2 facade appears to be between four and six stories in height. It towers over the rubble that is the remains of WTC towers 1 & 2. Immediately behind WTC 2 (left-center of the picture) is where WTC 3 (Marriott Hotel) once stood. The remains of WTC 6, an 8-story building, is in the upper right of the picture; the rubble in front of that building is the remains of WTC 1 (north tower). The eight story WTC 6 also towers over the remains of WTC 1.

If the pancake theory (or even traditional demolition) of the WTC towers were true, the rubble from the destruction of the towers should be 1/8 (12.5 %) the height of the original towers. Both WTC towers 1 & 2 were 110 stories in height. That means that the rubble from a pancake collapse (or traditional demolition) should have had a height of more than 13 stories. There were six sub-basements under the WTC complex. While the sub-basements suffered extensive damage, they did not suffer a collapse below street level. What is seen above ground in the picture depicts the height of the rubble from street level. Where did all of the rubble from the destruction of two quarter-mile high skyscrapers go? The towers appear to have turned to dust; the rubble in the picture is not sufficient to account for the material from the destruction of the massive buildings.[305]

Look at the height of the rubble from towers 1 and 2 in the picture below. The picture below was taken on September 14, 2001.[306] In this picture, the photographer is standing at the former entrance to the Plaza that was at Church St between Dey and Cortland, looking about northwest. The charred remains in the center of the photo are WTC 6, the remnant of the wall to the left of it closest to the camera is the eastern wall of WTC 1. The brown building to the right is WTC 5. In the upper part of the photo, in the background over the charred remains of WTC 6, is the top part of the Verizon building which was next door immediately to the west of what used to be WTC 7. The structure that can be seen in the haze in the background on the left upper portion of the photo is the back (west) wall of WTC 1. You can see the rescue workers are still on the site. There should be more than 13 stories of rubble from the two 110 story towers, yet the rubble is less than one story in height. The photographer was standing on the plaza itself, and the photo shows that he had a clear line of sight from the east wall of WTC Tower 1 all the way through the haze to the west wall of Tower 1. There is no rubble blocking his view of the back wall. The bronze ball in the plaza, which is only about 15 feet tall, towers over the rubble. You can see the rescue workers standing on the rubble at the base of the ball. Where is the expected 13 story-high mass of 1 million tons of steel and concrete from WTC Towers 1 and 2?

WTC Plaza on 9-14-01

On the whole, the rubble piles from WTC towers 1 and 2 are less than 7 % of their expected 13-story height. More than 93% of the mass of the two towers is missing. The mass of the towers seems to have been turned to dust. Below is a picture showing all of Manhattan engulfed in fine particles of dust. That is where the mass of WTC towers 1 and 2 ended up. What could cause more than one million tons of steel and concrete to turn to dust? The only thing that could cause two massive buildings to turn to dust would be a directed energy weapon.

Manhattan engulfed in ultra-fine dust on 9-11-01

Figure 75: Notice the melted truck, but unsinged paper mixed with steel dust from the towers is everywhere on the ground.

Notice in figure 75 at left how the truck near the WTC Towers appears to have melted as though from fire, but yet there is paper everywhere that is not even singed.[307] The dust from the dissolved towers is everywhere. How does one explain this strange phenomenon? It is similar in concept to the directed energy that a microwave oven uses to cook food. Directed energy acts differently than conventional carbon fuel fire and explains why when one puts an aluminum can or aluminum foil in a microwave oven it will spark and even flare up, however, when one puts a paper plate in the same oven it will not even get warm.

Yet, when one exposes the paper plate to the open flame of the stove top burner, it will catch fire, whereas the aluminum can or foil exposed to the open flame will get hot, but will not flare up or catch fire. On 9/11 there was the total dustification of solid steel from the towers and the melting of nearby vehicles, yet sheets of paper from the towers were seen floating to the ground and were not even singed. Such phenomenon suggests that directed energy was used to destroy the towers. A carbon-fueled fire would not "dustify" steel and leave paper unharmed; directed energy waves would do exactly that.

Figure 76 at right shows a strange phenomenon that was exhibited during September 11, 2001. Cars near the towers (and in some instances far away) blew up or spontaneously caught fire. The burning cars were often surrounded by the dust and paper from the dissolved towers. The strange thing is that there are no pictures of any of the paper burning. Even the paper very near the burning cars did not burn. These strange occurrences suggest that stray energy waves were striking the vehicles. That explains why there is no evidence of a single tree in New York having burned, and yet hundreds of cars were melted and burned. In figure 76, there are papers caught in the young tree, and the tree and the papers are unburned.[308] The smaller tree that is next to the raging car fire in the background is not burning.

ABC News Reporter Robert Krulwich gives an idea of the massive quantity of material that turned to dust:

Figure 76: Unburned paper mixed with tower dust surrounding burning cars.

> Engineers', at the firm that built the buildings, best guess to account for the missing 1200 feet of material from each tower is that large portions simply vaporized into the dust that rained down on New York immediately after the collapse. It was that powerful. We're talking here about 43,600 windows, 600,000 sq. ft. of glass, 200,000 tons of structural steel, 5 million sq. ft. of gypsum, 6 acres of marble, 425,000 cubic yards of concrete, turned in good part into a cloud, says Environmental Medical Doctor, Dr. Stephen Levin [from Mt. Sinai Hospital].[309]

Krulwich could not understand the mystery of the massive amounts of paper, in the wake of the disintegration into dust of the twin towers. He stated:

> But most interesting, in the mix, they are looking at specks of steel that used to be beams and elevators, marble from the lobby floor and facings. **So what were once the strongest architectural elements in the two towers were pulverized, large portions turned into clouds, like this one.**
>
> **Still there is this mystery, if some of the hardest materials were vaporized, how to account for the presence everywhere of paper, fully intact letters, business forms, stationary.** Paper is so fragile, and combustible, yet somehow, maybe because we have so much of it, it was everywhere.[310]

Directed energy perfectly explains the mystery of the unburned, intact paper simultaneous with the disintegration into dust of the massive amount of steel, concrete, windows, etc. in the towers. Microscopic analysis of the WTC dust and vapors revealed that steel and other materials were broken down to the atomic level (iron, manganese, sulfur, phosphorous, carbon, etc.). Dr. Wood concluded that it is impossible for burning fuel to burn hot enough to create atomic sized particles of iron.

In order for steel to break down to its atomic elements, it must be brought to a boil. Iron is the principal element in steel; most construction steel consists of 96% to 99% iron. The boiling point of iron is 4,982°F; 2,750°C. A hydrocarbon fire in the atmosphere burns at a maximum temperature of 1,517°F; 825°C, well short of what is necessary to boil iron. Do not confuse the boiling point of Iron with its melting point, which is 2,795°F; 1,535°C. The melting point of steel is approximately 2750°F; 1510°C. A hydrocarbon fire is not hot enough to melt steel, let alone boil it and break it down into its constituent atoms.

Temperatures hot enough to separate the iron atom from steel would certainly burn the paper that was seen mixed with the resulting molecular dust particles on 911. Paper ignites at the relatively low temperature of 451°F; 233°C. It is impossible that the collapse of the building was caused by heat, when paper was expelled from the same building (with a flashpoint of only 451°F; 233°C) at the same time with iron particles, and the temperature needed to heat the steel to produce the iron particles would have been 4,982°F; 2,750°C. Such temperatures would have completely consumed the papers, yet there were papers everywhere. Clearly, fire was not the cause of the collapse.

Furthermore, scientists found organic molecules along with atoms of iron, vanadium, etc. in the dust. Even if hypothetically there was a heat source hot enough to atomize metal, it would make it impossible for organic material to be present in the same sample. The organic material would never exist alongside the metals if the temperature was hot enough to atomize the metals (the boiling point of vanadium is 6,165°F; 3,407°C).[311] Dr. Wood concluded that some other mechanism, similar to that seen in cold fusion experiments, caused the simultaneous molecular disassociation of both metal and organic material.[312]

Almost all of the papers that were seen all over Manhattan came out of steel filing cabinets. There was only one remnant of a filing cabinet that survived the destruction of the twin towers. All other filing cabinets disappeared in a cloud of ultra-fine dust and vapor. The same cataclysmic event that caused the steel in the thousands of filing cabinets in the twin towers to dissolve and fall to the ground as a fine dust did not even singe the papers that were inside those thousands of file cabinets. Dr. Wood's conclusion is that directed energy caused the molecules in the cabinets and the building to lose their bond turning the steel and other materials to ultra-fine dust.

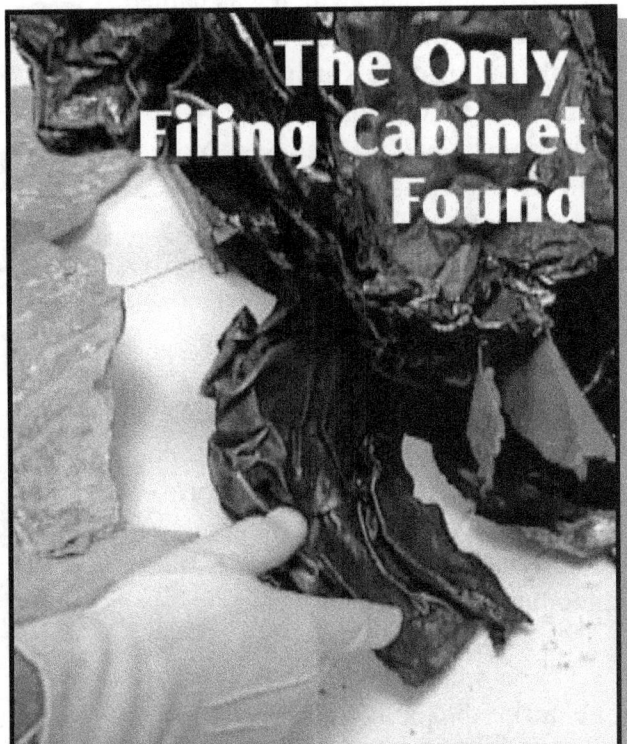

Figure 77 at right is the only part of a filing cabinet found in the WTC rubble. It is the remains of a two-drawer steel cabinet from the Ben & Jerry's ice cream shop located between WTC 1 and WTC 2. It was reduced to a shriveled ball of metal the size of a basketball. David Shayt, the curator for the Smithsonian Museum, revealed that the cabinet in figure 77 was found balled up with unburned paper money inside.[313] If heat caused the shriveling of the cabinet, the money would have been burned up. Shayt revealed that when he first saw the cabinet it was crumpled, but the metal was still shiny, however, within the space of two or three hours it began to rust. He had to spray oil on it to stop the rusting. Rapid rusting of steel is a common residual effect of exposure to high intensity directed energy. It is one of the many effects of exposure to directed energy collectively known as "The Hutchison Effect." The Hutchison Effect was named after Canadian researcher John Hutchison, who discovered strange effects (levitation, fragmentation, bending, and dissolving of metal, as well as the fusion of dissimilar materials) without any heat applied during his directed energy experiments. All of those Hutchison effects were seen at and around the WTC disintegration on 9/11. Notice in the picture how the red and blue folders that are attached to the shriveled cabinet still have their color.[314] That indicates that whatever shriveled the metal cabinet was not heat. Literally tons of paper were scattered all over the area surrounding the twin towers after the tower collapses, but the thousands of filing cabinets that held the papers disappeared! Whatever was used to destroy the towers vaporized the steel filing cabinets but did not harm any of the papers that were inside

Figure 77: Thousands of filing cabinets held tons of paper in the WTC Towers, yet this shriveled piece is all that remains. The papers that were in the thousands of cabinets floated to the ground unburned.

those steel filing cabinets. Obviously, heat did not destroy the filing cabinets; temperatures sufficiently hot to make the steel filing cabinets vaporize would have consumed the papers inside the cabinets. Directed energy is the only plausible explanation for the vaporization of thousands of steel filing cabinets with the paper contents emerging unscathed.

Almost nobody in New York, or anywhere in the United States for that matter, knew of a significant event that had been kept secret by the major media. There was a category three hurricane with winds reaching 120 mph that was on a direct path toward New York in the days leading up to 9-11-2001. Why did the media not report this hurricane?

The hurricane, which was named Hurricane Erin, was by all measures larger than Hurricane Katrina that devastated New Orleans in 2005. If Hurricane Erin had reached New York, it would have devastated the city because large areas of New York City are only 5 feet above sea level. A storm surge from a category two hurricane can be as much as 15 to 20 feet, which would have flooded a large portion of New York City. Hurricane Erin was a category three hurricane, which began on or about September 1, 2001 as a tropical storm. It reached hurricane status on September 8th and remained a hurricane until September 15th.

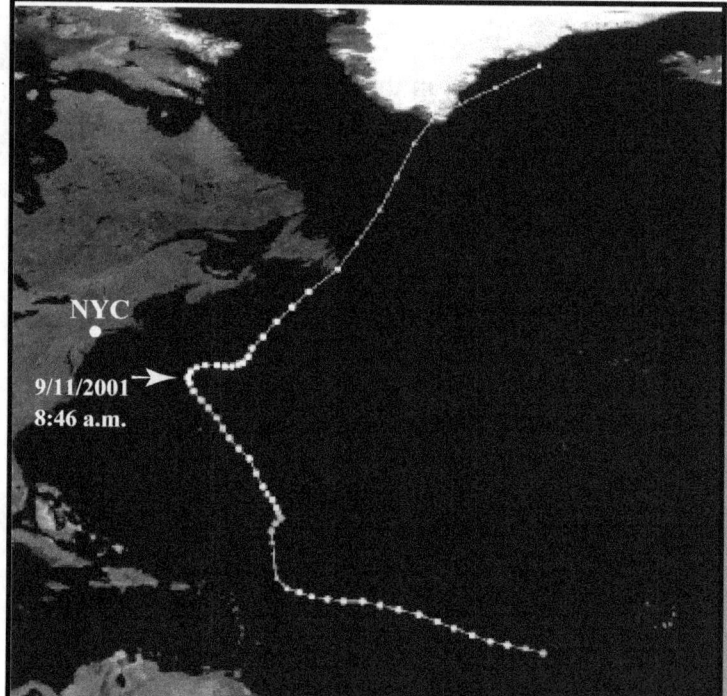

Figure 78: Plot chart showing the path of Hurricane Erin leading up to 9/11/2001, and its path thereafter. Notice the sudden change in direction on 9/11/2001. The hurricane was at its closest point to New York City at 8:46 a.m. on 9/11/2001, which was the exact moment WTC 1 exploded.

The picture in figure 78 shows a plot chart of the path of Hurricane Erin leading up to 9/11/2001 and its path thereafter.[315] On 9/11/2001 Hurricane Erin abruptly changed course and turned 90 degrees away from New York. The hurricane was at its closest point to New York City at 8:46 a.m., which was the precise moment that WTC 1 exploded. What are the chances of such a confluence of events?

The odd thing about the path of Hurricane Erin is that it was closest to New York City on 9/11/01 and grew to its largest status on that date (although wind speeds were greater the day before). Figure 79 below is a picture of Hurricane Erin shortly after the collapse of the towers on 9-11-2001.[316] The photo inset shows the plume of material from the destroyed WTC Towers wafting skyward.

Figure 79: Satellite photo of Hurricane Erin off the east coast at its closest point to New York on 9-11-2001. The fumes from the collapse of the towers can be seen wafting skyward in the inset blowup picture. Pictures broadcast by the media on 9/11 from the international space station cropped out any view of Hurricane Erin.

Figures 80 and 81 show weather maps from television weather reports on 9/11/2001.[317] Notice that there is no indication that there is a hurricane off the coast of New York. How can the networks broadcast a weather report and not discuss a category three hurricane bearing down on New York and the east coast? The presence of a hurricane should have been the focal point of any weather report and indeed headline news. With the exception of one network, the major news outlets blacked out any mention of a hurricane approaching New York and the east coast. The non-reporting of Hurricane Erin was clearly purposeful.

One major network mentioned Hurricane Erin on September 10th; CNN briefly mentioned the hurricane but with the assurance that "it posed no immediate threat to land on Monday."[318] That was the day before 9/11 and the hurricane was on a direct course at that time for New York and the east coast. How did CNN know on 9/10 that it "posed no immediate threat to land?" How did CNN know that Hurricane Erin would not make landfall and cause catastrophic loss of life and property? How did they know that Hurricane Erin would turn 90 degrees on 9/11 and thus not strike New York?

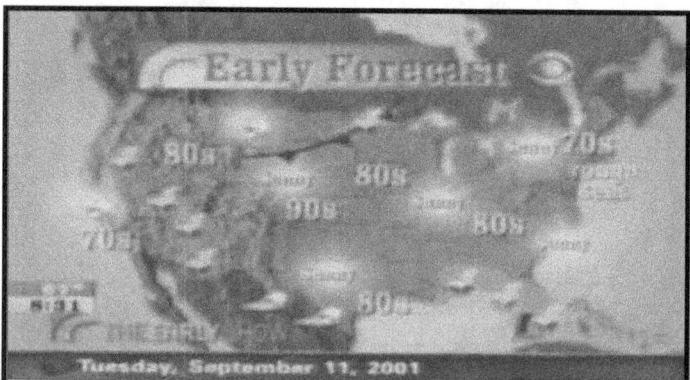

Figure 80: Actual weather map from CBS broadcast on 9/11/2001 at 8:31 a.m. not showing Hurricane Erin

Figure 81: Actual weather map from NBC broadcast on the morning of 9/11/2001 not showing Hurricane Erin

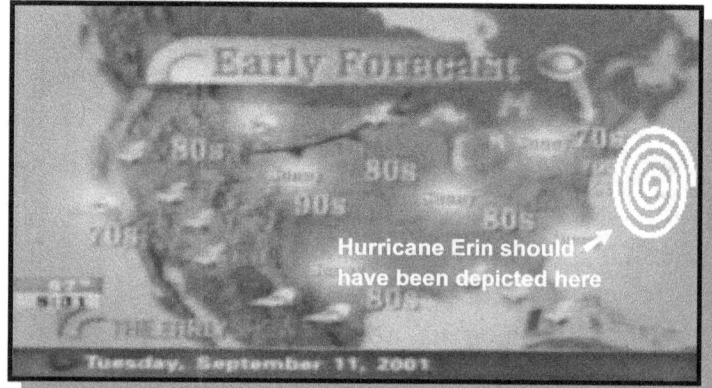

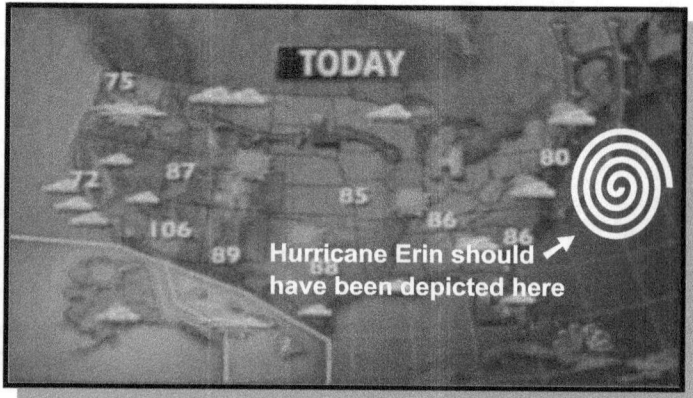

Why would the major media outlets keep the existence of a hurricane secret? There is

something about Hurricane Erin that they do not want the ordinary public to know. They must have known that the hurricane would not hit landfall, otherwise they would not have kept its existence secret. Dr. Judy Wood theorizes that Hurricane Erin acted as a massive Tesla coil creating field effects used by directed energy weapons on 9/11/2001.

> [T]he use of directed energy technology on the huge scale of its use on 9/11 might very well have had weather-altering effects. Such technology might have been able to draw upon the vast energies and field effects of the enormous Tesla Coil known as Hurricane Erin. Thoughts of this kind are justified, even necessitated, by the fact of Erin's having been treated as a carefully kept secret, much like a state secret.[319]

Dr. Wood's theory suggests that Hurricane Erin was created and controlled by some secret technology. The creation and control of Hurricane Erin is not wild science fiction. On March 3, 2000, Leonard David, senior space writer for Space.com, revealed the existence of advanced weather altering technology:

> A blast of microwave energy beamed down from a space satellite could be used to tame the destructive nature of a tornado, a scientist said this week.... But the tornado-nuking concept advocated here this week flies in the face of being at the mercy of Mother Nature's fury. Called a Thunderstorm Solar Power Satellite, the concept was presented at the Space 2000 Conference and Exposition on Engineering, Construction, Operations and Business in Space, sponsored by the American Society of Civil Engineers. The proposal calls for beaming microwave energy into the cold, rainy downdraft of a thunderstorm where a tornado could originate. That pulse of power would disrupt the convective flow needed to concentrate energy that forms a tornado, said Bernard Eastlund, president of Eastlund Scientific Enterprises Corporation, based in San Diego, California. He has teamed up with Lyle Jenkins, a 37-year NASA veteran who now heads his own firm, Jenkins Enterprises in Houston, Texas. The two researchers envision surgical strikes of microwave energy that could modify the temperature and fine structure of storm systems. "We call it taming the tornado," Jenkins said. "With just a little burst of microwave energy, we think we see a way to negate the trigger point in tornado creation."[320]

Bernard Eastlund, the developer of this weather altering technology, is not some wacky scientist. He is a physicist who is an expert on electromagnetism. He was the former head of nuclear fusion research for the U.S. Atomic Energy Commission.[321] He was inspired to use microwave energy beams to zap tornadoes by his work in the Strategic Defense Initiative (SDI), commonly referred to as the Star Wars missile shield.[322] It seems that part of the SDI research involved directed energy weaponry, which included weather modification and augmentation. The abstract of the scientific research presented by Eastlund and Jenkins explains that "[T]he concept consists of orbiting solar collectors that provide electricity to microwave generators. An antenna array of these microwave generators forms a beam to direct the energy to a 'rectenna' receiver on the surface of the Earth."[323] A rectenna is a special antenna that turns microwave energy into electricity. The immense power from the microwave beam would be turned into electricity and be directed in a powerful beam of energy.

Eastlund and Jenkins made the following statement in their abstract, which indicates that this is not just a theory. "With the critical points identified, the necessary space system requirements to deliver an energy beam with the duration and accuracy needed to interfere with the formation of the tornado can be defined."[324] How are they able to say with such certainty that they can define the space system needed for such a project? It is reasonable to conclude that they had knowledge that such a system in fact already existed. They submitted their proposal to the American Society of Civil Engineers at the Space 2000 conference in March 2000, more than a year before the 9/11/2001 events.

Eastlund holds many patents. He and others believe that one of his patents is the foundation for the HAARP project.[325] HAARP stands for High Frequency Active Auroral Research Project, and it is funded jointly by the U.S. Navy, Air Force, the University of Alaska, and the Defense Advanced Research Projects Agency (DARPA). Eastlund has a patent (# 4,686,605) that is described as a "Method and Apparatus for Altering a Region in the Earth's Atmosphere, Ionosphere; and/or Magnetosphere."[326] The patent was initially sealed as a state secret by the U.S. Government. Researchers have uncovered a cluster of other patents that are also alleged to be the basis for HAARP. Those patents describe "nuclear-sized explosions without radiation," "power-beaming systems," and "electromagnetic pulses previously produced by thermonuclear weapons."[327]

Eastlund's patent was later unsealed. The following is an excerpt from the patent:

> Thus, this invention provides the ability to put unprecedented amounts of power in the Earth's atmosphere at strategic locations and to maintain the power injection level particularly if random pulsing is employed, in a manner far more precise and better controlled than heretofore accomplished by the prior art, particularly by detonation of nuclear devices of various yields at various altitudes.[328]

Eastlund's invention is described as having the power of a nuclear device, but that it is more precise and controlled. Could the technology that is at the core of Eastland's invention have been used to direct massive energy at the World Trade Center Towers to cause them to disintegrate into dust at the molecular level? It is significant that Eastlund's research involved both directed energy and weather modification, and there was evidence of both things happening on 9/11/2001, with Hurricane Erin and the Hutchison Effect.

Dr. Judy Wood concludes that if one can stop a tornado one can start one. If the technology existed in 2000 to start and stop a tornado, it is not unreasonable to infer that the technology exists to start and turn a hurricane. Dr. Wood opines that the abundance of evidence of the Hutchison Effect in the area of the WTC towers before, during, and after their disintegration suggests that there was some radio frequency energy being used within a static field. Hurricane Erin seems to have acted as a massive Tesla coil creating that static field. Dr. Wood explains:

> The static field used by John Hutchison is produced by a Tesla Coil or by a Van de Graaf generator. In Chapter 18 [of *Where Did the Towers Go?*], it was shown that Hurricane Erin was centered just outside of New York City on the morning of 9/11/2001 with her outer bands reaching over Cape Cod as well as reaching the end of Long Island. On 9/11, thunder, which is evidence of an electrical field, was reported at JFK, LaGuardia, and Newark Airports, the three major airports around New York City. In Chapter 19, it was shown that magnetometer readings in Alaska exhibited excursions of the earth's magnetic field that were coincident with the time of the event at the WTC on 9/11. And we know that rotating electrical fields can produce a magnetic field. And an interference of these fields can cause molecular dissociation. And, referring to the article quoted on page 450, if it is possible to stop a vortex, then it is certainly possible to start one. And levitation as well as fusion of dissimilar materials and destruction of materials can result from an energy vortex.[329]

The magnetometer readings referenced by Dr. Wood are yet more evidence that directed energy weapons were used on 9/11/2001. Immediately prior to the explosion in WTC 1 at 8:46 a.m. magnetometer readings at the Geophysical Institute Magnetometer Array (GIMA) began to fluctuate dramatically from normal.[330] GIMA measures deviations in the Earth's magnetic field. There was yet another dramatic deviation from normal at 9:03 a.m., which was when WTC 2 exploded. That was followed by another significant deviation at 9:59 a.m., which was when WTC 2 turned to dust. The notable significant fluctuations continued until after 5:21 p.m., when the WTC 7 fell to the ground. There is a correlation between magnetism and electricity. It seems that the discharge of the directed energy weapons at the WTC towers in turn caused a dramatic deviation from normal of the Earth's magnetic field.

14 The Destruction After the Destruction

The remaining rubble from the WTC complex was hurriedly destroyed. The destruction of the crime scene without a proper crime survey is not an indication of incompetence but rather culpability. Identify the characters involved in the destruction of the evidence and you have identified the perpetrators. Christopher Bollyn puts the destruction of the evidence into perspective:

> According to the U.S. indictment against the alleged terrorists, there were 2,976 "murder victims" on 9/11, of whom about 93 percent were murdered at the World Trade Center. This includes the 147 people said to have been on the two airliners that struck the buildings plus the 2,605 victims trapped in the towers when they were demolished. This makes the demolition of the Twin Towers the largest case of mass murder in U.S. history, but that's not how it was handled by the authorities of the federal government or New York City. What is most appalling about the 9/11 case is how the most crucial evidence from the crime scene was confiscated and destroyed before it could be properly examined.[331]

Oddly, on September 25, 2001, New York City Mayor Rudolph Giuliani banned all photography or video recording at the scene of the 9/11 attacks at the WTC complex unless authorized by the police commissioner. Signs were posted warning the public that it was a class-B misdemeanor to take photographs of the rubble. The claimed reason was that it was a crime scene. Of course it was a crime scene, but that does not explain why the public could not take photographs. Taking a photograph in no way contaminates the crime scene. Furthermore, banning the taking of a photograph from a public place of a public place, crime scene or not, is quite simply unconstitutional and unprecedented. The order prohibiting taking photographs only makes sense as a way to conceal from the public the destruction of the crime scene. The reason Giuliani did not want the public taking photographs was that it became clear that the cleanup was revealing that directed energy was used in the WTC destruction.

Bollyn is one of the most capable investigative reporters of our time, but he is mistaken on one point. Bollyn relied on the work of Steven Jones and thus theorizes that "super thermite" was used to destroy the towers. He thinks that the quick destruction of the rubble was to conceal that fact. Because nano-sized thermite particles were found in the dust samples taken in the days and weeks after the attacks, Steven Jones opines that "super thermite" must have been used. What Jones ignores is that thermite was in fact used in the days after the attacks during clean up of the tower rubble, which could explain its presence in the samples. In addition, thermite may have also been used for the initial made-for-TV tower explosions. Super thermite (or even super-duper thermite) cannot explain the dustification of the towers; directed energy is the only plausible explanation.

The quick destruction of the steel was for the purpose of concealing the sparseness of the steel by arranging for a foreign company to take delivery of the metal and inflating the actual amount of the steel received. The New York and New Jersey Port Authority estimated that the rubble from the seven buildings in the WTC complex contained a total of 285,000 tons of steel (each of the twin towers alone contained 78,000 tons of steel). Robert A. Kelman, then Senior Vice President and General Manager of Hugo Neu, which was the principal contractor for the destruction of the steel from the WTC rubble, told the Associated Press in 2002 that Hugo Neu recycled 250,000 tons (88% of the total amount) of WTC scrap steel and had shipped it to 11 countries, including Malaysia, China, South Korea, and Japan. There is no way that the remaining rubble contained anywhere near the 250,000 tons of steel that Kelman claimed was recycled by Hugo Neu. Kelman's statement was unaccompanied by any verifiable documentation and was a cover story to explain where the towers went.

Bollyn came across Israeli nationals and dedicated Zionists at every key point of the criminal destruction of the steel from the World Trade Center. Bollyn discovered that the scrapyard that managed the destruction of most of the steel was controlled by a team of metal traders sent by a high-level agent of the Mossad to dispose of the steel by sending it to Asian smelters.[332]

Hugo Neu Schnitzer East and Metal Management Northeast, the two junkyards that processed the steel from the World Trade Center, were both controlled by Zionist Jews. Bollyn uncovered evidence that in 1999 two scrap iron traders who worked for Israeli citizen Marc Rich and his company, Glencore AG, were sent to New York to create an international trading division at Hugo Neu Schnitzer East. That is the company that two years later ended up managing the destruction of most of the steel from the World Trade Center. Marc Rich and his lieutenant Ivan Glasenberg, CEO of Glencore International, are not only both Israeli citizens, but they also have close ties to the Mossad. "The head of the Marc Rich Foundation in Israel is a former Mossad operative named Avner Azulay (also spelled Azoulai)."[333] Bollyn explains:

> The Marc Rich Foundation in Israel is run by Azulay working out of Shaul Eisenberg's Asia House in Tel Aviv. Eisenberg is the mega Mossad operative owner of Israel Corp., ZIM shipping, ATASCO, and hundreds of ventures in Asia, including Atwell

Security, the Mossad company that obtained the security contract for the World Trade Center in the 1980s.[334]

The destruction of the evidence could not have been pulled off without the authorization of the U.S. Department of Justice. That was ensured by Michael Chertoff, who was the head of the Criminal Division of the Department of Justice, which oversaw the FBI investigation of 9/11 and the collection of evidence. Bollyn explains:

> The two New Jersey junkyards who handled most of the steel from the World Trade Center were the final links in a secure system arranged by the Zionist masterminds behind 9/11 to destroy the crucial evidence. The highest agent in this system was Michael Chertoff, the Assistant Attorney General in charge of the Criminal Division of the U.S. Department of Justice. The FBI has special investigative jurisdiction in crimes of terrorism, and Chertoff, an Israeli national and son of a Mossad agent, was the senior official who oversaw the FBI investigation and the collection of evidence.[335]

Chertoff had responsibility to oversee the gathering of the evidence from the crime scenes of 9/11. Bollyn personally asked Chertoff if he authorized the destruction of the steel. Chertoff wrote back to Bollyn answering that he did not authorize the destruction and further that he had no idea who had done so. Bollyn properly concluded:

> If the criminal destruction of the evidence from the World Trade Center were to be prosecuted as it should be, Chertoff should be charged with criminal negligence because it was his official duty to oversee the proper collection and protection of evidence to prosecute those behind 9/11.[336]

It is clear that the masterminds "put in place a network to manage the destruction of the steel, the solid evidence that could expose their crime."[337] Bollyn asks the obvious rhetorical question:

> What does this fundamental part of the 9/11 cover up tell us about who is really behind the crime? If Osama Bin Laden and 19 Arab hijackers truly brought down the World Trade Center, why was a network of Israeli intelligence agents engaged in a concerted effort to destroy the evidence?[338]

It is obvious that Israeli intelligence did not mastermind the hasty destruction of the steel from the World Trade Center in order to cover up the involvement of Osama Bin Laden in the crime. Rather, the Zionist Jews destroyed the evidence to cover up the involvement of Israel and treasonous accomplices in the U.S. government. The quick destruction of the rubble was needed to conceal the fact that so little of the building remained after directed energy weapons brought down the towers. They had to protect the conspiracy lie that Arab terrorists were to be blamed for the deaths of nearly 3,000 people on 9/11. Bollyn concluded:

> The physical evidence of the towers was hastily destroyed by a network of Zionist agents because it could expose the falsity of their interpretation of events. Indeed, the fact that a Zionist network had been established in order to manage the destruction of the evidence confirms the hypothesis that 9/11 was a false-flag terror atrocity carried out by Israeli intelligence and their agents in the U.S. government.[339]

The perpetrators had to destroy the rubble to keep secret their method of destruction. They could not, however, destroy all of the evidence in all of its many forms. Sometimes, the fact that an item that is expected to be found is not found is evidence that can point to the method of destruction. How could they explain that only one small portion of one of the thousands of metal file cabinets that were in the twin towers of the World Trade Center survived the destruction? How could they explain that not a single telephone, faucet, metal door, door handle, or even an ink pen survived the destruction of the twin towers, and yet tons of paper scattered all over New York City survived the destruction? The only plausible scientific explanation is that directed energy was used to destroy the towers.

All litigation involves a process called discovery, where during discovery a party is able to compel the opposing party to turn over evidence that is relevant to his claim. The discovery process would reveal evidence of directed energy and the involvement of Israeli and treasonous U.S. government officials in the destruction of the towers. The conspirators had to plan ahead to ensure that the revelation of incriminating evidence would not find its way into court, where it could be verified. In order to do that, they needed a judge in their back pocket to keep a lid on any revelation of an international conspiracy to destroy the towers through directed energy. Enter federal judge Alvin Hellerstein. Bollyn explains Hellerstein's tactics:

> Alvin K. Hellerstein has blocked a 9/11 trial for years by waging a judicial war of attrition against the victims' families, forcing all but one into out-of-court settlements. Hellerstein's son lives in Israel and works for a law firm that represents the parent company of one of the key defendants in the 9/11 litigation. This glaring conflict of interest is ignored by the media.
>
> Although 96 families who lost loved ones on 9/11 chose to litigate rather than accept the government payout, Judge Hellerstein waged a prolonged war of attrition against the families forcing all of them, with only one exception, to settle out of court. The family of Mark Bavis of Boston, a passenger on Flight 175, is the only family that will have a 9/11 trial to determine who was responsible for their

loss. Hellerstein, however, has imposed a most arbitrary and unusual time limit for the only 9/11 trial that will be held to determine who is responsible for the loss of life. He will only allow one month for the entire trial with only 50 hours allowed for each side.

As an orthodox Jew and a Zionist, Judge Hellerstein has a serious conflict of interest that should have prevented him for hearing any 9/11 cases. Israel, through its intelligence agency the Mossad, is a key defendant in the 9/11 litigation. Hellerstein and his immediate family are devoted supporters of the state of Israel. This presents an obvious conflict of interest that should have kept Hellerstein from overseeing the 9/11 tort litigation in the first place.

Furthermore, Judge Hellerstein's son, Joseph, lives in Israel and works for an Israeli law firm that represents the parent company of one of the defendants in the 9/11 tort litigation, Mossad's "security" company International Consultants for Targeted Security (ICTS NV). ICTS owns Huntleigh USA, the airport security company responsible for screening the passengers that boarded the planes on 9/11. The fact that Hellerstein is a religious Zionist with a close family connection to one of the defendants should disqualify him from managing the 9/11 litigation, but it has not.[340]

It is unconscionable that Judge Hellerstein would preside over the 9/11 litigation in view of his glaring conflict of interest. The silence of the press about this state of affairs speaks loudly about the scope of the conspiracy and the power of the conspirators.

15 What Did Bush Know and When Did He Know It?

President George W. Bush stated the following during his November 10, 2001, address before the UN General Assembly: "Let us never tolerate outrageous conspiracy theories concerning the attacks of September the 11th - malicious lies that attempt to shift the blame away from the terrorists themselves, away from the guilty."[341]

Why was George Bush so concerned about discussions of a conspiracy? The answer will become apparent as you read Illarion Bykov and Jared Israel recount the chronology of events on 9-11-01, which reveal George Bush's suspicious conduct that day:

> Associated Press reporter Sonya Ross was one of the journalists covering Bush's trip to Florida on the morning of 9-11. Ms. Ross was either on her way to the Booker School or already there when she learned of the first WTC crash: "My cell phone rang as President Bush's motorcade coursed toward Emma E. Booker Elementary School in Sarasota, Fla. A colleague reported that a plane had crashed into the World Trade Center in New York. No further information. I called the AP desk in Washington, seeking details. Same scant information. But I knew it had to be grim. I searched for a White House official to question, but none was on hand until 9:05 a.m." Ms. Ross searched for a White House official, because she knew Bush's people would be better informed than the Associated Press.
>
> President Bush is not an ordinary person. He travels with an entire staff. They are responsible for receiving, filtering and conveying administrative and military information. Chief of Staff Andrew Card organizes and coordinates these staff members and communicates with the President. In addition, Bush has the Secret Service, which is responsible for his safety. The members of this support team have the best communications equipment in the

world. They maintain contact with, or can easily reach, Bush's cabinet, the National Military Command Center (NMCC) in the Pentagon, the Federal Aviation Administration (FAA), and Secret Service agents who have stayed behind at the White House, etc.

Since the President's information system is far more extensive and sophisticated than what is available to a reporter, it seems more than plausible that by the time Ms. Ross heard about the first WTC crash - that is, as the Bush motorcade was speeding to Booker Elementary School - the president already knew about this tragic event. Public sources confirm this. ABC journalist John Cochran was traveling with the President. He reported on ABC TV on Tuesday morning, [here he is talking to Peter Jennings]: "Peter, as you know, the president's down in Florida talking about education. He got out of his hotel suite this morning, was about to leave, reporters saw the White House chief of staff, Andy Card, whisper into his ear. The reporter said to the president, 'Do you know what's going on in New York?' He said he did, and he said he will have something about it later. His first event is about half an hour at an elementary school in Sarasota, Florida." So Bush knew about the first WTC incident before leaving his hotel.

What else did he [Bush] know? This question is answered by something Vice President Richard Cheney revealed, probably unwittingly, on MEET THE PRESS, Sunday, September 16th. Even without John Cochran's report on ABC, Cheney's comments constitute evidence that before President Bush went to the Booker School he knew a plane had been hijacked and then crashed into the WTC. Cheney was talking with MEET THE PRESS journalist Tim Russert about the flight path of American Flight 77, which struck the Pentagon. Here's the exchange:

"VICE PRES. CHENEY: ...As best we can tell, they [American Flight 77] came initially at the White House and...

"MR. RUSSERT: The plane actually circled the White House?

"VICE PRES. CHENEY: Didn't circle it, but was headed on a track into it. The Secret Service has an arrangement with the F.A.A. They had open lines after the World Trade Center was... "

"MR. RUSSERT: Tracking it by radar.

"VICE PRES. CHENEY: And when it entered the danger zone and

looked like it was headed for the White House was when they grabbed me and evacuated me to the basement... (Etc.)" MEET THE PRESS Transcript

It appears that Cheney may have blurted out the crucial fact that the Secret Service had an open line to the FAA, then realized he was talking too much and stopped before completing his sentence. But if he did indeed talk too much, he also stopped talking too late. It is obvious that the sentence should have ended with the word 'hit' or something similar.

* * *

Therefore, by the time American Flight 11 crashed into the World Trade Center, around 8:46, and most likely before that happened, the Secret Service knew what the FAA knew. So, what did the FAA know? The FAA admits that at 8:20 it 'suspected' that American Flight 11 had been hijacked. And according to the official story released Sept. 14th: "8:40 [the] FAA notifie[s] NEADS (the Northeast Air Defense Sector) of NORAD, the military's civil defense system, about Flight 11, [i.e., that it had been hijacked.]" Newsday 23 September 2001.

Therefore, based on the official story, the Secret Service knew by 8:40 or before that Flight 11 had been hijacked. And since the FAA was tracking Flight 11, as was the National Military Command Center, which is notified of hijackings and has access to radar from all over the country, it is definite that at 8:46 the Secret Service knew a hijacked plane had crashed into the World Trade Center.

So according to the official story, before the President entered the Booker School, indeed, apparently before he left his hotel, the Secret Service knew that, for the first time in US history, the country had been attacked by terrorists from the air.

The Secret Service, which employs more than 4,000 people, has several responsibilities. The most important is protecting the President. And surely, this means first of all keeping him out of unnecessary danger because prevention is better than cure. This is especially true in regard to certain dangers:

"During the cold war, when security agents used to play war games involving terrorist threats to the White House, the one unsolvable problem was a commercial airliner loaded with explosives working its way into the landing pattern at Washington National Airport, then veering off for a suicide plunge into the White House." (TIME Magazine) The Secret Service has long been aware that one of the trickiest security dangers is posed by a suicide attack from a hijacked commercial airplane from a nearby airport. On a day when planes were being hijacked from different airports and crashing into buildings, a top security precaution would be to keep the President away from a publicly announced appointment at a building near an airport. The Booker School is fewer than 5 miles from the Sarasota-Bradenton International Airport.[342]

Why did they allow President George Walker Bush to keep his scheduled plan to appear at the school? Perhaps he knew more about the intended targets and knew he was in no danger. How could I say such a thing? Let us look at Bush's conduct that day. The Associated Press reported on September 12th the following: "In Sarasota, Florida, Bush was reading to children in a classroom at 9:05 a.m. when his chief of staff, Andrew Card, whispered into his ear. The president briefly turned somber before he resumed reading. He addressed the tragedy about a half-hour later."[343]

Did you catch that? Bush is now notified that a second plane has crashed into the WTC and he continues to read a children's story. As we have established, he likely already knew that the first strike was in fact a terrorist attack and now it is confirmed with a second plane hitting the second tower, and he reacts to this by resuming his reading of a children's story! Why would the President of the United States not immediately take action? The answer did not come until two months later during a December 4, 2001, town meeting in Sarasota, Florida. Let's read what he said directly from the official transcript on the White House web site:

> Well, Jordan, you're not going to believe what state I was in when I heard about the terrorist attack. I was in Florida. And my Chief of Staff, Andy Card -- actually, I was in a classroom talking about a reading program that works. I was sitting outside the classroom waiting to go in, and I saw an airplane hit the tower -- the TV was obviously on. And I used to fly, myself, and I said, well, there's one terrible pilot. I said, it must have been a horrible accident. But I was whisked off there, I didn't have much time to think about it. And I was sitting in the classroom, and Andy Card, my Chief of Staff, who is sitting over here, walked in and said, "A second plane has hit the tower, America is under attack."[344]

George Bush said that he saw on TV the first plane hit the first tower. Whose video was he watching? No media outlet in the country had a video of the first alleged plane crash available to broadcast until the next day, yet Bush is watching the alleged crash within minutes. The only people who would have had a video available that quickly would have been those who knew in advance what was going to happen and were set up to create the computer generated image (CGI) of the plane hitting the building.

Furthermore, Vice President Cheney stated they had a direct line with the FAA who is portrayed as having suspected at 8:20 a.m. that the first alleged plane was hijacked and notified NORAD of that fact at 8:40 a.m. The alleged highjacking of the supposed plane was thought confirmed when it was portrayed as having allegedly plowed into the first WTC tower at 8:46 a.m. Yet President Bush, who is a pilot, upon viewing the film has the bizarre reaction: "I said, well, there's one terrible pilot. I said, it must have been a horrible accident." He already knew the story that the alleged plane had been hijacked, because the Secret Service had an open line with the FAA who had information that the alleged plane was hijacked before it allegedly hit the tower. Yet upon seeing a video showing a CGI of an allegedly hijacked plane crash into the largest man made free standing structure in the world on a clear day with miles of visibility, he said: "there's one terrible pilot" and further said that "must have been a horrible accident." That does not sound credible.

It gets worse; when he is told about the purported second plane crash and is explicitly told by his chief of staff that "America is under attack," he continues to read a children's story. That is not the conduct of a leader, it is the conduct of a puppet, who is pretending not to know what is really happening and is waiting for instructions on what he should do next. He is so controlled and his conscience so seared that one of the most horrendous attacks to befall this great country does not even faze him.

Remember, before he was told of the second explosion, he had seen a video of the first CGI plane crash, and his response had been to do nothing regarding the clear national security issues. Then, when he is told that there has been a second crash, he didn't miss a beat, he continued where he left off reading the children's story. He displays absolutely no curiosity about the unfolding tragedy!

Most have focused on the pathetic and suspicious conduct of President Bush. What has gone largely unexplained, however, was the equally suspicious behavior of Andy Card. Card does not wait for instructions as to what actions to take. Card walks up and spends less than three seconds whispering in the ear of the President of the United States (who is the Commander and Chief of the U.S. Armed Forces) that America is under attack and immediately steps away. He did not hesitate in his exit; it was immediate.

How did Card know that President Bush would not reply with instructions on what actions to take? It appears, upon viewing the video, that Card was not making a revelation of an unfolding tragedy so that the President could respond with instructions. Card was simply giving a progress report of events that were expected to happen; Card then immediately walked away. It is clear that he knew that President Bush had no instructions to give.

There has not been a single word about Bush's or Card's conduct on 9-11-2001 in the mass media. The puppet masters not only control Bush, they control the media. President Bush has not been asked a single question about his bizarre conduct or his incredible statements. That should give the reader some idea of the power and control of the conspirators.

Stanley Hilton, former chief of staff to Senator Robert Dole, represents over 400 plaintiffs in a seven billion dollar class action lawsuit against President George Bush, Vice President Richard Cheney, National Security Advisor Condoleezza Rice, Secretary of Defense Donald Rumsfeld, FBI Director Robert Mueller, and others in high government office, alleging that they planned and orchestrated the 9/11 attacks.[345]

Mr. Hilton has documentary proof and eyewitnesses that President George Bush personally ordered the 9/11 attacks. Furthermore, he has eyewitnesses and documentary evidence that the U.S. Air Force and NORAD conducted 35 drills over the two months prior to 9-11-01 rehearsing attacks by airliners against various targets, including specific drills where the World Trade Center was to be the target of attacks by airplanes.[346]

In fact, on 9-11-01 there were five drills being conducted by NORAD and the Air Force involving attacks by commercial airliners.[347] The 35 rehearsals by the U.S. Government for attacks by airliners impeaches the credibility of National Security Advisor Condoleezza Rice, who said during a May 16, 2002 press briefing: "I don't think anybody could have predicted that these people would take an airplane and slam it into the World Trade Center, take another one and slam it into the Pentagon; that they would try to use an airplane as a missile, a hijacked airplane as a missile."[348] Why would she say such a thing when it is so clearly false? Because she did not think that anyone would ever find out about the prior rehearsals. Now that the rehearsals have leaked out the conspirators have a problem.

16 Mossad Involvement in the 9/11 Attacks

In December 2001, investigative reporter Christopher Bollyn spoke with Eckehardt Werthebach, the former head of the *Verfassungsschutz*, the domestic branch of German intelligence, about the terror attacks of 9-11.[349] Werthebach stated that the deathly precision and the magnitude of planning behind the 9/11 attacks would have required years of planning. He explained that such a sophisticated operation would have required the fixed frame of a state intelligence organization.

Werthebach said that is not something that is found in the loose group like the one allegedly led by Mohammed Atta while he studied in Hamburg. The nebulous *Al Qaida* and the Taliban of Afghanistan lacked the fixed frame of a state intelligence organization. He stated that many people would have been involved in the planning of such an operation and the absence of leaks was a further indication that the attacks were state organized actions. That raises the question: which state?

Former Italian President Francesco Cossiga has told Italy's oldest and most widely read newspaper, *Corriere della Sera*, that the 9-11 terrorist attacks were run by the Mossad, which is Israel's foreign intelligence service.[350] President Cossiga stated in that newspaper that the Mossad's perpetration of the 9/11 attacks was common knowledge among global intelligence agencies. President Cossiga stated that the attacks were designed to blame the Arab countries and induce the western powers to invade Iraq and Afghanistan.[351]

In an interview only weeks after 9-11, Hamid Gul, former head of Pakistani intelligence (ISI) from 1987-1989, told UPI reporter Arnaud de Borchgrave that the Mossad and its accomplices were the perpetrators of 9/11. Gul pointed out that the U.S. spent $40 billion per year on intelligence prior to 9-11-2001 and yet claims that it was taken by surprise. Within 10 minutes of the attacks, however, the government and the media had decided that Osama Bin Laden was the perpetrator. Gul stated that pinning the 9/11 attacks on Osama Bin Laden was a planned piece of disinformation. Gul further stated: "It created an instant mindset and put public opinion into a trance, which prevented even intelligent people from thinking for themselves."[352]

Andreas von Buelow, the former head of the parliamentary commission that oversaw the German intelligence agencies, told Christopher Bollyn that he believed that the Mossad was behind the terror attacks of 9-11.[353] Von Buelow explained that a sophisticated false-flag operation like 9/11 has an organizational structure with three basic levels: 1) architectural, 2) operational, and 3) working. He said that Atta and the 19 Arabs blamed as the hijackers of 9/11 were part of the working level. Von Buelow explained that the alleged hijackers were simply part of the deception. That is, after all, how false-flag terror works. The 9/11 attacks were designed to turn public opinion against the Arabs, and to boost military and security spending.

Von Buelow further explained: "You don't get the higher echelons," which is the architectural level that masterminds such false-flag terror attacks. At that level, the organization doing the planning, in this case the Mossad, is primarily interested in affecting public opinion, and it goes without saying that the mass media must be tightly controlled in order for such large-scale deception to succeed. He opined that "ninety-five percent of the work of the intelligence agencies around the world is deception and disinformation."[354] He stated that the deception is widely propagated in the mainstream media, which creates an accepted version of events. One can see it in the reporting. Von Buelow explained that is why journalists don't even raise the simplest questions. He said that those who do deviate from the official story are labeled as crazy.

Dr. Alan Sabrosky stated unequivocally:

> What we need to stand up and say is that not only did they [Israel] attack the USS Liberty, they did 9/11. They did it.
>
> I have had long conversations over the past two weeks with contacts at the Army War College, at the Headquarters Marine Corps, and I have made it absolutely clear in both cases that it is 100% certain that 9/11 was a Mossad operation. Period.[355]

Who is Dr. Sabrosky? Alan Sabrosky (Ph.D., University of Michigan) was for five years the Director of Studies for the Strategic Studies Institute at the U.S. Army War College. In his capacity as director, he received the Superior Civilian Service Award. While in government service, he held concurrent adjunct professorships at Georgetown University and Johns Hopkins University School of Advanced International Studies (SAIS). Dr. Sabrosky's teaching and research appointments have included the United States Military Academy, the Center for Strategic and International Studies (CSIS), Middlebury College, and Catholic University. He was also holder of the General of the Army Douglas MacArthur Chair of Research. He is listed in WHO'S WHO IN THE EAST (23rd ed.) and is a Marine Corps Vietnam veteran and a 1986 graduate of the U.S. Army War College.[356]

Dr. Sabrosky's credibility is further enhanced by the fact that he is part Jewish. He has a grandparent who was a Jew and some in his extended family are Jewish. He acknowledged that if the American people find out that Israel did 9/11 he will suffer right along with the other Jews. Dr. Sobrosky, however, states that he has a duty to the United States and if it means that he suffers for protecting America he is willing to do that. Dr. Sabrosky stated: "If this explodes I am going to go down with the rest of them, and I know this. I flat out know this."[357]

Being Jewish, Dr. Sabrosky has every motive to conceal this information. He feels compelled by patriotism as an American first to expose the truth of the matter. Dr. Sabrosky's allegiance is to the U.S., but as he explains "a large majority of American Jews give their allegiance to a foreign country, and they have American citizenship, but their allegiance is to Israel."[358]

The U.S. Military is fully aware of the Mossad's capabilities and ruthlessness. On September 10, 2001, the Army School of Advanced Military Studies issued a report written by elite U.S. army officers. The report was made public just prior to 9-11-2001. The report described the Mossad as follows: "Wildcard. Ruthless and cunning. Has capability to target US forces and make it look like a Palestinian/Arab act."[359] The Mossad not only has the capability of attacking U.S. forces, it has a history of doing that very thing. Israel using unmarked military jets to attack and attempt to sink the U.S.S. Liberty is just one example.

Is there evidence that supports the conclusions of these government officials? In fact there is. Angry witnesses reported seeing three separate groups of men at three different locations celebrating as they watched the September 11, 2001, attack on the World Trade Center. One group of men were seen celebrating in Union City. The witnesses reported their license plate to the police, who later arrested the men. Witnesses also saw three men in Liberty State Park in Jersey City filming the attack on the World Trade Center. After the attack the men were seen cheering and jumping up and down. Those men were also caught by the police and arrested several hours after the attack. Sources close to the investigation stated that it appeared that the men were involved in the attack and knew ahead of time what was going to happen.

Witnesses saw another group of five who were filming the smoking New York skyline. The men seemed quite happy with the spectacle of the burning towers. A neighbor witnessed the men shouting cries of joy and mockery. They all had prior knowledge of the 9/11 attacks and were set up in advance to film the World Trade Center explosions. The fact that the group was set up in advance to film the explosions in the WTC Towers was confirmed by CIA Field Agent Robert Baer.[360]

One of the "be on lookout"(BOLO) messages from the FBI was: "Three individuals with van were seen celebrating after initial impact and subsequent explosion. FBI Newark Field Office requests that, if the van is located, hold for prints and detain individuals."[361] Another FBI BOLO was: "Vehicle possibly related to New York terrorist attack. White, 2000 Chevrolet van with New Jersey registration with 'Urban Moving Systems' sign on back seen at Liberty State Park, Jersey City, NJ, at the time of first impact of jetliner into World Trade Center."[362]

At approximately 3:56 p.m. five men were found in the described white van and arrested.[363] It turned out to be the van from Liberty Park; apparently they had picked up two more passengers. They were found to possess maps and other evidence that linked them to the attack. One of the arrestees had $4,700 in cash hidden in his sock. Another passenger was carrying two foreign passports. As reported by ABC News:

> [P]erhaps the biggest surprise for the officers came when the five men identified themselves as Israeli citizens. According to the police report, one of the passengers told the officers they had been on the West Side Highway in Manhattan "during the incident" - referring to the World Trade Center attack.[364]

It turns out that the white van was in fact at Liberty Park, N.J. during the "incident"and not on the West Side Highway in Manhattan as deceptively portrayed by the passenger.[365] Why would the Israeli passenger lie about where they were when the "incident" happened? Apparently, he was trying to conceal his whereabouts. Deception about one's whereabouts at the time of a crime is evidence of guilt.

ABC News reported that the driver of the van told the officers: "We are Israeli. We are not your problem. Your problems are our problems. The Palestinians are the problem."[366] That is an odd statement under the circumstances, because the passengers at that time had not been told why they were being arrested. ABC News also reported that: "The FBI also questioned Urban Moving's owner. His attorney insists that his client answered all of the FBI's questions. But when FBI agents tried to interview him again a few days later, he was gone."[367] The owner had cleared out of his New Jersey home and hurriedly fled with his family back to Israel.[368] Three months later, ABC News program 20/20 photographed the inside of Urban Moving. "[I]t looked as if the business had been shut down in a big hurry. Cell phones were lying around; office phones were still connected; and the property of dozens of clients remained in the warehouse."[369]

It is suspicious enough that each of these men were Israelis linked to Israeli owned moving companies out of New York and New Jersey.[370] The real smoking gun is the fact that at least two of the arrested Israeli citizens were confirmed to be Mossad agents, and the moving company for which they worked was determined to be a Mossad front operation.[371]

Christopher Ketcham reports on the initial statements of the arrested Israelis:

> Remarkably, the Urban Moving Systems Israelis, when interrogated by the FBI, explained their motives for "celebration" on the New Jersey waterfront, a celebration that consisted of cheering, smiling, shooting film with still and video cameras and, according to the FBI, "high-fiving" - in the Machiavellian light of geopolitics. "Their explanation of why they were happy", FBI spokesman Margolin told me, "was that the United States would now have to commit itself to fighting [Middle East] terrorism, that Americans would have an understanding and empathy for Israel's circumstances, and that the attacks were ultimately a good thing for

Israel". When reporters on the morning of 9/11 asked former Israeli Prime Minister Benjamin Netanyahu about the effect the attacks would have on Israeli- American relations, he responded with a similar gut analysis: "It's very good", he remarked. Then he amended the statement: "Well, not very good, but it will generate immediate sympathy [for Israel from Americans]".[372]

The most telling thing about the celebration by the Israelis was the timing of their celebration. Christopher Ketcham explains:

> What is perhaps most damning is that the Israelis' celebration on the New Jersey waterfront occurred in the first sixteen minutes after the initial crash, when no one was aware this was a terrorist attack. In other words, from the time the first plane hit the north tower, at 8:46 a.m., to the time the second plane hit the south tower, at 9:02 a.m., the overwhelming assumption of news outlets and government officials was that the plane's impact was simply a terrible accident. It was only after the second plane hit that suspicions were aroused. Yet if the men were cheering for political reasons, as they reportedly told the FBI, they obviously believed they were witnessing a terrorist act, and not an accident.
>
> After returning safely to Israel in the late autumn of 2001, three of the five New Jersey Israelis spoke on a national talk show that winter. Oded Ellner, who on the afternoon of September 11 had, like his compatriots, protested to arresting officer Sgt. Dennis Rivelli that "we're Israeli", admitted to the interviewer: "We are coming from a country that experiences terror daily. Our purpose was to document the event." By his own admission, then, Ellner stood on the New Jersey waterfront documenting with film and video a terrorist act before anyone knew it was a terrorist act.[373]

That is clear evidence that those Israelis were directly involved as conspirators in the 9/11 attacks. The implications are clear: the attack was a false-flag operation conducted by Israel in order to prompt the U.S. to militarily attack Israel's enemies. The U.S. Government responded on cue to the stimulus, like a Pavlovian-rabid dog.

An indication of the power and control of Israel over the U.S. Government is the fact that all of the Israeli Mossad agents who were caught celebrating over the carnage of the burning twin towers were deported back to Israel. Incidently, the United States has no extradition treaty with Israel, so the deported culprits will never be brought to justice in this world. The U.S. government was under no legal compulsion to deport the Mossad agents. In fact, the U.S. is now holding many suspects indefinitely without filing any charges against them and without allowing them legal counsel, because they are considered illegal enemy combatants of war. It is no surprise that none of those detained enemy combatants are Jews.

Who was behind the release of the Israeli spies? Michael Chertoff, as head of the Criminal Division of the Deptartment of Justice, had control over the entire investigation (read: cover-up) into 9-11. Chertoff obstructed justice by ordering the return of the spies to Israel. Why would Chertoff do such a thing? He is a dual citizen of Israel. His real loyalties are with Israel.

In 2005, Christopher Bollyn exposed the fact that Michael Chertoff was an Israeli national. Chertoff was the Assistant Attorney General responsible for the Criminal Division of the U.S. Department of Justice during and after the 9-11-2001 attacks.[374] Israel made certain it had key people in place to ensure that there would be no blow-back on Israel. Chertoff was one of those key men.

Bollyn was able to substantiate his allegation that Chertoff is an Isreali national; Bollyn obtained a flight manifest that showed that Chertoff spent part of his childhood in Israel.[375] The flight manifest from El Al flight LY207/17 from Israel to New York on 18 August 1955 indicates passenger # 28 was Michael Chertoff. Chertoff would have been approximately three years old at that time. Chertoff travelled with his father, Gershon Baruch Chertoff, an orthodox rabbi, who sat in seat # 26 and his Israeli mother Livia Eisen Chertoff, who sat in seat # 27.

Assistant Attorney General Chertoff remained at his post until 2003. Chertoff was appointed to the position of the Director of the U.S. Department of Homeland Security in 2005. Bollyn explained that the Chertoff family involvement in Israeli intelligence affairs has deep roots. Chertoff's mother was the first hostess on El Al and was involved in secret Mossad missions. In fact, her obituary in the December 21, 1998, (Newark, N.J.) Star-Ledger specifically mentions her involvement in Operation Magic Carpet.[376]

The influence of Israel over the U.S. Government is evidenced by the fact that there is no mention of the arrest of the Mossad Agents on 9-11-2001 in the 9/11 Commission Report. With the exception of the initial report by ABC News, and one other report by Fox News, there has been a virtual news blackout of the subject. In fact, there was significant pressure brought on ABC News to kill the story before it even ran. A former ABC News employee high up in the network newsroom told Ketcham that when ABC News ran its June 2002 exposé on the celebrating New Jersey Israelis, "Enormous pressure was brought to bear by pro-Israeli organizations." The odd thing was that the pressure began months before the piece was even close to airing. ABC News employees wondered how the pro-Israel organizations found out that ABC was going to air the story.

ABC management was getting bombarded by protest calls. ABC News to its credit ran the story on or about June 2002.[377] Of course, as with any article that implicates Israel in 911, ABC found it necessary to include a conclusion that there was no evidence that the Israeli arrestees had foreknowledge of 911. ABC News has Vince Cannistraro, a former chief of operations for counterterrorism with the CIA, as their consultant. Cannistraro was quick to cover for Israel by coming to a conclusion that is unsupported by the evidence. Cannistraro concluded that "after all the polygraphs, all of the field work, all the cross-checking, [and] the intelligence work, they probably did not have advance knowledge of 9/11."[378] The evidence contradicts the conclusion of Cannistraro and indicates that the arrested Israelis had advance notice. Christopher Ketcham has spoken to reliable sources that revealed to him that the Israelis were on the scene even before the first crash.[379] Ketcham's sources were corroborated by eyewitnesses and by CIA Field Agent Robert Baer.[380] That is clear evidence of advance knowledge.

Cannistraro's spinning of the evidence to point away from Israeli prior knowledge is one example of how the media bias toward Israel is played out. The pro-Israel media bias is often achieved by the many journalists reporting for the American and Western media who have close ties to Israel. Alison Weir "was astounded to learn how many of the allegedly 'objective' journalists in the region reporting for American media have close ties to the Israeli military. Ethan Bronner, New York Times bureau chief, has a son in the Israeli army. Others have themselves served in the Israeli military. 'Pundit' Jeffrey Goldberg, who is often interviewed for commentary on U.S. mainstream news broadcasts, served in the Israeli military."[381]

Fox News and Carl Cameron were attacked over the reports about Israeli spying in the U.S. and their surveillance of the alleged 9/11 hijackers prior to 9-11-2001. Christopher Ketcham explains:

> The attack against Cameron and Fox News was spearheaded by a pro-Israel lobby group called the Committee for Accuracy in Middle East Reporting in America (CAMERA), which operated in tandem with the two most highly visible powerhouse Israel lobbyists, the Anti-Defamation League (ADL) and the American Israel Public Affairs Committee (itself currently embroiled in a spy scandal connected to the Defense Department and Israeli Embassy). "CAMERA peppered the shit out of us," Carl Cameron told me in 2002, referring to an e-mail bombardment that eventually crashed the Fox News.com servers. Cameron himself received 700 pages of almost identical e-mail messages from hundreds of citizens (though he suspected these were spam identities). CAMERA spokesman Alex Safian later told me that Cameron's upbringing in Iran, where his father traveled as an archeologist, had rendered the reporter "very sympathetic to the Arab side". Safian added, "I think Cameron, personally, has a thing about Israel"--coded language implying that Cameron was an anti-Semite. Cameron was outraged at the accusation.
>
> According to a source at Fox News Channel, the president of the ADL, Abraham Foxman, telephoned executives at Fox News' parent, News Corp., to demand a sit-down in the wake of the Cameron reportage. The source said that Foxman told the News

Corp. executives, "Look, you guys have generally been pretty fair to Israel. What are you doing putting this stuff out there? You're killing us".[382]

What finally happened after the sit-down with Foxman was that only four days after Cameron's series about Israeli spying was posted on Fox News.com, the transcripts of the story disappeared. They were replaced by the message: "This story no longer exists."[383]

Christopher Ketcham did a first rate job of investigative reporting on the Israeli spying, but very few people know about it. That report was offered to both the Nation and Salon, but they declined to publish it because they felt it was not newsworthy. It was finally published by Counterpunch. One of the non-newsworthy things that Ketcham reported was that there was a connection between the alleged 9/11 hijackers and Urban Moving, the Mossad front company that employed the celebratory Israelis arrested on 9-11-2001. Ketcham revealed:

> All five future hijackers of American Airlines Flight 77, which rammed the Pentagon, maintained addresses or were active within a six-mile radius of towns associated with the Israelis employed at Urban Moving Systems. Hudson and Bergen counties, the areas where the Israelis were allegedly conducting surveillance, were a central staging ground for the hijackers of Flight 77 and their fellow al-Qaeda operatives. Mohammed Atta maintained a mail-drop address and visited friends in northern New Jersey; his contacts there included Hani Hanjour, the suicide pilot for Flight 77, and Majed Moqed, one of the strongmen who backed Hanjour in the seizing of the plane.

Ketcham asked the rhetorical question: "Could the Israelis, with or without knowledge of the terrorists' plans, have been tracking the men who were soon to hijack Flight 77?" Apparently, it is impolite to allege complicity by Israel in the 9/11 attacks, and so the most Ketcham will allow himself to say is that maybe the Israelis were "tracking" the alleged hijackers. Why not ask: "Were the alleged hijackers being controlled by the Mossad?" If he had asked that question in his article, the article would no doubt never have seen the light of day on Counterpunch or anywhere else. His reporting would be exposed only to those few who would read his personal internet posting.

It seems likely that the Mossad knew exactly what was going to happen and when, which suggests that the attacks were their plan. After all, the Mossad Agents were in place to see the 9/11 attacks and seemed quite pleased by the outcome. This does not appear to be merely a case of a failure to inform the U.S. about an attack by a loose knit group of Arab terrorists, but rather a planned attack by Israel on the U.S., with the Alleged Arab terrorists being controlled by the Mossad to be set up as patsies to take the blame. It is possible that many of the Arab terrorists were being portrayed by Mossad agents, who had assumed false identities and immediately after the attacks assumed other false identities and fled the United States back to Israel.

Ketcham revealed that there was no real investigation of the arrested Israelis. The rank-and-file FBI Agents who were trying to investigate the case were frustrated by the FBI administration that prevented any real investigation. The official FBI position was that the Mossad was not conducting espionage in the U.S.; the rank-and-file FBI Agents, however, knew that was not the case. A former CIA counter-terrorism officer told Ketcham that there was no question but that the White House ordered the investigation closed down. The CIA immediately assumed that there was going to be a cover-up so that the Israelis would not be implicated in any way in 9/11.

Another aspect of the Israeli arrests on 9-11-2001 is the earlier reported attempts by Israeli operatives approaching Drug Enforcement Administration (DEA) facilities and agents through a ruse of being art students selling art. The Israeli "art students" visited a total of twenty-eight DEA offices and twenty-nine private residences of DEA employees throughout the country. It was obvious that the art student status was just a cover for an intelligence operation, because their backgrounds in the Israeli military were incongruent with being art students. As noted in a leaked DEA report, many of the "art students" had training as intelligence and electronic intercept officers in the Israeli military or were associated with Israeli wiretapping and surveillance firms; they had training and experience far beyond the compulsory military service mandated by Israeli law.

Ketcham reveals that suspected Israeli spy Tomer Ben Dor, who was questioned at Dallas-Fort Worth Airport in May 2001, worked for the Israeli wiretapping and electronic eavesdropping company NICE Systems Ltd. Ketcham points out that "NICE Systems' American subsidiary, NICE Systems Inc., is located in Rutherford, New Jersey, not far from the East Rutherford site where the five Israeli "movers" were arrested on the afternoon of September 11."[384]

In his book *Solving 9/11 - The Deception That Changed the World*,[385] Christopher Bollyn reveals that NICE Systems, Inc., is the wholly owned U.S. subsidiary of an Israeli company with the same name. In 2001, when the "art students" were trying to infiltrate DEA and other government buildings, NICE was headed by Israeli Brigadier General Shlomo Shamir. In April 2001 he became President and Chief Executive Officer of NICE. General Shamir constructed and led the planning division in the IDF (Israeli military) headquarters. He also served as Israel's military attaché to Germany until 1994.[386]

Another Israeli art student was Michal Gal, who was arrested by DEA Agents in Irving, Texas, in the spring of 2001. He was released on a $10,000 cash bond posted by Ophir Baer.[387] Baer is an employee of the Israeli telecommunications software company Amdocs Inc., which provides phone-billing technology to clients that include the largest phone companies in the United States and U.S. government agencies.[388] Amdocs' executive board is heavily stocked with retired and current members of the Israeli military intelligence. Amdocs has been investigated at least twice in the last decade by U.S. authorities on charges of espionage-related leaks of data.[389] A number of senior corporate officers of Amdocs, all Israelis, regularly move between NICE Systems, ViryaNet Ltd., and Guardium, which are all Israeli technology companies closely associated with former Israeli military and intelligence officers.[390]

Ketcham revealed that a large number of the purported "art students" operated out of Hollywood, Florida. In fact, thirty of the approximately 120 Israeli operatives posing as art students lived in the Hollywood area. That fact alone is significant when juxtaposed against the fact that Hollywood was one of the chief staging points for the patsies alleged to have hijacked the alleged planes that supposedly crashed into World Trade Center and in Pennsylvania. Hollywood was home to fifteen of the nineteen alleged hijackers; nine of them lived in Hollywood, with six living in the surrounding area. Ketcham explains:

> One "art student" was a former Israeli military intelligence officer named Hanan Serfaty, who rented two Hollywood apartments close to the mail drop and apartment of Mohammed Atta and four other hijackers. Serfaty was moving large amounts of cash: he carried bank slips showing more than $100,000 deposited from December 2000 through the first quarter of 2001; other bank slips showed withdrawals for about $80,000 during the same period. Serfaty's apartments, serving as crash pads for at least two other "art students", were located at 4220 Sheridan Street and 701 South 21st Avenue. Lead hijacker Mohammed Atta's mail drop was at 3389 Sheridan Street--approximately 2,700 feet from Serfaty's Sheridan Street apartment. Both Atta and Marwan al-Shehhi, the suicide pilot on United Airlines Flight 175, which smashed into World Trade Center 2, lived in a rented apartment at 1818 Jackson Street, some 1,800 feet from Serfaty's South 21st Avenue apartment.[391]

That is not all. Ketcham discovered what he conservatively describes as "an improbable series of coincidences." Ketcham read through a leaked 2001 DEA report, the 9/11 Commission's staff statements and final report, FBI and Justice Department watch lists, hijacker time-lines compiled by major media, and statements by local, state and federal law enforcement personnel. He discovered that in at least six urban centers, suspected Israeli spies and 9/11 hijackers and/or al-Qaeda connected suspects lived and operated near one another. These areas included northern New Jersey, Hollywood, Florida, Arlington and Fredericksburg, Virginia, Atlanta, GA, Oklahoma City, Los Angeles, and San Diego. In some instances the Israeli spies and the purported terrorists lived less than a half mile apart during the run-up to the 9-11-2001 attacks.

Ketcham reports that Khalid al-Mihdhar and Nawaf al-Hazmi, who are alleged to have eventually hijacked the Pentagon plane, were among the alleged hijackers who operated in close proximity to both the Israeli spies acting as art students in Hollywood, Florida, and to the Urban Moving Systems Israelis in northern New Jersey. Coincidently, Hazmi and at least three Israeli art students visited Oklahoma City on almost the same dates, from April 1 through April 4, 2001.[392]

Below is a map showing the improbable correlation between the Israeli intelligence operatives masquerading as art students trying to infiltrate DEA facilities and the alleged 9/11 hijackers.[393] The close proximity of the Israeli spies to the alleged hijackers prior to 9-11-2001 suggests that the Israeli operatives were the controlling agents for the patsies (or fellow Mossad agents assuming false identities and portraying Arab terrorists) who would later be accused of the supposed 9/11 hijackings. That map was contained in a report submitted by Gerald Shea on September 15, 2004, to the National Commission on Terrorist Attacks upon the United States (a/k/a the 9/11 Commission), The Senate Select Committee on Intelligence, and The House Permanent Select Committee on Intelligence.[394] Shea's 166 page report details the activities of the Israeli spies and their correlation to the alleged 9/11 hijackers.

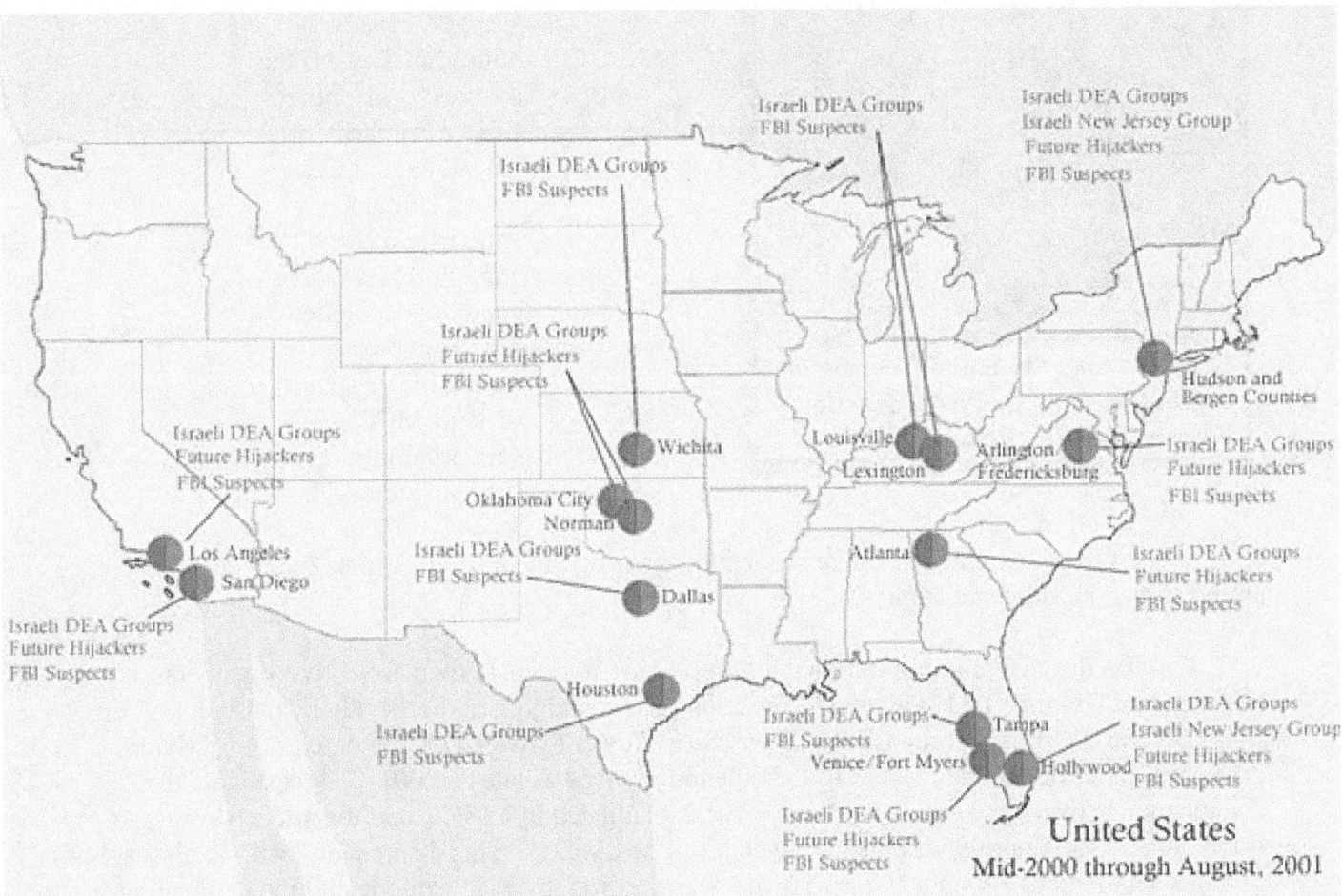

Jonathan Elinof discovered evidence that "art students" were in New York and they actually lived in the World Trade Center as part of the World Views program that was located in the Lower Manhattan Cultural Council (LMCC). Elinof reported that those art students occupied floors 90 and 91 in the North Tower of the WTC.[395] There has been no reliable evidence that has yet been uncovered that links the Israeli art students to the art students who resided in the North Tower. That is not to say there is no link, just that there is no clear evidence of a link. The close connection of both groups of art students to the target of the 9/11 attacks at about the same time frame is a notable coincidence.

The LMCC described the World Views program as being on the 91st and 92nd floors of the North Tower.

Gelatin "Arts Students" Peering out a Window from the WTC North Tower (Note the Boxes)

From 1997 to 2001, LMCC's first studio residency program, World Views, was housed in Tower One of the World Trade Center primarily on the 91st and 92nd floors. The Port Authority of New York and New Jersey generously donated raw, temporarily vacant office spaces, which LMCC converted into artists' studios.[396]

The LMCC explains that a key aspect of the program was that "artists received 24/7 access to the building and studios."[397]

It was through that program that a group of art students known collectively as Gelatin (also spelled Gelitin[398]) were given construction passes and joined the 14 other "art students" on floors 90 and 91 of the World Trade Center North Tower (Tower 1) some date prior to March 2000 and spanning until at least May 1, 2000 and perhaps as late as 2001.[399] Please note the discrepancy between the access to floors 91 and 92 alleged by LMCC and the alleged access to floors 90 and 91 (floor 90 was outside the control of LMCC). This discrepancy will be discussed in more detail later. Tower 1 (North Tower) was the first tower to explode and the explosion in the North Tower spanned from the 92nd floor to the 98th floor.

The Gelatin "art students" wrote and published a book on or before July 2001 titled *The B-Thing*, which explained their stunt performed in March 2000 of removing a window from the 91st floor of the North Tower of the World Trade Center and walking out on a constructed platform to be photographed from a helicopter.[400] A summary of the description of the book prepared by the publisher describes the event as having occurred not in March 2000, but rather in

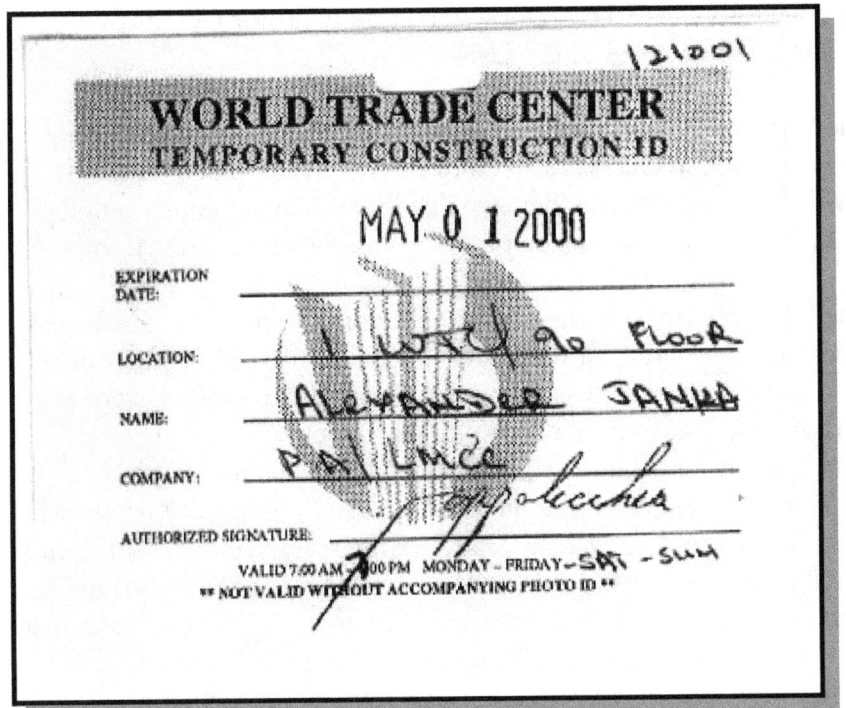

Construction Pass for Alexander Janka for the 90th Floor of WTC Tower 1 (North Tower) Obtained by Jonathan Elinof Through a Confidential Source

June 2000.[401] In an August 18, 2001, review of the book by The New York Times, the "art students" were described as "Vienna-based artists known collectively as Gelatin."[402] The LMCC lists Gelatin as taking part in World Views from winter 1999 until spring 2000.[403] In several of the pictures in the book boxes can be seen stacked floor-to-ceiling; it is not known what was in those boxes.

One indication that the Gelatin group was a cover for some other objective is that the crude drawings contained in *The B-Thing* book demonstrate that the Gelatin group, which was supposed to be a troupe of artists, lacked any artistic talent. Most of the drawings contained in the book appeared to have been drawn by a talentless 12-year-old school child. They were clearly not art students.

If the Gelatin group was not a group of art students, what was it? The construction passes are the smoking gun as to what they were really doing in the World Trade Center. Why was it necessary for the Gelatin group, which was supposedly made up of art students, to receive construction passes? Construction passes are not just handed to anybody. In order to receive a construction pass, approval must have been received from the high officials in the management of the World Trade Center. Obviously, something more than a prank was afoot.

The LMCC identified their program as involving the 91st and 92nd floors, however, Elinof alleges that Gelatin occupied the 90th and 91st floors. That seemingly suggests that perhaps Elinof has his facts wrong about Gelatin. Elinof, however, has been able to corroborate his claim by producing a construction pass in the name of Alexander Janka for the 90th floor of the WTC.

Alexander Janka was identified as a member of Gelatin, and The New York Times even interviewed him for their article regarding Gelatin's book about their stunt at the World Trade Center.[404] The construction pass given to Janka was amended to give him access to the 90th floor seven days a week, rather than the usual five days a week. The construction pass identifies the company for which he worked as "PA/LMCC." Clearly, the members of the Gelatin group were getting special privileges and access within the WTC. The special treatment for Gelatin is notable, since the 90th floor was outside the control of the LMCC.

Furthermore, access to the 90th floor was completely unnecessary for the prank, since according to The New York Times article and Gelatin's website the stunt took place on the 91st floor of the North Tower of the WTC.[405] Why would they need access (let alone construction passes) to the 90th floor if their whole purpose was to step out of a window on the 91st floor?

Not only was access to the 90th floor unnecessary, but Gelatin could not even gain access to the 90th floor through the World Views program of the LMCC, because the LMCC did not have control over the 90th floor. In order to gain access to the 90th floor, Gelatin had to get approval from the management of the WTC itself. The approval was given with the understanding that the art students worked for "PA/LMCC." The LMCC is an art program; a construction pass is unnecessary for art students. Who gave this bunch of supposedly fringe art students construction passes to the 90th floor of the World Trade Center? The very idea of doing such a thing does not pass the smell test. The construction passes gave these supposed fringe "art students" access to areas within the infrastructure of the building, which would be inaccessible to an ordinary tenant. The fact that the Gelatin "art students" had access to the 90th floor, which was outside the control of the LMCC, reveals the LMCC grant of access as a poorly framed cover story.

A foreign intelligence agency, like the Mossad, while running a false flag operation, must have a cover-story in the event that their activities are discovered. In order to *appear* as helpful to an ally, but not actually *be* helpful, Israel provided cryptic information in such a fashion that it would be of no help to the U.S., but at the same time allow Israel to claim later that they warned the U.S. On August 23, 2001, the Mossad briefed the CIA. A day after the Mossad's briefing, Mihdhar and Hazmi were placed by the CIA on a terrorist watch list. On August 27, 2001, the CIA warned the FBI about Mihdar and Hazmi.

The information provided by the Israelis was timed so that it would be completely ineffective, because by the time they briefed the CIA the patsy cell was already in hiding, being prepared by the Mossad for their role as patsies in the 9/11 attacks. The warning was timed so that it would be completely useless. The purpose of the warning was to provide Israel with plausible deniability over their role in the 9/11 attacks.

Part and parcel of the Israeli spy network are several Israeli government subsidized telecommunications companies, where many of the "art students" worked. Most of these companies have interlocking relationships. Amdocs is one of those companies. Amdocs provides billing and directory assistance for 90% of the phone companies in the United States.

"Amdocs' main computer center for billing is actually in Israel and allows those with access to do what intelligence agencies call 'traffic analysis'; a picture of someone's activities based on a pattern of who [sic] they are calling and when. Another Israeli telecom company is Comverse Infosys, which subcontracts the installation of the automatic tapping equipment now built into every phone system in America. Comverse maintains its own connections to all this phone tapping equipment, insisting that it is for maintenance purposes only. However, Comverse has been named as the most likely source for leaked information regarding telephone calls by law enforcement that derailed several investigations into not only espionage, but drug running as well. Yet another Israeli telecom company is Odigo, which provides the core message passing system for all the 'Instant Message' services. Shortly after 9-11-2001 Odigo was acquired by Comverse.[406] Two hours before the attacks on the World Trade Towers, Odigo employees received a warning. Odigo has an office 2 blocks from the former location of the World Trade Towers."[407]

Christopher Bollyn explains the role of Odigo in warning Israelis of the 9-11-2001 attacks:

> In the first days and weeks after 9-11, I paid very close attention to the large number of Israeli terror suspects arrested, which was more than two hundred by November 2001, and investigated the published reports that an Israeli instant text message service had been used to warn Israelis of the attacks in New York, hours before they occurred. Many Israelis were evidently forewarned of the attacks through an Israeli instant messaging service called Odigo. This story, which presents the clearest evidence of Israeli prior knowledge of the attacks, was reported only very briefly in the U.S. media – and then forgotten.
>
> According to the published reports, Israel-based employees of Odigo reported having received warnings of an imminent attack at the World Trade Center hours before the first plane hit the north tower. Odigo, an Israeli-owned company, had its U.S. headquarters two blocks from the World Trade Center, but the forewarned Odigo employees did not pass the terror warning on to the authorities in New York, an act that would have saved thousands of lives.
>
> Two weeks after 9-11, Alex Diamandis, Odigo's vice president, said, "The messages said something big was going to happen in a certain amount of time, and it did – almost to the minute." "It was possible that the attack warning was broadcast to other Odigo members, but the company has not received reports of other recipients of the message," Diamandis said. Four thousand Israelis were expected to have been working at the World Trade Center on 9-11, yet only one was reported to have died at the complex. Based on the Israeli government figure that 4,000 Israelis were expected to have been at the World Trade Center at the time of the attacks, it seems evident that many Israeli Odigo users got the message of

warning.

> Odigo, which offers real-time messaging, has a feature called "People Finder" which allows a user to send an instant message to a large group based on a common characteristic, such as Israeli nationality. "People Finder" allows Odigo users to search for online "buddies," with filters like Israeli nationality, while maintaining user privacy at all times. The message was probably sent in Hebrew. The Internet address of the sender of the warning was allegedly given to the FBI. Two months later it was reported that the FBI was still investigating the matter. Since then there have been no further media reports about the Odigo warning of 9/11.
>
> These two news stories about the fake Israeli "movers" and the Odigo messages, which clearly indicated that some Israelis had very specific prior knowledge of the attacks, were published in American and Israeli newspapers shortly after 9-11. Had the recipients of these Odigo instant messages contacted the New York police department, thousands of lives could have been saved. The question that has not been asked is, why didn't they?[408]

Bollyn explained in an article he wrote in 2005 that "Odigo, like many Israeli software companies, is based and has its Research and Development (R&D) center in Herzliya, Israel, the small town north of Tel Aviv, which happens to be where Mossad's headquarters are located."[409] Regarding the 4,000 Israelis that worked in and around the World Trade Center, the internet version of the Jerusalem Post reported on September 12, 2001:

> The Foreign Ministry in Jerusalem has so far received the names of 4,000 Israelis believed to have been in the areas of the World Trade Center and the Pentagon at the time of the attack. The list is made up of people who have not yet made contact with friends or family, Army Radio reported.[410]

That Jerusalem Post report is believed by most to be the original basis for the reported 4,000 Israelis who absented themselves from the World Trade Center on 9-11-2001. Not surprisingly, that article has since been removed from the Jerusalem Post website. In 2003, Bret Stephens, editor-in-chief of the Jerusalem Post, confirmed the accuracy of the report: "Whether this story was the origin of the rumor, I cannot say. What I can say is that there was no mistake in our reporting."[411] One aspect of the report that is overlooked by most is that the 4,000 figure was obtained from a list of "Israelis" who have not made contact with friends or family. That indicates that it is only a smaller subset of all of the Jews that worked in and around the World Trade Center and the Pentagon. The point being that there were more than 4,000 Jews who would have been endangered by the attacks if they had been at work in those areas on 9-11-2001.

Twenty citizens of Colombia and 15 citizens from the Philippines died in the World Trade Center attacks. The death toll for Israeli citizens would be expected to be much higher than that. New York is the center of international Jewish financial power, and the World Trade Center is at its epicenter. The international Jewish involvement in banking and finance is legendary. Two of the largest and richest firms in New York are Goldman-Sachs and Solomon Brothers. Both firms had offices in several floors in the twin towers of the World Trade Center. Many executives in those firms regularly commute to and from Israel conducting international banking and business. Many Jews are dual U.S./Israeli citizens. One would expect the Israeli death toll to be catastrophic.[412] Yet, Alon Pinkas, Israel's consul general confirmed that only three Israelis were killed in the 9-11-01 WTC attacks. Two Israelis were killed in the two purported planes which supposedly crashed into the towers, and one Israeli, who had been visiting one of the World Trade Center towers on business, was killed.

Only three of potentially thousands of Israelis working in the WTC were killed on 9-11![413] How is that possible? 9-11-01 was not a Jewish holiday; so where were the 4,000 Israelis who ordinarily would have been working in or around the World Trade Center? The Odigo warning would seem to explain the absence of any significant Israeli casualties on 9-11-2001.

The Bush Administration was concerned over the strange appearance of so few Israeli losses on 9-11. Christopher Bollyn reveals: "Although a total of three Israeli lives were reportedly lost on 9/11, speech writers for President George W. Bush grossly inflated the number of Israeli dead to 130 in the president's address to a joint session of Congress on September 20, 2001."[414] Another curious fact is that the Israeli who was identified as being allegedly killed aboard American Airlines Flight 11, Daniel Lewin, was an officer in Sayeret Matkal, which is the most elite secret anti-terrorism commando unit in the Israeli Defense Forces.

The fortuitous narrow escape of 200 employees of an Israeli government run company called ZIM Israel Navigational is very intriguing indeed. Just one week before the 9-11 attacks, ZIM Navigational moved its offices and more than 200 workers out of the World Trade Center.[415]

Why the rush to move out of the WTC only months before the lease was up and incur $50,000 in penalties in the process? What fortunate timing, moving out of the building just days before it and its twin tower collapsed! Questions regarding ZIM Navigational's sudden move from the WTC were referred to the WTC lease owner, Silverstein Properties, who in turn referred inquiries to their public relations firm, Howard J. Rubinstein. Interestingly, Howard J. Rubinstein is also the public relations firm for the state of Israel.[416]

The $50,000 penalty was peanuts compared to the extra costs that ZIM incurred at the other end of their move. A little known fact about the ZIM move is that it was not a sudden decision. The company planned on moving out of the WTC over a year ahead of time. ZIM contracted with an architectural and construction firm to build their new building in Norfolk, Virginia. One of the stipulations in the contract for construction, which was the essence of the contract, was a hard deadline that the building be move-in ready prior to September 2001. The time frame for the design and construction of the building was so short that several architectural firms turned down the contract before ZIM finally found a firm that agreed to the stipulated time frame. To compress an architectural and construction contract increases the cost of construction significantly. ZIM paid a huge premium for the expedited construction schedule. In hindsight, it is clear why ZIM was willing to incur the extra costs at both ends. ZIM knew about the planned attacks on 9-11-2001 and wanted out of the WTC. How did the Israeli state owned ZIM know? ZIM knew, because Israel planned it.

      A spokesman for ZIM stated that the reason for the sudden move was to save on rent.[417] The claim that a major global shipping firm, backed up by government money, needed to save a few bucks on rent lacks credibility. That explanation is particularly incredible in light of the fact it cost the company $50,000 to break their lease with the World Trade Center, which was to run until the end of the year, and they incurred huge extra construction costs for expediting the construction of their new facility in Norfolk, Virginia.[418] The provable fact that ZIM lied about their reasons for moving is yet more proof that ZIM knew about the 9-11-2001 attacks and that Israel was behind the attacks.

17 Able Danger

The actions of the Israeli "art students" correlates closely in time with the circulation of information in the U.S. intelligence community gained from the U.S. Military's Special Operations Command project called "Able Danger." Able Danger was an electronic search and linking project that was able to identify Mohamad Atta and three other of the named hijackers before the 9/11 attacks. However, between December 2000 and March 2001 the program was ordered shut down and all records that were compiled were destroyed. Apparently, Able Danger was coming too close to the mark.

The 9/11 Commission never mentioned Able Danger in its report even though its executive director, Philip Zelikow, and other staff members were briefed on the project.[419] The failure of the 9/11 Commission to even mention Able Danger is yet more evidence of a cover-up. The 9/11 Commission's sweeping mandate in pertinent part was to "investigate facts and circumstances relating to the terrorist attacks of September 11, 2001, including those related to intelligence agencies, law enforcement agencies."[420] The Able Danger information was clearly prior intelligence involving at least four of the alleged hijackers.

A Defense Intelligence Agency (DIA) source revealed to Wayne Madsen that in 2000 Able Danger established links between the CIA and Israeli intelligence agents and Mohammed Atta and other members of his alleged hijacking team.[421] The best proof of those links is the hurried shut down of Able Danger and destruction of 2.5 terabytes of data. Was Israel tipped off about the Able Danger data? Were the Israeli "art students" trying to make it appear that the indication of terrorist activity was actually drug activity or other criminal conduct, thus clouding the terrorist conclusions drawn from the Able Danger data and throw the Able Danger team off their trail?

Reporter Mike Kelly interviewed a member of the Able Danger Team on or before August 14, 2005:

> In those horrific weeks after the attacks, the official story line was that U.S. counterterror officials had no idea who Atta was before

that murderous plot unfolded - or where he was before 9/11. Only
after the attacks could authorities track Atta's movements. Now
that story seems to be false.[422]

The Able Danger team was able to identify four of the 9/11 alleged hijackers in advance of 9-11-2001: Mohammed Atta, Marwan al-Shehhi, Khalid al-Mihdar and Nawaf al-Hazmi. *Der Spiegel* and *Die Zeit* in October 2002 reported that on August 23, 2001, the Mossad gave the United States the exact same four names: Atta, al-Shehhi, al-Mihdar and al-Hazmi as part of a list of nineteen men the Israelis said were planning a terror attack in the United States.[423]

Assuming Israel, through its electronic eavesdropping and human intelligence assets, knew what was revealed by Able Danger, it perfectly explains why the Mossad would give the United States that list of names. Israel knew what the United States already knew; the Mossad simply waited until August 23, 2001 to confirm the information, so that at that late date it would be impossible to find the subjects (patsies) before 9-11-2001.

Kelly explains the detail of the Able Danger information:

> The connect-the-dots tracking by the team was so good that it even knew Atta conducted meetings with the three future hijackers. One of those meetings took place at the Wayne Inn. That's how close all this was - to us and to being solved, if only the information had been passed up the line to FBI agents or even to local cops.
>
> This new piece of 9/11 history, revealed only last week by a Pennsylvania congressman and confirmed by two former members of the intelligence team, could turn out to be one of the most explosive revelations since the publication last summer of the 9/11 commission report.
>
> The information not only undermines key commission findings that Atta and others were undetected, but it again raises a question that continues to haunt the 9/11 tragedy:
>
> Why is our government so incompetent?[424]

Kelly is giving the government the benefit of the doubt, when he alleges incompetence. An objective view of the Able Danger fiasco strongly suggests something much more sinister. The very competent officers on the Able Danger project knew something big was going to happen and wanted to go to the FBI with the information, so that they could round up the culprits and stop their plan, but as Kelly reports: "A former member of the military intelligence team told me in an interview that it had enough data to raise suspicions. 'But we were blocked from passing it to the FBI.'"[425]

Blocking information about a terrorist plan from being sent to the FBI is not incompetence, it is obstruction. That conclusion is compelled when the actions blocking the FBI from access to the information is added to the fact that the government subsequently ordered all the information obtained from the investigation (2.5 terabytes) destroyed.

The Able Danger Team knew that they were onto something big which is why they wanted to go operational by having the FBI step in to stop whatever was being planned. Kelly reports:

> By mid-2000, the Able Danger team knew it had important information about a possible terrorist plot. Because of a peculiar series of computer links that went through Brooklyn, the team began referring to the four future hijackers as the "Brooklyn cell." Their movements and communications were raising too many suspicions.[426]

Lt. Col. Anthony Shaffer, who was a member of the Able Danger Team, said that an unnamed two-star general above him was very adamant about not looking further at Mohammed Atta. Shaffer stated that he was directed several times to ignore Atta; at one point the general had to remind Shaffer that he was a general and Shaffer was not, and that Shaffer would essentially be fired if he continued to track Atta.[427]

If the Able Danger Team was able to forward their intelligence to the FBI, it may have thwarted the 9/11 attacks. Rep. Curt Weldon (R), who in 2005 helped bring to light the existence of Able Danger, stated:

> Obviously, if we had taken out that cell, 9/11 would not have occurred and, certainly, taking out those three principal players in that cell would have severely crippled, if not totally stopped, the operation that killed 3,000 people in America.

Able Danger uncovered evidence that Mohamed Atta and Marwan Alshehhi were living in Wayne, New Jersey for 12 months prior to the September 11, 2001 attacks. That is contrary to evidence that generally places those two alleged terrorists in Florida from July 2000 until shortly before 9/11.[428] Those facts only represent a conflict to those who do not understand how intelligence communities establish patsies for pre-planned crimes.

Often, intelligence agencies while controlling the unwitting patsy will have an operative assume the identity of the patsy. That way they can sheep-dip the patsy by having the similar looking operative engage in suspicious and incriminating conduct that can be later used to prove that the now dead patsy was a heartless terrorist, as called for by the script. It can always be claimed that the target patsy moved back and forth between locations which would nicely explain how he could be living in two places. Sometimes there is a slip-up that reveals that there are two persons using the same identity. That seems to have happened in the case of Atta. The FBI timeline shows that Atta was in two places at once in the spring of 2000.[429]

Once the story about Able Danger broke two members of the Able Danger project came forward. Lieutenant Colonel Anthony Shaffer, a civilian employee of the Defense Intelligence Agency and reserve officer within the U.S. Army, and Mr. James Smith, a defense contractor at the time with Orion Scientific Systems. Both of those Able Danger members, however, were forbidden by the Department of Defense from testifying before Congress about Able Danger. Consequently, on September 21, 2005, their lawyer, Mark Zaid, testified in their stead before Congress.

> In the most understandable and simplistic terms, Able Danger involved the searching out and compiling of open source or other publicly available information regarding specific targets or tasks that were connected through associational links. No classified information was used. No government database systems were used. In addition to examining Al Qaeda links, Able Danger also handled tasks relating to Bosnia and China. The search and compilation efforts were primarily handled by defense contractors, who did not necessarily know they were working for Able Danger, and that information was then to be utilized by the military members of Able Danger for whatever appropriate purposes.
>
> * * *
>
> Again, what was being explored were associational links between individuals, meaning person "A" who was associated with Sheik Abdel-Rahman, and then identifying person "B" who was associated with person "A" and so on. Essentially, think in your mind how the game "Six Degrees of Kevin Bacon" operates. That is a simplistic explanation of part of Able Danger's activities.
>
> The compiled information would be uploaded into an interactive computer program designed by the contractor that would create depictions of the links accompanied by all the underlying data to support those links.
>
> * * *
>
> As part of their efforts multiple individuals associated with Able Danger have stated that they identified four of the terrorists, including Mohammed Atta, who subsequently were involved in the terrorist attacks on 9/11. At least one chart, and possibly more, featured a photograph of Mohammed Atta and had him linked through associational activities to the blind Sheik and others

operating in or around Brooklyn, New York.

On at least three occasions those involved with Able Danger attempted to provide the FBI with information they had obtained. Each attempt failed, as it has been said, as a result of Army lawyers who either precluded the sharing or prevented the Able Danger personnel from attending the meeting. The stated concern was whether legal limitations restricted Able Danger from compiling information on U.S. persons. Their definition apparently included foreigners legally present on our soil. Based on my understanding of the law surrounding Posse Comitatus and the relevant DoD regulations, it would appear such an interpretation was unduly restrictive.

* * *

Eventually during the period December 2000 and March 2001, all records [obtained through the Able Danger program], both electronic and hard copy, were destroyed under orders of the Army. Additionally, we just recently learned that duplicate documentation that was maintained by Lt Col Shaffer at his civilian DIA office was apparently destroyed – for reasons unknown – by DIA in Spring 2004.

* * *

First, those associated with Able Danger who remember the Atta photograph continue to believe that it was, in fact, the same Mohammed Atta who acted as one of the 9/11 hijackers. They specifically recall the photograph, which is not the same photograph published by any U.S. Government agency or the 9/11 Commission, because of the daunting and literally evil expression on his face.

Second, as has been stated repeatedly, Lt Col Shaffer met with staff members of the 9/11 Commission, to include its Executive Director, while serving on active duty in Afghanistan in October 2003. It is Lt Col Shaffer's specific recollection that he informed those in attendance, which included several Defense Department personnel, that Able Danger had identified two of the three successful 9/11 cells to include Atta. That statement is disputed by the 9/11 Commission and may never be resolved. Nevertheless, it is clear the 9/11 Commission took Lt Col Shaffer's comments, whatever the substance, very seriously and immediately attempted to obtain supporting documentation, which we now know had already been destroyed. Whatever documents the 9/11 Commission were given by the Department of Defense obviously did not support Lt Col Shaffer's statements. That is an issue best directed not at the 9/11 Commission but at the Department of Defense.

* * *

Where it would appear the Commission failed to fulfill its responsibility was to simply go back to Lt Col Shaffer and query him for additional information, such as to identify other members of Able Danger who could have supported his statements. Had they done that in January 2004 they would have been led directly to numerous individuals, including James Smith, Navy Captain Scott Philpott (who on his own initiative in July 2004 approached the Commission) and others, who would have confirmed Lt Col Shaffer's information. Thus, where we are today could have been investigated more than 18 months ago.

Third, while we have never claimed that Lt Col Shaffer's security clearance problems were connected to his work on Able Danger, the coincidences of the timing should not be overlooked. An investigation was initiated and his security clearance suspended by the DIA shortly after it became known that he had provided information to the 9/11 Commission. The revocation of his security clearance conveniently took place two days ago just as he was preparing for his testimony before this Committee. As part of my law practice I specialize in security clearance cases. That is why I was retained by Lt Col Shaffer in the first place. Based on years of experience I can say categorically that the basis for the revocation was questionable at best. I am authorized and would be happy to discuss the specifics of Lt Col Shaffer's security clearance during questioning.

Fourth, unfortunately we are not aware of the continuing existence of any chart containing Mohammed Atta's name or photograph. The copies that would have been in the possession of the U.S. Army were apparently destroyed by March 2001. The copies within Lt Col Shaffer's files were destroyed by the DIA in approximately Spring 2004. The destruction of these files is an important element to this story and I encourage the Committee to investigate it further. It would appear, particularly given the Defense Department's outright refusal to allow those involved with Able Danger to testify today, that an obstructionist attitude exists. The question for this Committee is to investigate how far that position extends and why.

* * *

[A]ccording to the key members of the Able Danger team they identified four individuals who later became 9/11 hijackers. Those individuals were on a chart that had as many as five dozen names.[430]

The Able Danger Agents' attorney, Mark Zaid, in that prepared statement before Congress, said: "At no time did Able Danger identify Mohamed Atta as being physically present in the United States." However, that statement contradicted statements made by one of his clients to Fox News on August 17, 2005: "[T]he intelligence agent [Lt. Col. Anthony Shaffer] is standing by his claim that he told them that the lead hijacker in the Sept. 11, 2001, terror attacks had been identified in the summer of 2000 as an Al Qaeda operative living in the United States."[431]

The strange activity of the "art students" at about the time that the Able Danger information was being circulated throughout the U.S. military and intelligence agencies, suggests that Israel was aware of Able Danger and attempting to swing interest away from the idea of a terrorist attack and divert U.S. Government attention to a drug or security issue. The Israeli operatives seemed to be in a sense saying "look over here, here we are." The art student ruse, which came on the heels of the Able Danger intelligence, appeared to be designed as a distraction to point the government in the direction of a drug investigation to avoid actions that would cause a premature take-down of the terrorist patsies by the U.S. Government.

On May 7, 2002, Salon reported that all of the Israeli "art students" claimed to have come from either Bezalel Academy or the University of Jerusalem. However, a review of the Bezalel database by Salon showed that not a single one of the "art students" attended school there. Furthermore, there is no such thing as the University of Jerusalem.[432] The article notes the sheer sloppiness and brazenness of the "art student" spy operation appears to be a great mystery, since the Mossad is renowned as one of the most secretive and competent spy agencies in the world. A government source for the Salon article concluded that the Israeli "art students" were actually a smoke screen. They were intended to be caught and identified by DEA in order to allow other Mossad operatives to complete other missions.

For Israel to front their operatives so obviously as portraying art students indicates that Israel was conducting a limited hang-out for damage control. Why would Israel do a limited hang-out? Because, if the 9/11 operation had been taken down by the FBI as advocated by the Able Danger operatives, the rank and file FBI would have found out that the Mossad had its operatives portraying Arab terrorists. Even the arrest of the unwitting patsies would have led to the Mossad.

The indiscreet and conspicuous conduct by the Israeli "art students" suggests that Israel was concerned that their involvement in the terror cells was already known. Wayne Madsen's discovery from his Defense Intelligence Agency (DIA) source that Able Danger had established links between Israel intelligence agents and Mohammed Atta adds further support to that conclusion.[433]

It can be inferred that Israel used its influence within the U.S. Government to kill Able Danger and at the same time it used the "art student" ruse as a limited hang-out to dress up the operation and make it appear as a drug and security operation rather than a terrorism operation. Israel needed the patsies in the alleged terror cells set up in advance of the 9/11 attacks. They had to have the patsies in place to draw the blame, however, Able Danger was a threat to the patsy end of the 9/11 attacks.

Justin Raimondo of Antiwar.com noticed the close correlation of the shut down of Able Danger and the appearance of the Isreali "art students." Raimondo wondered if the reason that Able Danger was shut down was because the surveillance of Arab terrorist groups in the U.S. was subcontracted out to the Israelis.[434] Raimondo asks if Able Danger was shut down with the knowledge and complicity of the CIA in order to prevent that program from poaching on the Israelis' preserve.

His question assumes that Israel is subordinate to the United States and would not desire to see terrorist attacks on the United States. Those are not fair assumptions. The more logical conclusion is that Able Danger was shut down because it posed a threat to the terrorist attacks that took place on 9-11, and that those terrorist attacks were conducted by the Mossad with the treasonous complicity of high officials in the U.S. Government.

18 A Nest of Spies

How could Israel so effectively shut down Abel Danger and control government officials like so many puppets on strings? Because Israel runs a very effective espionage operation, which gives them unparalleled access and even control over the military and intelligence apparatus of the U.S. Government. High military and civilian government officials have been completely compromised.

A low level translator in the FBI translation section stumbled upon a thread that when she pulled it unraveled the cloth that concealed a nest of spies within the U.S. Government. Israel and its operatives in the U.S. Government have tried to mend the curtain of secrecy that was rent by the patriotic translator.

After the 9/11 attacks, Sibel Edmonds was recruited by the FBI to help translate important national security wire intercepts. Shortly after working in the FBI translation section, Sibel Edmonds was in turn recruited by Douglas and Melek Can Dickerson, who were husband and wife, to spy on behalf of Turkey.[435] Melek Can Dickerson was a fellow translator with Sibel in the FBI translation section. Sibel was offered financial security in return for her espionage against the United States.

The organization that the translators mentioned as the funnel for funds to reward her for spying was the American Turkish Counsel.[436] Edmonds realized that the ATC was a front for criminal spy activity within the United States. Sibel Edmonds revealed the contact through her chain of command and was later retaliated against and ultimately fired by the FBI. She sued claiming that she was fired for revealing a security compromise.

The government responded to Edmonds's lawsuit not by contesting the accuracy of her claims but instead by having the Attorney General Ashcroft file court documents on behalf of the State Department and the Pentagon to have her case dismissed based upon the rarely asserted state secrets privilege. The Department of Justice stated that it was necessary to have the case dismissed to protect certain sensitive diplomatic relationships and certain foreign business relations of the United States. The Department of Justice has also obtained an order which not only silenced her, but also retroactively classified the statements she eventually made before the Senate Judiciary Committee and the 9/11 Commission. Interestingly, the State Department and the Pentagon, who made the request to have her gagged under the state secrets privilege, are the two government departments which Edmonds alleges are most compromised by the ATC.

There is a close connection between the ATC and the American Israel Public Affairs Committee (AIPAC), which is a powerful lobbying front for an Israeli espionage operation. There has been an historically cozy espionage relationship between Turkey and Israel, which has been nurtured by none other than Doug Feith, long-time Jewish lobby operative in Washington; he was the Defense Department's top policy officer and an architect of the U.S. led invasion of Iraq. Feith has long been suspected of being a conduit for passing classified information to Israel. In fact, when Feith was Defense undersecretary for policy under George W. Bush, Feith's subordinate at the Pentagon, Lawrence Franklin, was caught passing top secret documents to AIPAC, who in turn forwarded the documents to Israel.[437]

Feith was joined by Richard Perle, who was fired from Senator Henry Jackson's office in the 1970's after the National Security Agency (NSA) caught him passing highly classified national security documents to the Israeli Embassy. The powerful Israeli lobby protected Perle, and he was able to stick around Washington and ultimately became the Chairman of the Pentagon's Defense Policy Board under George W. Bush. Both Feith and Perle are dual U.S./Israeli citizens, and in 1989 they founded International Advisors, Inc. to increase defense technology transfers to Turkey. Mark Hackard explains:

> Throughout the 1990s and up to the present day the Israel lobby has provided groups like the American Turkish Council expertise in managing the cash flows that power K Street and Capitol Hill, as well as access to its networks in government and the defense industry. This assistance has ranged from the relatively overt business of influencing legislation (such as killing Armenian genocide bills) to joint intelligence collection of advanced U.S. weapons technologies. Needless to say, Israeli and Turkish espionage gets little play in the media. The success of both lobbies' political operations has led to a growing convergence of interests with lawmakers and the foreign policy establishment, so spy scandals are quickly swept under the rug.
>
> Besides Perle and Feith, other prominent partisans for Israel have been instrumental in securing U.S. support for Turkey. These include Paul Wolfowitz, the late Congressman Tom Lantos, and former ambassadors to Ankara Mort Abramowitz and Marc Grossman. According to the former FBI translator-turned-whistleblower Sybil Edmonds, many of these figures were also under investigation for their close contacts with Israel's Mossad and MIT, the Turkish intelligence service.

Even when examining the public side of influence campaigns, the intimate links between Israeli and Turkish lobbying organizations in the U.S. are immediately apparent. The Sunlight Foundation's 2008 record of Turkish embassy contacts is largely a story of meetings and communications with AIPAC, JINSA, the ADL, the American Jewish Council and similar parties.[438]

Gordon Duff concluded: "We know that a vast spy ring operates in Washington and that Israel is the center of it. We also know that Israel, Turkey, India, Pakistan, China and Russia trade American secrets back and forth like baseball cards. We know that AIPAC is deeply involved in this spying."[439] Philip Giraldi, a former CIA Officer who is presently a partner in Cannistraro Associates, an international security consultancy, reveals that Edmonds was able to confirm the close espionage relationship between ATC and AIPAC:

> The ATC, founded in 1994 and modeled on the American Israel Public Affairs Committee, was intended to promote Turkish interests in Congress and in other public forums. Edmonds refers to ATC and AIPAC as "sister organizations." The group's founders include a number of prominent Americans involved in the Israel-Turkey relationship, notably Henry Kissinger, Brent Scowcroft, Richard Perle, Douglas Feith, and former congressman Stephen Solarz. Perle and Feith had earlier been registered lobbyists for Turkey through Feith's company, International Advisors Inc. The FBI was interested in ATC because it suspected that the group derived at least some of its income from drug trafficking, Turkey being the source of 90 percent of the heroin that reaches Europe, and because of reports that it had given congressmen illegal contributions or bribes. Moreover, as Edmonds told the Times, the Turks have "often acted as a conduit for the Inter-Services Intelligence, Pakistan's spy agency, because they were less likely to attract attention."[440]

Giraldi explains that while a low-level contractor might seem poorly positioned to expose major breaches of national security, the FBI translators' pool was so riddled with corruption and nepotism that these secrets were kept from surfacing until Edmonds arrived.

> Edmonds's claims that the section was infiltrated by translators who should never have received security clearances and who were deliberately failing to translate incriminating material are supported by the Justice Department inspector general investigation and by an FBI internal investigation, which concluded that she had been fired after making "valid complaints." One translator, Melek Can Dickerson, who had worked for three Turkish front organizations under investigation—she failed to reveal this when applying for

employment—allegedly stamped many documents of interest "not pertinent," removed classified documents from FBI premises, and forged signatures on classified documents relating to 9/11 detainees. An Urdu translator was the daughter of a Pakistani Embassy employee who worked for Gen. Mahmoud Ahmad, the head of the Pakistani intelligence service who is accused of authorizing a $100,000 wire transfer to Mohammed Atta's Dubai bank account immediately before 9/11. The Justice Department IG report confirmed Edmonds's charge that translators' section managers issued a go-slow order shortly after the terrorist attacks to create an artificial backlog that would justify an increase in budget and manpower. Those managers are reportedly still in place. Some have been promoted.[441]

One of many allegations made by Edmonds is that diplomat Marc Grossman (dual U.S./Israeli citizen) ambassador to Turkey from 1994-97 and Undersecretary of State for Political Affairs from 2001-05, was being investigated by the FBI and had his phone tapped by the Bureau in 2001 and 2002. Giraldi explains that Edmonds discovered that Grossman was receiving cash payments from the ATC and was "instrumental in seeding Turkish and Israeli Ph.D. students into major American research labs by godfathering visas and enabling security clearances. She says that she reviewed transcripts in which the moles in the U.S. military and academic community involved in nuclear technology reportedly carried out several 'transactions' involving the sale of nuclear material or information relating to nuclear programs every month, with Pakistan being a primary buyer."[442]

Giraldi states that "Edmonds's revelations have attracted corroboration in the form of anonymous letters apparently written by FBI employees. There have been frequent reports of FBI field agents being frustrated by the premature closure of cases dealing with foreign spying, particularly when those cases involve Israel, and the State Department has frequently intervened to shut down investigations based on 'sensitive foreign diplomatic relations.'"[443] A Department of Justice Inspector General investigation and an internal FBI review into Edmonds' claims about the translations section have confirmed most of her allegations.[444]

19 Israel is Our Enemy

Why would Israel want to spy on and even attack its strongest ally in the world? That question assumes facts which are not true. While we consider Israel an ally, Israel only pretends to be our ally. Israel actually considers the U.S. an enemy.

Rafi Eitan, who is a Mossad spymaster, an advisor to Fidel Castro, and an Israeli cabinet minister told one of Israel's largest daily newspapers, *Yediot Aharonot*, in June 1997: "I failed in the Pollard affair, just as I failed in other intelligence operations beyond enemy lines."[445] Pollard is a Jewish spy who was caught spying on the U.S. for Israel. Joseph DiGenova, the U.S. attorney who prosecuted the case, said he was surprised that Eitan would admit that Pollard's spying was sanctioned by Israel, since the official government position taken by Israel is that Pollard was a rogue spy operation. DiGenova added: "But this is basically all stuff that the evidence in the case shows."[446]

The most notable aspect of Eitan's statement is his characterization of the United States as Israel's enemy. The most DiGenova could bring himself to say on that matter was the fact that Eitan "does not refer to the U.S. as an ally is regrettable." The political power of Israel is so great, there are limits to what a public servant will say about Israel, no matter how authoritative is the evidence. No matter what Israel says in its official pronouncements, the actions of Israel in the Pollard case are the actions of an enemy. "When Jonathan Pollard stole our nuclear secrets (which your taxes paid to develop) and sent them to Israel, Israel did not hesitate to trade those secrets to the USSR in exchange for increased emigration quotas."[447]

Spymaster Rafi Eitan's statement that Israel is the enemy of the United States is proven by the conduct of Israel toward the United States. Jack Bernstein stated that the 23 October 1983 suicide bombing attack on the U.S. Marine barracks in Lebanon where 241 Marine personnel were killed was planned by the Israeli military intelligence (the Mossad). Bernstein stated that the purpose for the attack on the marine base was to turn the American people against the Arabs in order to draw the United States into the war to help Israel.[448]

That 1983 Marine barracks bombing was not the first time that Israel has used *agent provocateurs*. In 1954 the U.S. was beginning to favor Egypt over Israel regarding some regional issues. The Israeli government decided to use eleven Israeli agents in Egypt to blow up some American buildings and blame it on Egyptian nationalists. The hope of the Israelis was to rupture the relationship between Egypt and the United States. The plot, however, was discovered and exposed. It was referred to as the Lavon Affair, after the Defense Minister of Israel, Pinhas Lavon, who was allegedly the mastermind behind the plot. Lavon denied he was involved in the plot and blamed the Israeli military intelligence, the Mossad. It was never completely resolved which of them was responsible. What is clear was that it was an official operation of the Israeli government.

The Israelis learned their lesson from the Lavon affair. They now use unwitting Muslim Arabs to do their dirty work. Some have alleged that the 1993 truck bombing of the World Trade Center was arranged by an operative of the Israeli Mossad. How many other bombings and highjackings have been perpetrated by Muslims who were tools of the Mossad?

The September 11, 2001 destruction of the World Trade Center (WTC) is also the work of the Mossad and the CIA, framing unwitting Arab terrorists as patsies in order to get the U.S. to wipe out the Arab resistance to their Zionist goals. In the shadowy world of terrorism one must ask: *cui bono* (who benefits)? Israel and their partner Zionists are the clear winners from the WTC destruction and it fits their *modus operandi*.

Another clear example of the truth of Israeli spymaster Rafi Eitan's statement that Israel is the enemy of the United States is the infamous attack on the USS Liberty. That attack also demonstrates the power of the Jews in the U.S. government. During the Israeli Six Day War, the USS Liberty, an American intelligence gathering ship, was sailing in international waters. Apparently the USS Liberty had discovered something that the Israeli Government did not want revealed. Israeli aircraft and torpedo boats attacked the Liberty. The attack lasted for 75 minutes, during which U.S. Defense Secretary Robert McNamara and Lyndon Johnson ordered the Admiral on a nearby aircraft carrier to recall his jets and NOT to come to the USS Liberty's aid.

Some have speculated that the Israelis may have been concerned that the Liberty might detect the cold-blooded murder of 150 Egyptian POWs by the Israelis. Others have suggested that the intent of the attack was to sink the vessel and kill the entire crew and then blame the massacre on the Egyptians; thus, the Americans would enter the conflict on the side of the Israelis. That theory is supported by the nature of the attack. Israeli aircraft flew approximately 13 close up reconnaissance sorties on a day with clear skies over the six hours between 6:00 a.m. and 12:00 p.m. Then at approximately 2:00 p.m. unmarked aircraft came in from all directions at once in a massive air attack that included machine gun fire, rocket attacks, and even the dropping of napalm bombs on the ship.

The aircraft had no identifying markings, which was in violation of the Geneva Convention. Because the aircraft were unmarked, the sailors on the USS Liberty did not know at the time of the attack who were the attacking forces. The objective of the first wave of attacks was to knock out the communications capability of the ship. The attackers succeeded, but the sailors on the Liberty were able to rig a communications antenna and transmit an S.O.S., which was received by the Sixth Fleet. However, MacNamara and Johnson treasonously recalled the American jets sent to defend the Liberty.

The initial air attack was followed by a torpedo attack by three torpedo boats, which fired six torpedoes at the Liberty, with one hit. The torpedo hit produced a huge gaping hole on the side of the ship, but miraculously it did not sink. The life rafts were launched, but they were immediately shot up by machine gun fire from the jets. It was clear to those on board the Liberty that the intent was to sink the ship and leave no survivors. An Israeli helicopter gun ship made an appearance and waited nearby expecting the Liberty to sink. The inferred mission of the gun ship was to machine gun any life boats and anyone who was floating in the water to ensure that there would be no survivors.

When the Liberty did not sink as expected, the helicopter flew off. If the Israelis had succeeded in their mission and there had been no survivors, the Israelis and the Zionists in the U.S. Government could lay the blame for the attack on Egypt and thus the U.S. would have been drawn into the war on the side of Israel. The attack on the USS Liberty could be just another case in the long history of Israel acting as *agent provocateur*.

David Lewis of Lemington, Vermont, was a sailor on the Liberty when it was attacked. In an interview, Lewis said Israel had to know it was targeting an American ship. He said a U.S. flag was flying that day and Israel shot it full of holes. He said that the sailors on the ship quickly hoisted another American flag, which was a much bigger one, to show Israel it was a U.S. vessel. "No trained individual could be that inept," said Lewis of the Israeli forces.[449]

It is not just the subjective opinion of one sailor that the attack was deliberate, it is also the considered conclusion reached by the lead investigators who interviewed the other witnesses and examined the evidence. Jews, however, had such complete control over the reigns of the U.S. government that they controlled the outcome of the military investigation into the attack on the USS Liberty. On October 22, 2003, Ward Boston, a retired captain and a former Navy lawyer who was the senior legal counsel in the military investigation of the June 8, 1967 Israeli attack on the USS Liberty released a sworn affidavit at a Capitol Hill news conference. In the affidavit Boston stated that former President Lyndon Johnson and defense secretary, Robert McNamara, ordered those leading the investigation into the Israeli attack on the USS Liberty to "conclude that the attack was a case of 'mistaken identity' despite overwhelming evidence to the contrary."[450] Boston said in the sworn statement that he stayed silent for years because he's a military man, and "when orders come, I follow them."[451]

He said he felt compelled to "share the truth" following the publication of a recent book, The Liberty Incident, by Jay Cristol, which concluded the attack was unintentional.[452] Cristol is a retired Navy pilot and member of the judge advocate's office. Boston further stated in his affidavit: "The evidence was clear. Both Admiral (Isaac) Kidd and I believed with certainty that this attack, which killed 34 America sailors and injured 172 others, was a deliberate effort to sink an American ship and murder its entire crew. I am certain that the Israeli pilots that undertook the attack as well as their superiors who had ordered the attack, were aware the ship was American."[453] His affidavit continued: "I am outraged at the efforts of apologists for Israel in this country to claim this attack was a case of 'mistaken identity,'" he wrote. In particular, the recent publication of Jay Cristol's book, the 'Liberty Incident,' twists the facts and misrepresents the views of those of us who investigated the attack. It is Cristol's insidious attempt to whitewash the facts that has pushed me to speak out."

Boston said "I saw the flag, which visibly identified the ship as American, riddled with bullet holes, and heard testimony that made it clear the Israelis intended there be no survivors."[454] Admiral Kidd and Boston traveled to Malta to conduct the inquiry into the attack. The USS Liberty had been taken to Malta for repairs and care of the wounded. Though both Kidd and Boston agreed the attack was intentional, Kidd prepared a report that went with the Israeli version of events. "I know from personal conversations I had with Admiral Kidd that President Lyndon Johnson and Secretary of Defense (Robert) McNamara ordered him to conclude the attack was a case of 'mistaken identity,'" Boston's affidavit said.[455]

There is additional clear and convincing evidence that proves beyond any doubt that the Israeli attack was intentional. Communications between the attacking Israeli jets and their headquarters were intercepted by U.S. Military electronic surveillance planes as the aircraft approached the USS Liberty. The Israeli pilots were clearly ordered by their controllers to find and quickly sink "the American ship" (the USS Liberty). Those intercepted communications were almost simultaneously translated and broadcast from a U.S. Air Force C130 surveillance plane flying near the scene to an intelligence site at Crete.

The communications were then immediately sent to Washington and to other stations as "Critical Intelligence" (known as CRITICs). CRITICs are sent via the fastest and most secure means available. These reports routinely arrived in the White House, State Department, and Pentagon within ten minutes or less of their interception. Israel was caught in the act and their treachery was known to the highest levels of the US government, before the attack was even completed.[456]

At the time Johnson talked to Admiral Geis nobody on the Liberty nor the Sixth Fleet knew who the attackers were, because the attacking Israeli jets were unmarked. The receipt of the CRITIC reports by Johnson (and the possibility of direct communications by him with Israel) would explain how President Johnson knew that the attack on the Liberty was an attack by an ally (Israel) when he ordered Admiral Geis not to defend the Liberty.

Former U.S. Air Force Intelligence Analyst Stephen Forslund recalls seeing the communication intercepts of the Israeli attack on the Liberty as follows:

> Much discussion has gone on about what the NSA archives hold
> about the Liberty attack. The latest I read stated that the only and

final "tapes" that the NSA has released show that helicopters sent by Israel to the site of the attack on the Liberty, after the attack, were unaware of her nationality. Much importance is put on this issue by different factions in this debate. Parties state that these are the only tapes of intercepts that exist. That may very well be true, now. Nothing I can say will change anyone's mind but I have to state, for my own peace of mind, what I witnessed as an all source intelligence analyst for the U.S. Air Force during the 6 day war.

There were other intercepts, and I and many others like me, read transcripts of the air-to-air and air-to-ground communications of the fighters who attacked the USS Liberty. We read these in real time during the day the attack occurred. These intercepts were preceded by many others we read that week that started with the opening attack by Israel in the war and included intercepts of messages between the USA and Israel in which our government stated their knowledge of the Israeli's pre-emptive attack that began the war and warned Israel to cease their activities.

On the day of the attack on the Liberty, I read yellow teletype sheets that spewed from the machines in front of me all day. We obtained our input from a variety of sources including the NSA. The teletypes were raw translations of intercepts of Israeli air-to-air and air-to-ground communications between jet aircraft and their ground controller. I read page after page of these transcripts that day as it went on and on. The transcripts made specific reference to the efforts to direct the jets to the target which was identified as American numerous times by the ground controller. Upon arrival, the aircraft specifically identified the target and mentioned the American flag she was flying. There were frequent operational transmissions from the pilots to the ground base describing the strafing runs. The ground control began asking about the status of the target and whether it was sinking. They stressed that the target must be sunk and leave no trace. The pilots stated they had made several runs and the target was still floating. The ground control station re-iterated that it was urgent that the target be sunk, leaving no trace. There was a detectable level of frustration evident in the transmissions over the fact that the aircraft were unable to accomplish the mission quickly and totally.

The aircraft eventually broke off and we received no further transcripts of the event. I have since learned in later descriptions of the attack that torpedo boats attacked the Liberty also. I saw neither intercepts nor analyses that addressed that attack. An hour or two

later I was discussing the event with a team member and he stated
they had received, during the time frame of the attack, an intercept
of a US State Department message to Israel stating that the United
States had full evidence of what had occurred in the attack on the
Liberty and strongly warning Israel to cease activities immediately.

Imagine my surprise when, upon going home that night, I was
watching the evening news and a short piece that gave vague
reference to a mistaken attack by Israel upon an American ship off
Sinai came on. The next day there was a small article buried in the
A section of the paper stating that there had been an accidental
attack on the USS Liberty and that the governments involved were
in discussions. I saw little mention after that in the popular press
and, of course, said nothing for the next 36 years.

I read these discussions debating whether Israel intentionally
attacked the USS Liberty and what their motivation would have
been for a deliberate attack. I can't debate their motivation. But, I
will carry the memory of those transcripts with me until I die. We
all lost our virginity that day.[457]

The statement of Intelligence Analyst Forslund is supported by James Ronald Gotcher, III, who was a Sergeant in the United States Air Force, assigned to the 6924th Security Squadron, Da Nang, in the Republic of Vietnam, when on June 8, 1967, CRITIC message that the USS Liberty was under attack by Israel. In Gotcher's September 2, 2003, sworn affidavit, quoted in part below, he states:

I, James Ronald Gotcher, do declare under penalty of perjury that
the following statement is true and complete, and based entirely
upon my personal knowledge gained through direct observation,
unless specifically stated otherwise:

* * *

7. It was clear from the explicit statements made by both the
aircraft crews and the controllers that the aircraft were flying a
planned mission to find and sink USS Liberty.
8. My understanding of what I read led me to conclude that the
Israeli pilots were making every effort possible to sink USS Liberty
and were very frustrated by their inability to do so.
9. Approximately ten days to two weeks later, we received an
internal NSA report, summarizing the Agency's findings. The
report stated, in no uncertain terms, that the attack was planned in
advance and deliberately executed. The mission was to sink USS
Liberty.
10. A few days after the report arrived, another message came

through directing the document control officer to gather and destroy all copies of both the rough and final intercept translations, as well as the subsequently issued report.

11. After the destruction of those documents, I saw nothing further on this subject.

12. I have read the translated transcripts, released by the Israeli government, which purport to be actual transcripts of the air to ground communications between the controllers and the attacking aircraft. I know this document to be a fabrication because I have read the actual intercepts and they were nothing like this. It is not possible that the differences could be due to different translations being used.

13. If called upon to testify, I am competent to testify to all of the foregoing on the basis of direct observation and personal knowledge.[458]

To add to the clear and convincing evidence that the attack on the Liberty by Israel was deliberate, we have former Israeli military personnel who were there on the scene and have since revealed the truth. James M. Ennes Jr, in his book *Assault on the Liberty*, reports the following:

> Fifteen years after the attack, an Israeli pilot approached *Liberty* survivors and then held extensive interviews with former Congressman Paul N. (Pete) McCloskey about his role. According to this senior Israeli lead pilot, he recognized the *Liberty* as American immediately, so informed his headquarters, and was told to ignore the American flag and continue his attack. He refused to do so and returned to base, where he was arrested.
>
> Later, a dual-citizen Israeli major told survivors that he was in an Israeli war room where he heard that pilot's radio report. The attacking pilots and everyone in the Israeli war room knew that they were attacking an American ship, the major said. He recanted the statement only after he received threatening phone calls from Israel.[459]

Lieutenant Commander David E. Lewis, the officer in charge of Liberty's Research Department, had a meeting with Rear Admiral Lawrence R. Geis shortly after the Liberty attack. Admiral Geis was the officer in charge of the embarked aircraft in both the USS America and USS Saratoga. Commander Lewis stated that Admiral Geis told him the following:

> Admiral Geis said that he wanted somebody to know that we weren't forgotten. . . . attempts HAD been made to come to our assistance. He said that he had launched a flight of aircraft to come to our assistance, and he had then called Washington. Secretary

McNamara came on the line and ordered the recall of the aircraft, which he did. Concurrently, he said that since he suspected that they were afraid that there might have been nuclear weapons on board he reconfigured another flight of aircraft. . . . strictly conventional weaponry. . . . and re-launched it. After the second launch, he again called Washington to let them know what was going on. Again, Secretary McNamara ordered the aircraft recalled. Not understanding why, he requested confirmation of the order, and the next higher in command came on to confirm that. . . . President Johnson. . . . with the instructions that the aircraft were to be returned, that he would not have his allies embarrassed, he didn't care who was killed or what was done to the ship. . . . words to that effect. With that, Admiral Geis swore me to secrecy for his lifetime. I had been silent up until I found out from Admiral Moorer that Admiral Geis had passed away.[460]

Thirty-four Americans were killed and 172 wounded in the attack. Israel claimed it was a case of mistaken identity. However, U.S. intelligence revealed that it was a deliberate attack ordered by Israeli General Moshe Dyan. Former Secretary of State Dean Rusk and former Joint Chief of Staff Chairman, Admiral Thomas Moorer have both stated that the Israeli attack was deliberate.[461] That incident gives some idea of the power and control that the Jews have in the U.S. government. They can control the very apex of the executive branch of government to order the military to stand by while navy sailors are being massacred by the Israeli military.

Most do not know that Johnson was a crypto-Jew. His policies and conduct toward Israel revealed him as an ardent Zionist. As Commander in Chief of the Army and the Navy, he treasonously prevented the defense of the USS Liberty while it was under attack by Israeli forces and then ordered that the official report of the incident conceal the deliberate nature of the attack. Presumably, Johnson had received the CRITIC communication and therefore knew that the Israelis intended to sink the ship, and he was willing to allow that to happen.

One overlooked aspect of the attack on the Liberty is that the Israelis would never have attacked the Liberty unless they could be certain that the Liberty would not be defended by the Sixth Fleet. The only reasonable conclusion is that there must have been coordination between the highest levels of the U.S. government and the Israeli government prior to and during the attack, whereby the Israelis were assured that the Liberty would not be defended. That is treason!

National disloyalty is the hallmark of a Zionist Jew. The disloyalty shown by President Lyndon Johnson towards his country during the attack on the U.S.S. Liberty is illustrative of that fact. As a Zionist, Johnson's first loyalty was to Israel. Although he was President of the United States, and as such Commander in Chief of the Army and Navy, he sided with Israel when Israel attacked the United States. Investigative writer, Salvador Astucia, in his book, *Opium Lords*, explains Lyndon Johnson's Jewish heritage:

According to Jewish law, if a person's mother is Jewish, then that person is also Jewish, regardless of the father's ethnicity or religion. The facts indicate that both of Lyndon Johnson's great-grandparents, on the maternal side, were Jewish. These were the grandparents of Lyndon's mother, Rebekah Baines. Their names were John S. Huffman and Mary Elizabeth Perrin. John Huffman's mother was Suzanne Ament, a common Jewish name. Perrin is also a common Jewish name. Huffman and Perrin had a daughter, Ruth Ament Huffman, who married Joseph Baines and together they had a daughter, Rebekah Baines, Lyndon Johnson's mother. The line of Jewish mothers can be traced back three generations in Lyndon Johnson's family tree. There is little doubt that he was Jewish.[462]

Lyndon Johnson's Jewish background explains his loyalty to Israel and also explains, in part, his involvement in the assassination of President Kennedy. One of Johnson's lawyers, Barr McClellan, who is also father of White House press secretary Scott McClellan and Food and Drug Administration Commissioner Mark McClellan, revealed with corroborative proof that Johnson was instrumental in the planning and cover-up of the Kennedy assassination. McClellan revealed that Edward A. Clark, the powerful head of Johnson's private and business legal team and a former ambassador to Australia, led the plan and cover-up for the Kennedy assassination.

Johnson, however, would not make a move without the authorization and backing of his Zionist handlers. Israel's involvement in the assassination of President Kennedy is one of the deepest-darkest secrets of our time. The Warren Commission cobbled together by Johnson made its judgment that Oswald was a lone assassin without even examining the autopsy photographs or x-rays.[463] The pathologist in charge of the autopsy at Bethesda Naval Hospital burned his notes after he heard that Oswald was killed by Jack Ruby.[464]

It was no coincidence that the Kennedy assassination took place in Dallas, a city over which Johnson had almost complete political control. The evidence reveal the complicity of the Dallas Sheriff's Department, the Dallas Police Department, the FBI, and the Secret Service in the assassination of President Kennedy. Other facts reveal the involvement of the CIA and the U.S. Military. The major media, controlled by Jews, have also been willing accomplices in the treasonous coverup of the John Kennedy assassination. NBC even went so far as to attempt to bribe a witness involved in New Orleans District Attorney Jim Garrison's prosecution of Clay Shaw.[465] NBC's involvement in the attempt to derail Jim Garrison's investigation reached to the very top of NBC. The president of NBC had discussions with the president of Equitable Insurance Company, the employer of the witness in question, Perry Russo. NBC tried to persuade Russo to go on national television and falsely say "I am sorry for what I said because I lied, some of what I said was true but I was doctored by the District Attorney's staff into testifying like I did."[466] Perry stated that James Phelan of the Saturday Evening Post told him that he was working hand-in-hand with NBC reporter Walter Sheridan and that they were going to destroy Jim Garrison and his probe into the Kennedy assassination.[467]

Jim Garrison was approached by John J. King, who at the time used the alias John Miller.[468] King (Miller) offered Garrison a federal judgeship if he would drop the investigation into Clay Shaw's involvement in the Kennedy assassination.[469] King made clear to Garrison that he was in a position to guarantee his immediate appointment to the federal bench.[470] Apparently, King was speaking for others, because in order to become a federal judge he must be appointed by the President of the United States with the advice and consent of the Senate. Some very powerful interests were behind King's offer.

Subsequent investigation revealed that King was a wealthy oilman from Denver, Colorado who was involved in lucrative Israeli oil projects.[471] Interestingly, one of King's business partners was Bernie Cornfield (alternatively spelled by some sources as: Cornfeld), who was the protegee and front man for Rabbi Tibor Rosenbaum.[472] Rosenbaum was the founder of the Bank De Credit International and the central financier behind Permindex.[473] Permindex was a joint CIA - Mossad front which played a prominent role in facilitating the Kennedy assassination. Clay Shaw was one of the Permindex directors.[474]

The fact that King could guarantee a federal judgeship to Jim Garrison in return for dumping his investigation of Clay Shaw gives one some idea of the powerful interests that were behind the cover-up of the Kennedy assassination. A November 1963 FBI teletype identified John J. King as a wealthy Dallas businessman who was a close friend to Jack Ruby.[475] Jack Ruby (whose real name was Jacob L. Rubenstein) was a Jewish gangster with connections to the CIA, the FBI, the Israeli Mossad, and the Dallas Police Department. His connections inside the Dallas Police Department allowed him access to kill Lee Harvey Oswald.

Ruby told his defense lawyer, William Kunstler: "I did this that they wouldn't implicate Jews."[476] Before Kunstler left Ruby after his last jail visit, Ruby handed him a note in which he reiterated that his motive was to "Protect American Jews from a pogrom that could occur because of anger over the assassination."[477] Ruby and his handlers knew that if Oswald were to be prosecuted for the assassination of President Kennedy, the evidence would not support his conviction but would rather have pointed directly to Israel.

It seems that Ruby was a Sayan who was pressed into service to eliminate a loose end (Oswald). Sayanim (plural for Sayan) are Jews living outside of Israel who are fanatically loyal to the Jewish state and have agreed to assist Israel. Their loyalty to Israel supplants any loyalty they have to the country in which they reside. Often, Sayanim are recruited by relatives living in Israel and are under the control of professional spy masters called "katsas." They do whatever is asked of them to assist Israel and the Mossad.

A fair view of the facts reveals that the assassination of President Kennedy was a *coup d'etat*. How were all these separate state and federal agencies and the news media tied together into one giant conspiracy? Michael Collins Piper in his book, *Final Judgment*, presents a compelling case that Zionists in general, and the Israeli Mossad in particular, played a primary role in the assassination of President John F. Kennedy, and the subsequent coverup. Piper's book is chock-full of sources and evidence, with over 1,000 endnotes, and 10 appendices. Other books have revealed the separate involvement of Lyndon Johnson, the Dallas Police Department, the CIA, the FBI, anti-Castro Cubans, French intelligence agencies, the U.S. Secret Service, and organized crime in the assassination of President Kennedy. Mr. Piper methodically explains how all of these persons and organizations were tied together in a conspiracy that at its core was set in motion by the Israeli Mossad.

The motives for the Kennedy assassination are manifold, but one of the key reasons was Kennedy's intent to put an end to the Israeli plans for developing their own nuclear weapons. The Jerusalem Post reported on July 25, 2004 that the jailed nuclear whistle blower, Mordechai Vanunu, revealed that the Israeli government was behind the assassination of President Kennedy.

> Comments by freed nuclear spy Mordechai Vanunu that Israel was behind the assassination of US President John F. Kennedy failed to bring smiles to government officials Sunday. Vanunu said that according to "near-certain indications," Kennedy was assassinated due to "pressure he exerted on then head of government, David Ben-Gurion, to shed light on Dimona's nuclear reactor."[478]

In addition, John Kennedy realized after the Bay of Pigs fiasco that he was not in control of the executive branch of government. He came to understand that Zionists had infiltrated the very warp and woof of government. Beginning with the CIA, Kennedy began to make dramatic changes to take the reigns of government back from the hidden treasonous cabal that was steering the United States toward destruction. Kennedy had even implemented a plan to wrestle control of U.S. currency from the Federal Reserve by issuing U.S. notes. Kennedy also planned on completely pulling all advisors out of Vietnam. Kennedy had the audacity to actually take control of government and act in the best interests of the citizens who elected him. The shadow government simply would not stand for a President who would not be their puppet and act in their interests. In their eyes there was no alternative; Kennedy had to go. Immediately upon the assassination of President Kennedy there was a 180-degree reversal of many of U.S. policies instituted by Kennedy, particularly the U.S. policy toward Israel.

One of the key players in the conspiracy to assassinate Kennedy was Meyer Lansky, the Zionist Jewish gangster, who Piper reveals was the de facto head of organized crime in the United States. Piper explains how Lansky had deep and continuing working relationships with both the CIA and the Israeli Mossad. Although Piper's book deals with the assassination of President Kennedy, which happened over 40 years ago, the lessons he imparts are important and topical today for all American citizens who love their liberty. Piper's book is an autopsy which dissects the putrid body of a world conspiracy that is so pervasive, so intrusive, so powerful, it can assassinate the President of the most powerful country in the world and then conceal its involvement in that crime by controlling the mass media and even the very organs of that government. Piper takes off the blindfold and pins the tail on the donkey. His book is aptly titled; it is truly the Final Judgment in the assassination of our beloved President, John F. Kennedy, who valiantly and selflessly tried to wrestle the control of the U.S. government from a Zionist cabal. After assassinating President Kennedy that cabal resumed control of the government, which they have maintained to this day.

The best evidence of the Zionist control over our government is the 1964 Warren Commission and its fraudulent report pinning the Kennedy assassination on the patsy, Lee Harvey Oswald. The next best evidence is the U.S. House Committee on Assassinations report. The committee's 1979 report determined that there was probably a conspiracy to assassinate President Kennedy. One would think that such a finding would result in a monumental investigation to find the culprits. However, Congress apparently had no interest in finding out who was behind the assassination. The committee ran out of money and Congress was not going to continue funding a committee that might actually find the culprits. Instead, the committee turned over its findings to the U.S. Department of Justice for further investigation. In its report the committee criticized the investigation into the Kennedy assassination conducted by the FBI, but that did not stop them from turning the investigation back over to the Department of Justice, of which the FBI is part.

Once the investigation was referred to it, the Department of Justice also seemed not to have any curiosity in finding out who was really behind the assassination of President Kennedy. To this day, no resources of any significance have been devoted to any legitimate investigation of the Kennedy assassination by any organ of the Department of Justice. In fact, there is an abundance of documented proof that long prior to the referral to the Department of Justice by the U.S. House Committee on Assassinations, the FBI has been engaged in a concerted effort to conceal evidence and obstruct any investigation into the Kennedy assassination. The fact that the U.S. Congress and the U.S. Department of Justice have not shown any interest in finding out who assassinated the President of the United States and in actuality have engaged in concealing evidence and obstructing the investigation suggests that the culprits that were behind the assassination also control the very powers of government.

President Kennedy realized full well the nature and scope of the Zionist conspiracy lined up against him and the American people. He is reported to have stated: "The high office of President has been used to foment a plot to destroy the Americans' freedom, and before I leave office I must inform the citizen of his plight." His aim to do something about the conspiracy was the reason he was targeted for assassination. In a speech given at the Waldorf-Astoria Hotel New York City, April 27, 1961 Kennedy explained the nature and scope of the conspiracy:

> For we are opposed around the world by a monolithic and ruthless conspiracy that relies primarily on covert means for expanding its sphere of influence--on infiltration instead of invasion, on subversion instead of elections, on intimidation instead of free choice, on guerrillas by night instead of armies by day. It is a system which has conscripted vast human and material resources into the building of a tightly knit, highly efficient machine that combines military, diplomatic, intelligence, economic, scientific and political operations. Its preparations are concealed, not published. Its mistakes are buried, not headlined. Its dissenters are

silenced, not praised. No expenditure is questioned, no rumor is printed, no secret is revealed. It conducts the Cold War, in short, with a war-time discipline no democracy would ever hope or wish to match.[479]

President Lincoln also knew full well of the treachery of the money power. He was viewed as a formidable obstacle to their plans and so was assassinated. Lincoln stated:

The money powers prey upon the nation in times of peace and conspire against it in times of adversity. It is more despotic than a monarchy, more insolent than autocracy, and more selfish than bureaucracy. It denounces as public enemies all who question its methods or throw light upon its crimes. I have two great enemies, the Southern Army in front of me and the bankers in the rear. Of the two, the one at my rear is my greatest foe.

Another example of both the control of the Jews over those in government and the international (translation: anti-national) nature of Jews is the Marc Rich case. In the early 1980's billionaire Marc Rich and his partner were under investigation for violations of U.S. federal law as a result of a criminal scheme he conducted through his commodities trading firm Marc Rich & Co., A.G. When in June 1983 Rich and his cohorts realized that they were going to be indicted, they fled from the United States.[480] In September 1983, a federal grand jury issued a 51-count indictment against Marc Rich, his partner Pincus Green, and others for wire fraud, mail fraud, racketeering, racketeering conspiracy, tax evasion, and trading with the enemy. He traded with Iran while American hostages were being held captive during the Iran hostage crisis. Later, in March 1984, the Government filed a 65-count superseding indictment.

Both Rich and Green demonstrated their contempt for the United States by forfeiting their U.S. citizenship and acquired Israeli citizenship. Rich also became a citizen of Spain. The Spanish and Israeli governments refused to extradite Rich or Green to the United States to face prosecution. Because Rich's attorneys could not convince the U.S. Attorney in New York to dismiss the charges, they decided to obtain a pardon from the President of the United States, Bill Clinton. Rich's wife, Denise Rich, donated $450,000 to the Bill Clinton library fund and $1.1 million to Democratic causes, including Hillary Rodham Clinton's Senate campaign.[481] Next, Rich hired former Clinton White House Counsel Jack Quinn to help with the negotiations.[482] Perhaps most telling regarding the Jewish element in the pardons was the enlistment of then-Israeli Prime Minister Ehud Barak and former Israeli Prime Minister Shimon Peres, each of whom contacted President Clinton to lobby for Rich and Green to be pardoned.[483]

On January 20, 2001, Bill Clinton's last day as President of the United States, he granted a full and unconditional pardon to 140 people, including Marc Rich and Pincus Green. Rich and Green were pardoned in violation of the Rules Governing Petitions for Executive Clemency, which required that the pardon petition be submitted to the Department of Justice Pardon Attorney.[484] Further, the federal rules required an investigation of the petition.[485] Neither of those things was done. Perhaps most shocking is that Rich and Green were pardoned while still fugitives from justice. Prior to Clinton's pardon of Rich and Green, no President in the history of the United States had ever pardoned a fugitive from justice.

Clinton stated that he pardoned Rich partly "because I had received a request from the government of Israel."[486] Why would Israel be so interested in gaining a pardon for Rich? Because Rich was not only a Zionist Jew, he was also a Mossad asset.[487]

The efforts of Rich on behalf of Israel paint an interesting picture of that conduct of an *agent provocateur*. In January 2000, which was shortly before Clinton pardoned Rich, the Senate Judiciary Committee received documentary evidence that Rich played a crucial role in helping the Bank of Credit and Commercial International (BCCI) (a notorious bank involved in illegal drug money laundering) arrange for the world infamous terrorist Abu Nidal to receive hundreds of millions of dollars in illegal arms.[488] As revealed by respected investigative journalist Gordon Thomas for *American Free Press*: "A sworn affidavit by Ghassan Quassem, for 17 years a senior officer with BCCI, states: 'British weapons secretly destined for Abu Nidal were financed through BCCI offices and shipped under export documents that Marc Rich knew to be phony. My role at the bank was to handle the Nidal account. I later became a spy for the CIA and MI6.'"[489]

Why would Rich, who is a Zionist Jew, help a terrorist, who has been generally viewed as one of the most notorious anti-Israel terrorists in the world, obtain weapons presumably to use against Israel? The answer is that in order for Israel to justify its oppressive subjugation and expulsion of the Palestinian population in Israel, they need an excuse to act. If the Palestinians won't provide the terrorist attacks that would justify a martial response, the Israelis will create and fund a terrorist who will. Enter Abu Nidal. He is just one in a long line of past and future *agent provocateur* Frankenstein monsters created in the laboratories of the Israeli Mossad. And Marc Rich helped.

20 Silverstein and Friends

The managing leaseholder of the World Trade Center is Silverstein Properties, whose chief executive officer and owner is Larry Silverstein. Silverstein Properties took over the World Trade Center by agreeing to a 99-year lease on July 26, 2001. Where was Larry Silverstein on 9-11-2001? Since becoming the managing leaseholder in July 2001, Silverstein kept a regular schedule of having breakfast every morning at the World Trade Center. The WTC restaurant, Windows on the World, was located in the 107th floor of the North Tower. Silverstein would eat breakfast there and spend the next several hours meeting with his tenants. On 9-11-2001, however, he deviated from his regular schedule and did not eat breakfast at Windows on the World. In fact, he did not show up anywhere at the World Trade Center that morning. This is how he explained to the Wall Street Journal his absence from the WTC on 9-11-2001:

> His own life, he says, was spared "by a miracle, an absolute miracle." On the morning of 9/11 his wife insisted he make a dermatologist's appointment and skip a breakfast with tenants at the Windows on the World in the North Tower.[490]

Silverstein's deviation from his regular schedule was so unusual that even he calls it "a miracle." There were other "miracles" in the Silvertein family that morning. Not only did Larry Silverstein deviate from his regular schedule, but his son and daughter also happened to be missing from the World Trade Center on 9-11-2001.[491] Silverstein's son, Roger, and his daughter, Lisa, were working for him in temporary offices on the 88th floor of the WTC North Tower. However, both Roger and Lisa were running late that day and were not in the building when the 9/11 attacks happened. The Silversteins were either blessed by miracles on 9/11 or they knew not to come to work on 9-11-2001.[492]

According to Luke Rudkowski, Larry Silverstein and his daughter got a warning on the morning of 9-11-2001 not to come to work that day. Rudkowski explains: "We talked to their private security staff, we talked to people who were there with Larry on 9/11 - they said he got a phone call telling him not to show up to work and he called his daughter up and his daughter also never showed up to work."[493]

Silverstein is a Jew and an ardent Zionist, with close ties to Israel. It is no surprise then that his public relations firm is also the public relations firm for the state of Israel; their motives are the same. Sara Leibovich-Dar an Israeli reporter for the Jewish news service, Haaretz, verified the close ties that Silverstein has with high-level politicians in Israel.

> Shortly after the events of September 11, Prime Minister Ariel Sharon called Larry Silverstein, a Jewish real estate magnate in New York, the owner of the World Trade Center's 110-story Twin Towers and a close friend, to ask how he was. Since then they have spoken a few more times. Two former prime ministers - Benjamin Netanyahu, who this week called Silverstein a "friend," and Ehud Barak, whom Silverstein in the past offered a job as his representative in Israel - also called soon after the disaster. Yaakov Terner, the mayor of Be'er Sheva, sent a letter of condolence.
>
> Many Israeli politicians are acquainted in one degree or another with the 70-year-old Silverstein. For 10 years, he tried to bring about the establishment of a free-trade zone in the Negev, until the project fell apart. "This is a tragedy," Silverstein, deeply disappointed, said then.[494]

Silverstein's ties to the hierarchy of power in Israel run deep. Leibovich-Dar explains:

> The two [Silverstein and Netanyahu] have been on friendly terms since Netanyahu's stint as Israel's ambassador to the United Nations. For years they kept in close touch. Every Sunday afternoon, New York time, Netanyahu would call Silverstein. It made no difference what the subject was or where Netanyahu was, he would always call, Silverstein told an Israeli acquaintance.[495]

One of the most astounding revelations in the article is that within two days after the tragedy Silverstein mounted a campaign to rebuild the property. The rescue efforts were still under way and all Silverstein could think about was campaigning to rebuilt the towers. "From that moment [two days after 9-11], Silverstein launched a campaign to restore his property - a campaign that is generating public opposition and mounting criticism."[496]

While Silverstein was full steam ahead planning the rebuilding of the towers, former Israeli Prime Minister and good friend of Silverstein, Benjamin Netanyahu, was thinking of the benefits to Israel. The New York Times filed the following report regarding Netanyahu's response to the 9/11 attacks on September 12, 2001, the day after the attacks.

> Asked tonight what the attack meant for relations between the

United States and Israel, Benjamin Netanyahu, the former prime
minister, replied, "It's very good." Then he edited himself: "Well,
not very good, but it will generate immediate sympathy."[497]

In fact, it seems that Israel is the only country that has benefitted from the 9/11 attacks. That should be a clue as to who was behind the attacks. Over seven years after the 9/11 attacks former Israeli Prime Minister Netanyahu confirmed that Israel has benefitted from those attacks. The Israeli news service, Haaretz, reported:

The Israeli newspaper Ma'ariv on Wednesday reported that Likud
leader Benjamin Netanyahu told an audience at Bar Ilan University
that the September 11, 2001 terror attacks had been beneficial for
Israel.

"We are benefitting from one thing, and that is the attack on the
Twin Towers and Pentagon, and the American struggle in Iraq,"
Ma'ariv quoted the former prime minister as saying. He reportedly
added that these events "swung American public opinion in our
favor."[498]

Interestingly, it has been revealed that Netanyahu was in New York the day of the attacks on September 11, 2001.[499] Netanyahu stuck around and on September 20, 2001, gave a speech to the US House of Representatives' Government Reform Committee. During Netanyahu's harangue he named the states that he felt should be attacked economically, politically, and militarily in the war on terror: Iran, Iraq, Syria, Afghanistan, the Sudan, and Yasser Arafat's Palestinian Authority.[500]

Netanyahu pushed for a preemptive military attack, without waiting for any indication of an imminent threat from the country to be attacked. The philosophy of preemptive attack can only be described as moral degeneracy, and in a bygone era it was considered a war crime against humanity. In fact, it was one of the charges leveled against the Nazis at the Nuremberg trials after World War II. Since Netanyahu's speech, preemptive attack has become the official policy of the United States.

Netanyahu's rant had an ominous tone; he predicted dire consequences if immediate actions were not taken by the U.S. Government. He predicted that without immediate action that the United States would be the target of nuclear and biological attacks that could kill hundreds of thousands or even millions of citizens. The certainty with which he spoke was rather suspicious. It seems that all of the countries he mentioned as targets had one thing in common, they were all either threats to or opponents of Israel. Netanyahu clearly was there to give the orders to his subordinates in the U.S. Congress to commit our armed forces against the enemies of Israel. The Congress dutifully followed the orders and ultimately gave President George W. Bush an unconstitutional blank check to fight the war on terror. That forged check included the dictatorial authority to level preemptive attacks.

In addition to former Israeli Prime Minister Benjamin Netanyahu being in New York on 9-11-01, Christopher Bollyn found out that "Ehud Olmert, the right-wing Likud politician who is currently prime minister of Israel [and on 9-11-01 was the Mayor of Jerusalem], was in New York on September 10, 2001, the day before 9-11, meeting with supporters of the Israeli terrorist gang of the Irgun (Betar)."[501]

Olmert's presence in New York on 9-10-01 was inadvertently confirmed in a Jerusalem Post article on July 23, 2004 where it was reported that three years earlier Betur, a Jerusalem football team, was sold to a consortium of businessmen "following a meeting in New York with then-mayor Ehud Olmert on September 10, 2001."[502] When the significance of that revelation became known, that article disappeared from the Jerusalem Post.

Other than the slip up by the Jerusalem Post, Olmert's presence in New York on 9/11 was not reported in any media outlets and Olmert has done everything to conceal his presence in New York on the day before 9-11-2001. In fact, there was no mention of Olmert in the U.S. media until September 17, 2001, when the Associated Press reported that he telephoned Mayor Rudolph Giuliani 5 days after the attack.[503] Why did Olmert wait five days to call Mayor Giuliani, when Olmert was in New York on the day before the attacks? Why has Olmert concealed his presence in New York on the eve of the 9/11 attacks?

The rather suspicious secrecy about Olmert's presence in New York on the day before the attacks, suggests that he has something to hide. Christopher Bollyn makes an inescapable deduction: "My friends, the conspiracy is quite clear. The fascist mayor-cum-prime minister is at the center of the false-flag terror of 9-11. He does not reveal his presence because he was much more than a spectator – he was a participant in the 'false-flag' terrorism that changed America."[504]

There is evidence that Olmert was in New York on 9-10-01, and yet there is a blackout of that significant fact by major media outlets. The secrecy surrounding his presence in New York suggests that fact is just too much to let out; it exposes Israel and its role in the 9/11 attacks, and therefore that information must be kept from the masses. The evidence indicates that the 9/11 attacks were false flag attacks by Israel. Lo and behold, who do we find in New York on the days surrounding the false flag attack? Two Israeli Prime Ministers (one a past and the other a future prime minister).

The major media outlets will not investigate Olmert's presence in New York on 9-11-2001, because those outlets are controlled by Zionist interests. It is not hyperbole that the Jews control the major media outlets. John Whitley revealed in 2003 that "seven Jewish Americans run the vast majority of US television networks, the printed press, the Hollywood movie industry, the book publishing industry, and the recording industry."[505] He explained that "[m]ost of these industries are bundled into huge media conglomerates." He listed the Jewish men and stated that "[t]hose seven Jewish men collectively control ABC, NBC, CBS, the Turner Broadcasting System, CNN, MTV, Universal Studios, MCA Records, Geffen Records, DGC Records, GRP

Records, Rising Tide Records, Curb/Universal Records, and Interscope Records."[506]

Whitley's research concluded that "[m]ost of the larger independent newspapers are owned by Jewish interests as well. An example is media mogul Samuel I. 'Si' Newhouse, who owns two dozen daily newspapers from Staten Island to Oregon, plus the Sunday supplement Parade; the Conde Nast collection of magazines, including Vogue, The New Yorker, Vanity Fair, Allure, GQ, and Self; the publishing firms of Random House, Knopf, Crown, and Ballantine, among other imprints; and cable franchises with over one million subscribers."[507] Whitley's conclusions are as valid today as they were in 2003. Whitley explains why: "I could add that Michael Eisner could depart Disney tomorrow but the company will remain in the hands of Shamrock Holdings, whose principal office is now located in Israel."[508]

The major news outlets are extensions of the entertainment and special effects that flow from Hollywood. Who is in control of Hollywood (and indeed the media in general) becomes significant when we examine evidence of Israeli involvement in the 9/11 attacks. There is no question that Jews control Hollywood. Jewish writer Joel Stein wrote the following article in response to a recent poll that showed that only 22% of Americans believe that the Jews control the movie and television industries:

> I have never been so upset by a poll in my life. Only 22% of Americans now believe "the movie and television industries are pretty much run by Jews," down from nearly 50% in 1964. The Anti-Defamation League, which released the poll results last month, sees in these numbers a victory against stereotyping. Actually, it just shows how dumb America has gotten. **Jews totally run Hollywood.**
>
> How deeply Jewish is Hollywood? When the studio chiefs took out a full-page ad in the Los Angeles Times a few weeks ago to demand that the Screen Actors Guild settle its contract, the open letter was signed by: News Corp. President Peter Chernin (Jewish), Paramount Pictures Chairman Brad Grey (Jewish), Walt Disney Co. Chief Executive Robert Iger (Jewish), Sony Pictures Chairman Michael Lynton (surprise, Dutch Jew), Warner Bros. Chairman Barry Meyer (Jewish), CBS Corp. Chief Executive Leslie Moonves (so Jewish his great uncle was the first prime minister of Israel), MGM Chairman Harry Sloan (Jewish) and NBC Universal Chief Executive Jeff Zucker (mega-Jewish). If either of the Weinstein brothers had signed, this group would have not only the power to shut down all film production but to form a minyan with enough Fiji water on hand to fill a mikvah.
>
> The person they were yelling at in that ad was SAG President Alan Rosenberg (take a guess). The scathing rebuttal to the ad was

written by entertainment super-agent Ari Emanuel (Jew with Israeli parents) on the Huffington Post, which is owned by Arianna Huffington (not Jewish and has never worked in Hollywood.)

The Jews are so dominant, I had to scour the trades to come up with six Gentiles in high positions at entertainment companies. When I called them to talk about their incredible advancement, five of them refused to talk to me, apparently out of fear of insulting Jews. The sixth, AMC President Charlie Collier, turned out to be Jewish.

As a proud Jew, I want America to know about our accomplishment. Yes, we control Hollywood.[509]

Vice President of the United States Spiro Agnew, as with all politicians in Washington, was well aware of the power and control the Jews have over the national media. He was different from most politicians, however; he tried to warn the American people about the Jewish threat to their freedom.

President of the United States Richard Nixon was planning on taking action against the treasonous activities of some powerful Jews and their fellow travelers; Nixon therefore was targeted for removal from office by powerful Jews. The Jews, however, did not want Agnew to assume the presidency, because they viewed him as more of a threat than Nixon.

They had to remove Agnew from office before taking on Nixon. They dug around and found evidence of tax evasion for something Agnew had done six years earlier. They dusted off the evidence, brought tax evasion charges against Agnew, which in turn forced Agnew to resign from office. With Agnew out of the way, they then set their sights on Nixon, and the rest is history. Below is a quote from a 1976 Newsweek article, where Agnew stridently discusses the Jewish control of the major media outlets:

> The people who own and manage national impact media are Jewish and, with other influential Jews, helped create a disastrous U.S. Mideast policy. All you have to do is check the real policy makers and owners and you find a much higher concentration of Jewish people than you're going to find in the population.
>
> By national impact media I am referring to the major news wire services, pollsters, Time and Newsweek Magazines, the New York Times, Washington Post, and the International Herald Tribune. For example, CBS' Mr. (William) Paley's Jewish. Mr. Julian Goodman, who runs NBC, and there's a Leonard Goldenson at ABC. Mrs. Katherine Graham owns the Washington Post and Mr. Sulzberger the New York Times. They are all Jews!

> You go down the line in that fashion. . . . not just with ownership but go down to the managing posts and discretionary posts. . . . and you'll find that through their aggressiveness and their inventiveness, they now dominate the news media. Not only in the media, but in academic communities, the financial communities, in the foundations, in all sorts of highly visible and influential services that involve the public, they now have a tremendous voice.
>
> Our policy in the Middle East in my judgment is disastrous, because it's not even handed. I see no reason why nearly half the foreign aid this nation has to give goes to Israel, except for the influence of this Zionist lobby. I think the power of the news media is in the hands of a few people. . . . it's not subject to control of the voters, it's subject only to the whim of the board of directors.[510]

The candor of former Vice President Agnew was rare. The subject of Jewish control of the media today is usually off-limits for discussion. Any attempt to discuss Jewish media control is met with immediate reprisals from the Jewish financial and media interests. For example, when CNN news anchor Rick Sanchez stated that American television networks are run by Jews he was summarily fired.[511] The media tried to characterize the firing as being because he called Jon Stewart (born Jonathan Stuart Leibowitz) a bigot because of his unfair media treatment of non-Jews.

It was clear, though, that the reason Sanchez was fired was that he had the temerity to say on a radio broadcast what everyone who is in the media knows is the truth. The fact of Jewish media control must be kept a secret from the masses, and the Jewish controlled network for whom he worked made an example out of him for revealing it. John Stewart, who is a comedian, decided to rub it in and said this after Sanchez was fired: "If you went on radio and said the Jews control the media. . . . you may want to hold on to your money."[512] Stewart was trying to be funny, but sometimes there is truth in sarcasm.

The irrefutable fact of media control by the Jews is why they must keep a lid on the use of CGIs for the plane attacks on 911. If it became generally known that the media was part and parcel of the attacks, it would be a matter of logical deduction to discover who was behind the attacks. Pulling on that thread of media involvement in the 9/11 attacks would unravel the entire conspiracy and indeed open the eyes of the population of how they have been controlled for so long like brute beasts by their Jewish overlords.

21 Osama Bin Patsy

The assertions by Francesco Cossiga, former President of Italy, Hamid Gul, the former chief of Pakistani intelligence (ISI), and Andreas von Buelow, the former head of the parliamentary commission that oversaw the German intelligence agencies, that the 9/11 attacks were the works of state intelligence agencies, primarily the Mossad, worried the conspirators behind the attacks. They could not allow word to get out to the general public that Israel was behind the attacks. They decided to quickly jimmy up a phoney video in order to bring the focus back on their patsy, Osama Bin Laden. The video depicts someone portraying Osama Bin Laden admitting that he masterminded the 9/11 attacks.

Osama Bin Laden   **Actor portraying Bin Laden in video tape**

The picture above on the right is a picture of the person that is identified as Osama Bin

Laden in the "smoking gun"[513] tape trotted out by the U.S. government that allegedly showed Osama Bin Laden confessing to the 9-11 attacks. The tape was made public on December 13, 2001, just in time to rebut the claims made by foreign officials that 9/11 was an attack orchestrated by Israel to involve the U.S. in asserting the Israeli hegemony over the Middle East.

The picture above on the left is the real Osama Bin Laden. Check out the differences in the noses and the ears! It is obvious that these are two different people. President Bush said the following in defense of the video: "Those who contend it's a farce or a fake are hoping for the best about an evil man. This is Bin Laden unedited. This is. . . . the Bin Laden who murdered the people. This is a man who sent innocent people to their death." Do you believe your own eyes, or do you believe George W. Bush?

US Senator Ron Wyden, after seeing the video tape, made a public statement that he hoped it would remove suspicions in countries such as Pakistan that the 11 September attacks were an Israeli plot aimed at drawing the United States into a war with Islamic countries.[514] As the queen in Hamlet observed, so I also observe, that Senator Wyden "doth protest too much, methinks." He reveals too much about the hoped effect of the tape. Clearly the tape is a fraud. The conspirators produced the tape in the hopes that the tape would turn suspicions away from the evidence that Israel was behind the 9/11 attacks and bring the focus on the chosen patsies, Osama Bin Laden and the Taliban.

The appearance of the video with the actor portraying Bin Laden taking credit for the 9/11 attacks coincided with the reported date that Bin Laden died. Many reliable sources reported that Bin Laden died on December 13, 2001. In fact, Bin Laden's death on December 13, 2001, was announced in newspapers throughout Pakistan. It was no coincidence that December 13, 2001, was the day that the fake video was trotted out by the CIA and portrayed as a genuine video of Bin Laden taking credit for 911. It makes sense that the CIA would wait until after Bin Laden was dead to circulate a fake video. If they circulated the fake video while Bin Laden was still alive, Bin Laden would then be in a position to issue his own video refuting the CIA video as fake. The CIA simply could not allow that. The issuance of the fake video on December 13, 2001, marks that date as the last possible date that Bin Laden was alive.

The following page is a May 2, 2011, screen capture of the pertinent section of the FBI-Wanted-Poster as it was depicted on the FBI website for Osama (a/k/a Usama) Bin Laden. The poster shows that until May 2, 2011, which is the day after the U.S. Government alleges Bin Laden was killed by U.S. military forces, he was never indicted or even officially identified by the FBI as being involved in the 9/11 attacks.

Osama Bin Laden is listed as one of the FBI's Ten Most Wanted Fugitives. He is wanted for the "August 7, 1998, bombings of the United States embassies in Dar Es Salaam, Tanzania, and Nairobi, Kenya."[515] There is no mention on Bin Laden's wanted poster of his involvement in the 9/11 attacks, which the Bush Administration claims he masterminded.

FBI TEN MOST WANTED FUGITIVE

Murder of U.S. Nationals Outside the United States; Conspiracy to Murder U.S. Nationals Outside the United States; Attack on a Federal Facility Resulting in Death

USAMA BIN LADEN

Date of Photograph
Unknown

Multimedia: Images

Aliases:
Usama Bin Muhammad Bin Ladin, Shaykh Usama Bin Ladin, the Prince, the Emir, Abu Abdallah, Mujahid Shaykh, Hajj, the Director

DESCRIPTION

Date(s) of Birth Used:	1957	Hair:	Brown
Place of Birth:	Saudi Arabia	Eyes:	Brown
Height:	6' 4" to 6' 6"	Complexion:	Olive
Weight:	Approximately 160 pounds	Sex:	Male
Build:	Thin	Nationality:	Saudi Arabian
Occupation:	Unknown		

Scars and Marks: None known

Remarks: Bin Laden is the leader of a terrorist organization known as Al-Qaeda, "The Base". He is left-handed and walks with a cane.

CAUTION

Usama Bin Laden is wanted in connection with the August 7, 1998, bombings of the United States Embassies in Dar es Salaam, Tanzania, and Nairobi, Kenya. These attacks killed over 200 people. In addition, Bin Laden is a suspect in other terrorist attacks throughout the world.

On June 5, 2006, investigative reporter Ed Hass contacted the FBI headquarters and spoke with Rex Tomb, chief of investigative publicity for the FBI. Haas asked Tombs why Bin Laden's Ten Most Wanted poster did not mention the 9/11 attacks as being among his crimes. Tomb told Haas: "The reason why 9/11 is not mentioned on Osama Bin Laden's Most Wanted page is because the FBI has no hard evidence connecting bin Laden to 9/11."[516] The next day Claire Brown, a reporter for the I.N.N. World Report, contacted Rex Tomb and he confirmed the statement he made to Haas.[517]

What is missed by most is the significance of Tomb's elaboration during the conversation. Tomb stated that in order for a charge to appear on the FBI Wanted poster the suspect must be indicted for that charge. He explained that in order to charge Bin Laden, the U.S. Department of Justice must bring the case before a grand jury with evidence linking him to the crime. What most do not realize is that the burden of persuasion to indict a person is only probable cause, which is essentially a reasonable belief.[518] Think about it; George Bush alleged that the evidence of Bin Laden's culpability in the 9/11 attacks was compelling enough for him to order an invasion of Afghanistan, yet the FBI does not think there is enough evidence to even establish a reasonable belief that Bin Laden was implicated in those attacks.

George Bush as President of the United States is the chief executive of the federal government and as such has taken an oath to faithfully execute the laws of the United States.[519] The FBI is an agency in the U.S. Department of Justice over which he has supervisory authority through his appointed Attorney General. The FBI is funded for the very purpose of investigating federal crimes, including terrorism. Yet the investigative agency, whose very function is investigating terrorism, does not believe that there is sufficient evidence to reasonably believe that Osama Bin Laden was behind the 9/11 attacks. The FBI is now on record exposing as liars George Bush and the Zionist war mongers in his administration.

The Zionist controlled media has hidden these facts from the people. The Washington Post reported on the issue of the 9/11 attacks missing from Bin Laden's wanted poster, however, their intent was only to feign a report in order obscure and conceal the matter. They interviewed Tomb, but never asked him about his statement that "the FBI has no hard evidence connecting bin Laden to 9/11."[520]

What did Osama bin Laden actually say about his involvement in the 9-11-2001 attacks? In an interview with a Karachi-based Pakistani daily newspaper, Ummat, on September 28, 2001, Osama bin Laden denied any involvement in the 9-11-2001 attacks. In that interview, bin Laden stated in pertinent part:

> I have already said that I am not involved in the 11 September attacks in the United States. As a Muslim, I try my best to avoid telling a lie. I had no knowledge of these attacks, nor do I consider the killing of innocent women, children and other humans as an appreciable act. Islam strictly forbids causing harm to innocent

> women, children and other people. Such a practice is forbidden even in the course of a battle. . . . The United States should try to trace the perpetrators of these attacks within itself; the people who are a part of the U.S. system, but are dissenting against it; or those who are working for some other system; persons who want to make the present century as a century of conflict between Islam and Christianity so that their own civilization, nation, country, or ideology could survive. They can be anyone, from Russia to Israel and from India to Serbia. In the U.S. itself, there are dozens of well-organized and well-equipped groups, which are capable of causing a large-scale destruction. Then you cannot forget the American Jews. . . . I have already said that we are not hostile to the United States. We are against the system, which makes other nations slaves of the United States, or forces them to mortgage their political and economic freedom. This system is totally in control of the American-Jews, whose first priority is Israel, not the United States.[521]

You won't read that interview in the major media. If bin Laden adamantly denied involvement in the 9-11-2001 attacks and stated that such attacks are against his Muslim beliefs, how could he be seen later on tape saying just the opposite and taking credit for the attacks? It makes no sense for someone to deny involvement in a crime and explain that it is against his religion and then later do an about face and admit he was the mastermind all along. The later tapes produced by the CIA are obvious fabrications; the person depicted on the tapes is an actor falsely portraying bin Laden taking credit for the attacks.

On May 1, 2011, it was announced that Osama Bin Laden was killed by U.S. forces. The alleged killing of Bin Laden was followed thereafter by a very odd series of events regarding the disposal of his remains. The Washington Post stated: "After he was killed at his compound in Abbottabad, Pakistan, Osama bin Laden's body was flown by helicopter to Afghanistan for identification, then airlifted to the aircraft carrier USS Carl Vinson in an undisclosed location on the Arabian Sea."[522] Ten hours after Bin Laden was allegedly killed, his supposed body was purportedly buried at sea.

Why would the U.S. fly Bin Laden's alleged body approximately 400 miles from Pakistan to Afghanistan and then fly the body another 600 miles across almost the full length of Afghanistan and part of Pakistan and bury it at sea? That conduct only makes sense if one were trying to prevent anyone from being able to verify that it was Bin Laden who was killed on May 1st. The next day the U.S. government did not release a picture of Bin Laden's body to the media; government officials were debating on whether to do so. The reason for so quickly disposing of Bin Laden's alleged remains is that Bin Laden was not killed on May 1, 2011, and therefore the U.S. did not have possession of his body. Bin Laden had been killed years earlier. The professed disposal at sea of Bin Laden's body is a cover-story to explain why the U.S. cannot produce his body.

Benazir Bhutto, who was twice elected Prime Minister of Pakistan by the National Assembly (1988-1990 and 1993-1996), revealed in a November 2, 2007, Al-Jezeera TV interview with David Frost that Bin Laden was dead.[523] She not only revealed that he was dead, but identified his killer as Omar Sheikh. Ahmed Omar Saeed Sheikh is one of those convicted of kidnapping and killing U.S. journalist Daniel Pearl. Typical of media mouthpieces, David Frost showed no curiosity over Bhutto's revelation and asked no follow-up questions. Seven weeks after the Frost interview, on December 27, 2007, Benezir Bhutto was assassinated during a political rally, where she was targeted with gunfire and bombs that killed her and 20 other people.

Many have said Bin Laden died from natural causes at his hideout in Tora Bora. Afghan President Hamid Karzai, Pakistan's President, Pervez Musharraf, and the FBI's counter-terrorism chief, Dale Watson, were all on record long before May 1, 2011, stating that Osama bin Laden was already dead.

Steve R. Pieczenik, who was the former Deputy Assistant Secretary of State under three different administrations, is also on record stating that Bin Laden has been dead since 2001.[524] Furthermore, Paul Joseph Watson reported that Pieczenik is prepared to tell a federal grand jury that a top general told him directly 9/11 was a false flag attack.

> Top US government insider Dr. Steve R. Pieczenik, a man who held numerous different influential positions under three different Presidents and still works with the Defense Department, shockingly told The Alex Jones Show yesterday that Osama Bin Laden died in 2001 and that he was prepared to testify in front of a grand jury how a top general told him directly that 9/11 was a false flag inside job.
>
> Pieczenik cannot be dismissed as a "conspiracy theorist." He served as the Deputy Assistant Secretary of State under three different administrations, Nixon, Ford and Carter, while also working under Reagan and Bush Senior, and still works as a consultant for the Department of Defense. A former US Navy Captain, Pieczenik achieved two prestigious Harry C. Solomon Awards at the Harvard Medical School as he simultaneously completed a PhD at MIT.
>
> Recruited by Lawrence Eagleburger as Deputy Assistant Secretary of State for Management, Pieczenik went on to develop, "the basic tenets for psychological warfare, counter terrorism, strategy and tactics for transcultural negotiations for the US State Department, military and intelligence communities and other agencies of the US Government," while also developing foundational strategies for hostage rescue that were later employed around the world.

Pieczenik also served as a senior policy planner under Secretaries Henry Kissinger, Cyrus Vance, George Schultz and James Baker and worked on George W. Bush's election campaign against Al Gore. His record underscores the fact that he is one of the most deeply connected men in intelligence circles over the past three decades plus.

The character of Jack Ryan, who appears in many Tom Clancy novels and was also played by Harrison Ford in the popular 1992 movie Patriot Games, is also based on Steve Pieczenik.

Back in April 2002, over nine years ago, Pieczenik told the Alex Jones Show that Bin Laden had already been "dead for months," and that the government was waiting for the most politically expedient time to roll out his corpse. Pieczenik would be in a position to know, having personally met Bin Laden and worked with him during the proxy war against the Soviets in Afghanistan back in the early 80's.

Pieczenik said that Osama Bin Laden died in 2001, "Not because special forces had killed him, but because as a physician I had known that the CIA physicians had treated him and it was on the intelligence roster that he had marfan syndrome," adding that the US government knew Bin Laden was dead before they invaded Afghanistan.

Marfan syndrome is a degenerative genetic disease for which there is no permanent cure. The illness severely shortens the life span of the sufferer.

"He died of marfan syndrome, Bush junior knew about it, the intelligence community knew about it," said Pieczenik, noting how CIA physicians had visited Bin Laden in July 2001 at the American Hospital in Dubai.

"He was already very sick from marfan syndrome and he was already dying, so nobody had to kill him," added Pieczenik, stating that Bin Laden died shortly after 9/11 in his Tora Bora cave complex.

"Did the intelligence community or the CIA doctor up this situation, the answer is yes, categorically yes," said Pieczenik, referring to Sunday's claim that Bin Laden was killed at his compound in Pakistan, adding, "This whole scenario where you see a bunch of people sitting there looking at a screen and they look as if they're intense, that's nonsense," referring to the images released by the White House which claim to show Biden, Obama and Hillary Clinton watching the operation to kill Bin Laden live on a television screen.

"It's a total make-up, make believe, we're in an American theater of the absurd....why are we doing this again....nine years ago this man was already dead....why does the government repeatedly have to lie to the American people," asked Pieczenik.

"Osama Bin Laden was totally dead, so there's no way they could have attacked or confronted or killed Osama Bin laden," said Pieczenik, joking that the only way it could have happened was if special forces had attacked a mortuary.

Pieczenik said that the decision to launch the hoax now was made because Obama had reached a low with plummeting approval ratings and the fact that the birther issue was blowing up in his face.

"He had to prove that he was more than American....he had to be aggressive," said Pieczenik, adding that the farce was also a way of isolating Pakistan as a retaliation for intense opposition to the Predator drone program, which has killed hundreds of Pakistanis.

"This is orchestrated, I mean when you have people sitting around and watching a sitcom, basically the operations center of the White House, and you have a president coming out almost zombie-like telling you they just killed Osama Bin Laden who was already dead nine years ago," said Pieczenik, calling the episode, "the greatest falsehood I've ever heard, I mean it was absurd."

Dismissing the government's account of the assassination of Bin Laden as a "sick joke" on the American people, Pieczenik said, "They are so desperate to make Obama viable, to negate the fact that he may not have been born here, any questions about his background, any irregularities about his background, to make him look assertive....to re-elect this president so the American public can be duped once again."

Pieczenik's assertion that Bin Laden died almost ten years ago is echoed by numerous intelligence professionals as well as heads of state across the world.

Bin Laden, "Was used in the same way that 9/11 was used to mobilize the emotions and feelings of the American people in order to go to a war that had to be justified through a narrative that Bush junior created and Cheney created about the world of terrorism," stated Pieczenik.

During his interview with the Alex Jones Show yesterday, Pieczenik also asserted he was directly told by a prominent general that 9/11 was a stand down and a false flag operation, and that he is prepared to go to a grand jury to reveal the general's name.

"They ran the attacks," said Pieczenik, naming Dick Cheney, Paul Wolfowitz, Stephen Hadley, Elliott Abrams, and Condoleezza Rice amongst others as having been directly involved.

"It was called a stand down, a false flag operation in order to mobilize the American public under false pretenses....it was told to me even by the general on the staff of Wolfowitz – I will go in front of a federal committee and swear on perjury who the name was of the individual so that we can break it open," said Pieczenik, adding that he was "furious" and "knew it had happened."

"I taught stand down and false flag operations at the national war college, I've taught it with all my operatives so I knew exactly what was done to the American public," he added.

Pieczenik re-iterated that he was perfectly willing to reveal the name of the general who told him 9/11 was an inside job in a federal court, "so that we can unravel this thing legally, not with the stupid 9/11 Commission that was absurd."

Pieczenik explained that he was not a liberal, a conservative or a tea party member, merely an American who is deeply concerned about the direction in which his country is heading.[525]

President Obama announced on May 4, 2011 that the administration would not release a photograph of Bin Laden's corpse that many want to see to verify that Bin Laden was in fact killed on May 1, 2011. U.S. Senator Scott Brown was among the high officials who had seen the photograph in question.

Mark Arsenault form the Boston Globe reported: "Having seen unreleased photos of Osama bin Laden's corpse, US Senator Scott Brown does not believe pictures of the dead terrorist leader should be made public, the Massachusetts Republican said in an interview on NECN.".[526]

In an on air interview with NECN Senator Brown stated: "Let me assure you that he is dead, that bin Laden is dead, I have seen the photos, and in fact we have received the briefing."[527] Brown's statement was made hours before President Obama declared that he would not release the photos of Bin Laden's corpse.

Brown repeated his statement to having seen the photo of Bin Laden in a separate interview with Fox-25 TV. "Listen, I've seen the picture," Brown said. "He's definitely dead. And if there's any conspiracy theories out there, you should put them to rest."[528] Oddly, within hours of having stated he saw the photograph of Bin Laden's corpse he revealed that the photo was in fact a fake. The Boston Globe reported:

> NECN posted a statement on its website, saying, "Senator Brown's office tells NECN this afternoon that the bin Laden photos the Senator mentions seeing about 2 minutes into the clip here were not authentic."
>
> Fox 25 posted an update on its website, saying Brown had told the station that, "the photo that I saw and that a lot of other people saw is not authentic."
>
> Brown's office is declining to explain who showed him the fake photos, why he would believe photos that didn't come directly from the administration, and why he had suggested he had seen them as part of an official briefing. Instead, Brown's office responded by releasing a one-sentence statement.
>
> "The photo that I saw and that a lot of other people saw is not authentic," the senator said in the statement.[529]

Clearly, Senator Brown was being shown a photograph from an official source and not from a public source, since he was arguing that the photo should not be released to the public. The context suggests that the official source was the Obama administration, since he was talking about being briefed continually by the administration. The photo the senator saw was apparently leaked to the media and exposed as a fake, which prompted the senator to come forward and admit he was duped by the same fake photo.

He was not the only senator duped.

> Sen. Saxby Chambliss (R-GA), the vice chairman of the Senate intelligence committee, said earlier today that he had seen a photo of a slain bin Laden, describing it in some detail without casting

any doubt on its authenticity. But sure enough, he now admits he saw a fake.[530]

Senator Chambliss now states that he was not shown the picture from an official source. It is not surprising that he would make that claim, since if he said otherwise, he would be pointing the finger directly to the U.S. government as the perpetrator of a fraud and raise serious questions about the authenticity of the alleged raid and killing of Bin Laden. His claim that he did not see the photo from an official source is just not credible. He is the Chairman of the Senate Intelligence Committee. He has direct access to the most up-to-date intelligence. Why would he even care to consider a photo from other than an official source, when he has ready access to the entire intelligence community?

When you read Senator Chambiss' comments in the morning of May 4, 2011, before he found out that the photo was fake, it is clear that he thought he was looking at an official government photo that had not yet been released to the public, because he was discussing whether it would ever be released to the public:

> Ranking member of Senate Intel committee Sen. Saxby Chambliss (R-Ga.) told NBC News Wednesday morning the photos are, "what you would expect. Somebody's been shot in the head. It's not pretty."
>
> When asked if the pictures should be held or released, he said, "one of these days they're going to be released. It's a question of whether to do it now on our terms or [let] somebody else do it."[531]

The U.S. government flies Bin Laden's alleged body almost a thousand miles to dump it in the sea, thus assuring that it can never be used for identification. The Obama Administration briefs senators and show them photos of Bin Laden's corpse. The senators think that they are being shown genuine photos of Bin Laden's corpse only to find out later after they are leaked to the media that the photos are fake.

The tyrants who are running the terror campaign against the American people could not allow the fiction of Bin Laden's May 1st killing to go without making the most of it. They justified the brutal torture of detainees by claiming that finding Bin Laden was the direct result of brutal torture. The Christian Science Monitor reported: "The question is at the core of a rekindled debate over the value of harsh interrogation tactics authorized under President George W. Bush. Claiming vindication, former Bush officials say the information gleaned years ago from the harsh techniques bore fruit."[532]

The Obama administration denied that torture was the basis for finding Bin Laden. However, when Eric Holder, Attorney General in the Obama administration, was asked if torture helped find Bin Laden, he was not so emphatic; he stated "I do not know."[533] The Christian Science Monitor then quotes former Bush Administration officials as being adamant that torture was how Bin Laden was found:

> Others say the Bush administration's aggressive approach to intelligence gathering in the wake of the 9/11 attacks created the massive pool of data that eventually allowed intelligence analysts to put together pieces of a puzzle that led to bin Laden.
>
> "President George W. Bush, not his successor, constructed the interrogation and warrantless surveillance programs that produce this week's actionable intelligence," wrote former Justice Department legal adviser John Yoo in a Wall Street Journal op-ed piece.
>
> "According to current and former administration officials, CIA interrogators gathered the initial information that ultimately led to bin Laden's death," Mr. Yoo said.
>
> In an interview with Time magazine, the former director of the CIA's counterterrorism center, Jose Rodriguez, said the first important leads about Kuwaiti came from alleged 9/11 mastermind Khalid Sheikh Mohammed (KSM) and Abu Farraj al-Libbi, the third-ranking Al Qaeda leader at the time of his capture. Both men were interrogated at secret CIA "black sites," where Mr. Mohammed was subject to waterboarding 183 times.
>
> "Information provided by KSM and [Mr. Libbi] about bin Laden's courier was the lead information that eventually led to the location of the compound and the operation that led to his death," Mr. Rodriguez is quoted as saying.
>
> Former Defense Secretary Donald Rumsfeld told Fox News's Sean Hannity that the Obama administration would not have had "the kinds of intelligence that was critically important," but for the aggressive efforts of the Bush administration.
>
> "Anyone who suggests that the enhanced techniques, let's be blunt – waterboarding – did not produce an enormous amount of valuable intelligence just isn't facing the truth," he said.[534]

All of the people in the above article that are justifying torture knew when making their comments that Bin Laden was already dead prior to his fictional killing on May 1st. Why, if they knew that torture played no role in finding Bin Laden, are they arguing that torture led the U.S. to Bin Laden? They must justify their use of torture. They need torture as a tool to produce confessed patsies for future false flag operations. Torture serves their depraved need to persuade innocent people to confess to crimes they did not commit and convince those patsies to accuse other innocent patsies of being their co-conspirators.

22 The Real Reason for the Invasion of Iraq

"The love of money is the root of all evil." 1 Timothy 6:10. The 9/11 attacks and the subsequent war on terror are the direct result of the love of money. The Bush Administration started with a list of 23 reasons to invade Iraq, which they publicly floated within a year after the 9/11 attacks, before settling on its top three.[535] The three main reasons given for the 2003 invasion of Iraq were 1) Iraq was seeking uranium from Africa to make nuclear weapons, 2) Iraq had amassed weapons of mass destruction, and 3) Iraq was an accomplice in the 9/11 attacks. All three of those reasons given for the invasion of Iraq were false.

On July 8, 2003, the White House acknowledged that President Bush was incorrect when he said in his State of the Union address that Iraq recently had sought significant quantities of uranium in Africa.[536] By that point the White House did not have much choice, overwhelming evidence surfaced that the story was not true. It was so clearly untrue, many wondered how anyone could believe it.

The most damning evidence was provided by former U.S. Ambassador Joseph Wilson, who over a year before Bush gave his State of the Union address reported directly to the CIA that his investigation of the matter showed that the uranium story was not true. After Mr. Wilson went public with his information that established that the President's uranium statement was false, Mr. Wilson's wife, Valerie Plame, was exposed as a CIA undercover agent by Vice President Cheney's Chief of Staff, Scooter Libby. The circumstances suggested that the exposure of Wilson's wife as a CIA Agent was a payback for having gone public with what he knew about the uranium fiction. Libby was later convicted of a federal crime for revealing Plame's status, but President Bush commuted Libby's 30 month prison sentence.

On August 21, 2006, George Bush also had to acknowledge that there were no weapons of mass destruction in Iraq.[537] Again, Bush had no choice but to admit the obvious, he was starting to look foolish trying to keep up the charade that WMDs were somewhere in Iraq.

At that same August 21, 2006, news conference, George Bush flat out admitted that Iraq had "nothing" to do with the 9/11 attacks.[538] Bush was a little late with that admission. Deputy Secretary of Defense Paul Wolfowitz, one of the main architects for the war in Iraq, during an interview with radio personality Laura Ingraham on or about August 1, 2003, stated: "I'm not sure even now that I would say Iraq had something to do with it [the 9/11 attacks]."[539] That statement by Wolfowitz was made 111 days after the invasion of Iraq by the U.S. military and directly contradicted the pre-invasion claims made by Vice President Dick Cheney and Secretary of Defense Donald Rumsfeld.

It is pretty clear to all except for slow learners that the reasons given to the public for the invasion of Iraq by the Bush Administration were trumped up justifications that were completely without any basis in fact. That raises a question. What was the real reason the Bush administration invaded Iraq? It all comes down to the love of money.

Oil has become the defacto currency of the world. There has been a virtual media blackout regarding the fact that the United States has more oil in Alaska than in all of Saudi Arabia. Lindsey Williams served as an on-site chaplain in the mid-1970s during the Trans-Alaska Oil Pipeline's construction. He was given executive status by Alyeska Pipeline Personnel Relations Manager R.H. King. The Alyeska Pipeline Service Company is a consortium of nine major oil companies that built the Alaska Pipeline. Williams was able to sit in on high-level meetings of oil executives during the pipeline's construction for a period of two-and-a-half years.

Williams found out that there is enough oil in just three of the fields that have been drilled and confirmed in Alaska to supply the needs of the United States for at least the next 200 years.[540] Below is a summary of oil in those three oil fields.

Field	Pay Zone Oil (Average depth of oil pool)	Area of Field
Prudhoe	600 Ft. of pay zone	100 square miles
Kuparuk	300 Ft. of pay zone	Twice the size of Prudhoe
Gull Island	1,200 Ft. of pay zone	At least four times the size of Prudhoe . . . Estimates are that it is the richest oil field on the face of the earth.

If what Williams says is true, why is the U.S. so dependant on foreign oil imports, and why are we paying almost $3 per gallon for gasoline today (November 2010), with the price to go much higher in the near future? Williams states that in the 1970s Henry Kissinger representing the United States negotiated with oil producing countries, most notably Saudi Arabia, to have them agree to transact their oil sales only in U.S. Dollars and further to use a portion of those dollars to purchase U.S. Treasury bonds. In return, the U.S. government agreed to keep the Alaskan oil off the market.

Since then, the U.S. Government has locked up the Alaskan oil fields and will not allow most of the oil to be pumped. The original plan of the Alyeska Pipeline Service Company was to have a total of three pipelines, two pipelines for oil and one for natural gas. The U.S. Government has not permitted the other two pipelines to be built. All of the hullabaloo over environmental concerns in Alaska has nothing to do with the environment; it has everything to do with keeping the Alaskan oil and natural gas off the market.

The oil flowing through the single pipeline that was ultimately built has slowed to a trickle, and is nowhere near the full flow capacity of 1.7 to 2 million gallons per day. Williams has been informed that the amount of oil flowing through the 800-mile-long pipeline is small enough to require the use of a "pig," which is a kind of pipe cleaner. It has become necessary to use a "pig" because under-utilizing the line by slowing the flow of oil allows foreign material to build up on the inside of the pipeline.[541]

In addition, most of what is flowing down the pipeline is being shipped to Japan and other overseas countries. The U.S. Government is keeping the American economy dependent on foreign oil in order to have those foreign oil producing countries as customers for the debt that it is incurring as a result of its persistent deficit spending. The media is painting the oil companies as evil price gouging capitalists, when in fact they are unwilling accomplices of the international bankers.

This scheme, which is being orchestrated by the bankers who own and control the Federal Reserve and in turn the U.S. Government, is designed to keep enriching these bankers on the backs of the American people. Without the foreign countries buying the U.S. Government debt the U.S. economy would collapse, because there would not be anyone who could purchase the mountain of debt that has been run up by the U.S. Government.[542] In order for the U.S. Government to engage in runaway deficit spending they must have customers with lots of money willing to buy that debt. In order for the bankers to ensure that their foreign customers have enough money, the international bankers rig the price of oil to rise high enough to allow for the debt purchases. As the debt increases, the oil price must necessarily increase to permit the purchase of the debt and to keep the deficit-spending-inflation scheme going.

The three largest oil deposits in the Middle East are 1) Saudi Arabia, 2) Iraq, and 3) Iran. Saudi Arabia agreed to the deal proposed by Kissinger in the 1970's. Iraq and Iran did not agree to the deal and both remained (somewhat) independent. Iraq was targeted for invasion in the first place because Saddam Hussein threatened to change the currency for Iraqi oil sales from the U.S. dollar to the Euro.

It is the acceleration of the debt burden that was the primary reason for the U.S. Invasion of Iraq. In 2002, William Clark wrote an award-winning online essay explaining that Saddam

Hussein sealed his fate when Hussein announced in September 2000 that Iraq was no longer going to accept dollars and instead switch to Euros for oil being sold under the UN's Oil-for-Food program.[543] That was the reason the U.S. decided to invade and occupy Iraq.

It is notable that by June 10, 2003, the U.S. occupation government switched the Iraqi oil transactions back to dollars.[544] That was done in the face of the fact that it made no economic sense to do so, since the Euro at that time was valued 13% higher than the U.S. dollar.[545] The move to the dollar does not make economic sense from the perspective of ordinary Iraqis or Americans. However, it makes perfect sense from the perspective of the international bankers controlling the Federal Reserve. They need to have customers to absorb the billions of U.S. dollars being inflated into the world economy by the crushing debt of the U.S. Government. Without countries willing to take dollars, which are becoming worth less and less (and ultimately will become totally worthless), the entire U.S. economy would collapse. The collapse of the U.S. economy is inevitable, however, the bankers are not yet fully prepared for the collapse just yet, and so they must keep the scam going until they get their economic ducks in row.

The Iraq invasion is only a part of an economic death spiral that will ultimately destroy the U.S. economy and our freedoms. The higher gas price paid at the pump is essentially a tax on the U.S. citizens to pay for the mountainous government debt, and that debt is being exacerbated by the U.S. invasions of Iraq and Afghanistan. With the U.S. funding Iraq and Afghanistan occupation armies, the debt is increasing at a break-neck speed. What do the minions of the Jewish money power think of the precious lives of our military soldiers who are dying by the thousands to enrich the international bankers? Bob Woodward and Carl Bernstein in their book *The Final Days* reveal the following about Jewish Secretary of State Henry Kissinger: "In Haig's presence, Kissinger referred pointedly to military men as 'dumb, stupid animals to be used' as pawns for foreign policy."[546]

23 Is Iran Next?

Why is there continual talk in the media and the government about the nuclear danger posed by Iran? Is there such a danger? The answer is no. Iran only poses a danger to the Zionist bankers who run the Federal Reserve bank. In February 2008 the Iranian Government began its Iranian Oil Bourse, which is a commodity exchange for oil transactions.[547] Iran has requested its oil customers not to use U.S. dollars in its oil purchases from Iran. The Iranian Bourse will transact oil sales in euros, yen, and Iranian rials. That is a direct threat to the demand for dollars. As reported by Press TV: "Some expert opinions hold inauguration of the [Iranian] bourse could significantly devalue the greenback."[548] There is no "could" about it. The Iranian Bourse is a direct threat to the dollar. That threat to the dollar in turn threatens the ability of the Zionist Jewish bankers to keep up their wholesale thievery of the American people.

William Clark was proven correct in his 2002 prediction that Iraq would be invaded (as it was in 2003) because Saddam Hussein decided to conduct his oil transactions in Euros. Clark has made another prediction. In 2005, he stated that Iran is now being targeted for invasion by the U.S. and the neoconservatives [Zionists] for the very same reason that Iraq was invaded in 2003. He notes that these facts surrounding the real reason for the invasion of Iraq and the reason for the impending attack on Iran have been completely ignored by the major media outlets.

> Not surprisingly, this detail has never been mentioned in the five U.S. major media conglomerates who control 90% of information flow in the U.S., but confirmation of this vital fact provides insight into one of the crucial – yet overlooked – rationales for the 2003 Iraq war.
>
> Concerning Iran, recent articles have revealed active Pentagon planning for operations against its suspected nuclear facilities. While the publicly stated reasons for any such overt action will be premised as a consequence of Iran's nuclear ambitions, there are

> again unspoken macroeconomic drivers underlying the second stage of petrodollar warfare – Iran's upcoming oil bourse. (The word bourse refers to a stock exchange for securities trading, and is derived from the French stock exchange in Paris, the Federation Internationale des Bourses de Valeurs.)
>
> In essence, Iran is about to commit a far greater "offense" than Saddam Hussein's conversion to the euro for Iraq's oil exports in the fall of 2000. Beginning in March 2006, the Tehran government has plans to begin competing with New York's NYMEX and London's IPE with respect to international oil trades – using a euro-based international oil-trading mechanism.[549]
>
> The proposed Iranian oil bourse signifies that without some sort of US intervention, the euro is going to establish a firm foothold in the international oil trade. Given U.S. debt levels and the stated neoconservative project of U.S. global domination, Tehran's objective constitutes an obvious encroachment on dollar supremacy in the crucial international oil market.
>
> From the autumn of 2004 through August 2005, numerous leaks by concerned Pentagon employees have revealed that the neoconservatives [i.e., Zionists] in Washington are quietly – but actively – planning for a possible attack against Iran.[550]

Notice that an attack on Iran was being planned as far back as 2004. The scary part is that the plans included a nuclear strike against Iran in the event of another 9/11 type terrorist attack against the United States, regardless of Iran's fault in the next attack against the United States. No doubt the expected attack (if it happens) will be orchestrated by Zionists acting as *agent provocateurs*, orchestrating a false flag attack, to be blamed on an innocent invasion target, which as of this writing (November 2010) seems to be Iran. You can bet that if an attack happens, the Zionists will do their best to pin any attack on Iran, however, just as with Iraq, the retaliation against Iran will not depend on any actual evidence that Iran was the attacker.

In an article in The American Conservative, titled "In Case of Emergency, Nuke Iran,"[551] intelligence analyst Philip Giraldi explained "the resurrection of active U.S. military planning against Iran – but with the shocking disclosure that in the event of another 9/11-type terrorist attack on U.S. soil, Vice President Dick Cheney's office wants the Pentagon to be prepared to launch a potential tactical nuclear attack on Iran – even if the Iranian government was not involved with any such terrorist attack against the U.S."[552] Giraldi detailed the plans to attack Iran:

> The Pentagon, acting under instructions from Vice President Dick Cheney's office, has tasked the United States Strategic Command

(STRATCOM) with drawing up a contingency plan to be employed in response to another 9/11-type terrorist attack on the United States. The plan includes a large-scale air assault on Iran employing both conventional and tactical nuclear weapons. Within Iran there are more than 450 major strategic targets, including numerous suspected nuclear-weapons-program development sites. Many of the targets are hardened or are deep underground and could not be taken out by conventional weapons, hence the nuclear option. **As in the case of Iraq, the response is not conditional on Iran actually being involved in the act of terrorism directed against the United States.** Several senior Air Force officers involved in the planning are reportedly appalled at the implications of what they are doing – that Iran is being set up for an unprovoked nuclear attack – but no one is prepared to damage his career by posing any objections.[553]

Do not think that simply because Bush and Cheney are no longer in office that the plans have been scuttled. The same Zionists who ran the Bush administration, also run the Obama administration, and will run the next administration after that. Proof that the Obama administration is run by Zionists is that his chief of staff for the first two years of Obama's Presidency was Rahm Emanuel.

Rahm Emanuel is a dual citizen of Israel. His father was a member of the Irgun, a Zionist terror gang. Emanuel's father took part in the successful plot to assassinate Count Bernadotte, a Swedish diplomat and United Nations envoy who tried to broker peace in Palestine.[554] What are Emanuel's loyalties? During the 1991 Gulf War, he served in the Israeli Defense Forces (IDF).[555] The fact that Rahm Emanuel is no longer chief of staff for President Obama may indicate that the Zionist Jews are losing control of President Obama. Texe Marrs has issued a report indicating that may be happening.[556] While President Obama may resist the Zionist control, there has yet to be any real moderation in his pro-Israel policies.

On or about August 4, 2010, President Obama held a press briefing where he said the United States would use "all options available to us to prevent a nuclear arms race in the region and to prevent a nuclear-armed Iran."[557] Those words of Obama were reported by the far left wing communist *World Socialist Web Site*.[558] The statement by Obama was confirmed by Andrew Parasiliti of the International Institute for Strategic Studies,[559] and by Jeffrey Goldberg of the Atlantic, who reported:

> Tony Blair recently said in a telephone conversation, "personally, I think Israel would not allow Iran to get nuclear weapons." In March, Joseph Biden declared that "the United States is determined to prevent Iran from acquiring nuclear weapons, period." Barack Obama has repeatedly called a nuclear Iran "unacceptable." Just a few weeks ago, Obama reiterated to a group of reporters in the

White House that he would use "all options available to us to prevent a nuclear arms race in the region and to prevent a nuclear-armed Iran."[560]

Other than those three cited references, Obama's statement was not reported by any major media outlets. Robert Kagan of the Washington Post reported on the press briefing, but omitted the important statement from Obama.[561] That statement simply states that "all options," presumably including military options, are available. Those words do not mean that Obama is definitely going to attack Iran. Even a statement by Admiral Mike Mullen, chairman of the U.S. Joint Chiefs of Staff, days before Obama's statement did not definitely call for a military attack. Admiral Mullen simply stated that the risk of Iran's developing a nuclear weapon is unacceptable and that the military options have been on the table and remain on the table.[562]

What makes Obama's statement suspiciously ominous is that the Jewish controlled media has blacked out any mention of the statement; they are not ready for the masses to hear Obama suggest a military option. It seems something is afoot, but they do not want to wake the public from its slumber to the risk of war with Iran. Doing so, might throw a monkey wrench in their plans. There is no telling if the war plan comes to fruition. The Bush Administration and Israel had big plans of war with Iran, but events prevented it from happening. Hopefully, Obama and Israel will be no more successful in their attempts to incite a war with Iran.

David Broder of the Washington Post has added to the Zionist chorus calling for a military war with Iran. He suggests the war option as a Machiavellian way for President Obama to win reelection. Broder argues he is not calling on Obama to incite a war with Iran. But what he says clearly hints at that option. He states that Obama will be helped politically as war tensions rise and the country prepares for war, because the war effort will help the economy, the Republicans will support his efforts, and the country will rally around Obama. Broder states that if Obama confronts Iran and contains its nuclear ambitions (i.e., goes to war with Iran), he "may be regarded as one of the most successful presidents in history."[563] Broder is a shill media cheerleader for the Zionists.

Republican Senator Lindsey Graham said his fellow Republican conservatives, fresh from their historic elections romp in November 2010, support "bold" action to deal with Iran. What does he mean by bold action? He means war! He said that America does not need another war, but made it clear that trying to contain Iran short of war is "off the table."[564] That is scary.

The Iranian Oil Bourse is why the Bush Administration, the Obama Administration, and Israel have been sabre rattling toward Iran.[565] That is why Israel and the U.S. Government are falsely portraying Iran as a Nuclear threat, thus necessitating a preemptive attack against Iran. On June 6, 2008, the British Telegraph reported:

> On the Iranian front, [Israeli Prime Minister] Mr. Olmert privately pronounced himself happy after his visit to the White House that Israel and America are of one mind over the possibility of military

intervention against Tehran's nuclear programme.

In President George W Bush, Israel has a firm ally who shares its belief that Iran must be stopped at all costs from becoming a nuclear power.

One of Mr. Olmert's party deputies, Shaul Mofaz, kept up the pressure on Iran saying an Israeli attack on Iranian nuclear sites looked "inevitable" given the apparent failure of diplomatic and economic sanctions on Tehran.

"If Iran continues with its programme for developing nuclear weapons, we will attack it," he said.[566]

The drums of war were being beaten by Israel and the U.S. in the face of a 2005 National Intelligence Estimate (NIE) of Iran's nuclear program, which revealed that, "Iran is about a decade away from manufacturing the key ingredient for a nuclear weapon, roughly doubling the previous estimate of five years."[567] National Intelligence Estimates represent the official opinion of the U.S. intelligence agencies. "NIEs are produced by the National Intelligence Council and express the coordinated judgments of the United States Intelligence Community, the group of 16 U.S. intelligence agencies."[568]

In view of the NIE, it is clear that the saber rattling against Iran by the U.S. and Israel has nothing to do with a nuclear threat posed by Iran. The war plans have everything to do with an increasingly fragile U.S. economy on the edge of collapse under the crushing weight of the national debt and the dollar being inflated to worthlessness.[569] If the international community switches from the dollar, the demand for the dollar will dry up and the game that the Federal Reserve has been playing since its founding in 1913 will come to a sudden and catastrophic end. At this time the Jewish bankers are not fully ready for the scam to end and so they are doing all they can to keep it going, by hook or by crook (or by war).

Protocol VII of the Protocols of the Learned Elders of Zion states:

> 3. We must be in a position to respond to every act of opposition by war with the neighbors of that country which dares to oppose us: but if these neighbors should also venture to stand collectively together against us, then we must offer resistance by a universal war.
> 4. The principal factor of success in the political is the secrecy of its undertakings: the word should not agree with the deeds of the diplomat.
> 5. We must compel the governments of the GOYIM to take action in the direction favored by our widely conceived plan, already approaching the desired consummation, by what we shall represent

> as public opinion, secretly promoted by us through the means of that so-called "Great Power" - THE PRESS, WHICH, WITH A FEW EXCEPTIONS THAT MAY BE DISREGARDED, IS ALREADY ENTIRELY IN OUR HANDS.[570] (emphasis in original)

Proof of the hidden hand of Zionist Jews behind the Iraq war plans comes through Air Force Lt. Colonel Karen Kwiatkowski. Colonel Kwiatkowski worked in the office of Undersecretary for Policy, Douglas Feith. Colonel Kwiatkowski worked specifically with a secretive Pentagon organization run by Feith called the Office of Special Plans (OSP). She revealed that Zionist Jews within the Pentagon referred to as "neoconservatives" pushed for the Iraq war. There is such fear of the Jews within the government that when military and political leaders criticize them they are careful to call them "neoconservatives" rather than "Jews." The major news outlets controlled by Zionist Jews would not touch Colonel Kwiatkowski's revelations. She was relegated to being interviewed on an internet news site that the Jews in their Protocol VII states "may be disregarded." Colonel Kwiatkowski stated in the interview:

> From May 2002 until February 2003, I observed firsthand the formation of the Pentagon's Office of Special Plans and watched the latter stages of the neoconservative capture of the policy-intelligence nexus in the run-up to the invasion of Iraq. This seizure of the reins of U.S. Middle East policy was directly visible to many of us working in the Near East South Asia policy office, and yet there seemed to be little any of us could do about it. I saw a narrow and deeply flawed policy favored by some executive appointees in the Pentagon used to manipulate and pressurize the traditional relationship between policymakers in the Pentagon and U.S. intelligence agencies. I witnessed neoconservative agenda bearers within OSP usurp measured and carefully considered assessments, and through suppression and distortion of intelligence analysis promulgate what were in fact falsehoods to both Congress and the executive office of the president.[571]

The neoconservative Zionists in control of the military intelligence network will no doubt massage the intelligence information to justify an invasion of their next target, which as of this writing (November 2010) looks as though it could be Iran. The major media outlets, which are controlled by the Zionist Jews, will ensure that the masses of Americans will be deceived to believe the fabricated intelligence.

24 The Media Lap Dogs

If there is an invasion of Iran, it will be based upon media hype of some mythical or orchestrated threat that justified the invasion. Any evidence that would point to the innocence of Iran will be ignored or downplayed. That is what happened with the invasion of Iraq. The Jewish controlled media deliberately downplayed a story that Iraq had no weapons of mass destruction. In its March 3, 2003, issue, *Newsweek* disclosed that the Bush Administration had deliberately suppressed information exculpating Iraq. As damning as this disclosure was, *Newsweek* chose to downplay it. Russ Baker of *The Nation* sets the scene:

> In the summer of 1995 Saddam's then-son-in-law, Lieut. Gen. Hussein Kamel, former minister of Iraq's military industry and the person in charge of its nuclear/chemical/biological programs, defected and provided what was deemed scrupulously accurate, detailed accounts of those weapons. **Kamel's information has been cited as central evidence and a key reason for attacking Iraq.** In his February 5 [2003] presentation to the UN Security Council, Secretary of State Colin Powell said: "It took years for Iraq to finally admit that it had produced four tons of the deadly nerve agent VX. A single drop of VX on the skin will kill in minutes. Four tons. The admission only came out after inspectors collected documentation as a result of the defection of Hussein Kamel, Saddam Hussein's late son-in-law."[572]

The problem with Powell's assertions about Iraq's alleged weapons of mass destruction is that they were false, and Powell knew it. He deliberately lied in order to justify invading Iraq. As revealed by *Newsweek*'s John Barry, the Administration had excised a central component of Kamel's testimony--that **he had personal knowledge that Iraq had "destroyed all its chemical and biological weapons stocks and the missiles to deliver them."** Kamel said that Iraq had not abandoned its Weapons of Mass Destruction ambitions and had retained the design and engineering details, but **his last information was that Iraq's VX arsenal no longer existed**.

Bush and his administration had been lying to the public about the threat posed by Iraq in order to justify their military invasion. The most disturbing thing about this is that the media has downplayed the significance of this information, which shows that Bush was rushing to war and lying about the real reasons for doing so.

The Newsweek article revealing that Iraq had no weapons of mass destruction appeared in the March 3, 2003, issue of the magazine; at that point the U.S. was only a few weeks from its planned invasion of Iraq, which took place on March 19, 2003. When the article appeared, the Bush Administration was still justifying its planned invasion of Iraq in principal part because of Iraq's alleged possession of weapons of mass destruction. This should have been the *Newsweek* cover story, but instead *Newsweek* only revealed it in a short 500 word item in its "Periscope" section. In that issue of *Newsweek*, the featured cover story was on the African-American gender gap in jobs, education and other areas. That story may be a worthy story, but with the U.S. on the precipice of war with Iraq, it was a story that could have waited a week. This is yet another example of the Jewish media control.

No other major media outlets have picked up on the administration deception. Of course it was Israel who was pushing for the war with Iraq, and it is Israel who benefitted from a U.S. military occupation of Iraq. That fact explains why the revelations about the U.S. administration lies were downplayed before the invasion. It was not until after the invasion of Iraq that the news media trumpeted the falsity of the weapons of mass destruction claim. By that point it was too late to close the barn door; the horse had already escaped.

Chris Smith reported further media manipulation surrounding the alleged threat posed by Iraq as follows:

> For months [prior to invading Iraq], administration officials had been touting a series of letters purporting to show Iraqi efforts to buy uranium from the African country of Niger. If the letters weren't exactly a smoking gun, Washington hawks contended, they were at least irrefutable proof that Iraq still had nuclear ambitions.
>
> Then, two weeks ago [on or about March 11, 2003, which was before the U.S. military invasion of Iraq], it all came crashing down. The letters, it was revealed, were hoaxes -- crude forgeries discredited by nuclear weapons experts and disowned by the Central Intelligence Agency. Further, the Agency asserted that it made its concerns known to administration officials in late 2001, shortly after telling the White House about the letters. **For more than a year, Washington had used evidence repudiated by its own intelligence advisors to build a case for war.**

The revelations could have delivered a damaging blow to the White House's political and diplomatic push for invasion. But the national media rapidly moved off the story, swept up in the administration's rush to war. And it all might have ended there, but for Congressman Henry Waxman. In a scathing letter sent to President Bush last week, the California Democrat demands an investigation into what Bush knew about the Niger forgeries and when he knew it. Waxman, who voted last year to give the administration authority to wage a war in Iraq, says there is reason to believe that he and other members of Congress have been misled.

"It is unfathomable how we could be in a situation where the CIA knew information was not reliable but yet it was cited by the President in the State of the Union and by other leading Administration officials," he says. "Either this is knowing deception or utter incompetence and an explanation is urgently needed."

Waxman, who says he signed on to Bush's war initiative in part because he was concerned about Iraq's nuclear aims, wonders how the forgeries could have been used as evidence of Iraqi malfeasance for so many months after they were officially debunked. At the very least, he writes, the recent revelations have created a perception that facts were withheld to bolster the President's case for war.

"It appears that at the same time that you, Secretary Rumsfeld, and State Department officials were citing Iraq's efforts to obtain uranium from Africa as a crucial part of the case against Iraq, U.S. intelligence officials regarded this very same evidence as unreliable," he writes in his letter to the president. "If true, this is deeply disturbing: it would mean that your Administration asked the U.N. Security Council, the Congress, and the American people to rely on information that your own experts knew was not credible."

So far, however, neither the White House nor the national media seem inclined to give Waxman's questions serious consideration.

The administration's response has been a deafening silence, and mainstream media outlets have all but ignored Waxman's missive. While the congressman's charges garnered a brief mention on ABC News, it was left to Tom Engelhardt to break the news in his web log, Tom Dispatch.com. Engelhardt, an editor, historian, teaching fellow at Berkeley's Graduate School of Journalism, and regular contributor to MotherJones.com, says that he is "staggered" by the media's silence -- especially given the prominence of Waxman, the House's Ranking Minority Member of the Committee on Government Reform.

"You might think that when, in the midst of war, a significant member of the minority party in Congress challenges the administration's explanation for why we acted, it might merit the odd line or two, somewhere or other," he wrote.

Waxman spokesperson Karen Lightfoot acknowledges the congressman has been disappointed by the indifferent reception.

"It definitely deserves more attention than it has received," she said.

Over the weekend, Waxman's letter finally made an appearance in the Washington Post, but only as a small item buried within a larger story on the CIA's handling of the Niger letters.

Norman Solomon argues that the mainstream media's treatment of the story fits an established pattern. Noting that the forged letters are just the latest in a string of discredited White House claims, he argues that the mainstream media has frequently been "behind the curve" in reporting on the administration's shortcomings. Solomon, a fellow at the media watchdog group Fairness and Accuracy in Reporting and author of "The Habits of Highly Deceptive Media," faults the press for "waiting to be tossed perspectives and critiques from the administration."

The last few months have witnessed a "slow motion Gulf of Tonkin," he says, "and with very few exceptions, the press is swallowing it."

Eric Alterman agrees. The media critic and author of "What Liberal Media?" says he isn't surprised by the dearth of coverage.

"It's important, but not to the White House," he said. "That's not the kind of thing they care about. And if the White House doesn't care, then most of the media doesn't care either."[573]

Scott McClellan gave his assessment of waging unprovoked war against Iraq, after leaving his position as White House Press Secretary for the Bush Administration:

> What I do know is that war should only be waged when necessary and the Iraq war was not. Waging an unnecessary war is a grave mistake. But in reflecting on all that happened during the Bush administration, I've come to believe that an even more fundamental mistake was made—a decision to turn away from candor and honesty when those qualities were most needed.[574]

McClellan was also critical of the media for being so deferential to the Bush Administration. From his vantage point in the White House, McClellan saw the media as "complicit enablers"[575] of Bush's war strategy that was forged by deceit and framed by fraud.

After the United States invaded Iraq, major news outlets carried stories about the preplanned attack on Iraq. However, the news seems always spun and characterized in terms of George Bush and his administration as the culprits. There was no mention of the influence played by the neo-conservative Zionists. For example, in an interview with Lesley Stahl on CBS 60 Minutes former U.S. Treasury Secretary Paul O'Neil stated that the Bush Administration began laying plans for an invasion of Iraq including the use of American troops within days of President Bush's inauguration in January of 2001. There is no mention of the fact that Zionist factions in the prior Clinton administration and Congress were engaged in the very same planning. In fact, the best U.S. Congress Zionist money could buy passed legislation authorizing President Clinton to engage in all manner of efforts to subvert and overthrow Saddam Hussein, including but not limited to the use of U.S. military training and armaments. The Iraq Liberation Act of 1998, Public Law 105-338, passed by Congress provides in pertinent part:

> Be it enacted by the Senate and House of Representatives of the United States of America in Congress assembled . . . It should be the policy of the United States to support efforts to remove the regime headed by Saddam Hussein from power in Iraq and to promote the emergence of a democratic government to replace that regime. . . . The President may provide to the Iraqi democratic opposition organizations designated in accordance with section 5 the following assistance: . . . The President is authorized to direct the drawdown of defense articles from the stocks of the Department of Defense, defense services of the Department of Defense, and military education and training for such organizations.

Former U.S. Treasury Secretary O'Neill, who was fired by the White House, is the primary source for an upcoming book, "The Price of Loyalty," written by Ron Suskind. O'Neill and other White House insiders gave him documents that prove that in the first three months of 2001 the Bush administration was looking at military options for removing Saddam Hussein from power and planning for the aftermath of Hussein's downfall.[576]

Suskind reviewed pre 9-11-01 official memos, one of them marked 'secret' and titled 'Plan for Post-Saddam Iraq.' Another document from the Pentagon was titled "Foreign Suitors For Iraqi Oilfield Contracts." It outlines areas of oil exploration and discusses contractors around the world from 30 to 40 countries and their intentions on oil in Iraq.[577] Bush and his administration at the outset was bent on invading Iraq. The tone of the Bush Administration toward Iraq was to find a way to invade Iraq. The 9/11 attacks provided just the political atmosphere for the Iraq invasion. The post 9/11 declared "war on terrorism," by the U.S. Congress gave the President a blank check to wage a preemptive war on any country his Zionist masters characterize as a "terrorist threat." The Zionists put Bush in power and he began doing his job as he saw it; he obeyed his political masters.

Bush, Congress, and the Jewish controlled media have tried to characterize the invasion of Iraq after the fact as being prompted by faulty intelligence; they claim that the war was all a big mistake. In fact, the reports cited by the U.S. Government to support their claim are simply attempts by the government to cover-up a premeditated plan to invade and wage an unjustified war on Iraq. Proof that President Bush and his trusted advisors lied the United States into an unnecessary war with Iraq is provided by Warren P. Strobel and John Walcott of Knight Ridder.

> A highly classified British memo, leaked in the midst of Britain's just-concluded [May 2005] election campaign, indicates that President Bush decided to overthrow Iraqi President Saddam Hussein by summer 2002 and was determined to ensure that U.S. intelligence data supported his policy.
>
> The document, which summarizes a July 23, 2002, meeting of British Prime Minister Tony Blair with his top security advisers, reports on a visit to Washington by the head of Britain's MI-6 intelligence service. The visit took place while the Bush administration was still declaring to the American public that no decision had been made to go to war.
>
> "There was a perceptible shift in attitude. Military action was now seen as inevitable," the MI-6 chief said at the meeting, according to the memo. "Bush wanted to remove Saddam through military action, justified by the conjunction of terrorism and WMD," weapons of mass destruction.
>
> The memo said "the intelligence and facts were being fixed around the policy."
>
> No weapons of mass destruction have been found in Iraq since the U.S. invasion in March 2003.
>
> The White House has repeatedly denied accusations made by

several top foreign officials that it manipulated intelligence estimates to justify an invasion of Iraq. It has instead pointed to the conclusions of two studies, one by the Senate Intelligence Committee and one by a presidentially appointed panel, that cite serious failures by the CIA and other agencies in judging Saddam's weapons programs.

The principal U.S. intelligence analysis, called a National Intelligence Estimate, wasn't completed until October 2002, well after the United States and United Kingdom had apparently decided military force should be used to overthrow Saddam's regime.

The newly disclosed memo, which was first reported by the Sunday Times of London, hasn't been disavowed by the British government. A spokesman for the British Embassy in Washington referred queries to another official, who didn't return calls for comment on Thursday.

A former senior U.S. official called it "an absolutely accurate description of what transpired" during the senior British intelligence officer's visit to Washington. He spoke on condition of anonymity.

A White House official said the administration wouldn't comment on leaked British documents.

In July 2002, and well afterward, top Bush administration foreign policy advisers were insisting that "there are no plans to attack Iraq on the president's desk." But the memo quotes British Foreign Secretary Jack Straw, a close colleague of then-Secretary of State Colin Powell, as saying that "Bush had made up his mind to take military action."

Straw is quoted as having his doubts about the Iraqi threat. "But the case was thin. Saddam was not threatening his neighbors, and his WMD capability was less than that of Libya, North Korea or Iran," the memo reported he said.

Straw reportedly proposed that Saddam be given an ultimatum to readmit United Nations weapons inspectors, which could help justify the eventual use of force.

Powell in August 2002 persuaded Bush to make the case against

Saddam at the United Nations and to push for renewed weapons inspections.

But there were deep divisions within the White House over that course of action. The British document says that the National Security Council, then led by Condoleezza Rice, "had no patience with the U.N. route."

Rep. John Conyers, D-Mich., the leading Democrat on the House Judiciary Committee, is circulating a letter among fellow Democrats asking Bush for an explanation of the document's charges, an aide said.[578]

The secret Downing Street memo[579] also reveals that on July 23, 2002 British Prime Minister Tony Blair and members of his cabinet were going along with Bush and devising a plan for a joint U.S./British military invasion of Iraq.[580] However, two days later Blair dissembled to the House of Commons by stating that "we have not got to the stage of military action . . . we have not yet reached the point of decision."[581]

Without question, the Downing Street memo was one of the most significant news events of the year. The memo presents clear evidence that the Bush Administration lied the U.S. into the Iraq War. Yet, media analysts at *Editor and Publisher* reported: "The liberal Web site Media Matters for America found that editorials in four of the five largest U.S. newspapers -- USA Today, The Wall Street Journal, The New York Times, and the Los Angeles Times - 'remained conspicuously silent about the controversy surrounding the document.'"[582]

Several editors blamed their own lack of coverage of the memo on the Associated Press' (AP) lack of coverage.[583] "The Associated Press is a not-for-profit cooperative, which means it is owned by its 1,500 U.S. daily newspaper members. They elect a board of directors that directs the cooperative."[584] Most U.S. Newspapers rely heavily on the reporting by the AP, especially regarding international news.

The Associated Press filters the news through its control bureaus; the Downing Street memo seems to have been one of many worthy news stories that never made it past the censors in the control bureau. AP's Middle East control bureau, which is located in Israel, demonstrates that the AP is controlled by Zionist Jews. Alison Weir explains that the AP Middle East control bureau "is staffed largely by Jewish and Israeli journalists, many with close family ties to the Israeli military. Their reporting invariably contains pro-Israel spin and context. Quite often, they don't even send out reports on newsworthy items that reveal negative facts about Israel."[585]

"Deborah Seward, Associated Press international editor, has told Eric Boehlert of Salon magazine that the AP 'dropped the ball' in failing to pick up the Downing Street memo story earlier. AP's deputy international editor, Nick Tatro, told Boehlert 'It was our intent to do a story, and it just didn't happen,' for a variety of reasons."[586] The AP is recognized for their unparalleled reach, with news sources throughout the world. It is astounding that their explanation for not reporting on this blockbuster story is that they "dropped the ball" and "it just didn't happen!" That does not pass the smell test.

Why can't the International Editor and the Deputy International Editor for the AP offer any explanation for not reporting the news of the memo other than to state that they just didn't do it? Obviously, the story was deliberately spiked by the AP, and they don't want to admit it. I perceive at work the hidden hand of the Zionists who control the AP. How many other stories have never seen the light of day because the AP deliberately "dropped the ball" or the reporting purposely "just didn't happen?" Former CIA Analyst, Ray McGovern, has labeled the major media outlets as "the domesticated press," for their purposeful efforts in avoiding any meaningful coverage of the Downing Street memo.[587]

Some leading lights of the Washington press corps have had the audacity to explain their disinterest in reporting on the July 23, 2002, Downing Street memo by making the incredible claim that the memo is really not important news. Joe Conason of Salon.com indignantly objected to that explanation. Conason pointed out that the major media's mooing plaintive chorus that the Downing Street memo wasn't news would only be true if the absence of news were defined by the press' refusal to report it.[588]

Even when a major media outlet like Knight Ridder did report on the memo, the news was spun away from the real culprits behind the war. Notice what is not mentioned in the above Knight Ridder article: the role of Israel and her agents in the U.S. government in pushing for the invasion of Iraq. The people are only allowed to see George Bush as the culprit. The people are led to believe that all we must do is throw the bum out of office and that will solve all our problems.

What the people do not realize is that the next political savior will be bought and paid for by the Zionist cabal, and the same process will begin all over again. We saw that with the election of George Bush. People clambered for a change from the communist policies of Bill Clinton, and then we ended up with George Bush and his fascist policies. Bush is supported by the very same scum who put Clinton into power. Obama is as much a puppet as was George Bush and his father before him. Whether we choose a conservative, liberal, socialist, fascist, or communist, it is all the same - Talmudic Zionism.

25   The Core of the Conspiracy

The attacks of 9-11-2001 illustrate how far the United States as a country has sunk. This is the end-game. All, however, is not lost. There is a strategy to wrest our sovereignty back and reap the blessings of our God-given rights.

The first step is to gain understanding. "My people are destroyed for lack of knowledge." Hosea 4:6. "Wisdom is the principal thing; therefore get wisdom: and with all thy getting get understanding." Proverbs 4:7. With that in mind, let us explore the nature of our foreign and domestic enemies.

Most have been misled into believing that the Jews follow the Old Testament law. John Chrysostom, a 4th century Christian, explains the fallacy that the Jews are followers of the God of the Old Testament:

> But at any rate the Jews say that they, too, adore God. God forbid that I say that. No Jew adores God! Who say so? The Son of God say so. For he said: "If you were to know my Father, you would also know me. But you neither know me nor do you know my Father." Could I produce a witness more trustworthy than the Son of God?

The Jews for approximately 2,000 years have expressly denied that Jesus is the Christ. The word of God makes it clear that those who deny that Jesus is Christ, as do the Jews, are liars and antichrist.

> Little children, it is the last time: and as ye have heard that antichrist shall come, **even now are there many antichrists**; whereby we know that it is the last time. They went out from us, but they were not of us; for if they had been of us, they would *no doubt* have continued with us: but *they went out*, that they might be

> made manifest that they were not all of us. But ye have an unction from the Holy One, and ye know all things. I have not written unto you because ye know not the truth, but because ye know it, and that no lie is of the truth. **Who is a liar but he that denieth that Jesus is the Christ? He is antichrist**, that denieth the Father and the Son. Whosoever denieth the Son, the same hath not the Father: *(but) he that acknowledgeth the Son hath the Father also.* (1 John 2:18-23 AV)

During the time of Christ, the Talmud existed only in oral form, which Jesus referred to as the traditions of the scribes and Pharisees. This early oral tradition is called the Mishnah. It was only after Christ's crucifixion that the Mishnah was reduced to writing. The rabbis later added rabbinical commentaries to the Mishnah, which are called the Gemara.[589] Together these comprise the Talmud, which is now a collection of books.

There are today two basic Talmudic texts, the Babylonian Talmud and the Jerusalem Talmud. The Babylonian Talmud is regarded as the authoritative version and takes precedence over the Jerusalem Talmud.[590] The Babylonian Talmud is based on the mystical religious practices of the Babylonians which were assimilated by the Jewish Rabbis during their Babylonian captivity around 600 B.C. The Rabbis then used these occult traditions in place of the word of God.

Among the Orthodox and Hasidic Jews the Talmud has authority over even the Old Testament.[591] There is a sect of Jews, the Karaites, that adhere to the authority of the Old Testament alone. The Karaites, historically, have been hated and severely persecuted by Orthodox and Hasidic Jewish rabbinate. Ethiopian Jews do not adhere to the Talmud either and consequently they are not accepted by the Talmudic Jews. Former Jew Benjamin Freedman, in his book *Facts are Facts,* authoritatively traced the lineage of modern day Talmudic Jews back to the Pharisees of Christ's time:

> The eminent Rabi Louis Finkelstein, the head of The Jewish Theological Seminary of America, often referred to as "The Vatican of Judaism," in his Foreword to his First Edition of his world famous classic "The Pharisees, The Sociological Background of Their Faith", on page XXI states:
>
> "... Judaism . . . **Pharisaism became Talmudism, Talmudism became Medieval Rabbinism, and Medieval Rabbinism became Modern Rabbinism. But throughout these changes in name ... the spirit of the ancient Pharisees survives, unaltered** ... From Palestine to Babylonia; from Babylonia to North Africa, Italy, Spain, France and Germany; from these to Poland, Russia, and eastern Europe generally, ancient Pharisaism has wandered "demonstrates the enduring importance which attaches to

Pharisaism as a religious movement ..."[592]

What did Jesus have to say about the religion of the Pharisees? Jesus said they masqueraded as religious men who have the oracles of God, but they were really irreligious, teaching instead the doctrines of men.

> Then came to Jesus scribes and Pharisees, which were of Jerusalem, saying, Why do thy disciples transgress the tradition of the elders? for they wash not their hands when they eat bread. But he answered and said unto them, **Why do ye also transgress the commandment of God by your tradition?** For God commanded, saying, Honour thy father and mother: and, He that curseth father or mother, let him die the death. But ye say, Whosoever shall say to *his* father or *his* mother, *It is* a gift, by whatsoever thou mightest be profited by me; And honour not his father or his mother, *he shall be free*. **Thus have ye made the commandment of God of none effect by your tradition.** *Ye* **hypocrites**, well did Esaias prophesy of you, saying, This people draweth nigh unto me with their mouth, and honoureth me with *their* lips; but their heart is far from me. But **in vain they do worship me, teaching** *for* **doctrines the commandments of men.** (Matthew 15:1-9 AV)

To what traditions was Jesus referring when he upbraided the Pharisees for using them to transgress and replace the laws of God? Can we find out about those traditions today? Yes; the Talmud is a codification of the traditions of the scribes and Pharisees to which Jesus spoke. Michael Rodkinson (M. Levi Frumkin), who wrote the first English translation of the Babylonian Talmud, states the following in his book *The History of the Talmud*:

> Is the literature that Jesus was familiar with in his early years yet in existence in the world? Is it possible for us to get at it? To such inquiries the learned class of Jewish rabbis answer by holding up the Talmud. **The Talmud then, is the written form of that which, in the time of Jesus, was called the Traditions of the Elders**, and to which he makes frequent allusions.[593] (emphasis added)

During the time of Christ the Scribes and Pharisees were constantly heckling and challenging Jesus, and it was they who plotted his crucifixion. Read what Jesus had to say to those Jews.

> They answered and said unto him, Abraham is our father. Jesus saith unto them, If ye were Abraham's children, ye would do the works of Abraham. But now ye seek to kill me, a man that hath told you the truth, which I have heard of God: this did not

> Abraham. Ye do the deeds of your father. Then said they to him, We be not born of fornication; we have one Father, *even* God. Jesus said unto them, If God were your Father, ye would love me: for I proceeded forth and came from God; neither came I of myself, but he sent me. Why do ye not understand my speech? *even* because ye cannot hear my word. **Ye are of *your* father the devil, and the lusts of your father ye will do.** He was a murderer from the beginning, and abode not in the truth, because there is no truth in him. When he speaketh a lie, he speaketh of his own: for he is a liar, and the father of it. And because I tell *you* the truth, ye believe me not. Which of you convinceth me of sin? And if I say the truth, why do ye not believe me? He that is of God heareth God's words: **ye therefore hear *them* not, because ye are not of God.** (John 8:39-47 AV)

In Matthew 23 Jesus has even stronger language to describe the scribes and Pharisees. Jesus called them serpents, vipers, blind guides, whited sepulchers, and hypocrites who will be damned to hell.

> Woe unto you, scribes and Pharisees, hypocrites! for ye pay tithe of mint and anise and cummin, and have omitted the weightier *matters* of the law, judgment, mercy, and faith: these ought ye to have done, and not to leave the other undone. *Ye* blind guides, which strain at a gnat, and swallow a camel. Woe unto you, scribes and Pharisees, hypocrites! for ye make clean the outside of the cup and of the platter, but within they are full of extortion and excess. *Thou* blind Pharisee, cleanse first that *which is* within the cup and platter, that the outside of them may be clean also. Woe unto you, scribes and Pharisees, hypocrites! for ye are like unto whited sepulchres, which indeed appear beautiful outward, but are within full of dead *men's* bones, and of all uncleanness. Even so ye also outwardly appear righteous unto men, but within ye are full of hypocrisy and iniquity. Woe unto you, scribes and Pharisees, hypocrites! because ye build the tombs of the prophets, and garnish the sepulchres of the righteous, And say, If we had been in the days of our fathers, we would not have been partakers with them in the blood of the prophets. Wherefore ye be witnesses unto yourselves, that ye are the children of them which killed the prophets. Fill ye up then the measure of your fathers. *Ye* serpents, *ye* generation of vipers, how can ye escape the damnation of hell? (Matthew 23:23-33 AV)

Why would Jesus use such strong language against the Pharisees and scribes? To answer that we should examine some of the Talmudic traditions that have developed over the years. For starters, the Talmudic Jews have a hatred for Gentiles. To them Gentiles are vile animals, who are unclean and have no legal rights.[594]

Citing Folio 114b of the Tractate *Baba Mezi'a* from the Babylonian Talmud, *The Jewish Encyclopedia* states that the Talmud only considers Jews as men; Gentiles are categorized in the Talmud as barbarians.[595] Elizabeth Dilling, in her book *The Jewish Religion: Its Influence Today,* explains the racial view adopted by Jews as codified in their Talmud:

> The basic Talmudic doctrine includes more than a "super-race" complex. It is an "only" race concept. The non-Jew thus ranks as an animal, has no property rights and no legal rights under any code whatever. If lies, bribes or kicks are necessary to get non-Jews under control - that is legitimate. There is only one "sin," and that is anything which will frighten non-Jews and thus make it harder for the Jewish "humans" to get them under control. "Milk the Gentile," is the Talmudic rule, but don't get caught in such a way as to jeopardize Jewish interests. Summarized, Talmudism is the quintessence of distilled hatred and discrimination - without cause, against non-Jews.[596]

The following passages from the Talmud attest to the Jewish hatred of Gentiles:

Baba Mezia 114b: Only Jews are men, gentiles ("heathen") are not men.

Baba Bathra 54b: Property of Gentiles is like the desert; whoever gets there first gets it.

Sanhedrin 57a: If a Gentile robs a Jew, he must pay him back. But if a Jew robs a Gentile, the Jew may keep the loot. Likewise, if a Gentile kills a Jew, the Gentile is to be killed. But if a Jew kills a Gentile, there is no death penalty.

Sanhedrin 52b: Adultery forbidden with the neighbor's wife, but is not forbidden with the wife of a heathen (gentile). The implication is that a heathen is not a neighbor.

The Talmud has a permissive attitude toward pederasty and sodomy. For example:

Sanhedrin 55b: It is permitted to have sexual intercourse with a girl three years and one day old. See also Yebamoth 57b, 60b; Abodah Zarah 37a.

Sanhedrin 54b: If a man has sex with a boy less than nine years old, he is not guilty of pederasty. He is only guilty of pederasty if the boy is over 9 years old.

Kethoboth 11b: When a grown-up man has intercourse with a little girl it is nothing, for when the girl is less than three years old it is as if one puts the finger into the eye, tears come to the eye again and again, so does virginity come back to the little girl under three years.

What are the consequences of such perverted religious doctrine? Ted Pike explains that "a number of Judaism's most venerable ancient rabbis, whose edicts are recorded in the 'Bible' of modern Judaism, the Talmud, were pedophiles."[597] Pike summarizes some of the history behind the longstanding pederasty in the Orthodox Jewish community and names some of the rabbis who promoted pederasty:

> Some of the earliest and very greatest sages, such as the "great" Simeon ben Yohai, encouraged rabbis to sexually assault ("marry") girls as young as three and permitted Jewish women to molest boys under the age of 9. (See, "Judaism and Homosexuality: A Marriage Made in Hell" and "Pedophilia 'Rampant' in Orthodox Judaism") Orthodox Judaism today reveals a disturbing trend: the more that Jewish leaders literally believe the Talmud, the more they are charged with sex crimes against minors.[598]

The permissiveness found in the Talmud toward pederasty has given rise to a child molestation scandal in the Orthodox Jewish community. Ted Pike reports:

> It is rare today that rabbis from the liberal branches of Judaism, which often "spiritualized" the Talmud, are accused of sex crimes against minors. (These are Reform, Conservative and Reconstructionist.) Yet in Orthodox Jewish centers such as New York and Israel, an escalating number of such Orthodox authorities are indicted as child molesters. **These rabbis do not merely theorize about the Talmud's encouragement of child sex but act on it.**
>
> Shmarya Rosenberg publishes Failed Messiah, a site devoted to ultra-Orthodox Judaism and exposing its sins. A former member of the Lubavitcher Hasidic movement who remains a practicing Orthodox Jew, he has published hundreds of posts about Orthodox molestation and says he gets dozens of tips per week.
>
> New York journalist and attorney Michael Lesher says, "A certain amount of sexual deviance is going to be found in any society. What is really shocking is the extent of license that's been extended to these people to victimize children and **if you are a pedophile, the Orthodox Jewish community is one of the best places you can be**…" (In The Wall of Silence, a Canadian TV documentary about haredi sexual abuse, part of a larger series.)
>
> Amy Neustein is an Orthodox Jew who wrote Tempest in the Temple: Jewish Communities and Child Sex Scandals. She says, "What outrages me most about pedophilia in the Orthodox Jewish

community is the systematic cover-up by its leaders of the ongoing crimes perpetrated against children. **Rabbis who have a lot of influence in the community systematically intimidate and threaten abuse victims, their advocates, their supporters and their therapist.** The abuse victims are left with no support and they're fighting a behemoth that's so strong they don't know where to turn."

But it is not only leaders who cover for abusers. An Orthodox rabbi, Yosef Blau, who counsels abuse survivors in New York, notes a significant difference between Catholic and Jewish sex abuse. **"In the Catholic Church, the issue was the cover-up by the church hierarchy. Here, it's the community, not the hierarchy. It's the whole community not wanting to admit trouble in our midst." Another difference is that pedophilia in the Catholic Church is condemned by church dogma. Child abuse in Orthodox Judaism, however, is commanded by its most authoritative religious source, the Babylonian Talmud.**

In 2008 a rabbi who investigates sex abuse in Orthodox communities was chased out of a synagogue by 200 Hasidic Jewish men in London, who formed a mob—even using their cell phones to call for backup—when they recognized him. (It is hardly possible to imagine this happening in a Catholic church.) Police had to intervene. The rabbi, Nachum Rosenberg, says he feared for his life.

Rosenberg has been investigating molestation in Orthodox communities for 18 months. He says, "These things are happening all the time, but the rabbonim prefer to take a quiet road." A victim abuse counselor in Brooklyn said, "Outside the Chasidic community no one has heard of Rabbi Rosenberg, but all the Chasidic communities know of his work." And they do not seem to appreciate it. When the attack outside the synagogue was reported on Jewish websites, there were hundreds of reader comments—mostly negative! Some called the rabbi a "pig," "sick" and "mentally retarded."

Washington Post reported on Rabbi Sidney Goldenburg, who had a 30-year religious career and spent it abusing children, shielded by the community as well as the hierarchy. He moved from place to place when whispers began. Not one family sued on behalf of their teenage daughters. Numerous authorities who knew of the multiple complaints against him did not

mention them when asked for a reference after he had moved. The law finally caught up with him but after a mere two years in prison, "Goldenberg can still call himself a rabbi, because Jewish authorities say ordination is like an academic degree -- once conferred, it cannot be revoked."

Failed Messiah reports that there are multiple religious obstacles for Jews who might otherwise report sex abuse. "The obstacles include traditional Jewish rules, adhered to in some pockets of the Orthodox world, such as a prohibition against 'chillul Hashem,' bringing shame on God's name, and against 'mesirah,' informing on fellow believers to secular authorities."[599]

Pike reveals that Mordechai Elon, who is one of the most powerful rabbis in the world, was investigated in 2010 in Israel for having sex with numerous male students, at least one by force. Since 2003, Elon's crimes against children had been addressed only by a Jewish non-government body established known as Takana. It was reported by Pike that all that had been required in the previous molestations was a promise from Elon that he would limit his contact with young men. Mordechai Elon is described by some as a "master and leader." His level of influence in Israeli families is far reaching. He is considered the Jewish "Billy Graham."

Why was Elon given such special treatment? Rabbis have a divine-like status among the Jewish faithful. When there is an insular Jewish community, as is the case in Israel, the child molesting rabbis are protected from prosecution by a special tribunal. Ted Pike explains:

> In ultra-Orthodox (Kabbalistic) culture, Talmudic sages are regarded as semi-divine, some having preexisted in heaven before bringing God's insight to earth. Ultra-Orthodox laity also regard themselves as the presence of divinity in this world. The mythical status of rabbis today gives them all the more power to abuse in secret. When they are found out, they are not responsible to the police.
>
> In Haaretz in 2010, Gideon Levy wrote that the Takana forum is an alternative law enforcement agency for religious Zionists. Levy explains, "A high school teacher at a secular school who sexually assaults his students would be turned over to the police. A rabbi at a yeshiva suspected of the same thing would be turned over to Takana." This body typically recommends distance from temptation or public life…not prison or public accountability! Even when authorities in Israel are contacted, permissiveness from the government continues. Apparently the Israeli attorney general also advocated silence in the Elon case.[600]

Below are some examples of Orthodox rabbis who were caught committing sex crimes. Because the Jewish culture systematically protects rabbinic child molestation, there is no telling how many more remain un-apprehended. This list is the tip of the proverbial iceberg.

1. "Rabbi Avrohom Mondrowitz, a Brooklyn based psychologist, was among the first of a series of high-profile rabbis or yeshiva teachers to be indicted on charges of sexual abuse that have rocked the Orthodox community in recent decades. Press reports have stated that the five-count indictment against him is based on complaints from more than one hundred victims." (Haaretz.com – N.Y. High Court Takes on Orthodox Sexual Abuse Scandal).

2. Rabbi Moshe Nussboim is currently on trial behind closed doors in Jerusalem, accused of sexually abusing three boys in his school between the years 2002 to 2008. (The Jerusalem Post - Sexual Abuse Case Sheds Light on Emmanuel's Ethnic Tensions).

3. Rabbi Nechemya Weberman, a prominent Brooklyn rabbi, was charged in 2011 with molesting a 12-year-old girl over three years. Weberman was charged with a criminal sex act, rape, endangering the welfare of a child and sexual abuse.

4. Rabbi Avrohom Reichman was temporarily removed as principal of a Brooklyn yeshiva after being accused of sexually abusing a student. The victim was pressured by all his religious leaders to be quiet about the incidents.

5. Rabbi Israel Weingarten was found guilty of molesting his daughter over a seven-year period by a Brooklyn Federal Court in 2009.

6. Rabbi Baruch Lebovits was convicted of repeatedly sexually abusing a 16-year-old classmate of his son. A Brooklyn jury found him guilty of eight counts of sexual abuse.

7. Rabbi Stanley Z. Levitt, in 2009, was charged with sexually assaulting two 11-year-old students while he taught at the Maimonides School in Brooklyn during the 1970s. In previous years, Levitt was also arrested on various charges related to claims of indecent assault against three other boys.

8. Rabbi Bryan Bramley was arrested in 2010 by U.S. Marshals for the rape of a 7-year-old girl in March 2000 in New York City.

9. Rabbi Yehuda Kolko pleaded guilty in 2008 to two counts of endangering the welfare of a child for molesting a 6-year-old boy. Another alleged victim stated that he personally knows of another 15 victims, and that he believes more than 100 other boys were molested by the rabbi.[601]

Talmudic Judaism has the most intense hatred for Jesus.[602] While some Jews will deny that the Talmud teaches such things, Benjamin Freedman, a former Talmudic Jew, stated that: "there have never been recorded more vicious and vile libelous blasphemies of Jesus, of Christians and the Christian faith than you will find between the covers of the 63 books of the Talmud which forms the basis of Jewish religious law, as well as being the textbook used in the training of rabbis."[603] For example:

Sanhedrin 106a & b: Mary was a whore; Jesus was an evil man.

Shabbath 104b: Jesus was a magician and a fool. Mary was an adulteress.

Sanhedrin 43a: Jesus was guilty of sorcery and apostasy; he deserved execution. The disciples of Jesus deserve to be killed.

Gittin 57b: Jesus was sent to hell, where he is punished by boiling excrement for mocking the Rabbis.

Out of the abundance of the heart the mouth speaks, and the Talmudic Jews have evil hearts. Winston Churchill had the following to say about them.

> It would almost seem as if the Gospel of Christ and the gospel of anti-Christ were designed to originate from the same people; and that this mystic and mysterious race had been chosen for the supreme manifestations, both of the divine and the diabolical......From the days of "Spartacus" Weishaupt to those of Karl Marx, and down to Trotsky (Russia), Bela Kun (Hungary), Rosa Luxembourg (Germany) and Emma Goldman (United States), this worldwide conspiracy for the overthrow of civilisation and for the reconstitution of society on the basis of arrested development, of envious malevolence and impossible equality, has been steadily growing. It played, as a modern writer, Mrs Nesta Webster, has so ably shown, a definitely recognisable part in the tragedy of the French Revolution. It has been the mainspring of every subversive movement during the nineteenth century; and now at last this band of extraordinary personalities from the underworld of the great cities of Europe and America have gripped the Russian people by the hair of their heads and have become practically the undisputed masters of that enormous empire. There

is no need to exaggerate the part played in the creation of Bolshevism and in the bringing about of the Russian Revolution by these international and for the most part atheistical Jews. It is certainly a very great one; it probably outweighs all others.[604]

The Pharisees also had other doctrines in addition to the Talmud. These other teachings were called the Cabala. The Cabala were occult oral traditions that were not shared with the general populace. The Cabala, as with the Talmud, has over time been reduced to writings which span numerous volumes. The Cabala is the source for the spiritual exercises of the Jesuits.

Magic and occult mysticism runs throughout the Cabala. Judith Weill, a professor of Jewish mysticism stated that magic is deeply rooted in Jewish tradition, but the Jews are reticent to acknowledge it and don't even refer to it as magic.[605] Gershom Scholem, Professor of Kabbalah at Hebrew University in Jerusalem, admitted that the Cabala contains a great deal of black magic and sorcery, which he explained involves invoking the powers of devils to disrupt the natural order of things.[606] Professor Scholem also stated that there are devils who are in submission to the Talmud; in the Cabala these devils are called *shedim Yehuda'im*.[607] The bible states clearly that such things are an abomination to the Lord.

> There shall not be found among you *any one* that maketh his son or his daughter to pass through the fire, *or* that useth divination, *or* an observer of times, or an enchanter, or a witch, Or a charmer, or a consulter with familiar spirits, or a wizard, or a necromancer. For all that do these things *are* an abomination unto the LORD: and because of these abominations the LORD thy God doth drive them out from before thee. (Deuteronomy 18:10-12 AV)

The Cabala, like the Talmud, graphically blasphemes Jesus. For example, in Zohar III, 282a, the Cabala refers to Jesus as a dog who resides among filth and vermin.[608]

According to John Torell, in the Jewish Cabala, God consists of one male being and one female being. The male part of God (called "En-Sof" by the Cabalists) withdrew himself into himself and created a vacuum in his own structure, which created a bottomless pit (this abyss is called the "kelipot" by the Cabalists). The Cabala teaches that the female part of God has fallen into this pit, and has taken the form of the "holy serpent." The Cabala further teaches that the "holy serpent" is surrounded by evil spirits and she is tempted at all times. The "holy serpent" is trying to set herself free from the bottomless pit. Once she does this she can enter the earth as "the messiah." Cabalists teach that "the messiah" will only appear on earth in one of two ways. One way is for the Cabalistic Jews to destroy all evil on the earth and make it totally good. The other alternative is for the Cabalistic Jews to destroy all good on earth and make it totally evil.[609]

The Cabalistic Jews have decided that is harder to make things good and so they have chosen the second alternative of destroying all goodness and making the world evil. This Cabalistic religion is grounded in the commission of sins in order to bring about the ascension of their messiah, the "holy serpent," out of the bottomless pit to make "her" appearance on earth. These Jews believe that only by breaking the laws of God can they serve their god. Do not think that Jews are ignorant of the fact that Satan is the god of their religion. Harold Wallace Rosenthal, Administrative Assistant to United States Senator from New York, Jacob K. Javits, in a 1976 interview with Walter White Jr. stated: **"Most Jews do not like to admit it, but our god is Lucifer."**[610] These modern day Pharisees go to great lengths not only to sin themselves, but also to lead as many others into sin as they serve their evil god, Satan. Jesus revealed their nature when he said to the Pharisees: "Woe unto you, scribes and Pharisees, hypocrites! for ye compass sea and land to make one proselyte, and when he is made, ye make him twofold more the child of hell than yourselves." (Matthew 23:15 AV)

This is confirmed by Jewish "rabbi" David Cooper, who spent eight years studying the Cabala in Jerusalem's Old City.

> The lesson is that even the heart of Satan has a divine spark; even the heart of evil yearns to be redeemed. This is important, because we learn that our job is not to set up the battleground to eradicate evil, but search out its spark of holiness. **Our task is not to destroy but to build.**[611]

* * *

> The mystical teaching of the Baal Shem Tov, however, presents us with a new paradigm. It says that evil has a divine nature within it. As the *Zohar* describes, 'there is no sphere of the Other Side (evil) that entirely lacks some streak of light from the side of holiness.' [Zohar II:69a-b] **Rather than destroy it, our task is to uplift it.**[612]

Surely Satan has an end in mind for constructing such a sinister religious doctrine. He does, and it is nothing short of the subjugation of all men under the dictatorial rule of his antichrist! He uses the escalating sin and crime in society as a justification to bring about more government regulation and control of the masses. As explained by Edmond Burke: "Men are qualified for civil liberty in exact proportion to their disposition to put moral chains on their own appetites. Society cannot exist unless a controlling power upon will and appetite be placed somewhere, and the less of it there is within, the more there is without. It is ordained in the eternal constitution of things that men of intemperate minds cannot be free. Their passions forge their fetters."

This evil doctrine can also be seen in the Talmud, where incest, fornication, adultery, etc. are promoted as virtues and something to be desired. It is difficult for the Gentile world to fully comprehend what is happening in this Jewish netherworld of conspiracy unless they understand the nature of Cabalistic Judaism. It is a religion that is based on the promotion, propagation, and commission of sin as a means to world domination.[613]

President George W. Bush, in his autobiography, *A Charge to Keep* stated: **"During my senior year I joined Skull and Bones, a secret society, so secret I can't say anything more."** What is so secret that he cannot speak any further about it? The secret is that in return for power, wealth, and fame, he must blindly obey his Satanic masters in their antichrist conspiracy to enslave and rule the world.

The initiation ceremony for Skull and Bones involves, but is not limited to, the inductees laying naked in a coffin and telling their deepest sexual secrets. Anton LaVey the founder of the Church of Satan in his *Satanic Rituals: Companion to the Satanic Bible* states that such a coffin ritual is a Satanic ritual common in many pagan orders. During the ritual a powerful spiritual force charges through the participants transforming their lives dramatically. This powerful spiritual force is a devil. The participants in these ceremonies end up possessed by a devil.

Evidence indicates that the Order of Skull & Bones founded at Yale in 1832 is a chapter of the Illuminati, which was originally founded in 1776 at the University of Ingolstadt in Germany.[614] From this we know that Skull & Bones is not American at all, but is a branch of a foreign secret society.[615] As with the Jesuits and the Illuminati, Skull & Bones has many ostensible Gentiles who are members. From this fact most people have mischaracterized the Skull & Bones as a purely Gentile organization. That is not true. Just as with the Illuminati and the Jesuits, the Skull & Bones is controlled by and serves the interests of Zionist Jews. George W. Bush is a prime example of a Gentile member of Skull & Bones who is acting in the interests of Israel to the detriment of the United States. He is completely controlled by Zionist Jews.

The Jewish control of Skull & Bones comes from its roots as a chapter in the crypto-Jewish Illuminati. Some of the practices and terms of the Skull & Bones reveal the Jewish nature of the Order. For example, those outside Skull & Bones are referred to by Skull & Bones members as vandals and **"Gentiles."**[616] Furthermore, in an attempt to conceal the meanings of their writings from any Gentile outsider who may obtain a copy, members of the Skull & Bones often obscure key words by deleting the vowels. For example, patriarchs would be written as p-tr–rchs, bones would be written as b-n-s.[617] The Hebrew alphabet does not have vowels, they use accent marks, and so Jews are accustomed to writing without using vowels. It is not surprising that they would follow that same practice when trying to conceal the meaning in their writings from the uninitiated Gentile world.

The Skull & Bones use the Hegelian dialectic to change society into a totalitarian state. Under Hegel's dialectic there must be a conflict, either real or perceived, between a thesis and an antithesis which is resolved by a synthesis of the two. The secret societies create these conflicts in order to move society regressively away from Christ and Christian principles and toward Satan and Satanic principles. One example of the dialectic in action is the orchestrated conflict between the German Nazis and Russian communists during World War II.

An American company, International Barnsdall, which was controlled by the members of the Order of Skull & Bones (the American chapter of the Illuminati) through the W.A. Harriman and Guaranty Trust companies, supplied the much needed equipment to Communist Russia in

1922 that allowed the communists to successfully exploit their oil reserves in the Caucasus.[618] This became a major reason for the Soviet economic recovery during that period. The oil supplied the largest single source of foreign exchange for the Soviets, accounting for 20% of the value of all Soviet exports.[619]

The W.A. Harriman and Guaranty Trust companies also financed the mechanization of the manganese mining operation in the Soviet Union.[620] The manganese mining income was second only to oil in foreign exchange income to the Soviets.[621] The assistance by W.A. Harriman and Guaranty Trust was instrumental in saving the communist revolution in Russia from certain economic collapse. This assistance was all done in clear violation of U.S. law.[622]

During the Lend Lease period, circa 1941 W.A. Harriman was appointed the Administrator of Lend Lease to Russia. The Lend Lease program was only supposed to allow the flow of military goods, however, government records reflect that extraordinary amounts of industrial equipment were also shipped to Russia. Amazingly, the Russians even received plates and ink for the German occupation currency redeemable in U.S. dollars.[623] It was estimated the redeeming of that money printed by the communist Russians cost the American citizens 250 million dollars.[624] Even more amazing was the revelation of Major George Racey Jordan that Lend Lease was used to secretly supply the Russians with our atomic secrets along with 2.2 pounds of uranium.[625] The total U.S. stock of uranium at the time was only 4.5 pounds.[626]

The Skull & Bones had nurtured and supported the Bolshevik revolution. With the establishment of communism in Russia they now needed an antagonist to communism in order to bring about world government.[627] The antithesis to the communist thesis would be the Nazi Party in Germany. W.A. Harriman and Guaranty Trust along with the Rothschild and Warburg banking interests and assisted by other firms controlled by members of Skull & Bones helped finance the Nazi Party in Germany in 1932.[628] In 1942 the United States Government seized the assets of Union Bank because it and its officers were found to have violated the Trading With the Enemy Act in their financing and support of Nazi Germany. The Union Banking Corporation was established in 1924 as a unit in the Manhattan offices of W.A. Harriman & Co. Prescott Bush was made vice president of W.A. Harriman & Co. in 1926. He was one of its directors when it was seized in 1942. Treason it seems is a deeply held Bush family value.

Skull & Bones member W. Averell Harriman founded W.A. Harriman & Co. in 1920; on January 1, 1931 it merged with Brown Brothers and became Brown Brothers, Harriman. During World War II, W. Averell Harriman was lend-lease administrator from 1941 to 1943; he then became ambassador to the Soviet Union (1943-46). Harriman next served as ambassador to Great Britain (1946), U.S. Secretary of Commerce (1946-48), and governor of New York State (1955-58). Notice, that when W. Averell Harriman had his assets in Union Bank seized by the U.S. Government because he was trading with the enemy (the Nazis), he was at that time (1942) the chief overseas administrator of the lend-lease program that was responsible for supplying the Russians with war supplies. He was profiting from the trade on both sides of the war.

Prior to and after the outbreak of World War II Harriman and Prescott Bush had close business relationships with the powerful Jewish banking house of Max Warburg, who, along with Harriman, was instrumental in financing the Nazis.[629] On March 29, 1933, Max Warburg's son, Erich Warburg, sent a cable to his cousin Frederick M. Warburg, who was a director of the Harriman railroad system.[630] He asked Frederick to use all his influence to stop all anti-Nazi activity in America, including atrocity news and unfriendly propaganda in foreign press, mass meetings, etc.[631]

The Warburgs, Harriman, and Prescott Bush all knew Hitler's plan for the Jews. The plan was to drive the Jews from Europe into Palestine in order to increase the population of Jews in Palestine and establish Jewish hegemony there. Two days after the cable from Erich Warburg to Frederick Warburg, on March 31, 1933, the American-Jewish Committee (controlled by the Warburgs) and the *B'nai B'rith*, issued a formal, official joint statement of the two organizations, counseling "that no American boycott against Germany be encouraged," and advising "that no further mass meetings be held or similar forms of agitation be employed."[632]

World War II would give birth to the synthesis, the United Nations. Notice that the same firms were involved in nurturing and supporting both Russian communism and German Nazism. In the end, the secret societies and their companies and banks made obscene profits from the war that they orchestrated. The Illuminati was able through the conflict between communism (international socialism) and Nazism (national socialism) to give birth to the United Nations (world socialism). You can count on further wars, perhaps culminating in a war between the United States and the United Nations in World War III, in an attempt to bring about a New World Order, which will be the rule of the antichrist under world Zionism.

Many think that Zionism is the struggle by the Jews for a homeland. Zionism is much more than the Jews establishing a Palestinian homeland. That is merely a cover for a much grander plan to rule the world. Zionism is the child of the Talmud, and Talmudism is communism. The communist revolution in Russia was planned and executed by Jews according to the doctrines of their Talmud. V.I. Lenin, supreme dictator, and Leon Bronstein (Trotsky), supreme commander of the Soviet Red Army, were both Jews.[633]

The Bolshevik revolution was Jewish from top to bottom. Of 556 leading conspirators in the Bolshevik state in 1918-19 there were 17 Russians, two Ukrainians, eleven Armenians, 35 Latvians, 15 Germans, one Hungarian, ten Georgians, three Poles, three Finns, one Czech, one Karaim, and 457 Jews.[634] As pointed out by Robert Wilton in his book The Last Days of the Romanovs, the communist revolution was not an insurrection by Russians, but rather a secret invasion by Jews. As of 1983, the Premier of the Soviet Union was a Jew (Andropov) and 23 out of 25 members of the Politboro (the Soviet ruling clique) were Jews. In addition, every top member of the military and of the Soviet police, were Jews.[635]

> The Germans knew what they were doing when they sent Lenin's pack of Jews into Russia. They chose them as agents of destruction. Why? Because the Jews were not Russians and to them the destruction of Russia was all in the way of business,

revolutionary or financial. The whole record of Bolshevism in Russia is indelibly impressed with the stamp of alien invasion. The murder of the Tsar, deliberately planned by the Jew Sverdlov (who came to Russia as a paid agent of Germany) and carried out by the Jews Goloschekin, Syromolotov, Safarov, Voikov and Yukovsky, is the act not of the Russian people, but of this hostile invader.[636]

Colonel Jack Mohr states: "One of the greatest difficulties of the Talmudic Pharisees has been that of bringing communism into power while trying to conceal its Talmudic origin."[637] However, the direct and circumstantial evidence that the communist revolution in Russia was a conspiracy perpetrated by Talmudic Jews is overwhelming. Circumstantial evidence that points to Jewish control of the communist revolution is that once the communists in Russia seized power, the first law they passed made anti-Semitism a crime punishable by death.[638] While Christian church buildings were turned into animal stables, slaughter houses, and dance halls, the Jewish synagogues were untouched.[639]

Christian pastors were removed from their pastoral duties and made to work on roads and in slave labor camps, yet the Jewish rabbis were permitted to continue their clerical duties.[640] "Some 200,000 (Christian) clergy, many crucified, scalped and otherwise tortured, were killed during the approximately 60 years of communist rule in the former Soviet Union, a Russian commission reported Monday (Nov. 27, 1995)...40,000 churches (were) destroyed in the period from 1922 to 1980..."[641]

Lenin's maternal grandfather, Israel Blank, was Jewish. Researcher Wayne McGuire of Harvard University wrote: "Lenin was a Jew by the standards of Israel's Law of Return: he possessed a Jewish grandparent."[642] Lenin, in apparent reference to himself, said: "The clever Russian is almost always a Jew or has Jewish blood in him."[643]

Historian Michael Hoffman II exposed the hidden meaning behind some of the bloodthirsty communist propaganda:

> Lenin declared, "We are exterminating the bourgeoisie as a class." His partner in crime, Apfelbaum (Zinoviev) stated: "The interests of the revolution require the physical annihilation of the bourgeoisie class." Who were these bourgeoisie? Certainly not Jews. Trotsky gave a clue to their identity in a 1937 interview in the New York Jewish newspaper, *Daily Forward:* "The longer the rotten bourgeoisie society lives, the more and more barbaric will anti-Semitism become everywhere."
>
> **Bourgeoisie was a Bolshevik code-word for Gentile.** The first law passed after the Communists seized power in Russia made anti-semitism a crime punishable by death. (*Izvestia*, July 27, 1918).

* * *

The Jewish Bolsheviks regarded politics as a branch of Gentile pest control. Hatred of Christians, especially the peasant "bourgeoisie" was their prime motivation. The systematic destruction of the Christian peasantry of Russia as so many vermin, beginning with Lenin's attack on them in the summer of 1918 and his forced starvation in 1921, has been almost completely ignored in Western history.[644]

Moses Mordecai Marx Levi, alias Karl Marx, was a Jew, a Satanist, and a member of the "League of the Just," which was a branch of the Illuminati.[645] In 1847, Marx was commissioned by the Illuminati to write the *Communist Manifesto*, which is an outline of their plans for world domination.[646]

Jews immediately retaliate against any gentile who reveals that a person in government or the media is a Jew, because the Jews want to keep concealed their behind-the-scenes involvement in the crimes of socialist and communist governments. "A man is considered an anti-Semite if he calls a Jew a Jew." Hilliare Belloc, Culture Wars (Sept. 2000).[647]

The reason that Jews do not want it revealed that they are Jews is that they do not want attention focused on what they are doing. That is because communism is Judaism, and the Jews are engaged in nefarious plans to enslave the gentile world. Jews fear that if the gentile majority woke up and understood what the Jews were doing, the gentiles would take steps to put a stop to it. Jewish media control is one of the ways that they keep a lid on their treasonous activities. Texe Marrs explains how the Jews will go to any lengths to conceal their secret involvement in socialism and communism.

> It was in 1990 that I first met the remarkable and brilliant Boris Lunachev. Aged, bent over slightly by repeated attacks of osteoporosis, Lunachev had asked to see me privately. He had, I understood, once been a most distinguished professor of Marxist doctrine at the prestigious Lenin Institute. He was a rising star on the Soviet political and educational scene. But in the late 70s, Lunachev was abruptly and unceremoniously ousted from his post and exiled to the West. Shaking the wisened old man's hand and seeking to inject a friendly tone into our conversation, I smiled and said, "So, you are a Russian, Dr. Lunachev?""Yes, I am a Russian," he answered.
>
> "But please, my dear friend," he continued. "Always remember, there are Russians and then there are Russians. And some who are Russian are not Russian." Confusing language, I thought, if intriguing. I made a mental note to later inquire further into the

nature of Lunachev's puzzling words. However, I soon discovered that follow up was not at all necessary. The good Professor Lunachev more than answered my curiosity with what he had to say.

Lunachev recounted his stellar career, beginning as a leader of the Communist Youth, his earning of high-level doctorate degrees, and his academic career, during which he was lauded and commended on a regular basis. Apparently, Lunachev was poised for further advancement; he was even being considered for a top political position in the Kremlin as a Marxist theoretician and was well rewarded economically by the elite intelligencia. Until...until he said something very, very vital—and very, very sensitive—to the wrong person.

It seems that a high-ranking Commissar had come from Moscow to the Institute to interview Lunachev for the Kremlin post. The Commissar, who was very pleased with Lunachev's deportment and his responses to standard questions, finally stated: "Professor Lunachev, is there any area of research or study that you have conducted that is unique or unusual?" "Yes," Lunachev replied. "I have recently been studying the field of race and biology. I have discovered that the great Karl Marx was a Jew and so was Comrade Lenin." "Comrade Stalin was an avid reader of the Jewish Talmud, and Comrade Khruschev's real surname was Perlmutter. He, too, was a Jew."

"I believe these facts of racial history need to be reported to the Soviet people and to the world," said Lunachev, "so everyone will recognize that the government of the USSR is not, as some have alleged, anti-Semitic." "Thank you for your time." retorted the now sober-faced and ashen Commissar. "You are dismissed."

That very evening, Boris Lunachev was accosted on his way home by Soviet secret police. He was taken promptly to a waiting aircraft and flown to Rome, Italy, where he was told by Soviet Embassy officials he would forever be persona non grata (unwelcome) in his native Russia. He had become an outcast. What was Lunachev's horrible crime, his unacceptable transgression against his Communist overseers? "My unpardonable crime," Lunachev said to me, "was to call a Jew a Jew."

Professor Lunachev, however, considered himself fortunate, indeed. "In 1917 in Soviet Russia," he explained, "one of the first laws passed by Lenin and the Bolsheviks was a law making anti-Semitism a crime punishable by death. In Rome, the KGB bluntly told me that to call a Jew a Jew, and especially to make public the name of a crypto-Jew, one who was hiding under an assumed Russian name, was clearly an act of anti-Semitism."

And so it was that Lunachev, by no means an anti-Semite in the real meaning of the term, a man who simply wanted to give Communism's founders and pioneers their due by recognizing their racial ancestry, became a feared and marked outlaw, a dangerous subversive to be banished and persecuted.[648]

Jews were behind the rise to power of Mao Tse Tung, the communist dictator of China, who tortured and murdered tens of millions of Chinese during his brutal reign. Sidney Shapiro, an American Jew, was in charge of China's propaganda organ. Another Jew, Israel Epstein, was Mao's Minister of Appropriations (Finance). Texe Marrs explains how the Pollard spy scandal sheds some light on the Jewish-communist connection:

> The covert Jewish control of Mao and the Chinese Communist Party (CCP) explains why convicted Jewish spy Jonathan Pollard, found guilty of stealing thousands of classified documents from the Defense Department where he worked, gave these materials to his masters, the Israeli Mossad operating in the U.S.A. The Israelis, in turn, transferred these valuable military secrets straight to Red Chinese dictators in Beijing.
>
> Pollard, a Jew born in Galveston, Texas, sits in a federal prison today. Recently, when Israeli Prime Minister Netanyahu came to America, he visited Pollard in prison and assured the despicable turncoat Israeli spy that the Israeli government was working behind-the-scenes with Obama's White House to pardon the convicted spy. Meanwhile, Pollard is a national hero in Israel—honored for stealing America's most precious military secrets which Israel gave to Communist China![649]

The Talmudic Jews have been successful in preventing any revelations about their involvement in establishing a new communist world order by labeling anyone who exposes their efforts an anti-Semite. What many do not understand is that many who claim to be objects of anti-Semitism are not Semites at all. Semites are those who are descended from Shem, the oldest son of Noah. Most Jews living in Israel and throughout the world today are eastern European converts to a religion that they call Judaism, but in fact is Babylonian Talmudism. The Europeans who later converted to this Babylonian form of Judaism are known as Ashkenazi or Khazar Jews.

Dr. Benjamin H. Freedman, who himself was born a Jew, states that the Khazars were a pagan nation whose religious worship was a mixture of phallic worship and other forms of idolatry. In the 7th century their King Bulkan chose Talmudism, which most now call Judaism, as the state religion.[650] Today Khazar Jews are called "Yiddish." In Revelation, God refers to these Talmudic Ashkenazi Jews as Jews who say they are Jews but are not, but rather are the "synagogue of Satan."

> I know thy works, and tribulation, and poverty, (but thou art rich) and ***I know*** **the blasphemy of them which say they are Jews, and are not, but** *are* **the synagogue of Satan.** (Revelation 2:9 AV)

> **Behold, I will make them of the synagogue of Satan, which say they are Jews, and are not, but do lie**; behold, I will make them to come and worship before thy feet, and to know that I have loved thee. (Revelation 3:9 AV)

These Ashkenazi Jews are people without any allegiance to any nation. Their primary objective is to own the entire world. To get an idea of the nefarious objective of these Talmudists, let us read an 1879 letter from Baruch Levy to Karl Marx:

> The Jewish people as a whole will be its own messiah. It will attain world dominion by the dissolution of other races, by the abolition of frontiers, the annihilation of monarchy, and by the establishment of a world republic in which the Jews will everywhere exercise the privilege of citizenship. In this new world order the children of Israel will furnish all the leaders without encountering opposition. The governments of the different peoples forming the world republic will fall without difficulty into the hands of the Jews. It will then be possible for the Jewish rulers to abolish private property, and everywhere to make use of the resources of the state. Thus will the promise of the Talmud be fulfilled, in which it is said that when the messianic time is come, the Jews will have all the property of the whole world in their hands.[651]

Many think that communism could not be the work of Talmudic Jews because Russia is allied with the Arab countries. Things, however, are not what they appear. Jack Bernstein, an American Ashkenazi Jew who moved to Israel shortly after its founding in 1948, returned in disgust to the United States after witnessing the duplicity of Israel. He revealed that the aboriginal Jews of Palestine, who are called Sephardic Jews, are discriminated against in modern Israel. They are second class citizens at the bottom strata of society in Israel, along with Christians and Muslims. In his book, *The Life of an American Jew in Racist Marxist Israel*, explains the Machiavellian strategy of Israel.[652]

Bernstein found out that it is not true that the Soviet Russians support the Arab countries. This subterfuge of support by the Soviets for the Arabs was simply a ploy which was instituted by Israel on or around 1949. At that time Golda Meir was Israel's first ambassador to the Soviet Union. As ambassador to the Soviet Union she met with Joseph Stalin. A secret agreement was entered into between Israel and Russia in which (1) Israel would not allow the U.S. or any western country to build military bases on Israeli territory; (2) Israel would allow an official Communist Party to function in Israel; (3) Israel would never make any agreement to solve the Palestinian problems; (4) Israel would work with world Jewry to influence Western governments to favor Israel over the Arabs; (5) Israel would continue its Marxist economic policies.[653]

In return for these concessions the Soviet Union was to (1) furnish military aid to the Arabs and Egypt, but never enough aid to allow them to destroy Israel; (2) encourage Jewish immigration to Israel from the Soviet satellite countries and if that was not sufficient they would allow immigration from Soviet Russia; and (3) guarantee the security of Israel and in order to do that they authorized the free exchange of intelligence reports between Israel and the Soviet Union.[654] Bernstein obtained this information directly from the horse's mouth: the Secretary-Treasurer of the Communist Party in Northern Tel Aviv.[655]

Bernstein pointed out that Israel presents itself as a democracy, but in fact Israel is a communist country to its core. He stated that Zionism and communism are one and the same. The purest form of communism is found in Jewish kibbutzim in Israel. Some have alleged that Bernstein was assassinated by the Israeli Mossad for revealing the truth about Israel. That, however, is probably not the case. This author has corresponded with Michael Collins Piper, who was a personal friend of Jack Bernstein. Piper stated that Bernstein died from an illness he incurred while traveling in the Phillippines. He stated that Bernstein himself did not think that the illness was the work of the Mossad. Piper himself is a highly respected investigative journalist. Piper reveals in his book, *Final Judgment*, that Israel's communist ties are not limited to the former Soviet Union. There has been a long, albeit secret, history of mutual cooperation between communist China and Israel in the development of nuclear and other military weapons. In fact, Israel has been cited as one of the primary conduits for the flow of U.S. and other western technologies to communist China.

Charles Cotesworth Pinckney, a delegate from South Carolina at the Philadelphia Constitutional Convention of 1787 recorded in his diary the following prophetic statement made by Benjamin Franklin during an intermission in the Constitutional Convention.

> I fully agree with General Washington, that we must protect this young nation from an insidious influence and impenetration. The menace, gentlemen, is the Jews.
>
> In whatever country Jews have settled in any great number, they have lowered its moral tone; depreciated its commercial integrity; have segregated themselves and have not been assimilated; have sneered at and tried to undermine the Christian religion upon

which that nation is founded, by objecting to its restrictions; have built up a state within the state; and when opposed have tried to strangle that country to death financially, as in the case of Spain and Portugal.

For over 1,700 years, the Jews have been bewailing their sad fate in that they have been exiled from their homeland, as they call Palestine. But gentlemen, did the world give it to them in fee simple, they would at once find some reason for not returning. Why? Because they are vampires, and vampires do not live on vampires. They cannot live only among themselves. They must subsist on Christians and other people not of their race.

If you do not exclude them from these United States, in their Constitution, in less than 200 years they will have swarmed here in such great numbers that they will dominate and devour the land and change our form of government, for which we Americans have shed our blood, given our lives our substance and jeopardized our liberty.

If you do not exclude them, in less than 200 years our descendants will be working in the fields to furnish them substance, while they will be in the counting houses rubbing their hands. I warn you, gentlemen, if you do not exclude Jews for all time, your children will curse you in your graves.

Jews, gentlemen, are Asiatics, let them be born where they will nor how many generations they are away from Asia, they will never be otherwise. Their ideas do not conform to an American's, and will not even though they live among us ten generations. A leopard cannot change its spots. Jews are Asiatics, are a menace to this country if permitted entrance, and should be excluded by this Constitutional Convention.[656]

Ben Franklin refers to the opinion of George Washington regarding the Jews. What was George Washington's opinion? "They (the Jews) work more effectively against us, than the enemy's armies. They are a hundred times more dangerous to our liberties and the great cause we are engaged in . . . It is much to be lamented that each state, long ago, has not hunted them down as pest to society and the greatest enemies we have to the happiness of America."[657]

Were Benjamin Franklin and George Washington anti-Semites? No, they simply understood the real dangers posed by the Talmudic Jews, who were not Semites at all. This Talmudic (communist) conspiracy continues today. In a 1971 White House recording released by the National Archives in 1999, President Richard Nixon revealed: "The only two non-Jews in the communist conspiracy were Chambers and Hiss...Every other one was a Jew and it raised hell with us."[658]

Why didn't the Jewish influence behind the communist infiltration of the U.S. Government come out? Because there is a conspiracy of silence on that issue among the major media outlets. When it became clear that almost all of the communist infiltrators being uncovered by Senator Joseph McCarthy were Jewish, McCarthy decided upon a political solution to deflect the charge of antisemitism. He appointed Jewish lawyer Roy Cohen to be the chief counsel of his Senate subcommittee investigating communist infiltration in the government. In the end, McCarthy's reputation was destroyed chiefly by the actions of Roy Cohen in coordination with the Jewish controlled media.

These Talmudic Jews have not only manifested their malevolence, they have put their plan for world domination in writing. THE PROTOCOLS OF THE LEARNED ELDERS OF ZION is an outline of a plan by Talmudic Jews to rule the world. The Protocols were drawn up by the International Jewish Council which met in Basle, Switzerland in 1879. The Protocols appear to be a summation of the conspiratorial plans that had been in existence long before they were memorialized at the 1879 meeting.

The Protocols contain the formula used by the megalomaniacal Zionists to launch their offensive to rule the world. While some Jews have claimed that the Protocols are a forgery, we should recognize that a forgery is merely an unauthorized copy of an original. The Talmudic Jews have never questioned the authenticity of the original Protocols, which were written in Hebrew, they have only attacked the English translation. Others, with absolutely no evidence to support their claim, have supposed that although the Protocols are genuine, at some point they were altered to refer to the Jews. Historical events have confirmed that Talmudic Jews are following the blueprint set forth in the Protocols.

In 1884 the daughter of a Russian general, Madamoiselle Justine Glinka, was endeavoring to serve her country in Paris by obtaining political information. She communicated her plans to General Orgevskii in St. Petersburg. For this purpose she employed a Jew, Joseph Schorst, member of the Mizraim Lodge (Oriental Rite of Freemasonry) in Paris. Schorst offered to obtain for her a document of great importance to Russia for the price of 2,500 francs. Mlle. Glinka received the money from St. Petersburg and obtained the document, which turned out to be the Protocols of the Learned Elders of Zion.

She forwarded the French original of the Protocols, accompanied by a Russian translation, to General Orgevskii, who in turn handed them to his superior, General Cherevin, for delivery to the Tsar. Cherevin, however, was under the control of wealthy Jews, and he consequently refused to transmit the Protocols. Cherevin merely filed the Protocols in the Russian archives.

Years later Mlle. Glinka gave a copy of the Protocols to the marechal de noblesse of her district, Alexis Sukhotin. Sukhotin showed the document to two friends, Stepanov and

Professor Sergius A. Nilus. Professor Nilus published the Protocols in Tsarskoe-Tselc (Russia) in 1901 in a book entitled *The Great Within the Small*. On or about August 10, 1906 a copy of the Protocols was deposited in the British Museum. In the meantime minutes of the proceedings of the Basle congress in 1897 had been obtained through Jewish members of the Russian police and these were found to confirm the plans set forth in the Protocols.

In January 1917, Professor Nilus had prepared a second edition of the Protocols, which were revised with further documentation, for publication. But before he could be get it to market, the Bolshevik Revolution of March 1917 took place. Kerenski came to power and ordered Nilus's book to be destroyed. In 1924, Professor Nilus was arrested by the Cheka (Russian Secret Police) in Kiev. He was imprisoned and tortured.

The best evidence of the authenticity of the Protocols is that the Jewish president of the court told Professor Nilus that the brutal treatment he received was as retribution for "having done them incalculable harm in publishing the Protocols." Professor Nilus was released for a few months, but was soon rearrested by the Cheka, this time in Moscow. He was confined in prison until February 1926. He died in exile in the district of Vladimir on January 13, 1929.

All copies of the Protocols that were known to exist in Russia were destroyed during the Kerensky regime. The law followed by Kerensky's communist successors to power was that the possession of a copy of the Protocols by anyone in the Soviet Union was a crime punishable by being shot on sight. The lengths that the communists went to eradicate the Protocols is evidence of the genuineness of the Protocols.

The authenticity of the Protocols can be further confirmed by reading the Talmud. The evil and blasphemous nature of the Talmud parallels much of what is found in the Protocols. The authenticity of the Protocols is further established by the fact that the details of the plan have been completely implemented before the eyes of the world in Russia, Eastern Europe, China, North Korea, and Vietnam. The plan is in the process of being implemented in Western Europe, South America, South Africa, the United States, and scores of other countries throughout the world.[659]

When one looks at the personages working for world communism, one sees Talmudic Jews and their fellow travelers, such as the Masons, just as the Protocols state. Benjamin Disraeli, himself Jewish, made the following statement in 1852 before the English House of Commons regarding the control of nations by the Talmudic Jews: "The world is governed by very different personages from what is imagined by those who are not behind the scenes.... The influence of the Jews may be traced in the last outbreak of the destructive principle in Europe. An insurrection takes place against tradition and aristocracy, against religion and property.... The natural equality of men and the abrogation of property are proclaimed by the secret societies who form provisional governments and men of Jewish race are found at the head of every one of them."

Renowned British author and World War II London Times journalist, Douglas Reed revealed:

> The money- power and the revolutionary – power have been set up and given share of the symbolic shapes ("capitalism" or "communism") and sharply defined citadels ("America" or "Russia"). Suitably to alarm the mass-minded, the picture offered is that of a bleak and hopeless enmity and confrontation. ... But what if similar men with a common aim secretly rule in both camps? ... I believe any diligent student of our times will discover that this is the case.[660]

Do we have examples of officials in the U.S. Government who are working toward a Zionist communist world government? President of the United States, Franklin Roosevelt, for one, was guided secretly by a communist agenda. Josephine Adams testified under oath before a subcommittee of the U.S. Senate that she acted as a courier between Earl Bowder, then Chief of the American Communist Party, and Franklin Roosevelt. She testified that she met with Roosevelt approximately 40 times during a three-year period prior to Roosevelt's death.[661] She testified that the meetings took place either in Roosevelt's Hyde Park home or the White House.[662] This testimony of Adams was later confirmed as true by Browder himself, who took pride in the fact that FDR appreciated the guidance Browder gave him.[663]

A Congressional investigation has revealed that in 1996 Vice President Al Gore peddled his influence to the Chinese Communist Government through an Israeli intermediary.[664]

Representative Louis T. McFadden in a May 2, 1934, radio address stated:

> It would be a monstrous mistake for any intelligent citizen of whatever nation to close his eyes to the evident fact that for nigh sixty years, the Jews have surely and rapidly though almost invisibly climbed to the heights of government wherefrom the masses are ruled. Politically, financially and economically they have seized the reigns of governments of all nations and their invasion in the realms of social, educational and religious fields not less important.[665]

Congressman McFadden, who was Chairman of the House Banking and Currency Committee, knew the power that the Jews wielded and the calamities that they caused. Just as the Protocols provided, the Talmudic Jews controlled the money supply through a central bank (The Federal Reserve Bank). Congressman McFadden stated: "It [the depression] was not accidental. It was a carefully contrived occurrence....The international bankers sought to bring about a condition of despair here so that they might emerge as the rulers of us all. ...The end result, if the Insiders have their way, will be the dream of Montagu Norman of the Bank of England that the Hegemony of World Finance should reign supreme over everyone, everywhere, as one whole super-national control mechanism."

Representative McFadden addressed the U.S. House of Representatives on June 10, 1932. "Some people think the Federal Reserve Banks are U.S. government institutions. They are not government institutions. They are private credit monopolies which prey upon the people of the U.S. for the benefit of themselves and their foreign and domestic swindlers, and rich and predatory money lenders."[666] In essence, the international Jewish money power used corrupt politicians to push through the Federal Reserve Act, which gave them a monopoly to print the money of the nation.[667] The Federal Reserve Act legalizes theft for a select few commercial banks that make up the Federal Reserve.

Woodrow Wilson, who spearheaded and signed into law the Federal Reserve Act, was oppressed and controlled by a sinister Zionist cabal, which he described in his 1913 book *The New Freedom*: "Since I entered politics, I have chiefly had men's views confided to me privately. Some of the biggest men in the U.S., in the field of commerce and manufacturing, are afraid of something. They know that there is a power somewhere so organized, so subtle, so watchful, so interlocked, so complete, so pervasive, that they had better not speak above their breath when they speak in condemnation of it."[668]

The political power and influence of the Jews stem directly from their control of banking. God explains in his word: "The rich ruleth over the poor, and the borrower is servant to the lender." The Jews have set up a system where the debt of individuals and nations can never be paid back because with the debt comes usury (i.e., interest). God admonished against the destructive practice of usury. See, e.g., Exodus 22:25, Leviticus 25:36-37, Deuteronomy 23:19, Nehemiah, Psalms 15:5, Proverbs 28:8.

The only way to free ourselves from underneath the power of the Jews is to take away from them the power of monopoly usury. President Jackson succeeded in doing that when he killed the first central bank in the United States. President Lincoln did it again during the civil war, when he printed Lincoln green backs rather than borrow from the bankers. President Kennedy tried to do that same thing, but he was assassinated by the bankers before his efforts bore fruit.

The monopoly power to print money must be taken away from the private banking cartel called the Federal Reserve and given back to the U.S. Government where it rightfully belongs.

The international Jewish money power used corrupt politicians to push through the Federal Reserve Act, which gave them a monopoly to print the money of the nation.[669] The Federal Reserve Act legalizes theft for a select few commercial banks that make up the Federal Reserve. McFadden exposed the methods that the Jews used to obtain their immense power over the government of the United States.

Representative McFadden revealed in a 1932 speech before the House of Representatives that the communist revolution in Russia was financed by the Federal Reserve.[670] In addition, billions of dollars and millions of ounces of the gold deposits of the United States were stolen by the Federal Reserve Banks and sent to Germany.[671] As he spoke in 1932, huge amounts of gold were being sent to Germany on a weekly basis. Why was this money being sent to Germany? To fund the Nazis. It was only a little over eight months later, on January 30, 1933, that Adolph Hitler was sworn in as Chancellor of Germany.

Within a year, Hitler had consolidated enough power, with the help of the Federal Reserve, that he declared himself "Fuhrer" (leader) of Germany. The gold he received from the Federal Reserve was used to build planes, ships, tanks, and guns that were used to kill brave Americans during World War II. The Federal Reserve Board and Banks funded both the communists in Russia and the Nazis in Germany, all at the expense of the hard labor of the American middle class.

Even during World War II, the United States funded the communist Russians through the "lend-lease" program. In addition to our own financial burdens of the war, the U.S. taxpayers funded the Germans and the Russians. The Jewish Bankers, having funded both sides of the war, made out like bandits.

As a consequence of Congressman McFadden's discovery of treasonous criminal conduct, on May 23, 1933, he brought formal criminal charges against the Board of Governors of the Federal Reserve Bank, the Comptroller of the Currency, and the Secretary of the United States Treasury. The petition for Articles of Impeachment was, thereafter, referred to the Judiciary Committee.

Representative McFadden was Chairman of the House Banking and Currency Committee and was in a position to do something about the banking monopoly. The Zionist Jews could not allow such a powerful person to oppose their plans. They tried several times to assassinate Representative McFadden. They were ultimately successful; in 1935 they poisoned him. After Representative McFadden's death, the bill introduced by him was pigeonholed in the Judiciary Committee and has never seen the light of day since.

God admonished man against the destructive practice of usury (i.e., interest). Why would the Jews ignore the commands of God against usury? Because the orthodox Jews do not follow the Old Testament. They have replaced God's laws with their traditions. They follow their oral traditions, which in part have been memorialized in the Talmud.

Israel Shahak explains that although the Talmud forbids a Jew, on pain of severe punishment, to take interest on a loan made to another Jew, the rabbis have figured a contrivance to get around that restriction.[672] A business dispensation called *heter 'isqa* was devised for an interest-bearing loan between Jews.[673] In any event, the Talmud grants a license to charge interest to gentiles; according to a majority of Talmudic authorities, it is a religious duty to take as much interest as possible on a loan made to a Gentile.[674]

The influence of the Talmud over the Jewish banking practices is witnessed by the fact that when Alan Greenspan, who is an atheist Jew, took his oath of office as Chairman of President Nixon's Council of Economic Advisers, he did so on a volume of the Talmud.[675] He later went on to be appointed Chairman of the Federal Reserve by Ronald Reagan.

Why would Greenspan, who is an atheist Jew, take an oath on the Talmud, which is a religious publication? Because within the Talmud is found the doctrine of the Devil that "ye shall be as gods." Genesis 3:5. That is why there are a great number of Jews who claim to be atheists. In fact, some Jewish rabbis are atheists. Rabbi Sherman Wine is one example. He was the rabbi of the Birmingham Temple in Michigan. Rabbi Wine stated: "I am an atheist."[676] He "expunged the name of God from all services at his temple."[677] Rabbi Wine had "a Jewish liturgy emphasizing Jewish culture, history and identity along with humanistic ethics while excluding all prayers and references to God."[678] Rabbi Wine is not alone. In December 2006, he traveled to Israel for the ordination of seven other atheist rabbis.[679] Rabbi Wine died in 2007. He is not an atheist anymore.

When the Jews thrive, then also does the nation in which they reside in like manner fade. The idea of a restored Israel with a resulting world of harmony and justice is just a cover story for the ignorant *goyim* to conceal the macabre plan for world dominion. Yesaiah Tishbi, who is a religious authority on the Jewish Kabbalah, reveals that "the presence of Israel among the nations mends the world, but not the nations of the world . . . it does not bring the nations closer to holiness, but rather extracts the holiness from them and thereby destroys their ability to exist. . . . (T)he purpose of the full redemption is to destroy the vitality of all the peoples."[680] This destructive influence stems from the Jewish core belief that the souls of non-Jews are evil.[681]

Knowledge is power. Jesus thought it important that we be wise about the source of our trials, but he also stated that Christians are to be harmless. "Behold, I send you forth as sheep in the midst of wolves: be ye therefore wise as serpents, and harmless as doves." (Matthew 10:16 AV)

Anti-Semitism has a manifold role in the Jewish scheme. False claims of anti-Semitism are used as a shield to protect the Jewish hierarchy when evidence of their crimes are uncovered. Former Israeli government official Shulamit Aloni succinctly described the epithet anti-Semite as "a trick, we [Jews] always use."[682] She explained that Jews hide behind it like a smokescreen, which is used to conceal evidence of Jewish malefaction.

Shulamit Aloni knows what she is talking about. She was a member of the Israeli Knesset from 1965 to 1969 and again from 1974 to 1996. She served on the Knesset Constitution Committee, Law and Justice Committee; State Audit Committee; Education and Culture Committee; and the Finance Committee. She served briefly as Minister without Portfolio from June to October 1974. From 1992 to 1996, Aloni served as Minister of Communications and the Arts, Science and Technology.[683]

By the trick of labeling a person as an anti-Semite, the accused person's credibility is undermined, and the focus shifts from the evidence against wrongdoing by Israel or the Jews to the motives of the accused anti-Semite. The Jewish controlled media then destroys the reputation of the accused anti-Semite, and he becomes an object lesson for anyone who might consider criticizing Israel or Jews.

So called antisemitism is also a tool of the Jewish hierarchy used to keep the common Jews in line. Do not fall for that trick. As Christians, we are to love our enemies. We are to be innocent in our conduct, but we should recognize and reprove the evils of Judaism. Do not allow the sin of hatred to overcome you. "Be ye angry, and sin not: let not the sun go down upon your wrath:" (Ephesians 4:26 AV) The only weapons and battlements to be used by Christians in this spiritual warfare is the gospel truth of Jesus Christ.

> Finally, my brethren, be strong in the Lord, and in the power of his might. Put on the whole armour of God, that ye may be able to stand against the wiles of the devil. For we wrestle not against flesh and blood, but against principalities, against powers, against the rulers of the darkness of this world, against spiritual wickedness in high *places*. Wherefore take unto you the whole armour of God, that ye may be able to withstand in the evil day, and having done all, to stand. Stand therefore, having your loins girt about with truth, and having on the breastplate of righteousness; And your feet shod with the preparation of the gospel of peace; Above all, taking the shield of faith, wherewith ye shall be able to quench all the fiery darts of the wicked. And take the helmet of salvation, and the sword of the Spirit, which is the word of God: Praying always with all prayer and supplication in the Spirit, and watching thereunto with all perseverance and supplication for all saints. (Ephesians 6:10-18 AV)

The Jewish hierarchy uses anti-Semitism to keep Jews from assimilating into gentile society; they want their Jews cloistered from gentiles. They also used anti-Semitism as a means of herding Jews to Israel. The organization *Jews Against Zionism* explains how anti-Semitism is used by Zionists to further their ends:

> Theodor Herzl (1860-1904), the founder of modern Zionism, recognized that anti-Semitism would further his cause, the creation of a separate state for Jews. To solve the Jewish Question, he maintained "we must, above all, make it an international political issue."

> Herzl wrote that Zionism offered the world a welcome **"final solution of the Jewish question."** In his "Diaries", page 19, Herzl stated "Anti-Semites will become our surest friends, anti-Semitic countries our allies."[684]

Notice the language used by Herzl long before World War II and the rise of the Nazis. He described the **"final solution of the Jewish question."** That language and concept did not originate with the Germans, it originated with Jewish Zionists. The "final solution" was not the extermination of the Jews, as is commonly believed; it was the persecution of the Jews in order to drive them out of Europe into Israel. The Nazis were simply unwitting tools in the hands of the Zionist Jews in their Machiavellian plan to gain hegemony over Palestine. All who engage in persecution of Jews, simply because they are Jews, are unwitting accessories to the Zionists.

Herzl explains how anti-Semitism furthers Zionist goals:

> "It is essential that the sufferings of Jews. . . become worse. . . this will assist in realization of our plans. . .I have an excellent idea. . . I shall induce anti-semites to liquidate Jewish wealth. . . The anti-semites will assist us thereby in that they will strengthen the persecution and oppression of Jews. The anti-semites shall be our best friends". (From his [Herzl's] Diary, Part I, pp. 16)[685]

To this day anti-Semitism is fostered by the Zionist hierarchy. A close examination of Neo-Nazi hate groups reveals that there are Jews throughout their leadership. The Neo-Nazis act as *agent provocateurs* in the hands of the controlling Jews in order to fan the flames of anti-Semitism. Jews are sent in to control the Jewish run gentile Neo-Nazi front.

If anti-Semitism is not that answer to the Jewish hatred of Christians and gentiles, what is the answer? Jesus provides the answer. It is not to strike back, it is to love your enemy and share with him the gospel of Jesus Christ. "But I say unto you, Love your enemies, bless them that curse you, do good to them that hate you, and pray for them which despitefully use you, and persecute you." (Matthew 5:44 AV) If you suffer persecution as a Christian at the hands of the Jews and their fellow travelers, rejoice and be glad that you are worthy to suffer for Christ's sake.

> Blessed are ye, when men shall hate you, and when they shall separate you *from their company*, and shall reproach *you*, and cast out your name as evil, for the Son of man's sake. Rejoice ye in that day, and leap for joy: for, behold, your reward *is* great in heaven: for in the like manner did their fathers unto the prophets." (Luke 6:22-23 AV)

Jesus explained that those who hate him also hate God the Father. The Jews hate Jesus and therefore they also hate the Father. The Jews reject Jesus, and therefore their god is not the Father. That leaves only Satan as their god. Do not be surprised by the unrelenting hatred of Jews toward Christians; Jesus clearly warned us that Christians would be hated by the Jews.

> If the world hate you, ye know that it hated me before *it hated* you. If ye were of the world, the world would love his own: but because ye are not of the world, but I have chosen you out of the world, therefore the world hateth you. Remember the word that I said unto you, The servant is not greater than his lord. **If they have**

persecuted me, they will also persecute you; if they have kept my saying, they will keep yours also. But all these things will they do unto you for my name's sake, because they know not him that sent me. If I had not come and spoken unto them, they had not had sin: but now they have no cloke for their sin. **He that hateth me hateth my Father also.** If I had not done among them the works which none other man did, they had not had sin: but now have they both seen and hated both me and my Father. But *this cometh to pass*, that the word might be fulfilled that is written in their law, They hated me without a cause." (John 15:18-25 AV)

The Talmud, which is the repository of many of the Jewish traditions, expresses hatred toward Christians. For Example:

Abodah Zarah 17a: Jews should stay away from Christians. Christians are allied with Hell, and Christianity is worse than incest.

Abodah Zarah 17a: Visiting the house of a Christian is the same as visiting the house of a prostitute.

Abodah Zarah 27b: It is forbidden to be healed by a Christian.

Sanhedrin 90a, 100b: Those who read the gospels are doomed to Hell.

Shabbath 116a: The New Testament is blank paper and are to be burned.

The admonition in the Talmud to burn New Testaments is not hyperbole. Orthodox Jews view the statement in Shabbath 116a as a command to burn New Testaments. On May 21, 2008, USA Today reported: "Orthodox Jews set fire to hundreds of copies of the New Testament in the latest act of violence against Christian missionaries in the Holy Land."[686] When Or Yehuda Deputy Mayor Uzi Aharon heard that hundreds of New Testaments were distributed by Christian missionaries, he took to the roads in a loudspeaker car and drove through the city urging people to turn over the New Testaments to Jewish religious students, who were going door to door to collect them. The New Testaments were then dumped into a pile and set afire in a lot near a synagogue. Aharon said it was a commandment to burn books that urge Jews to convert to Christianity.[687]

Why do the Jews hate Christians so much? It is because the children of the flesh will always hate the children of the spirit. **"But as then he that was born after the flesh persecuted him** *that was born* **after the Spirit, even so** *it is* **now."** (Galatians 4:29 AV)

Jews are victims of spiritual charlatans who have frightened them into following their heathen religion. Orthodox Jews are made by their religious leaders to hate Christ and Christians. Romans 11:28. Christians, however, are to love them and pray for them. "But I say unto you which hear, Love your enemies, do good to them which hate you, Bless them that curse you, and pray for them which despitefully use you." (Luke 6:27-28 AV) God has chosen a remnant of Jews for salvation. Christians should preach the gospel to the lost world, including the Jews.

Jews are powerful and ruthless, but they lack wisdom. That is their weakness. They have convinced the world through their control of the media that they are exceedingly intelligent. Nothing could be further from the truth. God tells us that "[t]he fear of the LORD *is* the beginning of wisdom: and the knowledge of the holy *is* understanding." (Proverbs 9:10 AV) The Jews reject the Lord and have no fear of him. They are in darkest ignorance. The Jewish leadership does not want the common Jew to see the light, which is why they prohibit Jews from reading the New Testament.

Our charge from the Lord is to preach God's word and reprove and rebuke those that have strayed from the sound doctrine of the Gospel of Jesus Christ. Jesus should be our model. He did not hesitate to rebuke the Jews for their religious errors. Jesus did not compromise and Christians are not to compromise with the world. We are not to be lukewarm about the gospel of Jesus Christ. Revelation 3:16. The gospel of Jesus Christ is the only effective weapon to the Jewish issue.

> For the word of God *is* quick, and powerful, and sharper than any twoedged sword, piercing even to the dividing asunder of soul and spirit, and of the joints and marrow, and *is* a discerner of the thoughts and intents of the heart. (Hebrews 4:12 AV)

Endnotes

1. William Norman Grigg, *Did We Know What Was Coming, The New American*, at 10,11, March 11, 2002.

2. At Least 7 of the 9/11 Hijackers are Still Alive, http://whatreallyhappened.com/WRHARTICLES/hijackers.html?q=hijackers.html (last visited on October 10, 2010).

3. David Harrison, *Revealed: the Men with Stolen Identities*, Telegraph, September 23, 2001, http://www.telegraph.co.uk .

4. The FBI Releases 19 Photographs of Individuals Believed to be the Hijackers of the Four Airliners that Crashed on September 11, 2001, September 27, 2001, http://www.fbi.gov/news/pressrel/press-releases/the-fbi-releases-19-photographs-of-individuals-believed-to-be-the-hijackers .

5. The FBI Releases 19 Photographs of Individuals Believed to be the Hijackers of the Four Airliners that Crashed on September 11, 2001, September 27, 2001, http://www.fbi.gov/news/pressrel/press-releases/the-fbi-releases-19-photographs-of-individuals-believed-to-be-the-hijackers.

6. The FBI Releases 19 Photographs of Individuals Believed to be the Hijackers of the Four Airliners that Crashed on September 11, 2001, September 27, 2001, http://www.fbi.gov/news/pressrel/press-releases/the-fbi-releases-19-photographs-of-individuals-believed-to-be-the-hijackers .

7. The FBI Releases 19 Photographs of Individuals Believed to be the Hijackers of the Four Airliners that Crashed on September 11, 2001, September 27, 2001, http://www.fbi.gov/news/pressrel/press-releases/the-fbi-releases-19-photographs-of-individuals-believed-to-be-the-hijackers .

8. Hijack 'Suspects' Alive and Well, BBC, September 23, 2001, http://news.bbc.co.uk/2/hi/1559151.stm.

9. The 9/11 Commission Report, at 2 (2004).

10. Steve Herrmann, 9/11 Conspiracy Theory, BBC, 27 October 2006, http://www.bbc.co.uk/blogs/theeditors/2006/10/911_conspiracy_theory_1.html.

11. Hijack 'Suspects' Alive and Well, BBC, September 23, 2001, http://news.bbc.co.uk/2/hi/1559151.stm.

12. Steve Herrmann, 9/11 Conspiracy Theory, BBC, 27 October 2006, http://www.bbc.co.uk/blogs/theeditors/2006/10/911_conspiracy_theory_1.html.

13. Steve Herrmann, 9/11 Conspiracy Theory, BBC, 27 October 2006, http://www.bbc.co.uk/blogs/theeditors/2006/10/911_conspiracy_theory_1.html.

14. Steve Herrmann, 9/11 Conspiracy Theory, BBC, 27 October 2006, http://www.bbc.co.uk/blogs/theeditors/2006/10/911_conspiracy_theory_1.html.

15. What Really happened to American Airlines Flights 11 and 77 on Sept 11, 2001. by Gerard Holmgren . November 13, 2003 (Slightly revised Sept 25, 2006), http://thewebfairy.com/holmgren/1177.html.

16. Bureau of Transportation Statistics, Detailed Statistics-Departure, http://www.bts.gov/xml/ontimesummarystatistics/src/dstat/OntimeSummaryDepatures.xml (last visited on October 17, 2010).

17. Evidence that Flights AA 11 and AA 77 Did Not Exist on September 11, 2001, http://www.serendipity.li/wot/aa_flts/aa_flts.htm (last visited on October 17, 2010).

18. Sheila Casey, *Flight 77 Cockpit Door Never Opened During 9/11 "Hijack"*, Rock Creek Free Press, http://rockcreekfreepress.tumblr.com/post/285492999/flt77fdr (last visited on November 3, 2010).

19. Sheila Casey, *Flight 77 Cockpit Door Never Opened During 9/11 "Hijack"*, Rock Creek Free Press, http://rockcreekfreepress.tumblr.com/post/285492999/flt77fdr (last visited on November 3, 2010).

20. Public domain work of a U.S. Army soldier or employee taken during the course of the person's official duties. http://commons.wikimedia.org/wiki/File:USAF_CT-43A_crash_1996.jpg (last visited on October 18, 2010). Other photographs contained in this book that are not in the public domain fall under the protection of the "fair use" doctrine in 17 U.S.C § 107, as they are being used for purposes of criticism, comment, news reporting, teaching, scholarship, and research on a topic of public interest where there is a need for the fullest information available. *See Time Inc. v. Bernard Geis Associates*, 293 F.Supp. 130 (S.D.N.Y. 1968).

21. Public Domain, U.S. Department of Defense, http://www.defense.gov/news/Sep2001/200109114a_hr.jpg (last visited on October 18, 2010).

22. Introducing the Amazing New Pentalawn 2000, http://killtown.911review.org/pentalawn.html (last visited on October 18, 2010).

23. Id.

24. Id.

25. Air Safety Online, http://web.archive.org/web/20010817121756/http://www.airsafetyonline.com/photos/vladivostokavia/7.shtml; AirDisaster.com (last visited on October 19, 2010);

http://www.airdisaster.com/photos/vl352/2.shtml (last visited on October 18, 2010).

26. American Airlines Flight # 77, Boeing 757, http://911research.wtc7.net/planes/evidence/docs/Flight77.png (last visited on April 30, 2011).

27. AirDisaster.com, http://www.airdisaster.com/photos/vl352/3.shtml (last visited on October 18, 2010).

28. http://i133.photobucket.com/albums/q62/chainsawmoth/FrustratingFraud/NEIT749_100-0028.jpg (last visited on October 19, 2001).

29. The Jamie Mcintyre Live Feed from Sept 11 2001, http://www.youtube.com/watch?v=TjlBpChvzD8 (last visited on October 18, 2010).

30. Physics 911, http://physics911.net/omholt (last visited on October 18, 2010).

31. By Robert Saiget, Safety Questions Swirl after China Plane Crash, August 25, 2010, http://www.mysinchew.com/node/43938. See also, China Uncovers 200 Fraudulent Airline Pilots, Malcolm Moore in Shanghai, Daily Telegraph, September 6, 2010, Morrison World Media, Morning Post, http://morrisonworldnews.com/?p=24479.

32. 9/11 Truth: Pentagon Eyewitness Bob Pugh Tells His Story, http://www.youtube.com/watch?v=-xtEJ4zrIPM&NR=1 (last visited on October 22, 2010).

33. Picture by Tom Horan, http://911review.org/brad.com/pentagonvideo_cctv_cam.html (last visited on October 22, 2010)

34. Above Top Secret, http://www.abovetopsecret.com/forum/thread349819/pg1 (last visited on October 22, 2010).

35. Major General Albert Stubblebine: Towers Fell Down Because of Explosives, World for 911 Truth, June 29, 2009, http://world911truth.org/major-general-albert-stubblebine-towers-fell-down-because-of-explosives/.

36. 911 and the Impossible, http://home.comcast.net/~skydrifter/exp.htm (last visited on October 23, 2010).;

37. Five Video Frames, Video Frames Leaked in 2002 Show Moments of the Pentagon Attack, http://911research.wtc7.net/pentagon/evidence/videos/fiveframes.html (last visited on October 23, 2010).

38. Pentagon Attack Footage, The Suppression of Video Footage of the Pentagon Attack, http://911research.wtc7.net/pentagon/evidence/footage.html#ref1 (last visited on October 23, 2010).

39. Pentagon Attack Footage, The Suppression of Video Footage of the Pentagon Attack, http://911research.wtc7.net/pentagon/evidence/footage.html#ref1 (last visited on October 23, 2010).

40. Pentagon Attack Footage, The Suppression of Video Footage of the Pentagon Attack, http://911research.wtc7.net/pentagon/evidence/footage.html#ref1 (last visited on October 23, 2010).

41. Better quality "Hotel" Pentagon Video w/ 'Official Flt Path', http://www.youtube.com/watch?v=n4O4R0LWCQ4&feature=related (last visited on October 23, 2010).

42. National Security Alert, http://www.citizeninvestigationteam.com (last visited on October 20, 2010).

43. Independent Investigation Into Pentagon Attack Yields Alarming Information, August 30, 2009, http://www.thepeoplesvoice.org/TPV3/Voices.php/2009/08/30/investigation-pentagon-attack-show-monst.

44. Washington DC Fox Affiliate Captures 2nd Explosion At Pentagon On 9/11, http://video.google.com/videoplay?docid=2912944806728436469# (last visited on October 23, 2010).

45. National Security Alert, http://www.citizeninvestigationteam.com/official-interviews.html (last visited on October 20, 2010).

46. 9/11 Pentagon Reality Check 13: Earwitness ERIC DIHLE, http://il.youtube.com/watch?v=tEyarCH2xYM (last visited on October 20, 2010).

47. FED. R. EVID. 803 (2).

48. Damage at the Pentagon, Associated Press, http://www.seattlepi.com/dayart/20010913/PentagonDamage.pdf (last visited on November 2, 2010).

49. The Pentagon Renovations Completed on 9/11/2001, http://whatreallyhappened.com/WRHARTICLES/911_pentagon_renovations.html?q=911_pentagon_renovations.html (last visited on November 2, 2010).

50. The Pentagon Renovations Completed on 9/11/2001, http://whatreallyhappened.com/WRHARTICLES/911_pentagon_renovations.html?q=911_pentagon_renovations.html (last visited on November 2, 2010).

51. Did Flight 77 Really Crash Into the Pentagon?, http://killtown.911review.org/flight77/claim.html (last visited on November 2, 2010).

52. Russell Pickering, *The Pentagon Exit Hole, More 9/11 Demolition?*, http://www.rense.com/general70/hole.htm (last visited on November 2, 2010).

53. Michael Meyer, *A Boeing 757 did not hit the Pentagon*, Scholars for 9/11 Truth, http://www.scholarsfor911truth.org/ArticlesMeyer3March2006.html (last visited on November 2, 2010).

54. Russell Pickering, *The Pentagon Exit Hole, More 9/11 Demolition?*, http://www.rense.com/general70/hole.htm (last visited on November 2, 2010).

55. Michael Meyer, *A Boeing 757 did not hit the Pentagon*, Scholars for 9/11 Truth, http://www.scholarsfor911truth.org/ArticlesMeyer3March2006.html (last visited on November 2, 2010).

56. Chairman Cox's Statement on the Terrorist Attack on America, Office of Representative Christopher Cox, September 11, 2001, http://web.archive.org/web/20011104161754/http://www.house.gov/cox/press/releases/2001/091101terroristattack.htm.

57. Chairman Cox's Statement on the Terrorist Attack on America, Office of Representative Christopher Cox, September 11, 2001, http://web.archive.org/web/20011104161754/http://www.house.gov/cox/press/releases/2001/091101terroristattack.htm.

58. Matthew Everett, *Donald Rumsfeld on 9/11: An Enemy Within*, May 30, 2007, http://onlinejournal.com/artman/publish/article_2026.shtml.

59. Complete 911 Timeline, Donald Rumsfeld's Actions on 9/11, History Commons, http://www.historycommons.org/timeline.jsp?timeline=complete_911_timeline&day_of_9/11=donaldrumsfeld (last visited on November 2, 2010).

60. Complete 911 Timeline, Donald Rumsfeld's Actions on 9/11, History Commons, http://www.historycommons.org/timeline.jsp?timeline=complete_911_timeline&day_of_9/11=donaldrumsfeld (last visited on November 2, 2010).

61. Complete 911 Timeline, Donald Rumsfeld's Actions on 9/11, History Commons, http://www.historycommons.org/timeline.jsp?timeline=complete_911_timeline&day_of_9/11=donaldrumsfeld (last visited on November 2, 2010).

62. Matthew Everett, *Donald Rumsfeld on 9/11: An Enemy Within*, May 30, 2007, http://onlinejournal.com/artman/publish/article_2026.shtml.

63. Statement of Principles, New American Century, January 3, 1997, http://www.newamericancentury.org/statementofprinciples.htm.

64. Rebuilding America's Defenses, Strategy, Forces and Resources for a New Century, A Report of The Project for a New American Century, at 51, September 2000, http://www.newamericancentury.org/RebuildingAmericasDefenses.pdf.

65. Rumsfeld Admits to Unaccounted, Missing 2.3 Trillion Dollars, http://video.google.com/videoplay?docid=-7904516028875682825# (last visited on October 23, 2010).

66. Barbara Honegger, *9-11 A Cheap Magic Trick, How False Flag Attacks are Manufactured by the World's Elite*, The Pentagon Attack Papers, http://911caper.com/2010/07/07/the-pentagon-attack-papers/ (last visited on October 22, 2010).

67. Jerry Mazza, Online Journal, *Following Zakheim and Pentagon Trillions to Israel and 9-11*, July 30, 2006, http://www.onlinejournal.com/artman/publish/article_1047.shtml.

68. Jerry Mazza, Online Journal, *Following Zakheim and Pentagon Trillions to Israel and 9-11*, July 30, 2006, http://www.onlinejournal.com/artman/publish/article_1047.shtml.

69. Rebuilding America's Defenses, Strategy, Forces and Resources for a New Century, http://www.newamericancentury.org/RebuildingAmericasDefenses.pdf (web address current as of June 18, 2005).

70. 9/11 Pentagon Survivor April Gallop on Alex Jones Show 1/4, http://www.youtube.com/watch?v=WCON1AncfoM (last visited on April 22, 2011).

71. Gallop v. Cheney, et al., http://willyloman.wordpress.com/2008/12/21/text-of-the-april-gallop-lawsuit/ (last visited on April 22, 2011).

72. 9/11 Pentagon Survivor April Gallop on Alex Jones Show 1/4, http://www.youtube.com/watch?v=WCON1AncfoM (last visited on April 22, 2011).

73. Bush Going to Court for 9/11 Cover Up, uploaded to YouTube April 6, 2011, http://www.youtube.com/watch?v=iU8aqx_PxnM.

74. Bush Going to Court for 9/11 Cover Up, uploaded to YouTube April 6, 2011, http://www.youtube.com/watch?v=iU8aqx_PxnM.

75. Judge John Walker, George Walker Bush's Cousin, Judges April Gallop's Suit, April 9, 2011, http://norcaltruth.org/2011/04/09/judge-john-walker-george-walker-bushs-cousin-judges-april-gallops-suit/.

76. Gallop v. Cheney, et al., http://willyloman.wordpress.com/2008/12/21/text-of-the-april-gallop-lawsuit/ (last visited on April 22, 2011).

77. Gallop v. Cheney, et al., http://willyloman.wordpress.com/2008/12/21/text-of-the-april-gallop-lawsuit/ (last visited on April 22, 2011).

78. Gallop v. Cheney, et al., http://willyloman.wordpress.com/2008/12/21/text-of-the-april-gallop-lawsuit/ (last visited on April 22, 2011).

79. Gallop v. Cheney, et al., http://willyloman.wordpress.com/2008/12/21/text-of-the-april-gallop-lawsuit/ (last visited on April 22, 2011).

80. Gallop v. Cheney, et al., http://willyloman.wordpress.com/2008/12/21/text-of-the-april-gallop-lawsuit/ (last visited on April 22, 2011).

81. Gallop v. Cheney, et al., http://willyloman.wordpress.com/2008/12/21/text-of-the-april-gallop-lawsuit/ (last visited on April 22, 2011).

82. Gallop v. Cheney, et al., http://willyloman.wordpress.com/2008/12/21/text-of-the-april-gallop-lawsuit/ (last visited on April 22, 2011).

83. Gallop v. Cheney, et al., http://willyloman.wordpress.com/2008/12/21/text-of-the-april-gallop-lawsuit/ (last visited on April 22, 2011).

84. www.pittsburglive.com (last visited on October 23, 2010).

85. Flight 93 Crash Site - No Plane!!!, http://www.spike.com/video/flight-93-crash-site/2693588 (last visited on October 23, 2010).

86. Us Mayor Says No Flight 93 Plane at Shanksville and No Bodies, http://www.youtube.com/watch?v=rqWEBo3da-Y&feature=related (last visited on October 23, 2010).

87. Us Mayor Says No Flight 93 Plane at Shanksville and No Bodies, http://www.youtube.com/watch?v=rqWEBo3da-Y&feature=related (last visited on October 23, 2010).

88. Peter Perl, *Hallowed Ground, Nobody Asked for This, but as September 11 Recedes, a Small Pennsylvania Town Finds Itself Guardian of an American Legend*, Washington Post, May 12, 2002, http://www.washingtonpost.com/ac2/wp-dyn?pagename=article&node=&contentId=A56110-200

2May8.

89. Robb Frederick, *the Day That Changed America*, September 11, 2002, Pittsburgh Tribune-Review, http://www.pittsburghlive.com/x/pittsburghtrib/s_90823.html. See also, Pennsylvania, Hunt the Boeing II, Shanksville Edition!, http://killtown.911review.org/htb2.html (last visited on October 23, 2010).

90. Robb Frederick, *the Day That Changed America*, September 11, 2002, Pittsburgh Tribune-Review, http://www.pittsburghlive.com/x/pittsburghtrib/s_90823.html.

91. Flight 93 Crash Debris, Photos of Wreckage From the Crash of Flight 93 Used as Trial Exhibits, http://911research.wtc7.net/planes/evidence/photos/padebris3.html (last visited on October 23, 2010).

92. Killtown Presents Hoodwinked at Shanksville, http://hoodwinkedatshanksville.blogspot.com/2007/03/back-in-black-boxes.html (last visited on October 23, 2010).

93. FAA Registry for N591UA, http://registry.faa.gov/aircraftinquiry/NNum_Results.aspx?NNumbertxt=N591UA (last visited on October 23, 2010).

94. The Cleveland Airport Mystery, http://911review.org/inn.globalfreepress/Cleveland_Airport_Mystery.html (last visited on April 22, 2011).

95. Christopher Bollyn, The Hollywood Fantasy of Flight 93, May 12, 2006, http://www.bollyn.com/the-hollywood-fantasy-of-flight-93-2.

96. The Cleveland Airport Mystery, http://911review.org/inn.globalfreepress/Cleveland_Airport_Mystery.html (last visited on April 22, 2011).

97. The Cleveland Airport Mystery, http://911review.org/inn.globalfreepress/Cleveland_Airport_Mystery.html (last visited on April 22, 2011).

98. Patrick O'Donnell, *Plane Diverted to Cleveland Triggers Alarm; FBI Finds Nothing Aboard Flight to L.A*, Cleveland Pain Dealer, http://911review.org/brad.com/Woodybox/CLEVELAND-PLAIN_NASA_9-12.html

99. Kymberli Hagelberg, Betty Lin-Fisher, and Mary Ethridge, *Chaos, Fear Land at Airports in Region Akron-canton Terminal Remains Open as Travelers Find Lodging, but Hopkins Closes and Evacuates*, Akron Beacon Journal, September 11, 2011, http://911review.org/brad.com/Woodybox/AKRON-TERMINAL-HOPKINS-EVACUATES.htm

l.

100. Flight 93, http://theredpill3.tripod.com/id3.html (last visited on April 23, 2011).

101. Devvy Kidd, FLIGHT 93 LAWSUIT UPDATE, News With Views, November 27, 2006, http://www.newswithviews.com/Devvy/kidd232.htm.

102. Cleveland-Hopkins Airport FAA Flight Arrival Record for September 10-11, 2001, http://www.devvy.com/pdf/2006_November/CLE_0911_Arrivals.pdf (last visited on April 27, 2001).

103. Cleveland-Hopkins Airport FAA Flight Arrival Record for September 10-11, 2001, http://www.devvy.com/pdf/2006_November/CLE_0911_Arrivals.pdf (last visited on April 27, 2001).

104. Cleveland-Hopkins Airport FAA Flight Arrival Record for September 10-11, 2001, http://www.devvy.com/pdf/2006_November/CLE_0911_Arrivals.pdf (last visited on April 27, 2001).

105. United Flight # 93, Boeing 757, http://911research.wtc7.net/planes/evidence/docs/Flight93.png (last visited on April 23, 2011).

106. Passenger Lists, Moussaoui Trial Exhibits, http://911research.wtc7.net/planes/evidence/passengers.html (last visited on April 23, 2011).

107. Excerpts from Trance-Formation of America (1995), http://www.bibliotecapleyades.net/sociopolitica/esp_sociopol_mindcon08.htm.

108. Brice Taylor, Thanks for the Memories (1999), at pp. 40, 71.

109. Traveling on Delta Flight 1989 on 9/11, http://256.com/gray/thoughts/2001/20010912/delta_flight_1989_9_11/travel.shtml (last visited on April 23, 2011).

110. Additional Details About Delta Flight 1989 on 9/11, http://256.com/gray/thoughts/2001/20010912/delta_flight_1989_9_11/details.shtml (last visited on April 23, 2011).

111. Traveling on Delta Flight 1989 on 9/11, http://256.com/gray/thoughts/2001/20010912/delta_flight_1989_9_11/travel.shtml (last visited on April 23, 2011).

112. September 11 Physics Cell Phones, http://911review.org/Wiki/Sept11PhysicsCellPhones.shtml (last visited on October 24, 2010).

113. A.K. Dewdney, *Project Achilles Report Parts One, Two and Three*, January 23, 2003, http://physics911.net/projectachilles.

114. The 9/11 Commission Report, at 12.

115. FBI Interview of Deena Bernett, http://intelfiles.egoplex.com/2001-09-11-FBI-FD302-deena-lynne-burnett.pdf (last visited on October 24, 2010).

116. David Ray Griffin and Rob Balsamo, *Could Barbara Olson Have Made Those Calls?,An Analysis of New Evidence about Onboard Phones*, http://pilotsfor911truth.org/amrarticle.html#sdfootnote39anc (last visited on October 24, 2010).

117. Flight Attendant Called Husband from Flight 93, http://www.youtube.com/watch?v=TBjgV1plf2M&feature=related (last visited on October 24, 2010).

118. F93 Attendent CeeCee Lyles Leaves a Message For Her Husband, http://www.youtube.com/watch?v=fUrxsrTKHN4 (last visited on October 24, 2010).

119. Flight 93 - Exposed -Smoking Gun Evidence, http://www.youtube.com/watch?v=mJzoGD_zsiM&NR=1 (last visited on October 24, 2010).

120. William M. Arkin, *When Seeing and Hearing Isn't Believing*, February 1, 1999, http://www.washingtonpost.com/wp-srv/national/dotmil/arkin020199.htm.

121. William M. Arkin, *When Seeing and Hearing Isn't Believing*, February 1, 1999, http://www.washingtonpost.com/wp-srv/national/dotmil/arkin020199.htm.

122. William M. Arkin, *When Seeing and Hearing Isn't Believing*, February 1, 1999, http://www.washingtonpost.com/wp-srv/national/dotmil/arkin020199.htm.

123. UNMASKING SEPTEMBER 11, 2001, http://www.apfn.org/apfn/unmasking.htm (last visited on October 24, 2010).

124. Phil Jayhan, Mark Bingham - Exif/IPTC Data 8/30/2001! 13 Days before 9/11!, August 6, 2010, http://letsrollforums.com/fl-93-mark-bingham-t22141.html.

125. Mark Bingham - Exif/IPTC Data 8/30/2001! 13 Days before 9/11!, http://www.coffinman.co.uk/mark_bingham.htm (last visited on April 25, 2011).

126. International Press Telecommunications Council (IPTC), http://www.iptc.org/site/Home/ (last visited on April 25, 2011).

127. International Press Telecommunications Council (IPTC), Photo Metadata, http://www.iptc.org/site/Photo_Metadata/Overview/ (last visited on April 25, 2011).

128. International Press Telecommunications Council (IPTC), Photo Metadata, http://www.iptc.org/site/Photo_Metadata/Overview/ (last visited on April 25, 2011).

129. Mark Bingham - Exif/IPTC Data 8/30/2001! 13 Days before 9/11!, http://www.coffinman.co.uk/mark_bingham.htm (last visited on April 25, 2011).

130. Some Interesting Facts about the Bingham IPTC Data, January 16, 2011, http://letsrollforums.com/fl-93-mark-bingham-t22141p7.html.

131. Some Interesting Facts about the Bingham IPTC Data, January 16, 2011, http://letsrollforums.com/fl-93-mark-bingham-t22141p7.html.

132. September 11, A Memorial, CNN.com, Wayback Internet Archive, June 11, 2009, http://replay.web.archive.org/20090611045126/http://www.cnn.com/SPECIALS/2001/memorial/lists/by-location/page98.html.

133. September 11, A Memorial, CNN.com, http://www.cnn.com/SPECIALS/2001/memorial/lists/by-location/page98.html (last visited on April 25, 2011).

134. September 11, A Memorial, CNN.com, Wayback Internet Archive, June 11, 2009, http://replay.web.archive.org/20090611045235/http://www.cnn.com/SPECIALS/2001/memorial/lists/by-location/page93.html.

135. September 11, A Memorial, CNN.com, http://www.cnn.com/SPECIALS/2001/memorial/lists/by-location/page93.html (last visited on April 29, 2011).

136. September 11, A Memorial, CNN.com, Wayback Internet Archive, June 11, 2009, http://replay.web.archive.org/20090611045123/http://www.cnn.com/SPECIALS/2001/memorial/lists/by-location/page96.html.

137. September 11, A Memorial, CNN.com, http://www.cnn.com/SPECIALS/2001/memorial/lists/by-location/page96.html (last visited on April 29, 2011).

138. September 11, A Memorial, CNN.com, Wayback Internet Archive, June 11, 2009, http://replay.web.archive.org/20090611045227/http://www.cnn.com/SPECIALS/2001/memorial/lists/by-location/page100.html.

139. September 11, A Memorial, CNN.com, http://www.cnn.com/SPECIALS/2001/memorial/lists/by-location/page100.html (last visited on April 29, 2011).

140. 9/11 Commission Report, at 10.

141. 9/11 Commission Report, at 14.

142. Dr. Daniel R. Bower, National Transportation Safety Board, Office of Research and Engineering, Radar Data Impact Speed Study, February 11, 2002, http://pilotsfor911truth.org/p4t/Radar_Data_Impact_Speed_Study--AA11,_UA175.pdf.

143. The 911 Aircraft Speed Lie, http://www.youtube.com/watch?v=fhUHxsOrz6g&feature=related (last visited on November 6, 2010).

144. The 911 Aircraft Speed Lie, http://www.youtube.com/watch?v=fhUHxsOrz6g&feature=related (last visited on November 6, 2010).

145. Impossible Plane Speed with "Boeing", http://www.youtube.com/watch?v=SrCqlr026W0 (last visited on November 6, 2010).

146. Impossible Plane Speed with "Boeing", http://www.youtube.com/watch?v=SrCqlr026W0 (last visited on November 6, 2010).

147. Impossible Plane Speed with "Boeing", http://www.youtube.com/watch?v=SrCqlr026W0 (last visited on November 6, 2010).

148. StillDiggin, Marcus Icke Writes a Review, http://911logic.blogspot.com/ (May 29, 2007).

149. 911 Commission Report, endnote 1, Chapter 9.

150. Twin Towers Construction, http://911research.wtc7.net/wtc/evidence/photos/construction.html (last visited on October 27, 2010).

151. http://www.pbs.org/wgbh/nova/wtc/sund-flash.html (last visited October 29, 2010). See also Reports of the Federal Building and Fire Investigation of the World Trade Center Disaster, http://wtc.nist.gov/NCSTAR1/ (last visited on October 29, 2010).

152. Aircraft Structural Design, http://adg.stanford.edu/aa241/structures/structuraldesign.html (last visited on October 30, 2010).

153. Aircraft Structural Design, http://adg.stanford.edu/aa241/structures/structuraldesign.html (last visited on October 30, 2010).

154. The Core Structures, The Structural System of the Twin Towers, http://911research.wtc7.net/wtc/arch/core.html (last visited on October 26, 2010).

155. The Core Structures, The Structural System of the Twin Towers, http://911research.wtc7.net/wtc/arch/core.html (last visited on October 26, 2010).

156. NIST Core Column Data, http://wtcmodel.wikidot.com/nist-core-column-data (last visited on November 1, 2010).

157. NIST Core Column Data, http://wtcmodel.wikidot.com/nist-core-column-data (last visited on November 1, 2010).

158. NIST Core Column Data, http://wtcmodel.wikidot.com/nist-core-column-data (last visited on November 1, 2010).

159. Towers' Design Parameters, Twin Towers' Designers Anticipated Jet Impacts Like September 11th's, http://911research.wtc7.net/wtc/analysis/design.html (last visited on October 31, 2010).

160. Towers' Design Parameters, Twin Towers' Designers Anticipated Jet Impacts Like September 11th's, http://911research.wtc7.net/wtc/analysis/design.html (last visited on October 31, 2010).

161. The Structural System of the Twin Towers, http://911research.wtc7.net/wtc/arch/perimeter.html (last visited on October 27, 2010).

162. The Structural System of the Twin Towers, http://911research.wtc7.net/wtc/arch/perimeter.html (last visited on October 27, 2010).

163. Rifle Plates Photo Gallery, http://www.bulletproofme.com/PHOTO%20pages/Rifle_Plates_PHOTOS.shtml (last visited on November 5, 2010).

164. Ballistic Vest, http://en.wikipedia.org/wiki/Ballistic_vest (last visited on Novemer 5, 2010).

165. Sources for Pictures: Impactos de pájaros, December, 2007, http://www.landingshort.com/2007/12/page/3/, Birds vs Planes, January 22, 2008, http://scienceblogs.com/tetrapodzoology/2008/01/birds_vs_planes.php.

166. http://www.takeourworldback.com/911/911fires3.htm (last visited on November 5, 2010).

167. The Webfairy, 2nd Hit - Pavel Hlava Shot, You Tube, http://www.youtube.com/watch?v=bwMWc-3H6v8 (visited on 5-25-08).

168. StillDiggin, Marcus Icke Writes a Review, http://911logic.blogspot.com/ (May 29, 2007).

169. Evan Fairbanks on 9/11, http://www.history.com/videos/evan-fairbanks-on-911#evan-fairbanks-on-911 (last visited on April 22, 2011). See also Evan Fairbanks NEW footage FULL, http://www.youtube.com/watch?v=4JwTXEJSr4A&feature=related (last viewed on April 21, 2011).

170. PumpItOut Jeff calls Evan Fairbanks, http://www.youtube.com/watch?v=7wMK1rmELtE (last visited on April 22, 2011).

171. Evan Fairbanks Is a Liar, September 16, 2008, http://www.youtube.com/watch?v=zsbIoMa-5mU&feature=related.

172. E. Fairbanks 9/11 WTC Footage, 22 minutes part 1, video uploaded to YouTube on May 1, 2010, http://www.youtube.com/watch?v=udVbDzN9Cgc.

173. Evan Fairbanks on 9/11, http://www.history.com/videos/evan-fairbanks-on-911#evan-fairbanks-on-911 (last visited on April 22, 2011).

174. Interview with Evan Fairbank, September 13, 2006, http://www.youtube.com/watch?v=HCDu2V3yjS4&NR=1.

175. 9/11 Evan Fairbanks 'We Have seen these images in movies and know that it is artificial' ABC 1030pm, http://www.youtube.com/watch?v=IYV-iX2GXB8&feature=related (last viewed on April 21, 2011).

176. BBC Reported Building 7 Collapse 20 Minutes Before It Fell, http://www.youtube.com/watch?v=C7SwOT29gbc&mode=related&search= (last visited on June 2, 2008).

177. Richard Porter, *Part of the conspiracy?*, BBC, February 27, 2007, http://www.bbc.co.uk/blogs/theeditors/2007/02/part_of_the_conspiracy.html.

178. Richard Porter, *Part of the conspiracy?*, BBC, February 27, 2007, http://www.bbc.co.uk/blogs/theeditors/2007/02/part_of_the_conspiracy.html.

179. BBC Anchor Agrees WTC-7 Collapse May Be a Conspiracy, May 2, 2008, http://noworldsystem.com/category/jane-standley/.

180. Richard Porter, *Part of the conspiracy?*, BBC, February 27, 2007, http://www.bbc.co.uk/blogs/theeditors/2007/02/part_of_the_conspiracy.html.

181. Paul Joseph Watson, *Time Stamp Confirms BBC Reported WTC 7 Collapse 26 Minutes In Advance*, February 28, 2007, http://www.prisonplanet.com/articles/february2007/280207timestamp.htm.

182. Information and Archive Policy Statements, BBC http://www.bbc.co.uk/guidelines/dq/pdf/media/policies.pdf (last visited on October 29, 2010).

183. Information and Archive Policy Statements, BBC http://www.bbc.co.uk/guidelines/dq/pdf/media/policies.pdf (last visited on October 29, 2010).

184. Steve Watson, *BBC Has Lost Tapes Of 21st Century's Defining Moment 9/11 coverage gone due to "cock up". Why is this not a world news headline?*, Prison Planet, February 28, 2007, http://infowars.net/articles/february2007/280207BBC.htm.

185. Richard Porter, *Part of the conspiracy?*, BBC, February 27, 2007, http://www.bbc.co.uk/blogs/theeditors/2007/02/part_of_the_conspiracy.html.

186. Steve Watson, *BBC Has Lost Tapes Of 21st Century's Defining Moment 9/11 coverage gone due to "cock up". Why is this not a world news headline?*, Prison Planet, February 28, 2007, http://infowars.net/articles/february2007/280207BBC.htm.

187. Richard Porter, *Part of the conspiracy?*, BBC, February 27, 2007, http://www.bbc.co.uk/blogs/theeditors/2007/02/part_of_the_conspiracy.html.

188. Richard Porter, *Part of the Conspiracy? (2)*, March 2, 2007, http://www.bbc.co.uk/blogs/theeditors/2007/03/part_of_the_conspiracy_2.html.

189. Richard Porter, *Part of the Conspiracy? (2)*, March 2, 2007, http://www.bbc.co.uk/blogs/theeditors/2007/03/part_of_the_conspiracy_2.html.

190. Richard Porter, *Part of the Conspiracy? (2)*, March 2, 2007, http://www.bbc.co.uk/blogs/theeditors/2007/03/part_of_the_conspiracy_2.html.

191. Art of a Woman II: DC's Fox 5 News Anchor Shawn Yancy Shares Her Passion for Her Art!, September 8, 2010, http://thedcladies.blogspot.com/2010/09/art-of-woman-ii-dcs-fox-5-news-anchor.html.

192. Reports of WT7 collapse BEFORE it COLLAPSED!!!, http://www.youtube.com/watch?v=VE9OP52H2E8 (last visited on October 27, 2010).

193. BBC denies 9/11 conspiracy, http://news.bbc.co.uk/2/hi/programmes/conspiracy_files/7483700.stm (page last updated on 2 July 2008). See also Mike Rudin, *Controversy and conspiracies III*, BBC 2 July 2008, http://www.bbc.co.uk/blogs/theeditors/2008/07/controversy_conspiracies_iii.html.

194. BBC denies 9/11 conspiracy, http://news.bbc.co.uk/2/hi/programmes/conspiracy_files/7483700.stm (page last updated on 2 July 2008).

195. Mike Rudin, *Controversy and conspiracies III*, BBC 2 July 2008, http://www.bbc.co.uk/blogs/theeditors/2008/07/controversy_conspiracies_iii.html.

196. Steve Watson, *BBC Has Lost Tapes Of 21st Century's Defining Moment 9/11 coverage gone due to "cock up". Why is this not a world news headline?*, Prison Planet, February 28, 2007, http://infowars.net/articles/february2007/280207BBC.htm.

197. CONG. REC. 2947-2948 (February 9, 1917) (speech of Rep. Callaway), http://www.iahf.com/media.html (current as of October 3, 2001).

198. Granville Williams, *Bestriding The World, Campaign for Press and Broadcasting Freedom*, New Internationalist magazine, http://www.mediachannel.org/ownership/granville.shtml (last visited on May 25, 2008). Christopher Bollyn, *Arnon Milchan & Israeli Control of the Media*, http://www.bollyn.com/index/?id=10568 (September 1, 2007).

199. CONG. REC. 2947-2948 (February 9, 1917) (speech of Rcp. Callaway), http://www.iahf.com/media.html (current as of October 3, 2001).

200. ERIC JON PHELPS, VATICAN ASSASSINS: "WOUNDED IN THE HOUSE OF MY FRIENDS," p. 465 (2001) (quoting A U.S. Police Action: Operation Vampire Killer, pp. 18-19 (1992)).

201. Tom Flocco, FBI Linguist Won't Deny Intelligence Intercepts Tied 911 Drug Money to U.S. Election Campaigns, TomFlocco.com, April 25, 2005, http://www.911truth.org/article.php?story=2005042520431369 (web address current as of May 12, 2005).

202. http://www.homelandsecurity.org/NewsletterArchives/080803.htm (web address current as of October 24, 2004).

203. http://archives.cnn.com/2001/SHOWBIZ/Movies/11/09/hollywood.war/ (web address current as of October 24, 2004).

204. Eye Witness Says it Was a Bomb, No Second Plane on 911, http://www.youtube.com/watch?v=XJjf7NRhCe0 (last visited on April 19, 2011).

205. Eye Witness Says it Was a Bomb, No Second Plane on 911, http://www.youtube.com/watch?v=XJjf7NRhCe0 (last visited on April 19, 2011).

206. Key 9/11 Witness commits suicide. RIP Kenny Johannemann, http://www.youtube.com/watch?v=yEuzU3LMgCA (last visited on April 19, 2011).

207. Key 9/11 Witness commits suicide. RIP Kenny Johannemann, http://www.youtube.com/watch?v=yEuzU3LMgCA (last visited on April 19, 2011).

208. 9/11 - Explosion Witness William Rodriguez, http://www.youtube.com/watch?v=b_LlJzR2oYI&feature=related (last visited on April 19, 2011).

209. Michael Daly, *9/11 Claims One More Victim*, New York Daily News, September 3, 2008, http://articles.nydailynews.com/2008-09-03/local/17905673_1_cell-phone-cat-maya.

210. 911 ABC Reporter Dan Dahler - An Eyewitness Saw No Plane, Only an Explosion, http://www.youtube.com/watch?v=XA8xD9CFu40 (last visited on April 19, 2011).

211. NBC Sept. 11, 2001 8:31 am - 9:12 am (September 11, 2001), Interview of Oberstein Starts at 23:32, Internet Archive, http://www.archive.org/details/nbc200109110831-0912.

212. NBC Sept. 11, 2001 8:31 am - 9:12 am (September 11, 2001), Interview of Oberstein Starts at 23:32, Internet Archive, http://www.archive.org/details/nbc200109110831-0912.

213. 911 BBC - Eye-witness Steve Evans Saw Second Explosion(s) but No Plane, http://www.youtube.com/watch?v=0YarBxlIzUk (last visited on April 19, 2011).

214. 911 CNN - an Eye-witness Heard a Sonic Boom, but No Plane, http://www.youtube.com/watch?v=d3LXJwI-7xY (last visited on April 19, 2011).

215. 911 Fake Witness - Mark Walsh a/k/a "The Harley Guy," http://wn.com/9_11_Fake_Witness__Mark_Walsh_aka_The_Harley_Guy (last visited on April 18, 2011).

216. 911 Fake Witness - Mark Walsh a/k/a "The Harley Guy,"http://wn.com/9_11_Fake_Witness__Mark_Walsh_aka_The_Harley_Guy (last visited on April 18, 2011).

217. 911 Fake Witness - Mark Walsh a/k/a "The Harley Guy,"http://wn.com/9_11_Fake_Witness__Mark_Walsh_aka_The_Harley_Guy (last visited on April 18, 2011).

218. Sean Murtagh's Pipe Dream, http://www.youtube.com/watch?v=ku9YslaObug (last visited on April 19, 2011).

219. Transcript of CNN Breaking News, Terrorist Attack on the United States, Aired September 11, 2001, 8:48 a.m., http://transcripts.cnn.com/TRANSCRIPTS/0109/11/bn.01.html.

220. Transcript of CNN Breaking News, Terrorist Attack on the United States, Aired September 11, 2001, 8:48 a.m., http://transcripts.cnn.com/TRANSCRIPTS/0109/11/bn.01.html.

221. Simon Shack, SEPTEMBER CLUES D, http://www.youtube.com/watch?v=HuB4jLAuVLk&feature=related (last visited on April 19, 2011). See also Ergenekon's Propaganda Power - DEEP STATE Brave TURKEY, April 2, 2011, http://u2r2h-documents.blogspot.com/.

222. Simon Shack, SEPTEMBER CLUES D, http://www.youtube.com/watch?v=HuB4jLAuVLk&feature=related (last visited on April 19, 2011). See also Ergenekon's Propaganda Power - DEEP STATE Brave TURKEY, April 2, 2011, http://u2r2h-documents.blogspot.com/.

223. Simon Shack, SEPTEMBER CLUES D, http://www.youtube.com/watch?v=HuB4jLAuVLk&feature=related (last visited on April 19, 2011). See also Ergenekon's Propaganda Power - DEEP STATE Brave TURKEY, April 2, 2011, http://u2r2h-documents.blogspot.com/.

224. Simon Shack, SEPTEMBER CLUES D, http://www.youtube.com/watch?v=HuB4jLAuVLk&feature=related (last visited on April 19, 2011). See also Ergenekon's Propaganda Power - DEEP STATE Brave TURKEY, April 2, 2011, http://u2r2h-documents.blogspot.com/.

225. Simon Shack, SEPTEMBER CLUES D, http://www.youtube.com/watch?v=HuB4jLAuVLk&feature=related (last visited on April 19, 2011). See also Ergenekon's Propaganda Power - DEEP STATE Brave TURKEY, April 2, 2011, http://u2r2h-documents.blogspot.com/.

226. Simon Shack, SEPTEMBER CLUES D, http://www.youtube.com/watch?v=HuB4jLAuVLk&feature=related (last visited on April 19, 2011). See also Ergenekon's Propaganda Power - DEEP STATE Brave TURKEY, April 2, 2011, http://u2r2h-documents.blogspot.com/.

227. Simon Shack, SEPTEMBER CLUES D, http://www.youtube.com/watch?v=HuB4jLAuVLk&feature=related (last visited on April 19, 2011). See also Ergenekon's Propaganda Power - DEEP STATE Brave TURKEY, April 2, 2011, http://u2r2h-documents.blogspot.com/.

228. Simon Shack, SEPTEMBER CLUES D, http://www.youtube.com/watch?v=HuB4jLAuVLk&feature=related (last visited on April 19, 2011). See also Ergenekon's Propaganda Power - DEEP STATE Brave TURKEY, April 2, 2011, http://u2r2h-documents.blogspot.com/.

229. New York 9/11 Photographer Did Not See 2nd Plane as He Photographed Explosion, http://www.youtube.com/watch?v=ulE9OiZqQwg (last visited on April 20, 2011).

230. WTC Impact Photo, January 1, 2007, http://www.zimbio.com/World+Trade+Center/articles/2/WTC+impact+photo.

231. No Plane Witnesses, May 7, 2007, http://www.livevideo.com/video/embedLink/83C0FA83D5E74E3F98B66F36DFF39F44/203582/no-plane-witnesses.aspx.

232. No Plane Witnesses, May 7, 2007, http://www.livevideo.com/video/embedLink/83C0FA83D5E74E3F98B66F36DFF39F44/203582/no-plane-witnesses.aspx.

233. No Plane Witnesses, May 7, 2007, http://www.livevideo.com/video/embedLink/83C0FA83D5E74E3F98B66F36DFF39F44/203582/no-plane-witnesses.aspx.

234. No Plane Witnesses, May 7, 2007, http://www.livevideo.com/video/embedLink/83C0FA83D5E74E3F98B66F36DFF39F44/203582/no-plane-witnesses.aspx.

235. World Trade Centre - 11th September 2001, http://www.cruzate.com/nyhell/ (last visited on April 20, 2011).

236. No Plane Witnesses, May 7, 2007, http://www.livevideo.com/video/embedLink/83C0FA83D5E74E3F98B66F36DFF39F44/203582/no-plane-witnesses.aspx.

237. What If The 911 Plane Witnesses Were Really Only Actors? 2/2, http://www.youtube.com/watch?v=O9VclcXNI9o&feature=related (last visited on April 21, 2011).

238. What If The 911 Plane Witnesses Were Really Only Actors? 2/2, http://www.youtube.com/watch?v=O9VclcXNI9o&feature=related (last visited on April 21, 2011).

239. NIST FOIA: Clifton Cloud Clips 1-3 (WTC2 Plane Impact, 9:03am), http://www.youtube.com/watch?v=A2unTcZnY30 (last visited on April 21, 2011).

240. NIST FOIA: Clifton Cloud Clips 1-3 (WTC2 Plane Impact, 9:03am), http://www.youtube.com/watch?v=A2unTcZnY30 (last visited on April 21, 2011).

241. 911 Witness: No Plane hit South Tower Cloud Clifton from NIST Release, http://www.youtube.com/watch?v=eL74ikIVDoE (last visited on April 21, 2011).

242. 911 Witness: No Plane hit South Tower Cloud Clifton from NIST Release, http://www.youtube.com/watch?v=eL74ikIVDoE (last visited on April 21, 2011).

243. 911 Witness: No Plane hit South Tower Cloud Clifton from NIST Release, http://www.youtube.com/watch?v=eL74ikIVDoE (last visited on April 21, 2011).

244. 911 Witness: No Plane hit South Tower Cloud Clifton from NIST Release, http://www.youtube.com/watch?v=eL74ikIVDoE (last visited on April 21, 2011).

245. 911 Witness: No Plane hit South Tower Cloud Clifton from NIST Release, http://www.youtube.com/watch?v=eL74ikIVDoE (last visited on April 21, 2011).

246. 911 Witness: No Plane hit South Tower Cloud Clifton from NIST Release, http://www.youtube.com/watch?v=eL74ikIVDoE (last visited on April 21, 2011).

247. 911 Witness: No Plane hit South Tower Cloud Clifton from NIST Release, http://www.youtube.com/watch?v=eL74ikIVDoE (last visited on April 21, 2011).

248. 9/11 Eyewitness Saw No Plane Hit WTC South Tower, January 17, 2009, http://www.youtube.com/watch?v=rGBiUbFZKD4.

249. South Tower Anomalies III - Addressing the Debunkers, December 4, 2007, http://www.youtube.com/watch?v=rh7cKDXnS_s.

250. 911 Chopper 4, August 5, 2009, http://www.youtube.com/watch?v=dbRD7ki8h0k.

251. NBC Sept. 11, 2001 11:48 pm - 0:30 am (September 12, 2001), Internet Archive (plane CGI at 37 minute mark of video), http://www.archive.org/details/nbc200109112348-0030.

252. Dylan Avery, Barry Jennings Uncut, http://blip.tv/file/1064938 (last visited on November 5, 2010).

253. Barry Jennings Mystery, December 31, 2009, http://barryjenningsmystery.blogspot.com/.

254. The NIST Investigation, National Institute for Standards and Technology Encounters Resistance, Pretends to Investigate, http://911research.wtc7.net/wtc/official/nist/index.html (last visited on November 6, 2010).

255. NIST and the World Trade Center, http://wtc.nist.gov/ (last visited on November 6, 2010).

256. NIST Final Report on the Collapse of World Trade Center Building 7, http://wtc.nist.gov/NCSTAR1/PDF/NCSTAR%201A.pdf (last visited on November 6, 2010).

257. Independent Research Letter Sent to NIST on September 15, 2008, http://911research.wtc7.net/letters/nist/WTC7Comments.html (last visited on November 6, 2010).

258. NIST Final Report on the Collapse of World Trade Center Building 7, at xxxvi, http://wtc.nist.gov/NCSTAR1/PDF/NCSTAR%201A.pdf (last visited on November 6, 2010).

259. NIST Final Report on the Collapse of World Trade Center Building 7, at xxxvii, http://wtc.nist.gov/NCSTAR1/PDF/NCSTAR%201A.pdf (last visited on November 6, 2010).

260. Barry Jennings: Dead Bodies?, http://www.youtube.com/watch?v=nyKtNHPeKxg (last visited on November 6, 2010).

261. Dylan Avery, Barry Jennings Uncut, http://blip.tv/file/1064938 (last visited on November 5, 2010).

262. Dylan Avery, Barry Jennings Uncut, http://blip.tv/file/1064938 (last visited on November 5, 2010).

263. NIST Final Report on the Collapse of World Trade Center Building 7, at xxxvi, http://wtc.nist.gov/NCSTAR1/PDF/NCSTAR%201A.pdf (last visited on November 6, 2010).

264. NIST Final Report on the Collapse of World Trade Center Building 7, at xxxvi, http://wtc.nist.gov/NCSTAR1/PDF/NCSTAR%201A.pdf (last visited on November 6, 2010).

265. NIST Final Report on the Collapse of World Trade Center Building 7, at xxxvi, http://wtc.nist.gov/NCSTAR1/PDF/NCSTAR%201A.pdf (last visited on November 6, 2010).

266. Independent Research Letter Sent to NIST on September 15, 2008, http://911research.wtc7.net/letters/nist/WTC7Comments.html (last visited on November 6, 2010).

267. Building 7, the Secrecy Shrouded Building Holding Guiliani's Command Center, http://911research.wtc7.net/wtc/background/wtc7.html (web address current as of October 24, 2004).

268. Rudolph Guiliani Interview, The Hall of Public Service, http://www.achievement.org/autodoc/page/giu0int-7 (web address current as of October 24, 2004).

269. Alexander James, *Proof of Demolition of WTC 1,2,6,7 by Internal Explosions*, July 11, 2004, http://newswire.indymedia.org/en/newswire/2004/07/805929.shtml (web address current as of October 24, 2004).

270. *The WTC Was Designed to Survive the Impact of a Boeing 767, So Why Didn't It?* http://hawaii.indymedia.org/news/2003/07/3257.php (web address current as of October 24, 2004).

271. Alexander James, *Proof of Demolition of WTC 1,2,6,7 by Internal Explosions*, July 11, 2004, http://newswire.indymedia.org/en/newswire/2004/07/805929.shtml (web address current as of October 24, 2004).

272. Alexander James, *Proof of Demolition of WTC 1,2,6,7 by Internal Explosions*, July 11, 2004, http://newswire.indymedia.org/en/newswire/2004/07/805929.shtml (web address current as of October 24, 2004).

273. Randy Lavello, *Bombs in the Building: World Trade Center 'Conspiracy Theory' is a Conspiracy Fact*, http://www.prisonplanet.com/analysis_lavello_050503_bombs.html (web address current as of October 24, 2004).

274. *WTC7: The Signature of a 9/11 Demolition*, http://www.whatreallyhappened.com/cutter.html (web address current as of October 24, 2004).

275. Photos of Damage to Nearby building and Southern Ground Zero, http://911research.wtc7.net/wtc/evidence/photos/gzrescue2.html (web address current as of

October 27, 2004); The World Financial Center, http://www.wirednewyork.com/wfc/3wfc/default.htm (web address current as of October 27, 2004).

276. NIST and the World Trade Center, http://wtc.nist.gov/ (last visited on November 6, 2010).

277. NIST Final Report on the Collapse of World Trade Center Building 7, http://wtc.nist.gov/NCSTAR1/PDF/NCSTAR%201A.pdf (last visited on November 6, 2010).

278. 9/11 Security Courtesy of Marvin Bush, http://whatreallyhappened.com/WRHARTICLES/911security.html?q=911security.html (last visited on November 10, 2010).

279. Wayne Madsen, Marvin Bush Employee's Mysterious Death – Connections to 9/11?, From the Wilderness, http://www.fromthewilderness.com/free/ww3/101003_bush_death.html (last visited on November 10, 2010).

280. William Norman Grigg, *Did We Know What Was Coming, The New American*, at 10,14, March 11, 2002.

281. William Norman Grigg, *Did We Know What Was Coming, The New American*, at 10,14, March 11, 2002.

282. Report of the U.S.. Senate Select Committee on Intelligence and U.S. House of Representatives Permanent Select Committee on Intelligence, Joint Inquiry Into Intelligence Community Activities Before and After the Terrorist Attacks of September 11, 2001, December 20, 2002, available at: http://www.gpoaccess.gov/serialset/creports/pdf/fullreport_errata.pdf.

283. William Norman Grigg, *Did We Know What Was Coming, The New American*, at 10,11, March 11, 2002.

284. Israel did 9/11 - ALL THE PROOF IN THE WORLD, May 06, 2009, http://theinfounderground.com/forum/viewtopic.php?p=20882 (last visited on November 10, 2010).

285. Israel did 9/11 - ALL THE PROOF IN THE WORLD, May 06, 2009, http://theinfounderground.com/forum/viewtopic.php?p=20882 (last visited on November 10, 2010).

286. Amy Goodman, "The White House Has Played Cover-Up"–Former 9/11 Commission Member Max Cleland Blasts Bush, Democracy Now, March 23, 2004, http://www.democracynow.org/2004/3/23/the_white_house_has_played_cover.

287. Amy Goodman, "The White House Has Played Cover-Up"–Former 9/11 Commission Member Max Cleland Blasts Bush, Democracy Now, March 23, 2004, http://www.democracynow.org/2004/3/23/the_white_house_has_played_cover.

288. MICHAEL SABA, THE ARMAGEDDON NETWORK (1984).

289. Ariel Sharon: *'We control America'*, October 3, 2001, http://americandefenseleague.com/onaleash.htm (web address current as of April 21, 2002).

290. NIST Final Report on the Collapse of World Trade Center Building 7, http://wtc.nist.gov/NCSTAR1/PDF/NCSTAR%201A.pdf (last visited on November 6, 2010).

291. Independent Research Letter Sent to NIST on September 15, 2008, http://911research.wtc7.net/letters/nist/WTC7Comments.html (last visited on November 6, 2010).

292. Christopher Bollyn, *Some Survivors Say 'Bombs Exploded Inside WTC'*, American Free Press, http://www.americanfreepress.net/10_22_01/Some_Survivors_Say__Bombs_Expl/some_survivors_say__bombs_expl.html (current as of October 27, 2001).

293. Woman Waving From WTC 1 Impact Area, http://whatreallyhappened.com/WRHARTICLES/wtc1_woman.html?q=wtc1_woman.html (last visited on November 7, 2010).

294. The Jet Fuel; How Hot Did it Heat the World Trade Center?, http://www.uscrusade.com/forum/config.pl/read/1064 (February 23, 2003).

295. Trade Center Hit by 6-Floor Fire, New York Times, http://www.nytimes.com/1975/02/14/nyregion/14WTC.html (last visited on November 7, 2010).

296. Christopher Bollyn, New Seismic Data Reputes Official Explanation, American Free Press, http://www.americanfreepress.net/09_03_02/NEW_SEISMIC_/new_seismic_.html (website address current as of April 1, 2003).

297. Twin Towers' Destruction, Photographic Evidence of the Fall of the Twin Towers, http://911research.wtc7.net/wtc/evidence/photos/collapses.html#north (last visited on November 7, 2010).

298. Twin Towers' Destruction, Photographic Evidence of the Fall of the Twin Towers, http://911research.wtc7.net/wtc/evidence/photos/collapses.html#north (last visited on November 7, 2010).

299. Judy Wood, *Where Did the Towers Go?, Evidence of Directed Free-Energy Technology on 9/11*, at 81 (2010).

300. Judy Wood, *Where Did the Towers Go?, Evidence of Directed Free-Energy Technology on 9/11*, at 90-91 (2010).

301. 9/11 Issues, http://www.drjudywood.com/ (last visited on May 3, 2008).

302. Directed Energy Weapon, http://en.wikipedia.org/wiki/Directed-energy_weapon (last visited on May 3, 2008).

303. Kirtland Air Fore Base, Directed Energy Directorate, http://www.kirtland.af.mil/afrl_de/ (last visited on May 3, 2008).

304. Morgan Reynolds, Judy Wood, Why Indeed Did the WTC Buildings Disintegrate?, A peer-review of Steven E. Jones' 9/11 Research, http://nomoregames.net/indcx.php?page=911&subpage1=trouble_with_jones (last visited on May 3, 2008).

305. Judy Wood and Morgan Reynolds, *The Star Wars Beam Weapons*, http://www.drjudywood.com/articles/DEW/StarWarsBeam3.html (last visited on May 3, 2008).

306. Dmytro Doblevych, A View From Ground Zero, A volunteer's account of September 11 aftermath, http://www.doblevych.com/english/about/writing/groundzero.html (last visited on May 3, 2008).

307. Judy Wood, Molecular Dissociation: from Dust to Dirt, May 16, 2007, http://www.drjudywood.com/articles/dirt/dirt2.html.

308. Judy Wood and John Hutchison, Anomalies at the WTC and the Hutchison Effect (part II), April 1, 2008, http://www.drjudywood.com/articles/JJ/JJ2.html.

309. Judy Wood, *Where Did the Towers Go?, Evidence of Directed Free-Energy Technology on 9/11*, at 298 (2010).

310. Judy Wood, *Where Did the Towers Go?, Evidence of Directed Free-Energy Technology on 9/11*, at 298 (2010).

311. Judy Wood, *Where Did the Towers Go?, Evidence of Directed Free-Energy Technology on 9/11*, at 330 (2010).

312. Judy Wood, *Where Did the Towers Go?, Evidence of Directed Free-Energy Technology on 9/11*, at 335 (2010).

313. Judy Wood, *Where Did the Towers Go?, Evidence of Directed Free-Energy Technology on 9/11*, at 362-63 (2010).

314. Judy Wood, "Aha!" Moments, October 6, 2008, http://www.drjudywood.com/articles/short/aha.html.

315. Judy Wood, 9/11 Weather Anomalies and Field Effects, May 19, 2008, http://www.drjudywood.com/articles/erin/erin1.html.

316. Judy Wood, 9/11 Weather Anomalies and Field Effects, March 25, 2008, http://www.drjudywood.com/articles/erin/index.html.

317. Judy Wood, 9/11 Weather Anomalies and Field Effects, May 19, 2008, http://www.drjudywood.com/articles/erin/erin1.html.

318. Judy Wood, *Where Did the Towers Go?, Evidence of Directed Free-Energy Technology on 9/11*, at 399 (2010).

319. Judy Wood, *Where Did the Towers Go?, Evidence of Directed Free-Energy Technology on 9/11*, at 410 (2010).

320. Leonard David, Taking the Twist Out of a Twister, http://beforeitsnews.com/story/598/774/Taking_the_Twist_Out_of_a_Twister.html, originally published at www.space.com on 3 March 2000.

321. Bill Rosato, Reuters, August 10, 2000, http://www.rumormillnews.com/cgi-bin/archive.cgi?read=4062.

322. Bill Rosato, Reuters, August 10, 2000, http://www.rumormillnews.com/cgi-bin/archive.cgi?read=4062.

323. Bernard J. Eastlund, (Eastlund Scientific Enterprises Corporation) and Lyle M. Jenkins, (Jenkins Enterprises), Concept for Disrupting Tornado Formation with Space Solar Power, Space 2000, Conference Paper, American Society of Civil Engineers, http://cedb.asce.org/cgi/WWWdisplay.cgi?120464 (last visited on June 16, 2011).

324. Bernard J. Eastlund, (Eastlund Scientific Enterprises Corporation) and Lyle M. Jenkins, (Jenkins Enterprises), Concept for Disrupting Tornado Formation with Space Solar Power, Space 2000, Conference Paper, American Society of Civil Engineers, http://cedb.asce.org/cgi/WWWdisplay.cgi?120464 (last visited on June 16, 2011).

325. Project HAARP: Overview, http://www.haarp.net/haarpoverview.htm (last visited on June 16, 2011).

326. Dr. Nick Begich and Jeane Manning, The Military's Pandora's Box, http://www.haarp.net/index.htm (last visited on June 16, 2011).

327. Dr. Nick Begich and Jeane Manning, The Military's Pandora's Box, http://www.haarp.net/index.htm (last visited on June 16, 2011).

328. Dr. Nick Begich and Jeane Manning, The Military's Pandora's Box, http://www.haarp.net/index.htm (last visited on June 16, 2011).

329. Judy Wood, *Where Did the Towers Go?, Evidence of Directed Free-Energy Technology on 9/11*, at 452 (2010).

330. Judy Wood, *Where Did the Towers Go?, Evidence of Directed Free-Energy Technology on 9/11*, at 413-430 (2010).

331. Christopher Bollyn, *Solving 9/11 - The Deception That Changed The World*, Chapter XV, The Destruction of the Evidence, May 17, 2010, http://www.bollyn.com/the-cover-up, also available at:
http://www.bollyn.com/public/Solving_9-11_-_The_Deception_That_Changed_The_World.pdf.

332. Christopher Bollyn, *Solving 9/11 - The Deception That Changed The World*, Chapter XV, The Destruction of the Evidence, May 17, 2010, http://www.bollyn.com/the-cover-up, also available at:
http://www.bollyn.com/public/Solving_9-11_-_The_Deception_That_Changed_The_World.pdf.

333. Christopher Bollyn, *Solving 9/11 - The Deception That Changed The World*, Chapter XV, The Destruction of the Evidence, May 17, 2010, http://www.bollyn.com/the-cover-up, also available at:
http://www.bollyn.com/public/Solving_9-11_-_The_Deception_That_Changed_The_World.pdf.

334. Christopher Bollyn, *Solving 9/11 - The Deception That Changed The World*, Chapter XV, The Destruction of the Evidence, May 17, 2010, http://www.bollyn.com/the-cover-up, also available at:
http://www.bollyn.com/public/Solving_9-11_-_The_Deception_That_Changed_The_World.pdf.

335. Christopher Bollyn, *Solving 9/11 - The Deception That Changed The World*, Chapter XV, The Destruction of the Evidence, May 17, 2010, http://www.bollyn.com/the-cover-up, also available at:
http://www.bollyn.com/public/Solving_9-11_-_The_Deception_That_Changed_The_World.pdf.

336. Christopher Bollyn, *Solving 9/11 - The Deception That Changed The World*, Chapter XV, The Destruction of the Evidence, May 17, 2010, http://www.bollyn.com/the-cover-up, also available at:
http://www.bollyn.com/public/Solving_9-11_-_The_Deception_That_Changed_The_World.pdf.

337. Christopher Bollyn, *Solving 9/11 - The Deception That Changed The World*, Chapter XV, The Destruction of the Evidence, May 17, 2010, http://www.bollyn.com/the-cover-up, also available at:
http://www.bollyn.com/public/Solving_9-11_-_The_Deception_That_Changed_The_World.pdf.

338. Christopher Bollyn, *Solving 9/11 - The Deception That Changed The World*, May 17, 2010, http://www.bollyn.com/solving-9-11-the-book#article_12159, also available at:
http://www.bollyn.com/public/Solving_9-11_-_The_Deception_That_Changed_The_World.pdf.

339. Christopher Bollyn, *Solving 9/11 - The Deception That Changed The World*, May 17, 2010, http://www.bollyn.com/solving-9-11-the-book#article_12159, also available at:

http://www.bollyn.com/public/Solving_9-11_-_The_Deception_That_Changed_The_World.pdf.

340. Christopher Bollyn, *Solving 9/11 - The Deception That Changed The World*, May 17, 2010, http://www.bollyn.com/solving-9-11-the-book#article_12159, also available at: http://www.bollyn.com/public/Solving_9-11_-_The_Deception_That_Changed_The_World.pdf.

341. William Norman Grigg, *Did We Know What Was Coming, The New American*, at 10,12, March 11, 2002.

342. http://www.emperors-clothes.com/indict/indict-3.htm#4 (current as of March 4, 2002).

343. http://www.davidicke.com/icke/articles3/bushlies.html (current as of March 4, 2002).

344. http://www.whitehouse.gov/news/releases/2001/12/20011204-17.html (current as of March 4, 2002).

345. Alex Jones Interviews Stanley Hilton, September 13, 2004, http://farshores.proboards6.com/index.cgi?board=conspiracy&action=display&num=1095696284 (web address current as of April 21, 2005).

346. Alex Jones Interviews Stanley Hilton, September 13, 2004, http://farshores.proboards6.com/index.cgi?board=conspiracy&action=display&num=1095696284 (web address current as of April 21, 2005).

347. Alex Jones Interviews Stanley Hilton, September 13, 2004, http://farshores.proboards6.com/index.cgi?board=conspiracy&action=display&num=1095696284 (web address current as of April 21, 2005).

348. Press Briefing by National Security Advisor Dr. Condoleezza Rice, May 16, 2002, http://www.whitehouse.gov/news/releases/2002/05/20020516-13.html (web address current as of April 21, 2005).

349. Christopher Bollyn, *Solving 9/11 - The Deception That Changed The World*, May 17, 2010, http://www.bollyn.com/solving-9-11-the-book#article_12159, also available at: http://www.bollyn.com/public/Solving_9-11_-_The_Deception_That_Changed_The_World.pdf.

350. Christopher Bollyn, *Solving 9/11 - The Deception That Changed The World*, May 17, 2010, http://www.bollyn.com/solving-9-11-the-book#article_12159, also available at: http://www.bollyn.com/public/Solving_9-11_-_The_Deception_That_Changed_The_World.pdf.

351. Christopher Bollyn, *Solving 9/11 - The Deception That Changed The World*, May 17, 2010, http://www.bollyn.com/solving-9-11-the-book#article_12159, also available at: http://www.bollyn.com/public/Solving_9-11_-_The_Deception_That_Changed_The_World.pdf.

352. Christopher Bollyn, *Solving 9/11 - The Deception That Changed The World*, May 17, 2010, http://www.bollyn.com/solving-9-11-the-book#article_12159, also available at: http://www.bollyn.com/public/Solving_9-11_-_The_Deception_That_Changed_The_World.pdf.

353. Christopher Bollyn, *Solving 9/11 - The Deception That Changed The World*, May 17, 2010, http://www.bollyn.com/solving-9-11-the-book#article_12159, also available at: http://www.bollyn.com/public/Solving_9-11_-_The_Deception_That_Changed_The_World.pdf.

354. Christopher Bollyn, *Solving 9/11 - The Deception That Changed The World*, May 17, 2010, http://www.bollyn.com/solving-9-11-the-book#article_12159, also available at: http://www.bollyn.com/public/Solving_9-11_-_The_Deception_That_Changed_The_World.pdf.

355. Transcript of Interview by Mark Glenn with Dr. Alan Sabroski and Phil Tourney, March 15, 2010, http://www.bibliotecapleyades.net/sociopolitica/sociopol_911zion_02.htm.

356. Alan Sabrosky, Zionism Unmasked: The Dark Face Of Jewish Nationalism, 11 March 2010, http://www.bigeye.com/sabrosky.htm.

357. Military Now Know Israel Did 911, http://www.youtube.com/watch?v=C9O5vQep-nM (last visited on December 12, 2010).

358. Transcript of Interview by Mark Glenn with Dr. Alan Sabroski and Phil Tourney, March 15, 2010, http://www.bibliotecapleyades.net/sociopolitica/sociopol_911zion_02.htm.

359. How 911 Was Done, http://how911wasdone.blogspot.com/, quoting the Washington Times, September 10, 2001.

360. 9/11: Core of Corruption - In the Shadows FULL HD, http://www.youtube.com/watch?v=ANMKiUwcEWo (last visited on April 26, 2011).

361. Albert D Pastore, Stranger Than Fiction, http://www.whatreallyhappened.com/NEWSTF/stfch2.htm (website address current as of March 28, 2003).

362. Albert D Pastore, Stranger Than Fiction, http://www.whatreallyhappened.com/NEWSTF/stfch2.htm (website address current as of March 28, 2003).

363. Christopher Ketcham, *High-Fivers and Art Student Spies: What Did Israel Know in Advance of the 9/11 Attacks?*, A CounterPunch Special Investigation, March 7, 2007, available at http://911notes.blogspot.com/2009/05/christopher-ketcham-on-dancing-israelis.html.

364. ABC News, The White Van, Were Israelis Detained on 9-11 Spies?, http://abcnews.go.com/sections/2020/DailyNews/2020_whitevan_020621.html (web address current as of October 9, 2003).

365. Christopher Ketcham, *High-Fivers and Art Student Spies: What Did Israel Know in Advance of the 9/11 Attacks?*, A CounterPunch Special Investigation, March 7, 2007, available at http://911notes.blogspot.com/2009/05/christopher-ketcham-on-dancing-israelis.html.

366. ABC News, The White Van, Were Israelis Detained on 9-11 Spies?, http://abcnews.go.com/sections/2020/DailyNews/2020_whitevan_020621.html (web address current as of October 9, 2003).

367. ABC News, The White Van, Were Israelis Detained on 9-11 Spies?, http://abcnews.go.com/sections/2020/DailyNews/2020_whitevan_020621.html (web address current as of October 9, 2003).

368. ABC News, The White Van, Were Israelis Detained on 9-11 Spies?, http://abcnews.go.com/sections/2020/DailyNews/2020_whitevan_020621.html (web address current as of October 9, 2003).

369. ABC News, The White Van, Were Israelis Detained on 9-11 Spies?, http://abcnews.go.com/sections/2020/DailyNews/2020_whitevan_020621.html (web address current as of October 9, 2003).

370. Christopher Bollyn, *Suspected Israeli Agents Held By the FBI*, American Free Press, October 1, 2001, http://worldcrossing.com/WebX?14@66.rj5EbyFu6NC^0@.eee90b0 (current as of October 5, 2001).

371. *Five Israelis Witness 9-11 Events and Celebrate Joyously, Criminal Politics*, p. 20, March 2002.

372. Christopher Ketcham, *High-Fivers and Art Student Spies: What Did Israel Know in Advance of the 9/11 Attacks?*, A CounterPunch Special Investigation, March 7, 2007, available at http://911notes.blogspot.com/2009/05/christopher-ketcham-on-dancing-israelis.html.

373. Christopher Ketcham, *High-Fivers and Art Student Spies: What Did Israel Know in Advance of the 9/11 Attacks?*, A CounterPunch Special Investigation, March 7, 2007, available at http://911notes.blogspot.com/2009/05/christopher-ketcham-on-dancing-israelis.html.

374. Christopher Bollyn, *Michael Chertoff's Childhood in Israel*, October 26, 2007, http://www.bollyn.com/michael-chertoffs-childhood-in-israel.

375. Christopher Bollyn, *Michael Chertoff's Childhood in Israel*, October 26, 2007, http://www.bollyn.com/michael-chertoffs-childhood-in-israel.

376. Christopher Bollyn, *Michael Chertoff's Childhood in Israel*, October 26, 2007, http://www.bollyn.com/michael-chertoffs-childhood-in-israel.

377. ABC News, The White Van, Were Israelis Detained on 9-11 Spies?, June 21, 2002, http://abcnews.go.com/2020/story?id=123885&page=1.

378. ABC News, The White Van, Were Israelis Detained on 9-11 Spies?, http://www.antichristconspiracy.com/HTML%20Pages/ABCNEWS_com_Were_Israelis_Detained_Sept_11_Spies.htm (last visited on November 8, 2010).

379. Christopher Ketcham on the Dancing Israelis, http://911notes.blogspot.com/2009/05/christopher-ketcham-on-dancing-israelis.html (last visited on November 8, 2010).

380. 9/11: Core of Corruption - In the Shadows FULL HD, http://www.youtube.com/watch?v=ANMKiUwcEWo (last visited on April 26, 2011).

381. Kourosh Ziabari, Criticize Israel and lose your career, Opinion Maker, July 7, 2011, http://www.opinion-maker.org/2011/07/criticize-israel-and-lose-your-career/.

382. Christopher Ketcham, *High-Fivers and Art Student Spies: What Did Israel Know in Advance of the 9/11 Attacks?*, A CounterPunch Special Investigation, March 7, 2007, available at http://911notes.blogspot.com/2009/05/christopher-ketcham-on-dancing-israelis.html.

383. Christopher Ketcham, *High-Fivers and Art Student Spies: What Did Israel Know in Advance of the 9/11 Attacks?*, A CounterPunch Special Investigation, March 7, 2007, available at http://911notes.blogspot.com/2009/05/christopher-ketcham-on-dancing-israelis.html.

384. Christopher Ketcham, *High-Fivers and Art Student Spies: What Did Israel Know in Advance of the 9/11 Attacks?*, A CounterPunch Special Investigation, March 7, 2007, available at http://911notes.blogspot.com/2009/05/christopher-ketcham-on-dancing-israelis.html.

385. Christopher Bollyn, *Solving 9/11 - The Deception That Changed The World*, May 17, 2010, http://www.bollyn.com/solving-9-11-the-book#article_12159, also available at: http://www.bollyn.com/public/Solving_9-11_-_The_Deception_That_Changed_The_World.pdf.

386. Christopher Bollyn, *Solving 9/11 - The Deception That Changed The World*, May 17, 2010, http://www.bollyn.com/solving-9-11-the-book#article_12159, also available at: http://www.bollyn.com/public/Solving_9-11_-_The_Deception_That_Changed_The_World.pdf.

387. Christopher Ketcham, *High-Fivers and Art Student Spies: What Did Israel Know in Advance of the 9/11 Attacks?*, A CounterPunch Special Investigation, March 7, 2007, available at http://911notes.blogspot.com/2009/05/christopher-ketcham-on-dancing-israelis.html.

388. Christopher Ketcham, *High-Fivers and Art Student Spies: What Did Israel Know in Advance of the 9/11 Attacks?*, A CounterPunch Special Investigation, March 7, 2007, available at http://911notes.blogspot.com/2009/05/christopher-ketcham-on-dancing-israelis.html.

389. Christopher Ketcham, *High-Fivers and Art Student Spies: What Did Israel Know in Advance of the 9/11 Attacks?*, A CounterPunch Special Investigation, March 7, 2007, available at

http://911notes.blogspot.com/2009/05/christopher-ketcham-on-dancing-israelis.html.

390. Christopher Bollyn, *Solving 9/11 - The Deception That Changed The World*, May 17, 2010, http://www.bollyn.com/solving-9-11-the-book#article_12159, also available at: http://www.bollyn.com/public/Solving_9-11_-_The_Deception_That_Changed_The_World.pdf.

391. Christopher Ketcham, *High-Fivers and Art Student Spies: What Did Israel Know in Advance of the 9/11 Attacks?*, A CounterPunch Special Investigation, March 7, 2007, available at http://911notes.blogspot.com/2009/05/christopher-ketcham-on-dancing-israelis.html.

392. Christopher Ketcham, *High-Fivers and Art Student Spies: What Did Israel Know in Advance of the 9/11 Attacks?*, A CounterPunch Special Investigation, March 7, 2007, available at http://911notes.blogspot.com/2009/05/christopher-ketcham-on-dancing-israelis.html.

393. Israeli Wiretappers, the NSA, and 9/11, January 5, 2008, http://www.infowars.com/israeli-wiretappers-the-nsa-and-911/. Map also available at: http://911blogger.com/node/18981, and Gerald Shea, Memorandum to the National Commission on Terrorist Attacks upon the United States, The Senate Select Committee on Intelligence, The House Permanent Select Committee on Intelligence, September 15, 2004, http://www.antiwar.com/rep2/MemorandumtotheCommissionandSelectCommitteesbold.pdf.

394. Gerald Shea, Memorandum to the National Commission on Terrorist Attacks upon the United States, The Senate Select Committee on Intelligence, The House Permanent Select Committee on Intelligence, September 15, 2004, http://www.antiwar.com/rep2/MemorandumtotheCommissionandSelectCommitteesbold.pdf.

395. Art Students in WTC Connected to Israeli Intelligence Serivice, http://www.newworldorderreport.com/News/tabid/266/ID/2411/Art-Students-in-WTC-Connected-to-Israeli-Intelligence-Service.aspx (last visited on April 27, 2011).

396. Lower Manhattan Cultural Council, http://www.lmcc.net/residencies/workspace/past_sessions/world_views (last visited on April 28, 2011).

397. Lower Manhattan Cultural Council, http://www.lmcc.net/residencies/workspace/past_sessions/world_views (last visited on April 28, 2011).

398. Gelitin, The B-Thing, http://www.gelitin.net/mambo/index.php?set_albumName=album03&option=com_gallery_proj144&Itemid=91&include=view_album.php (last visited on April 28, 2011).

399. Art Students in WTC Connected to Israeli Intelligence Serivice, http://www.newworldorderreport.com/News/tabid/266/ID/2411/Art-Students-in-WTC-Connected-to-Israeli-Intelligence-Service.aspx (last visited on April 27, 2011).

400. Shaila K. Dewan, *Balcony Scene (Or Unseen) Atop the World; Episode at Trade Center Assumes Mythic Qualities*, The New York Times, August 18, 2001, http://www.nytimes.com/2001/08/18/nyregion/balcony-scene-unseen-atop-world-episode-trade-center-assumes-mythic-qualities.html?src=pm.

401. Gelatin The B-Thing New Edition, http://www.boomerangbooks.com.au/Gelatin/Walther-Konig/book_9783883755076.htm (last visited on April 28, 2011).

402. Shaila K. Dewan, *Balcony Scene (Or Unseen) Atop the World; Episode at Trade Center Assumes Mythic Qualities*, The New York Times, August 18, 2001, http://www.nytimes.com/2001/08/18/nyregion/balcony-scene-unseen-atop-world-episode-trade-center-assumes-mythic-qualities.html?src=pm.

403. World Views Participating Artists, Winter 1999-Spring 2000, http://www.lmcc.net/residencies/workspace/past_sessions/world_views/participating_artists#y1997_98 (last visited on April 29, 2011).

404. Shaila K. Dewan, *Balcony Scene (Or Unseen) Atop the World; Episode at Trade Center Assumes Mythic Qualities*, The New York Times, August 18, 2001, http://www.nytimes.com/2001/08/18/nyregion/balcony-scene-unseen-atop-world-episode-trade-center-assumes-mythic-qualities.html?src=pm.

405. Gelitin, The B-Thing, http://www.gelitin.net/mambo/index.php?option=com_content&task=view&id=20&Itemid=1 (last visited on April 28, 2011).

406. Christopher Bollyn, *Mossad - The Israeli Connection To 911*, Exclusive to American Free Press, April 14, 2005, http://www.rense.com/general64/moss.htm.

407. The Israeli Spy Ring Scandal, http://www.whatreallyhappened.com/spyring.html (web page current as of May 9, 2002).

408. Christopher Bollyn, *Solving 9/11 - The Deception That Changed The World*, May 17, 2010, http://www.bollyn.com/solving-9-11-the-book#article_12159, also available at: http://www.bollyn.com/public/Solving_9-11_-_The_Deception_That_Changed_The_World.pdf.

409. Christopher Bollyn, *Mossad - The Israeli Connection To 911*, Exclusive to American Free Press, April 14, 2005, http://www.rense.com/general64/moss.htm.

410. Thousands of Israelis missing near WTC, Pentagon, Jerusalem Post, September 12, 2001, http://web.archive.org/web/20010913152700/http://www.jpost.com/Editions/2001/09/12/LatestNews/LatestNews.34656.html. Article deleted from original link at: http://www.jpost.com/Editions/2001/09/12/LatestNews/LatestNews.34656.html.

411. Christopher Bollyn, *Mossad - The Israeli Connection To 911*, Exclusive to American Free Press, April 14, 2005, http://www.rense.com/general64/moss.htm.

412. David Irving's Action Report, http://www.fpp.co.uk/online/01/11/WTC_DeathRoll2.html. (last visited on November 9, 2010).

413. David Irving's Action Report, http://www.antichristconspiracy.com/HTML%20Pages/Real%20History,%20Only%20One%20Israeli%20Died%20in%20WTC%20Attack.htm (website address current as of April 1, 2003).

414. Christopher Bollyn, *Mossad - The Israeli Connection To 911*, Exclusive to American Free Press, April 14, 2005, http://www.rense.com/general64/moss.htm.

415. Dr. Albert D. Pastore Phd., An Independent Investigation of 9-11 and the War on Terrorism, http://www.the7thfire.com/9-11/Pastore_Investigation_of_%209-11/chapter_14--Miracle_of_Passover.htm (web address current as of March 27, 2005).

416. Jim Marrs, INSIDE JOB, p. 95.

417. Dr. Albert D. Pastore Phd., An Independent Investigation of 9-11 and the War on Terrorism, http://www.the7thfire.com/9-11/Pastore_Investigation_of_%209-11/chapter_14--Miracle_of_Passover.htm (web address current as of March 27, 2005).

418. Jim Marrs, INSIDE JOB, p. 95.

419. Prepared Statement of Mark S. Zaid, Esq. Before the Committee on Judiciary, United States Senate, September 21, 2005, available at http://judiciary.senate.gov/hearings/testimony.cfm?id=1606&wit_id=4668.

420. 911 Commission Report, at xv.

421. Wayne Madsen, *Able Danger and Dia Had Advanced Knowledge of 9/11*, Online Journal, Sept 11th, 2009, http://onlinejournal.com/artman/publish/article_5116.shtml.

422. Mike Kelly, Deadly Tale of Incompetence, August 14, 2005, http://newsgroups.derkeiler.com/Archive/Alt/alt.religion.islam/2005-08/msg00949.html.

423. Able Danger Round-Up, September 3, 2005, http://www.911truth.org/article.php?story=20050830191215604.

424. Mike Kelly, Deadly Tale of Incompetence, August 14, 2005, http://newsgroups.derkeiler.com/Archive/Alt/alt.religion.islam/2005-08/msg00949.html.

425. Mike Kelly, Deadly Tale of Incompetence, August 14, 2005, http://newsgroups.derkeiler.com/Archive/Alt/alt.religion.islam/2005-08/msg00949.html.

426. Mike Kelly, Deadly Tale of Incompetence, August 14, 2005, http://newsgroups.derkeiler.com/Archive/Alt/alt.religion.islam/2005-08/msg00949.html.

427. Greg Kelly and Catherine Herridge, *Pentagon Probes Able Danger Claims*, Fox News, August 19, 2005, http://www.foxnews.com/printer_friendly_story/0,3566,166258,00.html.

428. Complete 911 Timeline, The Able Danger Program, http://www.historycommons.org/timeline.jsp?before_9/11=abledanger&timeline=complete_911_timeline (last visited on November 18, 2010)..

429. Able Danger Round-Up, September 3, 2005, http://www.911truth.org/article.php?story=20050830191215604.

430. Prepared Statement of Mark S. Zaid, Esq. Before the Committee on Judiciary, United States Senate, September 21, 2005, available at http://judiciary.senate.gov/hearings/testimony.cfm?id=1606&wit_id=4668.

431. Catherine Herridge, *Agent Defends Military Unit's Data on 9/11 Hijackers*, Fox News, August 17, 2005, http://www.foxnews.com/printer_friendly_story/0,3566,165948,00.html.

432. Dick Eastman, The 14 Israeli 'Art Students' Were Inside The WTC Towers Camping With Construction Passes, Part II, October 2, 2009, http://www.rense.com/general87/14_2.htm.

433. Wayne Madsen, *Able Danger and Dia Had Advanced Knowledge of 9/11*, Online Journal, Sept 11th, 2009, http://onlinejournal.com/artman/publish/article_5116.shtml.

434. Justin Raimondo, Israel and 9/11: New Report Connects the Dots, Antiwar.com, September 01, 2005, http://original.antiwar.com/justin/2005/08/31/israel-and-911-new-report-connects-the-dots/.

435. Sibel Edmonds Documentary - Kill The Messenger, http://www.youtube.com/user/pumpitoutdotcom#p/a/f/2/MiOtBqKyDYg , February 4, 2011.

436. Sibel Edmonds Documentary - Kill The Messenger, http://www.youtube.com/user/pumpitoutdotcom#p/a/f/2/MiOtBqKyDYg , February 4, 2011.

437. Barbara Ferguson, The Pentagon Spy Investigation: FBI Talks to Feith, Centre for Research on Globalization, September 1, 2004, http://www.globalresearch.ca/index.php?context=va&aid=649.

438. Mark Hackard, *The Israel Lobby's Turkish Connection*, Alternative Right, June 7, 2010, http://www.alternativeright.com/main/blogs/exit-strategies/the-israel-lobby-s-turkish-connection/.

439. Gordon Duff, Aipac Spying, Why Is the Fbi Looking the Other Way?, Veterans Today, November 23, 2011,

http://www.veteranstoday.com/2010/11/23/gordon-duff-aipac-spying-why-is-the-fbi-looking-the-other-way/.

440. Philip Giraldi, Found in Translation, FBI Whistleblower Sibel Edmonds Spills Her Secrets, The American Conservative, http://www.amconmag.com/article/2008/jan/28/00012/, January 28, 2008.

441. Philip Giraldi, Found in Translation, FBI Whistleblower Sibel Edmonds Spills Her Secrets, The American Conservative, http://www.amconmag.com/article/2008/jan/28/00012/, January 28, 2008.

442. Philip Giraldi, Found in Translation, FBI Whistleblower Sibel Edmonds Spills Her Secrets, The American Conservative, http://www.amconmag.com/article/2008/jan/28/00012/, January 28, 2008.

443. Philip Giraldi, Found in Translation, FBI Whistleblower Sibel Edmonds Spills Her Secrets, The American Conservative, http://www.amconmag.com/article/2008/jan/28/00012/, January 28, 2008.

444. Philip Giraldi, Found in Translation, FBI Whistleblower Sibel Edmonds Spills Her Secrets, The American Conservative, http://www.amconmag.com/article/2008/jan/28/00012/, January 28, 2008.

445. Christopher Bollyn, *Solving 9/11 - The Deception That Changed The World*, May 17, 2010, http://www.bollyn.com/solving-9-11-the-book#article_12159, also available at: http://www.bollyn.com/public/Solving_9-11_-_The_Deception_That_Changed_The_World.pdf.

446. Christopher Bollyn, *Solving 9/11 - The Deception That Changed The World*, May 17, 2010, http://www.bollyn.com/solving-9-11-the-book#article_12159, also available at: http://www.bollyn.com/public/Solving_9-11_-_The_Deception_That_Changed_The_World.pdf.

447. The Israeli Spy Ring Scandal, http://www.whatreallyhappened.com/spyring.html (web page current as of May 9, 2002).

448. DONN DE GRAND PRE, BARBARIANS INSIDE THE GATES, THE BLACK BOOK OF BOLSHEVISM, p. 314-15 (2000) (citing JACK BERNSTEIN, THE LIFE OF AN AMERICAN JEW IN RACIST MARXIST ISRAEL (1984)).

449. Associated Press, Lyndon Johnson Ordered Cover-up: Former Navy Lawyer, http://la.indymedia.org/news/2003/10/90418.php (web address current as of October 31, 2003).

450. Associated Press, Lyndon Johnson Ordered Cover-up: Former Navy Lawyer, http://la.indymedia.org/news/2003/10/90418.php (web address current as of October 31, 2003).

451. Associated Press, Lyndon Johnson Ordered Cover-up: Former Navy Lawyer, http://la.indymedia.org/news/2003/10/90418.php (web address current as of October 31, 2003).

452. Associated Press, Lyndon Johnson Ordered Cover-up: Former Navy Lawyer, http://la.indymedia.org/news/2003/10/90418.php (web address current as of October 31, 2003).

453. Nicholas M. Horrock, UPI Chief White House Correspondent, New Charges Vs. Israel in '67 Ship Attack, http://la.indymedia.org/news/2003/10/90418.php (web address current as of October 31, 2003).

454. Nicholas M. Horrock, UPI Chief White House Correspondent, New Charges Vs. Israel in '67 Ship Attack, http://la.indymedia.org/news/2003/10/90418.php (web address current as of October 31, 2003).

455. Nicholas M. Horrock, UPI Chief White House Correspondent, New Charges Vs. Israel in '67 Ship Attack, http://la.indymedia.org/news/2003/10/90418.php (web address current as of October 31, 2003).

456. http://www.itszone.co.uk/zone0/viewtopic.php?t=9139 (web address current as of 21 September 2003).

457. Statement of Steve Forslund, http://www.ussliberty.org/forslund.htm (web address current as of 21 September 2003).

458. Sworn Declaration of James Ronald Gotcher, http://www.ussliberty.org/gotcher.htm (web address current as of 21 September 2003).

459. JAMES M. ENNES JR, ASSAULT ON THE LIBERTY, http://www.washington-report.org/backissues/0693/9306019.htm (web address current as of September 21, 2003).

460. http://64.39.19.39/lewis.txt (current as of November 1, 2001). See also http://www.halcyon.com/jim/ussliberty/.

461. http://64.39.19.39/ (current as of November 1, 2001). See also http://www.halcyon.com/jim/ussliberty/.

462. Salvador Astucia, Opium Lords, http://www.jfkmontreal.com/johnson's_hidden_loyalties.htm#Secret%20Ethnicity (website current as of March 26, 2003).

463. JIM GARRISON, ON THE TRAIL OF THE ASSASSINS, pg. xiii (1988).

464. *See* JIM GARRISON, ON THE TRAIL OF THE ASSASSINS, pg. xiii (1988).

465. JIM GARRISON, ON THE TRAIL OF THE ASSASSINS, pg. 168 (1988).

466. JIM GARRISON, ON THE TRAIL OF THE ASSASSINS, pg. 168 (1988).

467. JIM GARRISON, ON THE TRAIL OF THE ASSASSINS, pg. 160-72 (1988).

468. MICHAEL COLLINS PIPER, FINAL JUDGMENT, pg. 204-05 (2004).

469. JIM GARRISON, ON THE TRAIL OF THE ASSASSINS, pg. 132-36 (1988).

470. JIM GARRISON, ON THE TRAIL OF THE ASSASSINS, pg. 132-36 (1988).

471. MICHAEL COLLINS PIPER, FINAL JUDGMENT, pg. 204-05 (2004).

472. MICHAEL COLLINS PIPER, FINAL JUDGMENT, pg. 204-05 (2004).

473. MICHAEL COLLINS PIPER, FINAL JUDGMENT, pg. 204-05 (2004).

474. MICHAEL COLLINS PIPER, FINAL JUDGMENT, pg. 259 (2004).

475. The JFK 100: Reprisals Against Jim Garrison, http://www.jfk-online.com/jfk100repris.html (web address current as of May 31, 2004)

476. William Kunstler, My Life as a Radical Lawyer, p. 158 (1994), quoted in Texe Marrs, Conspiracy of the Six Pointed Star, at 232 (2011).

477. William Kunstler, My Life as a Radical Lawyer, p. 158 (1994), quoted in Texe Marrs, Conspiracy of the Six Pointed Star, at 232 (2011).

478. Arieh O'Sullivan, *Vanunu: Israel behind JFK Assassination*, Jerusalem Post, Jul. 25, 2004.

479. President John F. Kennedy Waldorf-Astoria Hotel, New York, NY, April 27, 1961.

480. *In Re Grand Jury Subpoenas Dated March 9, 2001*, ___ F.Supp. ___, 2001 WL 1590541 (S.D.N.Y. 2001).

481. Greg B. Smith, *Denise Says Dem Gifts Solely Hers*, NEW YORK DAILY NEWS, May 25, 2001.

482. *In Re Grand Jury Subpoenas Dated March 9, 2001*, ___ F.Supp. ___, 2001 WL 1590541 (S.D.N.Y. 2001).

483. *In Re Grand Jury Subpoenas Dated March 9, 2001*, ___ F.Supp. ___, 2001 WL 1590541 (S.D.N.Y. 2001).

484. 28 C.F.R. § 1.1.

485. 28 C.F.R. 1.6(a).

486. Gordon Thomas, *Clinton's Pardoned Buddy Spied for Israel*, American Free Press, http://www.americanfreepress.net/10_07_03/Clintons_Pardoned/clintons_pardoned.html (web

address current as of March 3, 2004).

487. Gordon Thomas, *Clinton's Pardoned Buddy Spied for Israel*, American Free Press, http://www.americanfreepress.net/10_07_03/Clintons_Pardoned/clintons_pardoned.html (web address current as of March 3, 2004).

488. Gordon Thomas, *Clinton's Pardoned Buddy Spied for Israel*, American Free Press, http://www.americanfreepress.net/10_07_03/Clintons_Pardoned/clintons_pardoned.html (web address current as of March 3, 2004).

489. Gordon Thomas, *Clinton's Pardoned Buddy Spied for Israel*, American Free Press, http://www.americanfreepress.net/10_07_03/Clintons_Pardoned/clintons_pardoned.html (web address current as of March 3, 2004).

490. Matthew Kaminski, *The Man Who Is Rebuilding Ground Zero*, Wall Street Journal, Opinion Jounrnal, September 11, 2010, http://online.wsj.com/article/SB10001424052748703597204575483913446248440.html.

491. Howe 911 Was Done, http://how911wasdone.blogspot.com/ (last visited on November 9, 2010).

492. Howe 911 Was Done, http://how911wasdone.blogspot.com/ (last visited on November 9, 2010).

493. Paul Joseph Watson, *Claim: Silverstein Warned Not To Come To Work On 9/11*, Prison Planet, May 14, 2007, http://www.prisonplanet.com/articles/may2007/140507silversteinwarned.htm.

494. Sara Leibovich-Dar, *Up in Smoke*, Haaretz.com, http://www.haaretz.com/hasen/pages/ShArt.jhtml?itemNo=97338&contrassID=3&subContrassID=0&sbSubContrassID=0 (visited on May 25, 2008).

495. Id.

496. Id.

497. James Bennet, *A DAY OF TERROR: THE ISRAELIS; Spilled Blood Is Seen as Bond That Draws 2 Nations Closer*, New York Times, September 12, 2001, http://query.nytimes.com/gst/fullpage.html?res=9F07E4D91238F931A2575AC0A9679C8B63 (visited on May 25, 2008).

498. *Netanyahu Says 9/11 Terror Attacks Good for Israel*, Haaretz Service and Reuters, http://www.haaretz.com/hasen/spages/975574.html (April 16, 2008).

499. Larry Silverstein and 9/11, http://www.wakeupfromyourslumber.com/node/2210 (visited on May 25, 2008).

500. Benjamin Netanyahu, Speech to the US House of Representatives' Government Reform Committee, http://www.interesting-people.org/archives/interesting-people/200109/msg00429.html (last visited on May 26, 2008).

501. ChristopherBollyn, *Ehud Olmert Was in New York on 9-11*, http://www.rumormillnews.com/cgi-bin/archive.cgi?noframes;read=114367 (December 2, 2007).

502. ChristopherBollyn, *Ehud Olmert Was in New York on 9-11*, http://www.rumormillnews.com/cgi-bin/archive.cgi?noframes;read=114367 (December 2, 2007).

503. ChristopherBollyn, *Ehud Olmert Was in New York on 9-11*, http://www.rumormillnews.com/cgi-bin/archive.cgi?noframes;read=114367 (December 2, 2007).

504. Id.

505. John Whitley, *Seven Jewish American Control Most US Media*, Real News 24/7 (November 21, 2003), *available at* http://www.realnews247.com/seven_jewish_americans_control_media_rense.htm.

506. Id.

507. Id.

508. Id.

509. Joel Stein, Who runs Hollywood? C'mon, Las Angeles Times, December 19, 2008, http://articles.latimes.com/2008/dec/19/opinion/oe-stein19.

510. Texe Marrs, Conspiracy of the Six Pointed Star, at 108 (2011), quoting Newsweek, Vol. 87, 1976).

511. The Associated Press, Reuters and Haaretz Service, October 2, 2010, http://www.haaretz.com/jewish-world/cnn-s-sanchez-fired-after-calling-jon-stewart-a-bigot-1.316719

512. The Associated Press, Reuters and Haaretz Service, October 2, 2010, http://www.haaretz.com/jewish-world/cnn-s-sanchez-fired-after-calling-jon-stewart-a-bigot-1.316719

513. What Really Happened, The Fake 2001 bin Laden Video Tape, http://www.whatreallyhappened.com/osamatape.html (website last visited on May 3, 2008).

514. BBC, Tape 'proves Bin Laden's guilt', http://news.bbc.co.uk/1/hi/world/south_asia/1708091.stm (website last visited on May 3, 2008)

515. FBI Ten Most Wanted Fugitive (USAMA BIN LADEN), http://www.fbi.gov/wanted/topten/fugitives/laden.htm (last visited on June 4, 2008).

516. *Washington Post reporter, Dan Eggen, whistles government tune on Osama bin Laden*, The Jones Report (August 30, 2006), http://www.jonesreport.com/articles/300806_washpost_govt_tune.html (quoting The Muckraker Report, June 6, 2006).

517. Id.

518. United States v. Calandra, 414 U.S. 338 (1974) ("The grand jury's historic functions survive to this day. Its responsibilities continue to include both the determination whether there is probable cause to believe a crime has been committed and the protection of citizens against unfounded criminal prosecutions."). The Supreme Court has stated that "probable cause is a fluid concept - turning on the assessment of probabilities in particular factual contexts - not readily , or even usefully, reduced to a neat set of legal rules." Illinois v. Gates, 462 U.S. 213, 232 (1983). "These are not technical; they are the factual and practical considerations of everyday life on which reasonable and prudent men, not legal technicians, act." *Id* at 241. Probable cause does not mean that the outcome is more likely than not to occur, only that the likelihood of occurrence is sufficient to prompt a reasonably cautious law enforcement officer to take action. Probable cause is a reasonable belief. Zurcher v. Stanford Daily, 436 U.S. 547, 554 (1977).

519. U.S. Const. art. II, § 1.

520. *Washington Post reporter, Dan Eggen, whistles government tune on Osama bin Laden*, The Jones Report (August 30, 2006), http://www.jonesreport.com/articles/300806_washpost_govt_tune.html (quoting The Muckraker Report, June 6, 2006).

521. Carol A. Valentine, Bin Laden: Authentic Interview, October 16, 2001, http://www.public-action.com/911/oblintrv.html.

522. Closing in on bin Laden, Washington Post, http://www.washingtonpost.com/wp-srv/special/world/bin-laden-killed/ (last visited on May 2, 2011).

523. Benazir Bhutto Named Osama Bin Laden's Killer Before Her Death, January 15, 2008, http://english.pravda.ru/world/asia/15-01-2008/103426-benazir_bhutto_osama-0/. See also, Bhutto Confirms that Osama Bin Laden is Dead, http://video.google.com/videoplay?docid=8120236576648647371# (last visited on May 2, 2011).

524. Paul Joseph Watson, *Top Government Insider: Bin Laden Died In 2001, 9/11 False Flag Attack*, Centre for Research on Globalization, May 4, 2011, http://www.globalresearch.ca/index.php?context=va&aid=24622.

525. Paul Joseph Watson, *Top Government Insider: Bin Laden Died In 2001, 9/11 False Flag Attack*, Centre for Research on Globalization, May 4, 2011, http://www.globalresearch.ca/index.php?context=va&aid=24622.

526. Mark Arsenault, Brown: Don't show bin Laden Corpse to 'Sell Newspapers', Boston Globe, May 4, 2011, http://www.boston.com/news/politics/politicalintelligence/2011/05/brown_dont_show.html.

527. NECN interview of Senator Scott Brown, May 4, 2011, http://www.boston.com/news/politics/politicalintelligence/2011/05/brown_dont_show.html.

528. Michael Levenson, Brown Admits He Was Fooled by Fake Pictures of Bin Laden Body, Boston Globe, May 4, 2011, http://www.boston.com/news/politics/politicalintelligence/2011/05/brown_admits_he.html.

529. Michael Levenson, Brown Admits He Was Fooled by Fake Pictures of Bin Laden Body, Boston Globe, May 4, 2011, http://www.boston.com/news/politics/politicalintelligence/2011/05/brown_admits_he.html.

530. Susan Crabtree and Eric Lach, Senators Fall For Fake Bin Laden Death Photo, TPMDC, May 4, 2011, http://tpmdc.talkingpointsmemo.com/2011/05/senators-fall-for-fake-bin-laden-death-photo.php.

531. Ben Mayer, Who's really seen dead Bin Laden photos?, 11 Alive HD, A Gannett Company, May 4, 2011, http://www.11alive.com/news/article/189880/40/Whos-really-seen-dead-Bin-Laden-photos.

532. Warren Richey, Did harsh interrogation tactics help US find Osama bin Laden?, Christian Science Monitor, May 5, 2011, http://www.csmonitor.com/USA/Justice/2011/0505/Did-harsh-interrogation-tactics-help-US-find-Osama-bin-Laden.

533. Warren Richey, Did harsh interrogation tactics help US find Osama bin Laden?, Christian Science Monitor, May 5, 2011, http://www.csmonitor.com/USA/Justice/2011/0505/Did-harsh-interrogation-tactics-help-US-find-Osama-bin-Laden.

534. Warren Richey, Did harsh interrogation tactics help US find Osama bin Laden?, Christian Science Monitor, May 5, 2011, http://www.csmonitor.com/USA/Justice/2011/0505/Did-harsh-interrogation-tactics-help-US-find-Osama-bin-Laden.

535. William Raspberry, *The 23 Different Rationales for War*, The San Diego Union-Tribune, http://www.signonsandiego.com/uniontrib/20040601/news_mz1e1rasp.html (June 1, 2004).

536. *White House Admits WMD Error, Withdraws Claim That Iraq Tried To Buy Uranium From Africa*, CBS News, http://www.cbsnews.com/stories/2003/07/09/iraq/main562312.shtml (July 8, 2003).

537. *Bush: 'We're not leaving so long as I'm president'*, The Raw Story, http://www.rawstory.com/news/2006/Bush_calls_Lebanon_aid_troops_0821.html (August 21, 2006). *President Bush Holds a News Conference*, Washington Post, http://www.washingtonpost.com/wp-dyn/content/article/2006/08/21/AR2006082100469.html (August 21, 2006).

538. John Amato, *Bush says: "Iraq Had 'Nothing' To Do With 9/11,"* Crooks and Liars, http://www.crooksandliars.com/2006/08/21/bush-says-iraq-had-%E2%80%98nothing%E2%80%99-to-do-with-911/ (August 21, 2006). *President Bush Holds a News Conference*, Washington Post, http://www.washingtonpost.com/wp-dyn/content/article/2006/08/21/AR2006082100469.html (August 21, 2006).

539. Jason Leopold, Wolfowitz: Iraq Not Involved in 9-11, No Ties to al-Qaeda, AntiWar.com, http://www.antiwar.com/orig/leopold13.html (August 7, 2003).

540. Lindsey Williams, The Energy Non-Crisis, http://www.reformation.org/energy-non-crisis.html (last visited on June 6, 2008).

541. Mark Anderson, *Big Oil Spikes Easy Solution*, American Free Press, http://www.americanfreepress.net/html/big_oil_spikes.html (last visited on June 8, 2008).

542. Lindsey Williams, The Energy Non-Crisis - Part 8 of 8, http://www.youtube.com/watch?v=CC61X78-OI0 (last visited on June 6, 2008).

543. Peter Philips, *Censored 2004, The Top 25 Censored News Stories, Seven Stories Press*, (2003) General website for Project Censored: www.projectcensored.org/
Story #19: U.S. Dollar vs. the Euro: Another Reason for the Invasion of Iraq www.projectcensored.org/publications/2004/19.html .

544. Carol Hoyos and Kevin Morrison, "*Iraq Returns to the International Oil Market*," Financial Times, June 5, 2003.

545. William Clark, *Petrodollar Warfare: Dollars, Euros and the Upcoming Iranian Oil Bourse*, Energy Bulletin, http://www.energybulletin.net/7707.html (August 2, 2005) (citing Faisal Islam, *Iraq Nets Handsome Profit by Dumping Dollar for Euro*, [UK] Guardian, February 16, 2003, observer.guardian.co.uk/iraq/story/0,12239,896344,00.html).

546. Military Men Are Dumb, Stupid Animals, Portland Independent Media Center, http://portland.indymedia.org/en/2003/06/266114.shtml, quoting Bob Woodward and Carl Bernstein, The Final days, pp. 194-95 (1975).

547. Iranian Oil Bourse, Wikipedia, http://en.wikipedia.org/wiki/Iranian_oil_bourse (last visited on June 7, 2008).

548. Iran Oil Bourse to Deal Blow to Dollar, Press TV, http://www.presstv.ir/detail.aspx?id=37468&sectionid=351020103 (January 4, 2008).

549. William Clark, *Petrodollar Warfare: Dollars, Euros and the Upcoming Iranian Oil Bourse*, Energy Bulletin, http://www.energybulletin.net/7707.html (August 2, 2005) (citing "Oil bourse closer to reality," IranMania.com, December 28, 2004. Also see: "Iran oil bourse wins authorization," Tehran Times, July 26, 2005.).

550. William Clark, *Petrodollar Warfare: Dollars, Euros and the Upcoming Iranian Oil Bourse*, Energy Bulletin, http://www.energybulletin.net/7707.html (August 2, 2005).

551. Philip Giraldi, "In Case of Emergency, Nuke Iran," American Conservative, August 1, 2005.

552. William Clark, *Petrodollar Warfare: Dollars, Euros and the Upcoming Iranian Oil Bourse*, Energy Bulletin, http://www.energybulletin.net/7707.html (August 2, 2005).

553. William Clark, *Petrodollar Warfare: Dollars, Euros and the Upcoming Iranian Oil Bourse*, Energy Bulletin, http://www.energybulletin.net/7707.html (August 2, 2005) (quoting Philip Giraldi, "In Case of Emergency, Nuke Iran," American Conservative, August 1, 2005) (emphasis added).

554. Victor Thorn, *RAHM EMANUEL: Ardent Zionist called Obama's 'Svengali'*, American Free Press, http://www.americanfreepress.net/html/rahm_emanuel_157.html (last visited on November 13, 2010).

555. Rahm Emanuel, Obama's Pick for Chief of Staff, Is Tough, Direct and Wedded to His Jewish Roots, Jewish Journal, November 6, 2008, http://www.jewishjournal.com/nation/article/rahm_emanuel_obamas_pick_for_chief_of_staff_is_tough_direct_and_wedded_to_h/.

556. Texe Marrs, *Obama Tells Jews, "No More!"*, Power of Prophecy, http://www.texemarrs.com/102010/obama_tells_jews_no_more.htm (last visited on November 16, 2010).

557. Obama threatens Iran, World Socialist Web Site, 6 August 2010, http://www.wsws.org/articles/2010/aug2010/pers-a06.shtml.

558. Obama threatens Iran, World Socialist Web Site, 6 August 2010, http://www.wsws.org/articles/2010/aug2010/pers-a06.shtml.

559. Andrew Parasiliti, After Sanctions, Deter and Engage Iran, The International Institute for International Studies, http://www.iiss.org/publications/survival/survival-2010/year-2010-issue-5/after-sanctions-deter-a

nd-engage-iran/ (last visited on November 11, 2010).

560. Jeffrey Goldberg, Tony Blair: "Personally, I Think Israel Would Not Allow Iran to Get Nuclear Weapons", Oct 14 2010, http://www.theatlantic.com/international/archive/2010/10/tony-blair-personally-i-think-israel-would-not-allow-iran-to-get-nuclear-weapons/64615/.

561. Robert Kagan, *Obama's Briefing on Iran: It's about Pressure, Not Diplomacy*, August 6, 2010, http://www.washingtonpost.com/wp-dyn/content/article/2010/08/05/AR2010080504784.html.

562. Anne Gearan, *Joint Chiefs Chairman Says U.S. Has Plan to Attack Iran, Just in Case*, August 02, 2010, Associated Press, CBSNEWS.COM, http://www.cnsnews.com/news/article/70351.

563. David S. Broder, *The war recovery?*, Washington Post, October 31, 2010, http://www.washingtonpost.com/wp-dyn/content/article/2010/10/29/AR2010102907404.html.

564. Republican Senator urges Obama to support war with Iran, 'confrontation' with China, November 6th, 2010, http://www.rawstory.com/rs/2010/11/republican-senator-urges-obama-support-war-iran-confrontation-china/.

565. Pipes: Iran War Definite if Obama Wins, Press TV, http://www.presstv.ir/detail.aspx?id=58949&sectionid=351020101 (June 6, 2008).

566. Tim Butcher, *Israel Threatens War on Gaza and Iran*, Telegraph, http://www.telegraph.co.uk/news/worldnews/middleeast/israel/2085865/Israel-threatens-war-on-Gaza-and-Iran.html (June 6, 2008).

567. William Clark, *Petrodollar Warfare: Dollars, Euros and the Upcoming Iranian Oil Bourse*, Energy Bulletin, http://www.energybulletin.net/7707.html (August 2, 2005) (quoting Dafina Linzer, "Iran Is Judged 10 Years From Nuclear Bomb U.S. Intelligence Review Contrasts With Administration Statements," Washington Post, August 2, 2005; Page A01.).

568. National Intelligence Estimate, Wikipedia, http://en.wikipedia.org/wiki/National_Intelligence_Estimate (last visited on June 7, 2008).

569. Lindsey Williams, The Energy Non-Crisis - Part 7 of 8, http://www.youtube.com/watch?v=L5HGHsy3H_0 (last visited on June 6, 2008).

570. Protocols of the Learned Elders of Zion, Protocol VII, http://www.biblebelievers.org.au/przion1.htm (website address current as of March 27, 2003).

571. Karen Kwiatkowski, The New Pentagon Papers, *Salon.com*, http://www.salon.com/opinion/feature/2004/03/10/osp_moveon/ (web address current as of May

9, 2005).

572. Russ Baker, The Big Lie, The Nation, March 2, 2003, http://www.thenation.com/doc.mhtml?i=20030407&s=baker (website address current as of March 26, 2003).

573. Chris Smith, A Spurious 'Smoking Gun,' MotherJones.com, March 25, 2003, http://www.motherjones.com/news/update/2003/13/we_338_01.html (website current as of March 25, 2003).

574. Barney Brantingham, *Press Secretary McClellan's Latest Report*, Santa Barbara Independent, http://www.independent.com/news/2008/jun/05/press-secretary-mcclellans-latest-report/ (June 5, 2008).

575. Id.

576. http://www.quarterlifecrisis.com/forums/archive/index.php/t-2579.html (web address current as of May 7, 2005).

577. http://www.quarterlifecrisis.com/forums/archive/index.php/t-2579.html (web address current as of May 7, 2005).

578. Warren P. Strobel and John Walcott, Bush Made Intel Fit Iraq Policy, *Kansas City Star*, May 6, 2005, http://www.kansascity.com/mld/kansascity/news/politics/11574258.htm (web address current as of May 7, 2005).

579. The Secret Downing Street Memo, http://www.timesonline.co.uk/article/0,,2087-1593607,00.html (web address current as of May 9, 2005).

580. Michael Smith, Blair Planned Iraq War From Start, *Times Online*, May 1, 2005, http://www.timesonline.co.uk/article/0,,2087-1592724,00.html (web address current as of May 9, 2005).

581. Michael Smith, Blair Planned Iraq War From Start, *Times Online*, May 1, 2005, http://www.timesonline.co.uk/article/0,,2087-1592724,00.html (web address current as of May 9, 2005).

582. Editor and Publisher, Survey Finds Editorial Treatment of 'Downing Street Memo' Mixed, June 15, 2005, http://www.editorandpublisher.com/eandp/news/article_display.jsp?vnu_content_id=1000962804 (web address current as of June 18, 2005).

583. Editor and Publisher, Survey Finds Editorial Treatment of 'Downing Street Memo' Mixed, June 15, 2005,

http://www.editorandpublisher.com/eandp/news/article_display.jsp?vnu_content_id=1000962804 (web address current as of June 18, 2005).

584. Associated Press, http://www.ap.org/pages/about/faq.html#2, (web address current as of June 18, 2005).

585. Kourosh Ziabari, Criticize Israel and lose your career, Opinion Maker, July 7, 2011, http://www.opinion-maker.org/2011/07/criticize-israel-and-lose-your-career/.

586. Editor and Publisher, Survey Finds Editorial Treatment of 'Downing Street Memo' Mixed, June 15, 2005, http://www.editorandpublisher.com/eandp/news/article_display.jsp?vnu_content_id=1000962804 (web address current as of June 18, 2005).

587. Jan Herman, The Domesticated Press, http://blogcritics.org/straightup/2005/06/15/113743.php, (web address current as of June 18, 2005).

588. Tom Regan, Is 'Downing Street Memo' a Smoking Gun?, http://www.csmonitor.com/2005/0617/dailyUpdate.html, (web address current as of June 18, 2005).

589. Michael Hoffman & Alan R. Critchley, The Truth About the Talmud, http://www.hoffman-info.com/talmudtruth.html (current as of September 12, 2001).

590. Michael Hoffman & Alan R. Critchley, The Truth About the Talmud, http://www.hoffman-info.com/talmudtruth.html (current as of September 12, 2001).

591. Michael Hoffman & Alan R. Critchley, The Truth About the Talmud, http://www.hoffman-info.com/talmudtruth.html (current as of September 12, 2001).

592. Benjamin Freedman, Facts are Facts, http://www.biblebelievers.org.au/facts.htm#FACTS%20ARE%20FACTS%20-%20I (website address current as of April 2, 2003).

593. Michael L. Rodkinson: The History of the Talmud; http://www.come-and-hear.com/talmud/rodkin_ii3.html#E27 (web address current as of February 8, 2004).

594. Judaism vs. Christianity: The War The Lamb Wins, http://www.fixedearth.com/talmud.html (current as of September 11, 2001).

595. THE JEWISH ENCYCLOPEDIA, vol. V, p. 619 (1901-1906).

596. Elizabeth Dilling, THE JEWISH RELIGION: Its Influence Today, chapter IV, p. 41 (1964).

597. Ted Pike, Child Sex Indictments Plague Orthodox Judaism, National Prayer Network, 13 June 2011.

598. Ted Pike, Child Sex Indictments Plague Orthodox Judaism, National Prayer Network, 13 June 2011.

599. Ted Pike, Child Sex Indictments Plague Orthodox Judaism, National Prayer Network, 13 June 2011.

600. Ted Pike, Child Sex Indictments Plague Orthodox Judaism, National Prayer Network, 13 June 2011.

601. Ted Pike, Child Sex Indictments Plague Orthodox Judaism, National Prayer Network, 13 June 2011.

602. Judaism vs. Christianity: The War The Lamb Wins, http://www.fixedearth.com/talmud.html (current as of September 11, 2001).

603. DONN DE GRAND PRE, BARBARIANS INSIDE THE GATES, THE BLACK BOOK OF BOLSHEVISM, p. 209 (2000) (quoting BEJAMIN FREEDMAN, FACTS ARE FACTS (1954)).

604. Ivan Fraser, Protocols of the Learned Elders of Zion, Proofs of an Ancient Conspiracy, http://www.vegan.swinternet.co.uk/articles/conspiracies/protocols_proof.html (current as of September 10, 2001).

605. MICHAEL A. HOFFMAN, JUDAISM'S STRANGE GODS, at p. 88, (2000).

606. MICHAEL A. HOFFMAN, JUDAISM'S STRANGE GODS, at p. 88, (2000).

607. MICHAEL A. HOFFMAN, JUDAISM'S STRANGE GODS, at p. 91, (2000).

608. MICHAEL A. HOFFMAN, JUDAISM'S STRANGE GODS, at p. 92, (2000).

609. See John S. Torell, Showdown in Jerusalem, The Dove, winter 1995.

610. Walter White, Jr., The Hidden Tyranny, http://www.fourwinds10.com/corner/J224-ch4.pdf, http://www.antichristconspiracy.com/HTML%20Pages/Harold_Wallace_Rosenthal_Interview_1976.htm (web address current as of April 21, 2002).

611. RABBI DAVID A. COOPER, GOD IS A VERB, KABBALAH AND THE PRACTICE OF MYSTICAL JUDAISM, at 156 (1997) (emphasis added).

612. *Id.* at 160 (emphasis added).

613. See John S. Torell, Showdown in Jerusalem, The Dove, winter 1995.

614. ANTHONY C. SUTTON, AMERICA'S SECRET ESTABLISHMENT, AN INTRODUCTION TO THE ORDER OF SKULL & BONES, at p. 212 (1986).

615. ANTHONY C. SUTTON, AMERICA'S SECRET ESTABLISHMENT, AN INTRODUCTION TO THE ORDER OF SKULL & BONES, at p. 212 (1986).

616. ANTHONY C. SUTTON, AMERICA'S SECRET ESTABLISHMENT, AN INTRODUCTION TO THE ORDER OF SKULL & BONES, at p. 7 (1986).

617. ANTHONY C. SUTTON, AMERICA'S SECRET ESTABLISHMENT, AN INTRODUCTION TO THE ORDER OF SKULL & BONES, at p. 200 (1986).

618. ANTHONY C. SUTTON, AMERICA'S SECRET ESTABLISHMENT, AN INTRODUCTION TO THE ORDER OF SKULL & BONES, at p. 150 (1986).

619. ANTHONY C. SUTTON, AMERICA'S SECRET ESTABLISHMENT, AN INTRODUCTION TO THE ORDER OF SKULL & BONES, at p. 149 (1986).

620. ANTHONY C. SUTTON, AMERICA'S SECRET ESTABLISHMENT, AN INTRODUCTION TO THE ORDER OF SKULL & BONES, at p. 151 (1986).

621. ANTHONY C. SUTTON, AMERICA'S SECRET ESTABLISHMENT, AN INTRODUCTION TO THE ORDER OF SKULL & BONES, at p. 151 (1986).

622. ANTHONY C. SUTTON, AMERICA'S SECRET ESTABLISHMENT, AN INTRODUCTION TO THE ORDER OF SKULL & BONES, at p. 153 (1986).

623. ANTHONY C. SUTTON, AMERICA'S SECRET ESTABLISHMENT, AN INTRODUCTION TO THE ORDER OF SKULL & BONES, at p. 163 (1986). WILLIAM STILL, NEW WORLD ORDER: THE ANCIENT PLAN OF SECRET SOCIETIES, at p. 167 (1990).

624. WILLIAM STILL, NEW WORLD ORDER: THE ANCIENT PLAN OF SECRET SOCIETIES, at p. 167 (1990).

625. WILLIAM STILL, NEW WORLD ORDER: THE ANCIENT PLAN OF SECRET SOCIETIES, at p. 163-67 (1990).

626. WILLIAM STILL, NEW WORLD ORDER: THE ANCIENT PLAN OF SECRET SOCIETIES, at p. 167 (1990).

627. ANTHONY C. SUTTON, AMERICA'S SECRET ESTABLISHMENT, AN INTRODUCTION TO THE ORDER OF SKULL & BONES, at p. 164 (1986).

628. ANTHONY C. SUTTON, AMERICA'S SECRET ESTABLISHMENT, AN INTRODUCTION TO THE ORDER OF SKULL & BONES, at p. 164-174 (1986).

629. WEBSTER G. TARPLEY & ANTON CHAITKIN, GEORGE BUSH: THE UNAUTHORIZED BIOGRAPHY, http://www.tarpley.net/bush2.htm (website address current as of March 24, 2003).

630. WEBSTER G. TARPLEY & ANTON CHAITKIN, GEORGE BUSH: THE UNAUTHORIZED BIOGRAPHY, http://www.tarpley.net/bush2.htm (website address current as of March 24, 2003).

631. WEBSTER G. TARPLEY & ANTON CHAITKIN, GEORGE BUSH: THE UNAUTHORIZED BIOGRAPHY, http://www.tarpley.net/bush2.htm (website address current as of March 24, 2003).

632. WEBSTER G. TARPLEY & ANTON CHAITKIN, GEORGE BUSH: THE UNAUTHORIZED BIOGRAPHY, http://www.tarpley.net/bush2.htm (website address current as of March 24, 2003).

633. MICHAEL A. HOFFMAN II, JEWISH COMMUNISTS: THE DOCUMENTARY RECORD, http://www.hoffman-info.com/communist.html (website current as of March 5, 2003).

634. ROBERT WILTON, THE LAST DAYS OF THE ROMANOVS (1920).

635. Gordon "Jack" Mohr, The Talmudic Effect on Judeo-Christianity, http://www.christianbiblestudy.org/OPS/JM/jm0027c.htm (current as of September 19, 2001).

636. ROBERT WILTON, THE LAST DAYS OF THE ROMANOVS, p. 148 (1920).

637. COLONEL GORDON "JACK" MOHR, THE TALMUDIC EFFECT ON JUDEO-CHRISTIANITY, http://www.christianbiblestudy.org/OPS/JM/jm0027e.htm (current as of September 17, 2001).

638. *Izvestia,* July 27, 1918.

639. HENRY FORD, THE INTERNATIONAL JEW, vol. 1, p. 225 (1920).

640. HENRY FORD, THE INTERNATIONAL JEW, vol. 1, p. 225 (1920).

641. MICHAEL A. HOFFMAN II, JEWISH COMMUNISTS: THE DOCUMENTARY RECORD, http://www.hoffman-info.com/communist.html (website current as of March 5, 2003) (quoting The Christian News, Jan. 8, 1996, p. 2).

642. MICHAEL A. HOFFMAN II, JEWISH COMMUNISTS: THE DOCUMENTARY RECORD, http://www.hoffman-info.com/communist.html (website current as of March 5, 2003).

643. MICHAEL A. HOFFMAN II, JEWISH COMMUNISTS: THE DOCUMENTARY RECORD, http://www.hoffman-info.com/communist.html (website current as of March 5, 2003) (quoting Dmitri Volkogonov, *Lenin: A New Biography,* p. 112).

644. MICHAEL A. HOFFMAN II, JEWISH COMMUNISTS: THE DOCUMENTARY RECORD, http://www.hoffman-info.com/communist.html (website current as of March 5, 2003).

645. DES GRIFFIN, FOURTH REICH OF THE RICH, p. 62 (1976).

646. *Id.*

647. Texe Marrs, Conspiracy of the Six Pointed Star, at 165 (2011).

648. Texe Marrs, Conspiracy of the Six Pointed Star, at 165 (2011).

649. Texe Marrs, Conspiracy of the Six Pointed Star, at 201 (2011).

650. DONN DE GRAND PRE, BARBARIANS INSIDE THE GATES, THE BLACK BOOK OF BOLSHEVISM, p. 209 (2000) (quoting BEJAMIN FREEDMAN, FACTS ARE FACTS (1954)).

651. Baruch Levy, Letter to Karl Marx, `La Revue de Paris', p. 574, June 1, 1928. http://www4.stormfront.org/posterity/ci/tjg.html (current as of September 9, 2001). *See also* DON DE GRAND PRE, BARBARIANS INSIDE THE GATES, p. 64 (2000).

652. DONN DE GRAND PRE, BARBARIANS INSIDE THE GATES, THE BLACK BOOK OF BOLSHEVISM, p. 313-14 (2000) (citing JACK BERNSTEIN, THE LIFE OF AN AMERICAN JEW IN RACIST MARXIST ISRAEL (1984)).

653. DONN DE GRAND PRE, BARBARIANS INSIDE THE GATES, THE BLACK BOOK OF BOLSHEVISM, p. 313-14 (2000) (citing JACK BERNSTEIN, THE LIFE OF AN AMERICAN JEW IN RACIST MARXIST ISRAEL (1984)).

654. DONN DE GRAND PRE, BARBARIANS INSIDE THE GATES, THE BLACK BOOK OF BOLSHEVISM, p. 313-14 (2000) (citing JACK BERNSTEIN, THE LIFE OF AN AMERICAN JEW IN RACIST MARXIST ISRAEL (1984)).

655. JACK BERNSTEIN, MY FAREWELL TO ISRAEL THE THORN IN THE MIDEAST.

656. Ivan Fraser, Protocols of the Learned Elders of Zion, Proofs of an Ancient Conspiracy, http://www.vegan.swinternet.co.uk/articles/conspiracies/protocols_proof.html (current as of September 10, 2001).

657. http://www.biblebelievers.org.au/clilist.htm (current as of September 29, 2001).

658. MICHAEL A. HOFFMAN II, JEWISH COMMUNISTS: THE DOCUMENTARY RECORD, http://www.hoffman-info.com/communist.html (website current as of March 5, 2003) (citing N.Y. Times, Oct. 7, 1999 and Newsweek, Oct. 18, 1999, p. 30).

659. *See* Jack Mohr, *Satan's Kids*, http://www.christianbiblestudy.org/OPS/JM/JM0018c.htm (current as of September 9, 2001).

660. DONN DE GRAND PRE, BARBARIANS INSIDE THE GATES, THE BLACK BOOK OF BOLSHEVISM, p. 120 (2000) (quoting *The New York Times* 14 March 1935).

661. DONN DE GRAND PRE, BARBARIANS INSIDE THE GATES, THE BLACK BOOK OF BOLSHEVISM, p. 105 (2000).

662. Id.

663. Id.

664. DONN DE GRAND PRE, BARBARIANS INSIDE THE GATES, THE BLACK BOOK OF BOLSHEVISM, p. 296 (2000).

665. DONN DE GRAND PRE, BARBARIANS INSIDE THE GATES, THE BLACK BOOK OF BOLSHEVISM, p. 250 (2000) (quoting Representative Louis McFadden, radio address, May 2, 1934).

666. 75 Congressional Record 12595-12603.

667. See EDWARD GRIFFIN, THE CREATURE FROM JEKYLL ISLAND: A SECOND LOOK AT THE FEDERAL RESERVE (3RD Edition 1998).

668. Albert D Pastore, Stranger Than Fiction, http://www.whatreallyhappened.com/NEWSTF/stfch3.htm (website address current as of March 28, 2003).

669. See EDWARD GRIFFIN, THE CREATURE FROM JEKYLL ISLAND: A SECOND LOOK AT THE FEDERAL RESERVE (3RD Edition 1998).

670. CONG. REC. 12595-96 (1932) (speech of Rep. McFadden), *at* http://iresist.com/cbg/mcfadden_speech_1932.html (current as of September 30, 2001).

671. CONG. REC. 12595-96 (1932) (speech of Rep. McFadden), *at* http://iresist.com/cbg/mcfadden_speech_1932.html (current as of September 30, 2001).

672. Israel Shahak, Jewish History, Jewish Religion: The Weight of Three Thousand Years (1994), *available at* http//www.biblebelievers.org.au/jewhis3.htm#Orthodoxy%20and%20Interpretation.

673. Israel Shahak, Jewish History, Jewish Religion: The Weight of Three Thousand Years (1994), *available at* http//www.biblebelievers.org.au/jewhis3.htm#Orthodoxy%20and%20Interpretation.

674. Israel Shahak, Jewish History, Jewish Religion: The Weight of Three Thousand Years (1994), *available at* http//www.biblebelievers.org.au/jewhis3.htm#Orthodoxy%20and%20Interpretation.

675. Israel Shamir, Seven Lean Kine, November 28, 2008, *available at* http://www.thetruthseeker.co.uk/article.asp?ID=9743.

676. *Judaism: The Atheist Rabbi*, TIME, January 29, 1965, *available at* http://www.time.com/time/magazine/article/0,9171,839200,00.html.

677. *Judaism: The Atheist Rabbi*, TIME, January 29, 1965, *available at* http://www.time.com/time/magazine/article/0,9171,839200,00.html.

678. Amiram Barkat, *Rabbi Sherwin Wine, Founder of Humanistic Judaism, Dies at 79*, Haaretz, July 24, 2007, *available at* http://www.haaretz.com/hasen/spages/885330.html.

679. Amiram Barkat, *Rabbi Sherwin Wine, Founder of Humanistic Judaism, Dies at 79*, Haaretz, July 24, 2007, *available at* http://www.haaretz.com/hasen/spages/885330.html.

680. Michael Hoffman, *Judaism Revealed*, at 775 (2008) (quoting Yesaiah Tishbi, *Torat ha-Rave-Kelippah b-Kabbalat ha-Ari* ("The Theory of Evil and the Satanic Sphere in Kabbalah"), pp. 139-142 [1942; reprinted 1982]).

681. Michael Hoffman, *Judaism Revealed*, at 775 (2008) (quoting Yesaiah Tishbi, *Torat ha-Rave-Kelippah b-Kabbalat ha-Ari* ("The Theory of Evil and the Satanic Sphere in Kabbalah"), [1942; reprinted 1982]).

682. Shulamit Aloni: "It's a Trick We Always Use," http://wideeyecinema.com/?p=3804 (last visited on December 12, 2010).

683. Shulamit Aloni, Jewish Virtual Library, http://www.jewishvirtuallibrary.org/jsource/biography/aloni.html (last visited on December 12, 2010).

684. *Zionism Promotes Anti-Semitism*, Jews Against Zionism, *at* http://www.jewsagainstzionism.com/antisemitism/zionismpromotes.cfm (last visited on March 26, 2010).

685. *Zionism and Anti-Semitism*, Jews Against Anti-Semitism, *at* http://www.jewsagainstzionism.com/zionism/zanda.cfm (last visited on March 26, 2010).

686.*Israeli Youths Burn New Testaments*, USA Today, May 21, 2008, *at* http://www.usatoday.com/news/religion/2008-05-21-jewish-new-testament_N.htm.

687.*Israeli Youths Burn New Testaments*, USA Today, May 21, 2008, *at* http://www.usatoday.com/news/religion/2008-05-21-jewish-new-testament_N.htm.

www.ingramcontent.com/pod-product-compliance
Lightning Source LLC
Chambersburg PA
CBHW081839230426
43669CB00018B/2759